Disenchanted
Realists

Disenchanted Realists

Political Science and the American Crisis

Second Edition

Raymond Seidelman

With the assistance of Edward J. Harpham

Afterword by James Farr

Published by State University of New York Press, Albany

For information, contact State University of New York Press, Albany, NY
www.sunypress.edu

Production, Ryan Morris
Marketing, Anne M. Valentine

Library of Congress Cataloging in Publication Data

Seidelman, Raymond.
  Disenchanted realists: political science and the American crisis / Raymond Seidelman.—Second edition.
        pages   cm
  Includes bibliographical references and index.
  ISBN 978-1-4384-5573-0 (hc : alk. paper)—978-1-4384-5574-7 (pb : alk. paper)
  ISBN 978-1-4384-5575-4 (ebook)
1. Political science United States History 20th century. 2. Liberalism United States History 20th century. I. Title.
  JA84.U5S44 2015
  320.510973– dc23
                                                              2014017609

10 9 8 7 6 5 4 3 2 1

Contents

Foreword

Bruce Miroff and Stephen Skowronek

The authors of this foreword were long-time friends of Ray Seidelman and admirers of his most important scholarly work, *Disenchanted Realists*. Ray died in 2007 at age 56 after a four-year struggle with cancer. Subsequently, the political science editor at SUNY Press, Michael Rinella, suggested a second edition of *Disenchanted Realists* to bring Ray's provocative and insightful history of the political science discipline to a new generation of political scientists. James Farr, a distinguished student of the history of political science and another friend of Ray's, has written an afterword for this edition that situates the book among other disciplinary histories, assesses reactions to its arguments, and adds both a prequel and a sequel to the story it tells.

When *Disenchanted Realists* was published in 1985, it stood apart from prior and contemporaneous histories of political science. Other books on the history of the discipline—by Bernard Crick, Albert Somit and Joseph Tanenhaus, and David Ricci—primarily took a stand either in praise of or as a critique of the quest for a science of politics. Ray's work was concerned with the relationship between the scientific impulse in political science and the desire to influence the real world of American politics. He wrote about prominent political scientists who envisioned the creation of a "science of politics" that would simultaneously be "a science for politics." The purpose of political science, from their perspective, was not a detached body of objective truths but rather a growing repository of scientific knowledge that could reform and advance American democracy.

As the title of Ray's book indicates, the hopes that a "science of politics" would elevate public life in the United States repeatedly met with frustration, and the discipline's political ambitions gave way over time to a narrower pursuit of science for its own sake. Ray was nothing if not a political realist himself, and his history was not intended to be uplifting, much less for cheerleading about the progress of political science.

Nonetheless, *Disenchanted Realists* did not yield to cynicism; on the contrary, Ray admired most of the political scientists whose frustrations he depicted. The enduring power of his work is found not only in his insightful history of the discipline's struggle to combine science with democratic reform but equally in his insistence that his readers understand the nature of that struggle. Perhaps more than any other history of the discipline, *Disenchanted Realists* asks political scientists to reflect on the public meaning and significance of the work that they do.

Behind *Disenchanted Realists* lay Ray's experiences as a political activist while an undergraduate at the University of California at Santa Cruz. Even more important in the genesis of the book were his graduate years at Cornell University. Ray entered graduate school in 1973. Political science was then in an unsettled state, with scholars questioning received paradigms (pluralism, behavioralism) and looking for new directions. The nation was in an unsettled state as well. The movement politics of the 1960s was waning, and the travails of the Nixon administration were about to shake the government to its foundations. Ray was none too certain of his course. He was full of questions about where scholars fit into the emerging political scene and where he himself fit within political science's traditional divisions of labor.

Over the next several years, Ray took full advantage of the porous sub-field boundaries he found at the Government Department at Cornell. He set out to study political philosophy with Isaac Kramnick but ended up writing a dissertation in comparative politics on "Neighborhood Communism in Florence" under the direction of Sidney Tarrow. In the interim, he worked on a manuscript about the study of American politics, producing the first draft of what would become *Disenchanted Realists* under the supervision of Ted Lowi. Whatever pressures there were at Cornell to specialize, Ray successfully resisted them. His reluctance as a graduate student to declare himself a political theorist, or a "comparativist," or an "Americanist," would continue through the rest of his career. Attracted to all three areas but reluctant to commit to one over the others, he was more naturally disposed than most to think broadly about his chosen field of study and to engage political science as a discipline with a project all its own.

During his first year at Cornell, Ray met two other political theory graduate students, Edward Harpham and Stephen Skowronek, whose intellectual agendas had much in common with his own. Each was, in his own way, interested in working through the relationship between scholarship and political life. The three rented a house together in the summer of 1974, and over the next two years, while cramming for general examinations, they sustained a discussion about the bearing of theory on practice, ideas on action, norms on empirics, intellectuals on power. They approached Ted Lowi with the idea of a reading course that would focus on how political scientists in America had grappled with these questions in the past, and he agreed on the condition that they produce joint work commensurate in scope to three extended term papers. They ended up with about 200 pages loosely organized around the problems faced by political scientists who had self-consciously sought to direct the discipline toward the advancement of American democracy.

Each of the housemates took something essential to his later intellectual development from that experience. Harpham went on to write about Adam Smith's insights into the formation of a political economy; Skowronek, about the professional reform impulse in American state-building. By the time Ray returned from Florence and his study of the Italian left, all three were fairly far along on their own trajectories. Ray was eager to revive the joint project, to rework and expand its thesis, but in looking back at the old manuscript with the detachment of a few years, it was evident that pulling together a book would be an entirely new undertaking. Harpham agreed to help, but could not commit to the project full time. It was clear that if the idea was to bear fruit, Ray would have to take the lead and make it his own.

To write a history of the quest to combine "a science of politics" with "a science for politics," Ray turned to the careers of such political science luminaries as Woodrow Wilson, Charles Beard, Charles Merriam, Harold Lasswell, V. O. Key, and David Truman. Framing his history was his conception of a "third tradition" in American political thought. The first tradition, as he defined it, was the institutionalism of the Federalists, which aimed to channel and control unruly human nature through the political architecture of a national constitutional system. The second tradition, associated with the Anti-Federalists and their populist successors, criticized institutional controls as safeguards for aristocracy and promoted radical democracy from the bottom up. Ray perceived a third tradition among leading political scientists that sought to surmount the antagonism between the original two traditions by achieving a distinctive synthesis between institutionalism and popular democracy.

Starting with the early progressives, political scientists in Ray's narrative advocated a stronger national state in the vein of the Federalists, guided by trained experts such as public administrators. Yet these same political scientists sought to make this stronger state responsive and accountable through the ability of a reform political science to educate and cultivate an engaged democratic public. The vision of "third tradition" political science was the marriage of institutional expertise and popular input, of rationalized national institutions subject to the authority of a rational public. Political science would thus be both a force for modernization, overcoming the provincialism of the American past, and for harmonization, pulling together former political foes in new arrangements that served the common good. An autonomous discipline, priding itself on its objectivity, political science would do for democracy what ordinary political actors and agents had not accomplished.

But these hopes for "a science for politics" depended, as Ray observed, on several dubious assumptions. They assumed that even as the discipline of political science was becoming more professional and complex in its concepts and methods, there would be a public audience attentive to its findings. Moreover, they assumed that because the discipline carried the mantle of science, this public audience would defer to its expertise. Perhaps most questionable of all was the assumption that organized political and economic interests whose objectives were otherwise conflicting could be reconciled through the impartial guidance of an authoritative political science. Ray faulted "third tradition" political scientists for failing to grasp the recalcitrance of American political culture: political scientists might hope to educate citizens to recognize the value of an expert and benign state, but individualism and localism left most Americans hostile to centralized and bureaucratic government even as they benefited from its services. In their search for political harmony, political scientists also failed, in Ray's view, to come to grips with the inequalities of wealth and power that would leave their reform prescriptions stillborn in the academy.

As the story recounted in *Disenchanted Realists* moved from the 1880s to the 1980s, it uncovered a pattern of hope giving way to disappointment. Equally notable was the pattern of retreat and reentry: one generation of political scientists would abandon its effort to make a public difference and redirect its energies to pure science, yet the next generation would rediscover a democratic mission for the discipline and try all over again, albeit with new theories and methods. The final episode in the story Ray finished in the early 1980s told of two great "third tradition" scholars who are still with us: Theodore Lowi and Walter Dean Burnham. With these scholars, Ray concluded that the "third tradition" was reaching its end, dying off after a century of defeated aspirations for reform. What made his advance obituary for the "third tradition" especially poignant was the depth of admiration he felt for its final practitioners: Lowi had been Ray's teacher and Burnham remained one of his heroes.

The demise of the "third tradition" was, for Ray, hardly a cause for celebration. Devoid of its reformist hopes, American political science would increasingly close in on itself. Shorn of its direct engagement with questions about the vitality of the regime as a whole, the practical uses of the knowledge generated become largely strategic, offering insight for elites interested into how the system works and how to manipulate it. The concluding pages of *Disenchanted Realists* were bleak—but resolutely honest. They did not let anyone off the hook, including Ray himself: "The organization of modern political science may triumph over its original functions, becoming a mode of discourse of and for itself, heaving up great mounds of academic literature and specialized debate. Paradoxically, works like this one probably provoke interest only within the discipline they seek to criticize."

Almost a decade later, Ray revisited the themes of his book in an essay prepared for *Discipline and History: Political Science in the United States*, a volume he coedited with James Farr. In this essay he concluded that the reform impulse of the "third tradition" had gravitated to the field of political theory. It was in this field, distanced more than any other precinct of political science from the appeals of "scientism," that scholars still took seriously "the revival of an active citizenry." Using as his example Benjamin Barber's *Strong Democracy*, Ray was skeptical that political theorists could breathe new life into a dying tradition. The characteristic flaw in Barber's mode of democratic theory, he wrote, was its "curiously abstract nature" because it proposed a "disembodied ideal" unhinged from any empirical consideration of existing power relations or institutions.

Ray's insights into the historical appeal of the "third tradition" perhaps were more accurate than his pessimistic conclusions about its vanishing future. In recent years, not only political theorists but also scholars of American politics have once again aimed their work at a "science for politics." Amid the current crises of the American political order, proposals for institutional reform and for the revival of civic life have flowed from prominent political scientists such as Robert Putnam and Theda Skocpol. Nineteen political scientists contributed their efforts to *Democracy at*

Risk, edited by Stephen Macedo and published under the auspices of the American Political Science Association (APSA). Ray's skeptical spirit would suggest that the latest version of "third tradition" political science will be no more fecund than its predecessors in sparking democratic reform. Whatever the eventual fate of such scholarship, however, its reappearance does suggest that the hope of improving American democracy is so basic a part of the DNA of American political science that it will remain with us for the foreseeable future.

In the last decade and a half of his life, Ray's focus increasingly turned to the pedagogical practices of a "science for politics." He became one of three coauthors on multiple editions of an introductory textbook on American politics, *The Democratic Debate.* The debate at the center of the text was between "elite democrats" and "popular democrats," ideal types that closely followed the first two traditions in *Disenchanted Realists,* and the authors' approach toward the debate echoed the spirit of "third tradition" political science. One of Ray's innovations for the textbook was a unique chapter devoted to the puzzle of nonvoting, a subject that he regarded as essential to any realistic reckoning with the state of American democracy.

"A science for politics" was also at the heart of Ray's sense of mission as a teacher at Sarah Lawrence College. Primarily presenting courses on political economy, mass media, and civic participation, Ray brought unusual passion and energy to the discussion of political science. He was less concerned with questions of method than with matters of substance, aiming to instill in students the desire to connect what they learned in the classroom with what they encountered in the political world. Several generations of Sarah Lawrence students responded enthusiastically to Ray as an exemplar of political knowledge and commitment. He received the college's Lipkin Prize for Inspirational Teaching and became the Sara Yates Exley Chair in Teaching Excellence.

Although Ray shared with the "disenchanted realists" of his book an ultimate skepticism about the impact of political science on public life, he never grew disenchanted with democracy itself. In an address to a graduating class at Sarah Lawrence, Ray said: "Democracy is not what we have; it is what we aspire to be. So dare to aspire to it, for in the process you become a democratic citizen. It takes courage to live as a democratic citizen, and that's why we fight for it; this will involve you in great risks, but it's worth it because it will make you free." He encouraged his students to seek internships in community organizations or unions, and he accompanied them on road trips for both electoral mobilization and protest politics. Before he died, he requested that memorial contributions be directed to a scholarship fund established in his name to subsidize Sarah Lawrence graduates who took up low-paid positions as political organizers.

For the present generation of political scientists, many of whom have not been taught about the history of their discipline, Ray's *Disenchanted Realists* brings into sharp relief their forebears whose aspirations and frustrations, if not concepts and methods, illuminate a shared landscape that connects academic to political ground. Moreover, Ray's own career that combined scholarship, teaching, and democratic activism—the last of which might be termed "a science in politics"—illuminates one possible version of a life in political science. His scholarship on and his life in political science are, of course, not for everyone. But both can provoke any of us to think deeply about the public meanings of what we do in our own careers as political scientists.

Acknowledgments

This book has had many incarnations. It began humbly enough as a semester-long reading project among three Cornell graduate students. For good or ill, it slowly metamorphosed into a longish paper, a short monograph, and finally into three or four versions of the present work. The more we wrote, the more we limited our aims. No sane person we soon discovered could possess the patience or sustain the inclination to write a "complete" history of political science. There are too many tributaries and creeks that branch off from the mainstream, a surfeit of oddities that detract from any single concentration on the whole.

Instead, this is a modest history of the intertwined fate of political liberalism and some of the major leaders of American political science. We have tried to limit our claims about the discipline as a whole, even as we seek to avoid single intellectual biographies. If we have erred, we hope it is on the side of provocation rather than pedantry.

In part, our subject is the increasing insulation of political science from the realities of politics, power, and protest in twentieth-century America. There is an irony to this project: if political science is insulated, what is to be said about those who write about it? We venture the hope and expectation that this work will contribute in some small way to serious discussion about the connection of university academicians to the mainsprings of American politics, and that at minimum it rekindles self-examination within the political science discipline itself. In times when the American Right has achieved something close to a semimonopoly on public policy, inquiring about the fate of its liberal opponents, a group increasingly engaged in either talking to itself or apologizing for its past, might be useful.

No one in what we call here "third tradition" political science understands the liberal dilemma more than Theodore Lowi of Cornell University, who kept this work and its authors afloat despite the fact that both are frequently critical of his own studies. This is, of course, criticism that emerges from deep respect for Ted as a scholar and a person. His charm, wit, tolerance, critical abilities, and sheer enthusiasm kept this book going, and without those qualities this book would never have been written, much less published.

Our foremost intellectual debt is to Stephen Skowronek, now of the University of California at Los Angeles, who in the mid-1970s was a coequal participant in our research and writing. The completion of his doctoral dissertation and his book *Building a New American State* kept Steve occupied during the time we decided to alter and re-alter the thesis and kind of research presented here. Steve's insights and hard work remain, although he cannot be held responsible for any demerits that have later appeared in our chapters.

Others have graciously made extensive comments on this book at various stages. Luigi Graziano of the University of Turin, Bruce Miroff of the State University of New York at Albany, Douglas Jaenicke of the University of Manchester, Norman Jacobson of the University of California at Berkeley, Isaac Kramnick of Cornell University, Alan Stone of the University of Houston, Anthony Champagne of the University of Texas at Dallas, Paul Kress, and Bernard Johnpoll all deserve our thanks and gratitude. John Gunnell, editor of this series, has done more than anyone to keep our spirits high.

We would also like to thank Addie Napolitano for tolerating endless coughing and wheezing transmitted through the headphones of her Dictaphone.

We would like to thank Fay Chazin-Seidelman and Wendy Harpham for putting up with us during periods of sequestration in our respective offices.

Lastly, we feel the need to spell out the terms of our writing partnership. The thesis of this book and the treatment of the individuals discussed herein were developed jointly over several years when we were graduate students at Cornell University. After putting down the manuscript for several years in order to complete our doctoral dissertations, we returned to it in 1980. We decided to rewrite the entire manuscript because our ideas and foci had slightly altered and because we wanted to include an entirely new figure, V. O. Key. Although we both discussed the general outline of each chapter and exchanged preliminary drafts, we felt that the tasks of writing the chapters were distributed in such a way as to warrant assigning principal authorship to Raymond Seidelman, who wrote the bulk of this work. Edward Harpham was involved in the writing of significant parts of chapters 4 and 6, and was the primary author of chapter 5. Needless to say, both of us assume mutual responsibility for the entire contents.

Raymond Seidelman
Ossining, New York

Edward Harpham
Dallas, Texas

1
Introduction

"Liberalism" is something of a dirty word in America today. Reaganites scorn it as an unaffordable fad that could still wreck efforts to restore capitalist prosperity. Corporatist Democrats honor liberalism's past successes but now shun it as soft, mushy, and chickenhearted. Liberal doctrines are hardly adequate guides into the brave new world of the high-tech future. Democratic socialists trace the liberal philosophy's internal contradictions—liberals always seem to promise much more than they can deliver. Today, when choices between capitalist growth and democratic revival must be made, liberals can only shrug their shoulders. Whatever the American political future, our present political dialogue suggests that it is unlikely to be a liberal one.

Oddly, contemporary critics and supporters of liberalism alike seem to assume that it once was the preeminent public philosophy—that it succeeded in some fundamental way in shaping American politics to its prescriptions. There are many reasons to believe that this is indeed so. Liberals forged giant popular coalitions, staving off through timely reforms the growth of sizeable opposition to American capitalism. They built a welfare state with at least minimal protections against the ravages of the marketplace. They democratized American political institutions by extending civil and social rights to previously exploited groups and races. The litany could continue: Liberals most of all modernized American politics to fit the requirements of the twentieth century. If liberalism is now in eclipse, it is perhaps because most of its agenda has been successfully completed.[1]

Note: Bruce Miroff has made corrections to the text of the first edition of *Disenchanted Realists*, but the book has been neither updated nor revised; the second edition retains the late Ray Seidelman's distinctive argument and writing style.

1

Yet a historical perspective on liberalism's twentieth-century history might reveal that its successes were much more limited and tenuous, its aspirations and hopes more extensive, and its intellectual pretensions more ambitious than commentary suggests. A consistent undercurrent of anxiety and fear of failure exists among liberal intellectuals themselves, even as they have watched their reforms become public philosophy and policy. Just possibly, liberalism will not be eclipsed in America because it may not have ever possessed the popularity and power its supporters and detractors tend to assign it.

This book explores a single if crucial strain of disenchantment and disaffection with liberal politics among selected liberal thinkers themselves. Our subject is particular American scientists of politics and their connections with the vision, agenda, and methods of liberal politics. It is not a coincidence that a science of politics was born with the political movements and doctrines of modern liberalism. We argue that prominent political scientists have in fact helped to define the modern liberal view of democracy, society, and state in twentieth-century America. The consistency and aims of the arguments made by the political scientists discussed in this book have shaped the hopes, guided the forms, and suffered the consequences of reform politics from its birth in the late nineteenth century to the present impasse of the 1970s and 1980s. Much of the present crisis in liberal politics can be traced to the substance and disappointment of these hopes. A science of politics in America has encountered the same problems, crises, and successes as American reformers themselves. When liberalism falters, political science trembles.

Not all political scientists—perhaps not even most—have blended scholarship and political advocacy, a science of politics with a science "for" politics. For that reason, this book is not a history of a discipline, but rather a selected interpretation of those who built the discipline as a science for democracy, a way of linking objective professional political study with political reforms. This is a distinct group in political science history, including most of the more prominent scholars from Lester Ward to Theodore Lowi, from Charles Beard to Walter Dean Burnham, from Woodrow Wilson to V. O. Key.

Together, all these scholars have forged a reasonably coherent, consistent, and critical perspective on what they consider the main features of the American political tradition. All of them have seen political science as a nonrevolutionary alternative to the outdated political ideologies and practices of preindustrial America. Self-conscious modernists, they have been preoccupied with the absence of modernizing impulses in American political culture. Self-conscious revolutionaries in their scholarly methods, they are all self-conscious moderates and hopeful optimists about the ultimate victory and vindication of their notion of political truth. Anxious about the emergence of political extremes in America, they nonetheless have proposed far-reaching and ambitious reforms of political institutions and citizen attitudes. Impressed with their own cosmopolitanism, all of them have been eager to introduce European ideas and practices into our intellectual and political life. Yet they have all marveled at and complained about the "uniqueness" and peculiarity of American political development. The nation's peculiarities have been alternatively cursed and adored. Intent on maintaining objectivity in their studies, they have been supreme political advocates. Builders of a profession of political scientists, they have always sought to affect publics far beyond the ivory tower.[2]

Their seeming fondness for opposites suggests that their work embodies impossible contradictions and tensions. Ultimately, we hope to show that these contradictions and tensions are not to be found in their attempted union of facts and values, advocacy and objectivity, political and professional roles. Easy reconciliation of these opposites makes their work and lives exceptionally interesting and distinguishes their intellectual project from disciplinary drones and professional politicians. Their distresses are rather to be found in their basic claims about American politics and their consistent inability to reach and guide the publics they designate as the natural carriers of political reform.

Not surprising for such ambitious people, they have located a progressive dynamic of democratic modernization to which their brand of political science has been closely attached. Their scholarship has pretended to reveal the open vistas ahead for the modern American republic and has urged the polity on to this happy destiny. Above all, political scientists have tried but failed to modernize what they consider to be the retrograde and outdated aspects of two traditions of American political thought.

These traditions are appropriately labeled *institutionalist* and *radical democratic*. While the following chapters trace the personal and collective traumas of political scientists as they have confronted these two traditions, outlining the essentials of these traditions before we continue is worthwhile. Modern political science usually has been understood as a simple extension of one or the other of them. We argue that the political and intellectual departures from the past are more important than political science's continuity with older modes of American political thinking and acting.

Institutionalists and Radical Democrats

The institutionalist tradition—the dominant mode of American governmental organization and political thought in the late eighteenth and nineteenth centuries—is perhaps best captured in the victorious ideas of the Federalists and their 1787 Constitution. Norman Jacobson has called the political philosophy of the Constitution a "self-fulfilling prophecy" because the document not only established rules and procedures, but also has educated Americans and their perceptions of human nature in politics.[3]

Institutionalists like the Founders have been skeptical about human political capacities even when there has been evidence to the contrary. They have been preoccupied with the ubiquity of greed, avarice, and conflict in the history of republics, and fearful about the malevolent effects of majority rule on minorities and their rights. American institutions could be peculiar and unique, but not the citizens they governed. Eleven years after a revolution that some thought would "begin the world over again," John Adams still could say that Americans were after all "like all other people," that "they never merited the character of very exalted virtue" that enthusiastic revolutionaries liked to attribute to citizens of the new Republic.[4]

But the genius of the American Founders lay in their peculiar solutions to the riddles that befuddled past republican thinkers. Size, social diversity, and possessive individualism were not very appropriate building blocks for popular government, but the Founders turned these seeming vices into a novel theory and practice of republicanism. Rather than relying on community, public spiritedness, or social equality as foundations for republican government, Federalists held to "an amazing display of confidence in institutionalism, in the efficacy of institutional devices for solving social and political problems."

The Founders' science of politics entrusted to the impersonal artifice and mechanics of the Constitution's structures and procedures the virtuous qualities past republicans insisted must be instilled in citizens. In the famous argument of Federalist No. 10, the endless and natural pursuit of property is transformed into a mainstay of institutional stability. The geographical scope of America makes it difficult for coherent majorities to form around fundamental issues. Size expands the number of factions and makes communications between them remarkably difficult.

The Constitution extends the qualities started by nature. An imposing apparatus of checks and balances, divided powers, and complex procedures ensures that a common popular will might never gain the upper hand. At the same time, the supporters of the Constitution could tout their republican credentials by arguing that in the final analysis all government offices originated with the people. The result has been a federal government erected by the people but distant from their immediate concerns and malign passions: "Because the new federal government was designed to prevent the emergence of any passion or sense of oneness among large numbers of persons, men could now argue that 'virtue, patriotism or love of country never was nor never will be till men's natures are changed a fixed permanent principle and support of government.'"[5]

Faith in institutions as a source of order, control, and preservation of individual liberty is coupled with the Founders' trust in clipped and concise therapies for political diseases. Threatened with disorder, the institutionalist mechanism responded with a sudden harmony, with all its parts working together. Institutionalists, distrustful of common passions, were nonetheless precise when detailing how wars were to be declared and fought, taxes collected, black slaves counted, and rebellions quelled.

The institutionalist project establishes a political vocabulary of system, mechanism, control, realism, skepticism, and "facts." Suspicious of political associations, institutionalists have effectively bottled up those that have existed and deflected passions away from politics into the private realm. If collective passions were eliminated from politics, individual and group passions flourished in the economic marketplace. Assuming the undesirability and impossibility of changing human nature, institutionalists crafted and maintained the constitutional system as a permanent solution to innate human foibles as they manifested themselves in revolutionary America.[6]

As we shall see in a moment, political scientists have doubted the validity, efficacy, and utility of the institutionalist vision, even as they have had to confront it as the most powerful part of our political tradition. But they have also taken on an opposing vision of political society, as deeply engrained if not as successful as the first. From Thomas Paine to the Populists, from evangelicals to Locofoco craftsmen, radical democrats have challenged institutionalists and their self-proclaimed realism. To Paine, the purifying waters of revolution offered freedom from institutional entrapments. American society was "a blessing in every state, a loving and indulgent patron tolerant as nature herself of the variety of being and experience."[7]

To radical democrats such as Paine, political society did not need the imposition of an impersonal machine, but had to encourage the continuous experimentation and impromptu forms of popular power associated with equalitarian democracy. Popular virtue and sentiment—not neatly defined procedures—had to be the basis of republican community. And such energy was best expressed through political bodies close to the people, if not directly controlled by them. Protesting against the Constitution, western Massachusetts farmers declared it "absolutely necessary that the whole people should be active in the matter of government." Republicans "cannot surrender their privileges as citizens; they cannot be withheld from without."[8]

The Articles of Confederation may very well be the most characteristic document of radical democrats. In contrast to the present Constitution, the Articles' procedures were makeshift, and much was assigned to the Congress, the states, and their impromptu actions on the premise that the best government was one that was visible to and controllable by average citizens. To those concerned with national power and future expansion, the Articles offered few comforts. Only tentative and—to institutionalists—ultimately unworkable procedures were established for the collection of taxes, the making of war, the quelling of civil protests—all concerns much on the minds of the institutionalists. Trusting power to radical state legislatures, the Articles allowed what the Constitution forbade. In pre-Constitutional America, the specter of social leveling was as strong as the suspicion of a powerful national state.

The conflicts of institutionalists and democrats have formed the fundamental contours of American political debate and the extent of its future flexibility. As successful state builders, institutionalists have greased the wheels of their creation. The ubiquity of procedural battles, materialist analysis, and the self-interested conflict of factions and groups vindicates the institutionalists' claims about political society. But so, too, has the stream of radical democratic practice continued to flow, often below ground, but sometimes breaking through to the surface. The institutionalist logic has not entirely defeated what Norman Jacobson calls "the diffuse, protean, frequently contradictory demands of human nature." Nineteenth-century American political history is pockmarked with anomalies that defy the institutionalists' suspicion of collective political action. Religious evangelicals, utopian communitarians, abolitionists, Radical Republicans, populists, labor militants, and the dissenting youth of the 1960s—whatever the differences among them—continually sprout up in the formal gardens of the institutionalist republic of power, size, and grandeur.[9]

The Third Tradition: Beyond Mechanics and Spontaneity

Whatever the huge philosophical conflicts between institutionalists and radical democrats, leading political scientists have looked upon them as a kind of dialogue of the deaf. In their reciprocal archaism, both stand together as much as they conflict separately. Carried over to the profoundly transformed world of the late nineteenth and twentieth centuries, the modern proponents of each tradition have frozen structures, dispositions, and behavior into patterns of thought and practice formed in the agrarian republic. In their substitution of institutional contrivance for conscious human agency, in their fear of democratic majorities, and in their preoccupation with political order, institutionalists created and maintained a system that balanced power against power at the cost of neglecting the healthy and virtuous participation of citizens acting through politics. Almost by design, institutions in America have shredded political impulses of all kinds and have broken democratic majorities. Strangely, radical democrats started from different assumptions but created similar effects. Suspicious of concentrated power and distant institutions, they created a fondness for local democracy and hostility to national institutions. As the country grew, radical democrats immersed themselves in the effort to maintain face-to-face relations in communities that were being destroyed by forces beyond their control.

The consistent claims and most persistent definitions of a new science of politics in America rest heavily on replacing these two traditions with a new public philosophy. Not just a new method and organization of political studies, the American science of politics is also a kind of preventive medicine concocted for a sick polity. In place of the creaky and impersonal edifice of the nineteenth-century state, political scientists have sought a national state staffed by trained experts and supported by responsible and virtuous popular democratic majorities. If observers from Hegel to Samuel Huntington have noted the peculiar paradox of an innovative and changing American society contained within a stagnant and provincial polity, our political scientists have sought to close that gap between economic and social change and political provincialism. Firm admirers of political power carefully and judiciously exercised, enthusiastic about the rise of bureaucracies in the private and public world, liberal political scientists have wondered why elites and masses alike always divide, balance, and fragment political power, even as they adore private associations as the hallmark of "freedom."

But political scientists have not been American Bismarcks. Theirs is an attempt to mold a new state with what they see as native American forms of democratic legitimacy. The rough, autocratic, and militaristic image of the absolutist states of Europe need not appear here because state-building in America could only come at the crest of a popular democratic wave. In major part the impulse to found and practice a science of politics in America stems from this simple, if difficult, aim: How is it possible to build a sovereign, democratic, national state in a country whose major political traditions have defined democracy and limited power in ways contradictory to the effort?[10]

A particular definition and claim for the scientific outlook guides the answers political scientists have made to this question. Theirs is a cultural definition of the scientific ideal. Not only a method of study, social science is more important as a peculiarly American disposition to political thought and practice. Against divinely ordained ethics, opposed to all sanctification of authority, hostile to all determinisms, the "spirit" of the American science of politics is captured in its belief in the essential malleability of all social phenomena to human will and knowledge.[11] As humankind subjected natural forces to their will, so too could they channel social and economic processes to conscious and informed choices and purposes. There were compelling reasons to believe that a science of politics provided essential knowledge of previously uncontrollable social and economic processes. Democratic citizens, unlike bacteria, rocks, viruses, or microbes, were both the subject and object of investigation. If the forces shaping the modern world were presently mysterious and thus seemingly beyond human control, political science promised to end this unnecessary ignorance. Knowledge of these forces catalyzed a deeper collective search for destiny made possible by public awareness of the essential flexibility of modern societies to rational choices. In *Drift and Mastery*, Walter

Lippmann provides perhaps the clearest statement of the essentially democratic character of the scientific outlook:

> Science is the irreconcilable foe of bogeys, and therefore a method of laying bare the conflicts of the soul. It is the unfrightened, masterful and humble approach to reality—the needs of our nature and the possibilities of the world. The scientific spirit is the discipline of democracy, the escape from drift, the outlook of free men. Its direction is to distinguish fact from fancy, its enthusiasm is for the possible, its promise is the shaping of fact to a chastened and honest dream.[12]

Lippmann's juxtaposition of contemporary drift with the promise of future mastery indicates a fundamental disenchantment with the present. His ambition is typical of most liberal claims. In the last one hundred years, these claims have been comprehensive and extensive enough to warrant labeling them a distinctive public philosophy, a kind of "third tradition" dating from at least the late nineteenth century. It is the first concerted intellectual response to what Marx called the "creative destruction" capitalist industrialization in America spawned. As such, the third tradition takes its peculiar place among other historically rooted ways of thinking in America.

Scholars such as Woodrow Wilson, Lester Ward, Arthur Bentley, and Theodore Lowi can be brought together around not only what they oppose, but also around what they propose by means of their new science. At the very least, third tradition thought coheres around the following themes.

Modernism as Channeled Flux

As their critique of the American political past suggests, third tradition scholars have attributed to ignorance and false consciousness the features of industrial modernity that most Western European thinkers have seen as the inherent and structured conflicts, the pain and turmoil typical of mature capitalism. American scientists of politics have seen no systematic features of modernity that necessarily thwarted human freedom or progress. Against Marxian or Weberian thought, theirs is an unambivalent philosophy of triumphant modernism. The only impediments to historical progress are said to exist in the historical residue of premodern thinking as it works its dangerous way in the modern world. Once knowledge is accumulated and gained, conflicts thought to be endemic in modern society can be rationally controlled, mediated, and contained justly, equitably, and democratically. The essential harmony of industrial society is especially noteworthy in America where the absence of hard-and-fast class and religious divisions makes modern consensual democracy possible. Scientific knowledge helps Americans free themselves from the few constraints of their own history.[13]

Sovereignty and the State

To institutionalists, the state is ultimately a punisher. At best it prevents conflicts from reaching the political realm. To radical democrats, the state appears as a mailed fist, a basic violation of the fraternal instincts of democratic citizens. Third tradition political scientists have conjured up an image of the state as a benign and conscious reflection of, and actor for, an interdependent society. Among these third tradition political scientists is an almost complete absence of anxiety or fear about the role of any future American state. The despotic tendencies evident in state-building elsewhere can be easily avoided in America.

The new state in America has been an imperative and could be a blessing provided it could establish expertly organized instruments of domestic sovereignty and definitive spaces where authoritative decisions could be made about a whole range of increasingly politicized issues. Dear to political scientists has been the idea of separating the realm of politics from administration. More a desideratum than a datum, the concept is typical of the challenge offered to America's two traditions by political science modernizers. If the distinction were employed as public philosophy, it would revolutionize the practice of American government. The rule of law would return in the form of "democratic formalisms." Policy and legislation might be informed by expertise and implemented by a bureaucracy noted for its loyalty, accountability, and professionalism.

Some of the most trenchant critiques in political science history have explored the divergence of political practice from political potential. Bureaucratic advocates, political scientists have lamented the politicization and discretion of the bureaucracies they have advocated. Democratic devotees, political scientists have called on the president, Congress, and political parties to reassert their democratic authority.[14]

Citizenship and Legitimacy

Third tradition political scientists have been suspicious of static views of human nature, including those of institutionalists, radical democrats, socialists, and others. Citizens are thought to be neither benign, self-seeking, productive, nor innately incapable of judgment. Above all, they are malleable and flexible depending on the conditions of the epoch in which they live. Whatever else they are, citizens and their energies and support are deemed essential to the survival of modern democracy.

Inimical to the modern spirit is the idea that citizens are by nature greedy, self-seeking, and irredeemable. Citizens can be taught that the essence of democracy is rapt attention to national issues. They can be instructed in loyalty and prompted to use the state as their own instrument of experimentation and innovation. The problem, of course, is that Americans have been badly educated. They tend to equate democracy with individualism, the marketplace, and freedom from state control. But if citizens were better educated—if they were imbued with the rationality that comes from scientific thought—they could begin to make responsible choices. Narrow class interests, prejudices, ethnic loyalties, and all other provincial ideas might erode.

Interest group politics, federalism, hostility to modernism: All are the kinds of features that can be weeded out of the American political lexicon. The conflicts that people now take seriously are unnecessary because they are products of ideologies and false consciousness.[15]

Civic Education

No one has placed more confidence and hope in civic education as a vehicle for social change than liberal political scientists. Educators and schools have been assigned the task of creating a common national culture, captured in the ideas of innovation and experimentation—the spirit of science—that is said to be the essence of a free society. A reformed educational system has been assigned the task of weeding out archaic, premodern attitudes. To be sure, democratic educators avoid "value judgments." Far from propaganda, education in democracies shapes the individual's high sense of political efficacy. It creates an outlook free of rigid ideologies or irrational belief in messianic leaders. Charles Merriam, perhaps the most enthusiastic proponent of national civic education, well expresses the relationship between reform and educational innovation: "The broader education of humanity, the new forms of intercommunication, the larger resources of scientific inquiry—these are factors which are likely to force a readjustment of the bases of the political order and which require the development of techniques of government upon a wholly different plan from that upon which it has hitherto rested. . . . Politics as the art of the traditional advances to politics as the science of constructive intelligent social control."[16]

The Search for Reform Politics

The possibility of social and political harmony, the necessity of state-building, the scientization of public discourse, and the transformation of public associations all combine to form the public agenda of third tradition political scientists. Their definition of science itself promotes such hopes and claims because it promises a kind of intellectual order that dashes all hard-and-fast ideas about political association, even as it attacks all notions of necessary and inevitable revolutionary breaks with the past. But how could this ambitious agenda be realized? How could scientific politics be made real in the polity? Almost by the nature of the claims themselves, the success of political science has depended on communication to a wider audience and public outside the discipline. But which publics would most likely be receptive to this agenda? And how could intellectual influence be exerted on them to change their political direction?

While Western European intellectuals attached themselves to ongoing movements opposed to capitalism or put themselves at the service of the time-honored institutions of order and hierarchy, Americans, as usual, proved their own peculiarity by organizing themselves into autonomous professions. Modern professions emerged in America in the late nineteenth and early twentieth centuries. For social scientists, professional organizations became ways of establishing intellectual credibility and influence above "mere" partisanship and advocacy. The drive to professionalize, of course, implied insulation from the rough-and-tumble world of politics outside. Professionalism created a detachment said to be conducive to dispassionate research, observation, and studied reflection. But at least in political science and the other social sciences, this particular choice reflected a desire to establish forms of intellectual and political authority as truth-sayers as well as an attempt to influence the polity outside. Professionalism in American political science emerged not as a retreat from politics but as a way of expressing new and distinctive political claims.

At least in part, the drive for professionalism had its origins in forthright political choices—in roads *not* taken. There were few Karl Kautskys, Friedrich Engels, or Eduard Bernsteins in American political science. American political scientists shunned political parties as symptoms of a disease, not as vehicles for their philosophy of history. Labor and agrarian radical movements were culturally and politically alien to the temperament of the first social scientists as well, not necessarily because of their politics or their goals, but because of their stridency and methods. And, at least at first, few friends could be found among the elites of American politics and business. The American state bureaucracy was full of patronage appointees, people ill-disposed to bend to the rationalist claims of scientists. Robber barons were too selfish and narrow-minded to even care about attempts to achieve reforms and class conciliation. To form independent professions was more than anything a defensive choice, a recognition of nonpolitical alternatives. In the new universities of postbellum America, young scientists of society could conduct long-term, nonpartisan research. Political influence might come later by virtue of the obviously benign and reformist consequences that could be drawn from political research.[17]

This nineteenth-century choice has had a profound impact on the later rapport between political scientists and political reformers. Profession-builders became inextricably tied to the broader intellectual agenda of political research in America. The creation of universal standards for admission to and promotion within academia helped to flatten heterodox views among American intellectuals if only because heterodoxy could be channeled into research and work that met accepted standards of merit and "professionalism." Differences in opinion surely could exist, but they could not go too far beyond intellectual debate within the profession. The belief that there was, or could be, a "cumulative" science of politics in which each scholar's work responded to or built on that of his or her predecessors helped to establish a continuity of concerns and language among scientific students of society.

Third tradition political scientists have embraced professional organizations and standards. Adopting the professional ethos has enforced a consistency of political claims and a continuous perspective on the sources of disorder and crisis in America. Professional structures have also sustained a continuous view about how influence on the polity might be gained. Political advocacy always has taken place through the profession by combining advocacy with aspirations toward scholarly objectivity.[18]

But the very continuity of this shared perspective over the last hundred years suggests a gap between political and professional ambitions and claims on the one hand, and their extremely minimal impact on the course and direction of American political life on the other. Rather than a cumulative enterprise, political science is better seen as a repeating record with frequent variations on a theme. Successive generations of scholars return to older ideas and claims of their predecessors, often with the sense that they are making some path-breaking political and intellectual discovery. The source of these perpetual new beginnings is located in the failed aspirations of third tradition political science itself. Here is scholarship that depends for success on the vindication of its claims in the reconstruction of the American state and the reeducation of American citizens. The whole point of forming a profession has been to establish an authoritative voice to which ordinary citizens and elites alike defer. Lippmann referred to "the shaping of facts to an honest dream" as the spirit of science and of democratic politics. But when third tradition political scientists have made their forays into the world of politics, they have often encountered illusions and non-facts. Retreats and reentries into politics have characterized the professional life of the discipline's leading thinkers, and this cycle has been repeated often enough to call it a pattern. Political activity has thrust third tradition political scientists into public roles as sponsors of governmental reorganization, new economic and social planning schemes, and reforms of the two-party system. Retreat often comes after the success of policies and the failure of their overarching philosophies. The first to sponsor liberal legislation, political scientists have been the most trenchant and bitter critics of reform for its minimal effects.

The chapters of this book trace the democratic delusions of reform political scientists. Ultimately, the essential intractability of the American political character is what most depresses political scientists. Introspection always sets in when "scientifically" verified possibilities are ignored or mangled by the publics political scientists designate as reform vanguards. For some reason, these liberal publics always fail to heed the scientific message even though it is always advertised as the locomotive of history and the "science of the possible."

At least five distinct twists of this cycle can be identified. In chapter 2,

"The Impulse toward a Science of Politics, 1880–1900," our investigation begins with Lester Ward and Woodrow Wilson, among the most important founders of social science in late nineteenth-century America. Ward is usually considered the founder of American sociology, and Wilson refused to call himself a political scientist. Yet both of them were active in the professionalization movement of the 1880s and 1890s. Both men established an agenda for political studies in America. Advocates of the administrative state, they both predicted it would breathe "free American air." Critics of the status quo, they were optimistic about the prospects for reform. Each located reform publics, deeming them popular carriers of the scientific worldview into the wilderness of the contemporary American polity. Enthusiastic and hopeful in their youth, both lived to see their optimism dashed.

Chapter 3, "Science as Muckraking: The Cult of Realism in the Progressive Era," spans the early growth years of the political science profession between the turn of the twentieth century and World War I. The Progressive movement's apex fueled the enthusiasm of scientific reformers and raised expectations about a sea change in American political habits, thoughts, and practices. Charles Beard and Arthur Fisher Bentley are this movement's left-wing scholarly representatives. Beard and Bentley created a bare-bones science of politics whose mission was to strip institutions, ideologies, and seemingly random political processes of their ideological pretensions and ersatz justifications. Each dredged up disturbing facts about the forces behind the social and economic processes shaping American politics. Both highlighted these facts in order to stir popular outrage and catalyze political action. The great middle class, each believed, was the natural corrector of abuses.

Bentley's methods inspired future generations of professionals. Beard's political activities and didactic histories expanded the numbers and concentrated the activities of a growing and aggressive political science profession. Yet this radical political science always diverged from the designs of its architects. In the 1920s and 1930s, both Beard and Bentley became disillusioned with the profession they helped to build.

After World War I, political scientists responded to the failures of Progressivism by withdrawing into the university. Progressive political science was said to be methodologically immature and insufficiently organized to be effective in stirring reform. Chapter 4, "Reform and Disillusionment in the New Deal," looks at this scientific orientation, best represented in the works and lives of Charles Merriam and his student and colleague, Harold Lasswell. Theirs was a scientism designed to locate the secrets of political behavior in order to modify citizen attitudes. Both Lasswell and Merriam radically expanded the organization and influence of political science. The potential of a planned and expertly administered reform state was combined with efforts to transform citizen beliefs and eliminate premodern prejudices. Under Merriam's leadership, political science was supposed to become the "pure science of democracy," an alternative to the totalitarian sciences of Stalinism and fascism. Just revealing facts to a "reform public" was considered insufficient. Acting through the New Deal and Roosevelt's benign leadership, the new political scientists believed they could and would create a public respectful of science and democracy.

Most of Merriam's hopes for a liberal future died with the Second New Deal. Conservatives in Congress rejected his efforts to introduce peacetime economic planning and to implement a national policy of civic education. And the climate of post–World War II America was hardly hospitable to reformers and tinkerers such as Merriam. Chapter 5, "The Behavioral Era," is set in the era of the cold war and the great American celebration, when most of the critical perspectives in political science were replaced with an "objective orientation." Behavioralists of the 1950s and 1960s made Merriam look like a scientific primitive or a utopian dreamer. Behavioralists christened as the very definition of democracy the apathy and popular ignorance of politics Merriam derided. Still, there was an undercurrent of anxiety and fear in the writings of otherwise uncritical behavioralists. V. O. Key's and David Truman's works explored the "latent" manifestations of crisis and conflict beneath the seeming harmony of the period. Fearful that the American state was losing its legitimacy, Key and Truman worried about the rise of "potential interest groups," euphemisms for race and class conflicts.

Behavioralist quiescence combined with hyperspecialization to exclude from consideration most of the issues that had always worried political scientists—but not for long. Easy assumptions about the health of American democracy seemed a little ridiculous in the face of the events of the 1960s, 1970, and 1980s. The Vietnam War, Watergate, cultural turmoil, and a profound economic crisis all provoked deeper debate about the theory and practice of democracy in America.

In political science, these events reintroduced an older critical spirit, at least among a significant minority. Yet the "postbehavioral" period is aptly named, perhaps because the title reflects more what a segment of the profession rejected than what political science in America was supposed to be. Since the late 1960s, critics of behavioralism have multiplied. Appeals for radicalism have been mixed with appeals for relevance, and challenges to professionalism have been blended with efforts to make political science relevant again.

Many political scientists have welcomed such pluralism. Yet at the same time, such diversity reflects a great deal of disagreement and confusion about the purposes and aims of contemporary political science. Less and less, scholars talk of science itself as the language of political harmony and reform. More and more, they are skeptical about the validity and prospects of "interest group liberalism."

Increasingly, research seems to call into question previous hopes for liberal reform. A growing number of political scientists choose sides between philosophies that contradict the aspirations of third tradition scholars. Some conclude that "democracy" itself is to blame. Others fear repression in the form of capitalist reindustrialization and advocate less bourgeois forms of democratic life. Others disguise and dismiss political questions altogether, searching for mathematical formulas that will explain politics. An admirable spirit of mutual tolerance now prevails at professional meetings because each "subfield" is accorded its own panels attended by its own participants. What is clearly missing is that professional coherence that Wilson, Beard, Merriam, and others sought. As liberal assumptions erode in the polity, they die in political science.

Some measure of what has transpired can be seen in the works of Theodore Lowi and Walter Dean Burnham. They ask the same questions their third tradition predecessors asked, but they get very different answers. Lowi calls for "juridical democracy" in a work that shows why achieving it is impossible. Burnham discovers "critical elections" in the American past only to conclude that if we had one now, the results would be far from progressive. Radical liberal hopes are raised in their last chapters, only to be dashed by the discoveries of their own investigations.

In the 1980s, third tradition political scientists have become conscious of the scientific delusions of the past. The political confidence and aspirations of a once powerful strain of liberal thinking have already been shaken.

The present impasse, though, is nothing really new, for similar tensions have been evident throughout the history of political science. In brighter moments, third tradition political scientists have linked the growth of scientific scholarship to the achievements of the liberal agenda. No serious scholar is much inclined to that approach anymore. But to comprehend the present skepticism, the sources of historical overoptimism need to be analyzed.

2

The Impulse toward a Science of Politics, 1880–1900

The Founders crafted their Constitution for a nation with plantation slavery, small and relatively self-sufficient villages, tiny cities, expanding frontiers, and an ethnically homogeneous citizenry of white men. Radical democratic thought was forged in a similar world even though it drew different conclusions about citizens and their political capacities. Perhaps the ultimate vindication of both traditions is found in their longevity because if James Madison was somehow resurrected in postbellum America, he would have recognized little about the country except the political institutions he helped to design. But were these political institutions and the public philosophy they encouraged qualified to meet the profound new challenges and demands placed on them? Could institutional mechanisms or heartfelt passion for democratic community provide necessary coherence in the impersonal and interdependent society now spanning a continent?

These were the questions the first self-proclaimed social scientists at the end of the nineteenth century asked. For them, institutional longevity was hardly vindication, but rather was proof of political failure and impending crisis. Political conflict and debate seemed strangely out of touch with the American reality of the 1880s, and the gap between a stagnant political life, a dynamic society, and a transformed economy was only evidence that drift, discord, or even revolution might be the American political future. In America as in Europe, all that was solid was indeed melting into air. The disappearance of common customs, manners, and thought left political institutions, philosophies, and behavior without cultural underpinnings.[1]

Filling that gap was thought to require a complete understanding of social and economic processes operating in America. Such an understanding, social scientists believed, presented the opportunity for intelligent control of these processes. But there was opposition. Social scientists had to confront the American political traditions as they displayed themselves at that time. Contemporary political actors resisted the required adjust-ments; the resistance to new political knowledge might doom the polity altogether.

There were plenty of examples to distress thinking souls. By the end of Reconstruction, American politics seemed to have lost its bearings. Political life returned to the quaint provincialism of the antebellum days. Patronage-ridden parties, sectional politics, and immersion in localism and ethnic rivalries took hold of the political system, even as the society and economy were moving toward large corporate organizations, crowded and anonymous cities, a class system, and an interdependent economy that was both national and international in scope. As Europeans were building new states and imperial dominions in Africa and Asia, Americans were organizing their government—poorly—into competing patronage cliques. As grimy cities grew, the frontier closed, and self-sufficient villages and towns became increasingly part of the international economy, poli-ticians still pretended that the marketplace was beneficent and that there were no compelling reasons to regulate, much less control, the ravages of competition in the capitalist marketplace. Nor was the popular resistance to laissez-faire philosophy thought to be very comforting: Greenbackers and other agrarian radicals advocated panaceas to restore a bygone and outmoded way of life, not centralized political direction of large private organizations. Their desperation often produced only apocalyptic visions. As huge factories, corporate organizations, and a refined division of labor became commonplace, politicians still hawked "rugged individualism" and the virtues of "self-made men." Even as the world became filled with complicated processes incomprehensible to individuals, older scholars still spoke in the moral platitudes of natural law, divine commandments, sanctified political procedures, and legalisms.

Something had to give—or so most young and ambitious postbellum intellectuals believed. At the new American universities founded after the Civil War—Cornell, Stanford, Chicago, Johns Hopkins, Berkeley, and Michigan—the first self-proclaimed social scientists achieved marginal positions and tenuous badges of social respectability. Mostly European-ed-ucated and Northeastern-born, they were as impressed by the ubiquity of flux and change as they were confident about the prospects of ration-ally controlling their effects and tempo. Urban squalor, social inequality, and political corruption were all thought to be manifestations of a crisis in the way the world was understood. In contrast, complete knowledge of complex processes indicated that the world just did not have to work so poorly. For early social scientists, unraveling the diverse and tangled strands of social processes was taking a definitive step toward rational control over them, including prediction of their consequences and effects on the future. But before knowledge could be effective, archaic ideas about timeless "values" and sanctified social relations had to go. Oozing social processes could no more be stopped than biological evolution itself or the cycles of birth, life, and death. Social science promised to close the gap between premodern perceptions and obtrusive reality, as Thomas Haskell explains: "As causes recede and a growing interdependence introduces more and more contingency into each chain of causation, the realm of inquiry must expand and the conditions of satisfying explanation must change. Common sense fails and the claims of expertise gain plausibility. Explanation itself becomes a matter of special significance, because the explainer promises to put his audience back in touch with the most vital elements of a receding and increasingly elusive reality."[2]

The Attack on Amateurs

But what were satisfying explanations? The last quarter of the nineteenth century had no definitive answers. There was a deep-seated sense that groups of scholars had to try, and some certainty that existing explanations were untrue and superficial. In fact, the number of charlatans peddling explanations was by itself cause for intellectual indigestion. A quick survey of late-nineteenth-century lists of bestsellers in America reveals the depth of the intellectual crisis: To social scientists, snake oil salesmen had already invaded politics. Some, like Edward Bellamy in *Looking Backward*, promised utopian quick fixes: conflicts and tensions might be resolved in a single stroke. Others, such as Henry George or William "Coin" Harvey, sought to save society with panaceas. People such as Ignatius Donnelly predicted the imminent end of capitalist civilization in an Armageddon of barbarian outbreaks. Scholars might have snickered at Donnelly's prediction that an agrarian utopia would be founded by American survivors of the holocaust transported to Africa in captured blimps, but lots of people made lots of money as purveyors of such unscientific speculations.[3]

Meanwhile, unreconstructed apologists for unfettered capital accumulation justified the J. P. Morgans of the world as unwitting leaders of species development. Others, less ideological, ignored the rise of industrial civilization altogether. Books written by professors at Harvard, Yale, and Princeton still talked of the beauty of the polis, the rhetoric of Cicero, and the intricacies of common law. Unfortunately, those worlds existed only in libraries.

All the above qualified as enemies for young, ambitious, and worried social scientists, But there were closer contenders for the intellectual throne. Some competed with the new professionals for the mantle of "science," even though they misunderstood its principles. The American Social Science Association (ASSA), founded by former abolitionist Frank Sanborn in 1865, typified the kind of amateurism that the new professionals tried to combat.

Sanborn's organization united a large number of upper-class New England do-gooders and academic dilettantes. Their notion of scientific scholarship was predicated on the easy discovery of unchanging and benign laws governing the universal march toward plenty and progress. A science of society was no more than the application of Christian morality to the solution of practical problems. Well-meaning individuals could band together in voluntary organizations to redress grievances and ease obvious distresses. Sanborn's work in reorganizing charity efforts in Massachusetts suggested that organizational efficiency was replacing cleanliness as the virtue closest to godliness. To ASSA members, reality was not opaque or contingent. Social science was but the administration of shared and known moral precepts. Rather than encouraging serious scholarship, ASSA leaders assumed that doses of simple morality mixed with efficiency could reduce poverty, cure the mentally ill, house the homeless, and feed the hungry. Reform was a matter of educated personal morality, not the investigation and control of complex and impersonal social and economic processes.

Evangelical radicals, apocalyptic naysayers, advocates of quick fixes, nice but irrelevant social reformers—social scientists of the nineteenth century viewed them all as symptoms of modernism's dangers. In the absence of scholarly investigation, people inevitably grasped at straws. With the world unraveling, a "community of the competent" populated by trained and expert practitioners of scholarly research was urgently required. Just as the division of labor in the economy enabled an explosion of productivity, so too ought the study of society become a specialized task, a "vocation" as worthy as engineering, business administration, or physics. Specialists in explanation were as natural as trained specialists in any other endeavor, and humanitarian fervor was not a replacement for training, expertise, and universal standards of scholarly acceptability.[4]

The Profession Builders

Disenchantment with amateurs, impatience with supposed demagogues, and advocacy of professional standards and identities were the common currency of the young academics of the 1880s and 1890s. But the urge to establish intellectual credibility partly disguised radical differences among the founders of modern American social science. Today, these differences are often forgotten, even though splits in the modern profession tend to replicate older patterns. What we call "third tradition" scholarship formed as a kind of critical borrowing and selective synthesis of the various "extremes" among the new scholars. The unique perspectives of liberal Progressive political science emerged in the works of Lester Ward and Woodrow Wilson. But their view of the American political and intellectual crisis—as well as their definitions of science—had much to do with a rejection of extremes among early academics. Statism, socialism, and Social Darwinism were the most fashionable positions of "true" social scientists. But in Ward's and Wilson's thought, all these cross-currents were made to flow together harmoniously. Their pretenses to neutrality, however, did not emerge without political and intellectual struggles with other new academics.[5]

One group among the profession builders rejected the modern capitalist system altogether. In the 1870s and 1880s, young German-trained economic historians returned home and embarked on a series of studies of modern wage labor. Their studies predicted that America could hardly remain immune from the class struggles of Europe. The early works of scholars such as Richard Ely, Henry Carter Adams, and John Bates Clark traced the systematic inequality of the industrial capitalist system, an inequality that could not be tempered through halfway measures or conciliatory gestures and reforms. Hostile to centralized ownership of the means of production, Ely, Clark, and Adams perceived a gradual and ineluctable development of a "cooperative commonwealth" in America. Industrial capitalism would eventually have to be destroyed by workers' organizations and self-managing forms of production and consumption.

Their works were not mere political advocacy disguised as science, but among the most comprehensive academic treatises of late-nineteenth-century

America. Ely, Adams, and Clark, although rejecting Marxian socialism, centered on the division of labor as the central feature of industrial modernization. By nature, however, the growth of the division of labor was thought to prompt systematic political struggle as capitalists became increasingly superfluous to the maintenance of the society they presently controlled. Anticipating the work of Thorstein Veblen, all three predicted the demise of laissez-faire capitalism and the future happy union of engineer and laborer in a productive, democratic society.[6]

These tender shoots of native American socialist thought did not flourish, however. Neither Ely, nor Adams, nor Clark became American Fabians despite the historical and empirical arguments they all made for an American brand of socialism. One of the peculiar effects of the professional ethos they shared was to blunt frank political advocacy and active participation in the labor movements of the 1880s. Any anticapitalist tendencies in their writings were channeled into the safe and sane complexities of emerging academic discourse and professional social science. In a series of landmark academic freedom cases, their "socialist" social science was subtly transferred into respectability. All three men were forced to choose between contradictory alternatives: They could either leave academics for direct participation in labor struggles or "professionalize" and sanitize their discourse. Even in the 1880s and 1890s, this meant a moderation of language and a shift in emphasis. Ely, Adams, and Clark could express their political beliefs only as college teachers, not as partisans. For the first time, the call to science as a "vocation" excluded direct political advocacy. Ely, Adams, and Clark were made to believe that their credibility as scientists was much more important than direct political advocacy. In fact, they seemed to see their academic careers as ultimately much more political than abandoning academics.[7]

Socialist advocacy was one losing tendency among advocates of a professional science of society. Other, German-trained scholars imported a much more foreign social science into American academic life. Impressed by the close ties between the university and the German bureaucracy, men such as John Burgess and Andrew Dickson White were forthright statists.[8] Theirs was a formalist science, marked by enthusiasm about the prospects of state development in America as a solution to the problems of order and class conflict. White and Burgess exalted the virtues of a bureaucratic order. If America put a group of university-trained, morally upright, and technically proficient civil servants into power, then the reign of political parties and "dumb" immigrants might end. A new bureaucratic gentry could be established. Burgess, who founded the first graduate school in political science at Columbia, and White, Cornell's first president and ambassador to tsarist Russia, were as rabidly antisocialist as they were enthusiastic state-builders. What appeared to a later generation as intellectually empty justifications for racism were to these American statists preludes to a triumphant fusion of nationalism and imperialism.[9] To stem working-class anarchism, Burgess and White sought an academia frankly linked with imposed bourgeois order. Burgess and White were hardly optimistic about the future of democracy. Obsessed with finding a secular and "scientific" basis for elite rule, their allegiance to democracy was rhetorical. In their work, the claims of expertise always overrode the passions of the "ignorant" and "dangerous" classes.

The ubiquity and universality of social change prompted yet a third scientific response in the form of Social Darwinism. These thinkers discovered meaning in the otherwise mindless and uncontrolled processes of the marketplace. Competition among amoral entrepreneurs was the paradoxical source of moral progress itself. To Social Darwinists, progress was the ironic end of individual greed, avarice, and inequality. Human actions had an unintended if beneficent effect insofar as they were not subjected to conscious political machinations. Political action only held back the march of productivity and creativity. To William Graham Sumner, the foremost proponent of Social Darwinist thought in America, callousness and complacency might be reprehensible as moral qualities, but they created no problems warranting governmental action. Sumner's moral relativism turned the crisis of understanding into a positive virtue. It did not really matter if individuals or classes were caught in a world not of their own making or that the world's evolution had nothing to do with morality or divinely revealed principles. Aimless competition eventually fulfilled all purposes.[10]

The problem with all three of these sciences was their essential radicalism and pessimism. In one way or another, each invalidated the other. Each justified a sea change in American political life. If class conflict was inevitable, then it was no wonder that statists sought authoritarian order. If public morality was harmful, why not justify drift and discord? In all of them, the claims of particular social classes were given credence over and against the benign potential of interclass cooperation. Domination and submission were thought to be an integral part of the problematic dialectic of modernization. The scholarship of Lester Ward and Woodrow

Wilson drew heavily from each of these perspectives. But the radicalism of each one of them was carefully filtered out. From the socialists, Ward and Wilson borrowed a concern for issues of inequality between classes. Inherent class struggle was turned into a benign mediation of the state between groups. The call for a cooperative commonwealth gave way to liberal appeals for equality of opportunity.[11]

Ward and Wilson borrowed from the statists an admiration for autonomous bureaucracies and a preoccupation with political order and expertise. But the elitist and autocratic overtones of Burgess's and White's theories were castigated for their anti-American, pro-German "biases." If a strong state was to be introduced into America, it had to "breathe free American air"—it had to merge with a cultural predisposition for self-government, not fight this disposition.[12] If experts were to inhabit the state, they had to be drawn from all of America's social classes and had to be accountable to the commands of popularly elected institutions and leaders. Lastly, Social Darwinism provided both an intellectual foil and a source from which to borrow. In Ward's and Wilson's writings, mindless processes could be bent toward "creative evolution." Together, natural selection and survival of the fittest produced the potential of fruitful and conscious human control over the course of evolution itself.

The brief intellectual biographies that follow trace the formation of Ward's and Wilson's distinct perspectives. The battle against competing sciences as well as the utter disdain for a host of supposed intellectual "charlatans" helps to place both thinkers within the third tradition. Reformers, Wilson and Ward condemned radicalism and the status quo alike. Advocates of professionalism, both saw it as a way to reinstate intellectual authority in a country that lacked it. Perhaps professionalism was a way of isolating scholars from politics, but it was also a mode of increasing their credibility as objective truth-sayers. Claims of political order and resurgent democracy blended in their works as easily as did their advocacy of a union between science and sentiment.

The Strange Populism of the Founder of American Sociology

In 1883 an already distinguished group of youthful and ambitious scholars met in the opulent resort of Saratoga Springs, New York, to form the American Economic Association (AEA), the first "professional" social science organization in the United States. Despite the posh surroundings, or perhaps because of them, the AEA founders produced a founding platform that sharply attacked the then-leading intellectual advocates of laissez-faire capitalism. In a document later much revised to accommodate those less explicitly reform-minded, Woodrow Wilson and other AEA founders leveled a forceful attack on the excesses and antiquarianism of American political and economic ideas. Economist Richard Ely declared: "We regard the state as an ethical and educational agency, whose positive aid is an indispensable condition of human progress." Conventional wisdom was also dealt a blow by the founders of the newborn profession, who saw the previously accepted "laws" of economic behavior as mere claims demanding scientific verification: "We believe that political economy as a science is still in an early stage of its development . . . and we look not so much to speculation as to the historical and statistical study of actual conditions of economic life for the satisfactory accomplishment of this development."[13]

Although many of AEA's founders were probably not aware of it, Lester Frank Ward—one of their contemporaries—would later be heralded as the most systematic critic of laissez-faire economics, the Manchester School, and a whole tradition of American scholarship that perceived "positive government" as a violation of natural law or the imperatives of evolutionary progress. In the 1930s Ward was praised as "an American Aristotle."[14] New Deal ideologists resurrected his sociology because it posited the growth of "collective will" expressed through a governmental order both potent and benign. With the great revolution that justified the growth of the American state's scope and functions seemingly completed, Ward could indeed appear to be the happy warrior, the first to systematically weld a uniquely American equalitarian thrust to the positivist conservatism of Auguste Comte. To New Deal reformers, Ward's fusion of scientific study and political advocacy was all the more enchanting for its self-conscious concern for peculiarly American problems. But Ward's revival at the height of the New Deal is perhaps less indicative of a full understanding of his intellectual aims than it is of the proximity between government and social science sought by New Deal intellectuals. Ward's work led in directions far different than his New Deal admirers believed. Nearly a half-century before Franklin Roosevelt's reforms, he wrote accolades to the positive state and polemics against the class biases of laissez-faire thought. But his odd effort to join sociocracy with populism was a much more ambitious political project than the pragmatic aims of most New Deal intellectuals.[15]

Without a contextual and biographical understanding of Ward, under-standing why and how the conservative organicism of Auguste Comte was translated into a social science supportive of the demands of the working classes is difficult. Ward, unlike other social science notables of the late nineteenth century, was raised as a Locofoco Democrat, steeped in the belief that artisanal labor was the fountainhead of democracy. His fondness for "science" hardly contradicted his belief in a "natural" social harmony among simple, hard-working, self-sufficient citizens in a democratic republic. Ward's damning indictments of plutocratic wealth often recalled the vision of virtue and simple equality of frontier and farming America. The Locofoco dream of a democratic society composed of independent artisans perhaps explains why Ward flirted with, but ultimately rejected, theories favorable to technological utopianism and proletarian revolution. To Ward, class conflict was not an inevitable consequence of industrializa-tion in America. Struggles between classes were only aberrations provoked by the machinations of corrupt plutocrats. Republican virtue and natural social harmony might be restored by altering the functions and uses of government to modernize the American political character. In this country, natural political consensus need not have the conservative implications of Comtean hierarchy. In America, natural equalitarian order had been vio-lated only by a selfish few. Natural equality of opportunity, not hierarchy, stood as the basis of the modern republican order.[16]

Like many of the other professionals, Ward's own life is a story of social mobility. Only in middle age did Ward hold a teaching position at a major educational institution, Brown University. Born on the frontier into respectable poverty, Ward migrated east, found work in a factory, and simultaneously taught himself Greek, Latin, French, and German. An enlistee in the Union Army, Ward was wounded at Chancellorsville, and his experience netted him a job as a clerk in the Treasury Department after the Civil War. The bulk of his life was passed in the then tiny federal bureaucracy, as chief of the Division of Immigration and Navigation and as resident paleontologist in the U.S. Geological Survey. These positions allowed him to travel to every corner of the continental United States. With night-school degrees in law and science, Ward used federal service as an occasion to write *Dynamic Sociology*, his first great work in social science, begun in 1869 and finally published in 1883.

Ward's experience as a natural scientist and as a well-traveled public official suggested that government, if only it collected enough facts about social change, could reverse what he referred to as the "unthinking devastation of the forests" and "the depletion of the richest soils in the world." Ward's class origins gave an unusual popular caste to this hatred of waste and concern for conservation.[17]

Ward's positive science of society rejected all doctrines of historical necessity and human submission before the imperatives of one social or economic law or another. "Dynamic sociology," he believed, showed that the horrors of capitalist industrialization were simply not necessary. They were above all the results of sadly mistaken and ideologically charged philosophies that held back natural social evolution. Ward reversed Social Darwinist logic. Survival of the fittest and natural selection were the laws of nature and of society but with one important difference. Human evolution endowed societies with a collective mind. Their members could shape and choose their collective futures insofar as they had the knowledge of social and economic processes that social science could provide. The dream of consciously guiding and controlling human history, Ward believed, was now within the grasp of the most advanced part of the species.

Ward's work is as prone to biological metaphors as any other late-nineteenth-century writer. He was struck by the profligacy, waste, death, destruction, and random change in the world of plants and animals. But carried over to human history—especially present human history—biological theories became for Ward mere justifications for illegitimate authority. The distinctive quality of historical maturity was not competition, but rather cooperation in large organizations such as cities, government bureaucracies, and business corporations. Humans competed against natural forces, not against themselves. The immense productivity and interdependence of the industrial age led Ward to conclude that the ultimate criteria by which to judge human progress was found in the level of sharing it had achieved. From *Psychic Factors in Civilization*: "All human institutions—religion, government, law, marriage, custom—together with innumerable other modes of regulating social, industrial and commercial life, broadly viewed, are only so many ways of meeting and checkmating the principle of competition as it manifests itself in society."[18]

Ward attacked all "primitive" doctrines justifying competition, conflict, and natural hierarchy. Theories about the inviolability of property, the inevitability of class divisions, and the naturalness of poverty were not criticized, however, because they relied on evolutionary precepts, but precisely because they denied the potential created by human evolution itself. The workings of human invention and artifice against the competitive struggle of the natural world, Ward thought, *already* distinguished humankind from nature. Both the dilemma and the opportunity were to make human societies aware of their own cooperative potentialities, now disguised by amoral forms of capitalism and the laissez-faire ideologists who defended them.

Ward's sociology has often been perceived as a blistering and fundamental attack on laissez-faire doctrines. Yet it is the similarity between Ward's epistemology and that of his evolutionist adversaries that is significant. Ward neither disputed the view that certain evolutionary laws could be found at work in natural and human history, nor that the task at hand was to adjust and adapt human behavior to those laws. In all cases, the "natural laws" of social development held the key to the proper ends and means of intervention. These laws were discoverable through observation and controllable through human action and consciousness. Ward's sociology promised not to supplant evolutionary processes, but to discover and supplement them.[19]

Political science emerged as a subset of sociology. It was that part of "science" that builds the instruments of control and sets the terms of choice for evolutionary progress. The state, in his view, was itself a product of benign evolution. Its very emergence signaled the triumph of the cooperative ideal in human affairs, the union of knowledge with power. Rejecting W. G. Sumner's and Herbert Spencer's beliefs that "helping the weak and the unfit was a form of paternalism that in the long run would only cripple the race's progress," Ward proposed to show that the working class was weak only because capitalists had artificially twisted the laws of evolutionary change. In actual politics, capitalists used and needed the state as much as everyone else: "Nothing is more obvious today than the single inability of capital and private enterprise to take care of themselves unaided by the state; while they are incessantly denouncing paternalism—by which they mean the claim of the defenseless laborer and artisan to a share in this lavish state protection—they are all the while besieging legislatures for relief from their own incompetency, and 'pleading the baby act' through a trained body of lawyers and lobbyists."[20]

Ward saw late-nineteenth-century American society as fraught with "artificial" as opposed to "real" competition, "destructive" as opposed to "constructive" individualism, and unnecessary conflicts rather than national cooperation and harmony. All of these polarities highlighted the sources of his critical posture, even as they showed the political and intellectual boundaries beyond which Ward refused to go. The passion for property, Ward thought, was an essential and beneficial characteristic of evolutionary progress. Ironically, the business concentration promoted by the dynamics of capitalist industrialization set the conditions for social cooperation.

Competitive laissez-faire capitalism was merely a perversion of this passion for property and therefore an impediment to true progress and social harmony. Only unrestrained emotion, false consciousness, unfettered greed, and unrelieved ignorance created an irresponsible, competitive capitalism. Bad attitudes, not social laws, were the source of pigheaded provincialism. Change these attitudes and the findings revealed by science would become real; the cycle of destruction and waste would cease. Artificial barriers of class, status, wealth, and power would tumble because industrial civilization already had put an end to economic scarcity.[21] And collective will was to be found in society's brain—the state. Here, processes shaping the world would be understood and their tendencies shaped. Here, the unseen hand of the market would become the collective search for material and spiritual union.

By its nature, Ward's science of society thus involved a dual enterprise. The first was a concerted search for knowledge about social and economic interactions. Scientists compiled the facts and statistics regarding natural resources and their use, the distribution of wealth, the tempo of demographic change, and the secrets of technological progress and industrial growth. Scholars trained in the compilation of data explored the hidden possibilities of human intervention in heretofore uncontrolled social and natural processes.

But the mere compilation and collection of data were not enough. Scientists of society had to be educators. They had to change ingrained attitudes of fear of the state and rejection of collective governance. Divided social classes had to be taught that society, like the economy, was not an independent, uncontrollable entity distant from both passion and reason but rather was an instrument of human invention.

At this point Ward's thought most directly addressed the crisis in American institutions and democracy as they were conceived at the Founding. Who, Ward asked, would be the likely constituencies for the "scientific outlook" in late-nineteenth-century America apart from scientists themselves? If a government of society was the natural consequence of the "intellectual revolution" Ward sought to inspire, who would be the subjects of such a revolution in the world of politics? Characteristically, Ward here sought to locate two already active political tendencies that, once properly fused with the scientific outlook, would become the "conscious force of creative evolution." To Ward, the great popular labor and agrarian movements of his time, along with public spirited officials and elected office holders, comprised the democratic, scientific public. Republicanism and state power were to be fused in mutual admiration for the spirit of scientific experimentation.[22]

Ward's choice of the Knights of Labor and the Populists as the suitable constituencies for scientific politics typifies the outlook and hopes of third tradition political science. To him, the radical democratic sentiments of people victimized by industrial capitalism were indeed legitimate. Bolstered with the equalitarian impulses of the powerless, science could be introduced into American life as a fulfillment of the republican tradition. The vitality and spontaneity of political protest provided a superb opportunity to reverse the unnecessary excesses of capitalist growth: "All great movements in history," Ward held, "are preceded and accompanied by strong feeling. . . . Purely intellectual feeling is never sufficient directly to sway the multitude." Populist challenges to bankers and financiers, and industrial strikes were "precisely the way in which reform in the direction indicated should be expected to originate."[23]

But there was also hopeful calculation and some paternalism in Ward's democratic advocacy. Despite the justice of their grievances, protesters and their philosophies could not be accepted at face value. Their aims and methods had to "creatively evolve" away from their antiscientific, premodern distrust of the state and experts. Democratic sentiment was valuable in that it brought injustice to light, but it was a poor guide to necessary and possible reforms.

Populists and labor militants were suitable raw material for change, but their provincial, misdirected sentiments had to be "scientized" and "improved." Demands for political participation and nostalgia for honest country life needed to be transformed by intellect. Scientists, in short, were the vanguard of rational political protest. Democratic radicalism provided the proper emotions, but its advocates lacked reason:

> The problem is to apply the vast emotional forces which are ever
> striving to improve society, but failing for want of the proper intellectual

guidance, to some truly progressive system of machinery that shall succeed in accomplishing the desired end. . . . The only proper knowledge for this purpose is that which can be acquired of the materials and forces of nature . . . The diffusion of this kind of knowledge among the masses of mankind is the only hope we have of securing any greater social progress than that which nature itself vouchsafes through its own process of selection.[24]

The rapport of science and sentiment tapped an important vein in both Ward's thought and in the later history of reformers in political science. With utmost sincerity, Ward could write to his nephew, "I would probably go further toward populism than you. . . . No one is more anxious to throttle the money power." Yet simultaneously, Ward seriously misinterpreted the anti-institutional, communitarian strain in Populism as an outdated manifestation of agrarian nostalgia. If Populists deferred to scientists, they would be better led and more successful: impulses toward participatory democracy would become passé if not directed to their proper objects. Both labor and agrarian radicalism were understandable reactions, but intellectually they were immature. The interdependent economies of scale, the evolution of complex organizations, the inevitability of bureaucracy—Populists stubbornly resisted them all. To Ward, they failed to understand that all these forces could ultimately work in their favor. Ward's genuine hatred of injustice was thereby transformed into an attempt to alter the supposedly "premodern" attitudes of radicals. Democratic protest from below would be replaced by political engineering from above.[25]

Radical emotion had to give way to construction of a "new system of machinery" acting in the best "national interest." Not surprisingly his chosen vehicle for the birth of a new union between knowledge and protest and between intellectuals and Populism was his call for "popular scientific education."[26] To Ward, such education would redirect protest from its concern about a "lost" America in order to concentrate on the creative potentialities of modernism. Scientific education would level all hierarchies based on wealth and property, even as it taught the masses that intellectuals were their helpful big brothers, not snobbish interlopers. Destroying artificial hierarchies did not deter Ward from advocacy of a "true" meritocracy drawn from a "democratic pool of resources." Traditions of local control of education would fall with the class system. The popular classes would receive a "universal education," and the best among them would be selected for positions of economic and political leadership. Most important of all, education would transform the "antistate bias" of the plain people into a force for planning, control, and intervention on behalf of those crippled by laissez-faire capitalists and other corruptors of the republican spirit.[27]

The notion of popular scientific education thus can be seen as Ward's partial solution to the political contradictions of American society in transformation. Recurrent waves of popular protest, democratic senti- ment, and equalitarian yearnings were justifiable but immature reactions to a political order that was, somewhat ironically, the captive of a ruling class whose ideology only discredited the positive uses of government. If mutual antagonism was to cease, the terms of conflict had to change. Science had to direct mass protest to its proper object, which was surely not a return to the anarchy of enclosed island communities in an agrarian republic. Popular demand for a strong, coherent, and expert government "for" the people had to be generated.

But to Ward, the "scientific" direction of protest by definition had to be accompanied by a related and concurrent growth in the scope, functions, and autonomy of the American state. If science became the language of mature democracy, so too would it transform the structures of the state and the attitudes of those occupying it. The tangle of laws, procedures, and mechanisms by which state power in America had been crippled was to be thrown out. If the state was to become an ethical agency, then why distrust and fear the future wielders of democratic, scientific power? As scientific education was the form of knowledge and practice most suited to democratic citizens, so too was it necessary for the methods and prac- titioners of what Ward variously called "applied sociology" or "political science" to assume a direct and powerful role in the decisions of politi- cians and the disentanglement of the American state from its capitalist corruptors. Once again Ward recalled Comte, not to destroy democracy but to build a peculiar version of it. Just as there ought to be acknowledged experts in social processes, so too should there be experts in politics—"so- ciocrats," whose claims to lead rested on their transcendence of class interests and knowledge of the possibilities of social cooperation through political control:

> Most sciences are more or less practical; i.e., they furnish the principles which underlie the useful arts. From pure science to pure art there

are always three distinct steps. The first is the discovery of scientific principles; the second is the invention of the methods of applying these principles; the third is the actual application of the principles. . . . If, therefore, there is a political science, this must be also true of it. We will assume that there is such a science, that the operations of the state constitute a department of natural phenomena, which, like other natural phenomena, take place according to uniform laws. The intermediate or inventive stages embrace the devising of methods of controlling the phenomena so as to cause them to follow advantageous channels, just as water, wind and electricity are controlled. The third stage is simply the carrying out of the methods devised.[28]

More than any other American intellectual of his time, Ward linked the discoveries of political science with the day-to-day decisions of the politician. Knowledge, invention, and political application were stages in a single process, or at least they should and could be. Ward saw political science not only as a way of describing politics, but also as a way of acting in politics. If democratic radicals needed guidance, so too did the powerful: "As matters are now, governments have been a failure . . . because legislators as inventors, have proved mere bunglers, because they have known nothing of the laws of society. . . . Before progressive legislation can become a success, every legislature, as it were, must become a polytechnic school, a laboratory of philosophical research into the laws of society and human nature. . . . Every true legislator must be a sociologist and have his knowledge of that most intricate of all sciences founded upon organic and inorganic science."[29]

Perhaps Ward was never completely serious about the scientific legislature of the future. But evoking a union between science and office holding was an added salvo to Ward's blistering critique of what he viewed as the crude and mechanistic forms of American government as they had "artificially" evolved since the Founding. The whole system of checks and balances—and of confused lines of authority—limited the imagination of legislators and encouraged them to reflect the interests of factions, pressure groups, and big capital. In this process, "social will" was submerged, and even well-intentioned legislation became fragmentary, unscientific, and only accidentally purposive. Political scientists of later generations would make the same criticisms as Ward of American political institutions, but would perhaps blush at the naiveté behind Ward's "political science":

The true function of legislation is to remove all obstructions from social movements (those laws of movement discovered by statistics) and to cause their free operation to effect the least possible injury to public and private interests. . . .

Every movement of whatever nature going on in the country should have regularly reported to a central office and all such facts should be there systematically and elaborately published in tables, charts and diagrams, etc. and regularly laid before Congress for its use in framing laws for the benefit of the general public.[30]

In the 1930s Ward became something of a hero to those weekly commuters between Ivy League campuses and a national capital teeming with eager experts. In their quest for legitimacy, New Deal academics could easily dub Ward an "American Aristotle" and observe that the union of expertise with policy making was the essence of democratic decision making. Later, liberal historians whistled past some of Ward's "excesses," but they honored him as the father of American social sciences and the welfare state. Graduate schools of public affairs, municipal research bureaus, and legislative reference services were all baptized as children of Ward's "genius."[31]

Yet Ward's New Deal admirers seem to have forgotten many of his emphases and abandoned some of the assumptions that informed his perspectives on the nature, uses, and claims of "policy science." While there is no need to resurrect a "pure" Ward that contrasts with the interpretations of his later admirers, it is necessary to note the contradictions and unintended consequences of Ward's version of science. If Ward's admiration for the positive state was recalled by later political scientists, that many of the failures and contradictions of his science have been ignored is puzzling.

The effectiveness of Ward's dynamic sociology was premised on two distinct yet interrelated changes in the rapport between social science and society, changes that not even the New Deal achieved. Like his colleagues, Ward raised his voice in favor of a professionalized social science with its own journals, associations, curricula, and research institutes. To Ward, collecting the facts and statistics of social life and discovering the uniformities and regularities locked within them were unquestionably the activities of a specially educated and academically certified group of scholars. Yet the growth of professional standards and organizations was hardly an effort to isolate scientists from the outside world. Dynamic sociology made sense *only* if the voice of professional social science aided and educated reform movements on the one hand and legislators and administrators on the other. The justification of professionalism was to be found precisely in its impact on nonprofessionals, in the tasks of "scientizing" movement politics and governmental lawmaking and administration. Stated another way, the claims of professional social science were no less than to create a new and authoritative political language that would channel political protest into an effort to widen the scope, power, coherence, and legitimacy of a renewed American state.

Considered from this perspective, the supposed success of Ward's efforts may ring a little hollow. Whatever else might be said, Ward's effort to channel and moderate the spontaneity of agrarian and labor protest was a serious misunderstanding of the character of both Populism and the labor struggles of his time. Far from integrating into evolving political institutions informed by scientific expertise, the agrarian and labor movements maintained their own political demands and language. Democratic radicalism of the old variety remained strong, as did hostility to self-proclaimed leaders who told protesters how they had gone awry. Sentiment and scientific rationality did not mix well. When the scientific outlook accorded with the tamer and milder moods of middle-class reform, it was a success. The "gospel of efficiency"[32] behind the conservation movement of the late nineteenth century is a case in point. Yet when the authority of science and scientists locked horns in the 1880s over issues such as free silver, the moral decrepitude of Wall Street capitalism, or the racism and bankruptcy of the Democratic Party, Populism was more likely to be ignored or attacked. Alternatively, professional social scientific authority often appeared to popular protestors as just another effort to impose control on them, not an attempt to lead them to greener pastures. Mass popular education failed to level all artificial aristocracies or create that "democratic pool of resources" on which Ward wanted to rely.

The failure of Ward's science to live up to its own radical democratic aspirations would be repeated again and again in the later history of third tradition scholarship. Ward's science might have aided in the accumulation of "expert advice" that accompanied the growth of new state functions in America, but this is a "success" that Ward might have lamented because his science, to paraphrase a recent work, "triumphed over its own functions." This indeed might be considered fortunate by some since the dream of "sociocratic populism," if achieved, might have distorted Populism and the "second" tradition of democratic radicalism beyond all recognition. What is to be underscored is that Ward's science of society, despite his hopes to the contrary, only widened the gap between intellectual reformers and democratic protesters. If in Western European countries in the same period the cross-fertilization between intellectuals and the labor movement resulted in the formation of labor and socialist parties, in America the "science of society" helped preclude such development.

Ward's aspirations were disappointed in a second and equally important way. The findings of science for Ward were not to be introduced into politics and public policy piecemeal, but rather were to be the determining impulse behind the expansion of governmental purpose and functions. Just as scientific education would direct and crystallize popular protest, so too could it bridge the gap between popular sentiment and participation, and the imperative of institutional growth, coherence, and change. Ward's later admirers could indeed point at least to the partial success of his sociocratic vision. Progressive presidents might not be scientists in government, but they could at least tap the resources of scholars in universities, utilize Brookings Institution studies, and employ experts in the federal bureaucracy. Legislators, too, might remain mere politicians, but policy making was increasingly moved out of the "darkness" of "mere speculation" into the light supplied by the Brookings Institution, the Congressional Research Service, and numerous legislative reference services employing social scientists.

But all these supposed manifestations of the ultimate success of Ward's perspective disguise the profound failure to scientize governmental decision making and structures in the ways Ward had hoped. Social conflict, self-interest, and economic power were not removed from politics as Ward had hoped they would be. Instead, the science of politics began to reflect the very divisions it was supposed to transcend. Facts unearthed by scientists only produced "uniformities" whose impact was subject to the kind of political interpretation that defied the authoritative and sure scientific knowledge that Ward wanted to build. One person's true law of creative evolution is another's self-interested assertion, and insofar as the professional social science Ward helped to build relied on so simple an appeal to facts and natural uniformities, its relationship to political power would become one of subservience rather than leadership. Rather than the master of political discourse, science often became its servant.[33]

The fusion of the forces of mass protest and state-building through a neutral science was Lester Ward's response to the rise of American industrial civilization. In the face of the massive waste, inequality, and conflict created by capitalism, Ward's authoritative science promised democratic power informed by an all-embracing knowledge of moving social processes. A state made up of checks and balances, competing factions, and built-in competition was a symptom of ignorance and superstition, an unnecessary obstacle to an otherwise easy democratic modernization. It created a political culture built on impotent distrust of public authority and disdain for intelligent democratic aspirations.

Yet the call to science neither stirred the energies of democrats nor transformed the methods and outlook of emerging economic and political elites. A state bureaucracy was constructed in the twentieth century, but it was one hardly inclined to defy the imperatives of capitalist growth. Scientific experts appeared in government, but rarely as leaders of democratic movements. Ward is known as the "father" of American sociology. There is irony in his reputed paternity. A man who prided himself on the supposed realism and practicality of his outlook, Ward is perhaps better remembered for his faith, optimism, and enthusiastic scientific utopianism. Ward epitomizes those who dream of a political science that is as powerful, popular, and effective in transforming the human world as natural science is in transforming nature. After Ward, third tradition scholars could not sustain his impossible assumptions but tried to refine his science in order to make his politics more viable.

The Literary Politician and the Administrative Elite

At first glance, perhaps no two American intellectuals are as different in background, temperament, ambition, and style as Lester Ward and Woodrow Wilson. While Ward was something of a frontier populist who felt more at ease with ordinary people than with his fellow academicians, Wilson was a Virginia gentleman born into comfort and status. Ward admired the great system builders of the French revolutionary tradition, while the Anglophile Wilson spurned "speculation," instead finding wisdom in the conservative historicism of Edmund Burke. Despite his relative obscurity, Ward exuded intellectual confidence and personal enthusiasm. A brilliant career as scholar and politician notwithstanding,

Wilson was prone to continual self-doubt and brooding introspection. Ward's sociocracy was designed as a nonrevolutionary alternative to the existing political and economic hierarchies of laissez-faire capitalism. Wilson's reformism appears as an effort to effect changes without radical disturbances. Most important of all, Ward and Wilson stand at odds on their receptivity to popular democratic movements challenging nineteenth-century American capitalism. To Wilson, such movements were mere symptoms of a disease. To Ward, they were harbingers of future progress. Ward saw social scientists as the vanguard channeling democratic sentiment to its proper objects. Wilson saw political study as a means of warning elites before it was too late.

Differences in political temperament and attitude between the two extend to their claims and definitions of a new science of society and its relationship to the real world. Modern critics of scientism and behavioralism might find an early ally in Wilson because he resisted the notion that political behavior could or should be quantified, or that politics should be reduced to the fulfillment of historical laws discovered by social scientists. In contrast to Ward, Wilson favored the detachment of students of politics from any direct role in shaping politicians and the political world. In the final analysis, history was moved forward by "leaders of men" with intuition, independence, and vision, and not by abstract "material" or evolutionary forces. Wilson spoke of the "study of politics" instead of a "science of politics" because for him politics had to remain a "creative act," the unique and special sphere of the literary politician and statesman who understood the complex motivations and capacities of human beings. Wilson flatly rejected "sociocracy" as impossible and undesirable because it denied validity to the moral purposes and vision of leaders of liberal reform.

Yet the two men's shared sense of urgency, anxiety, and hope about America's future course holds them together. Wilson shared with Ward the concern to effect a great change in the methods, organization, and goals of political and social studies in America. For Wilson as much as for Ward, the "blind forces of evolution" had created dilemmas and opportunities unknown to the politician-scholars of the simpler world of the early Republic. Industrialization required profound changes in American institutions and conceptions of democracy, whether desired or not. Like Ward, Wilson perceived the growth of scholarly study as a way to understand the increasingly complex fabric of social life that could no longer be captured by formalistic descriptions of institutions or references to an abstract "political" or "economic" man. The problem with American political institutions was their inability to produce coherent policies that allowed purposive human control of the vast social and economic changes occurring in modern America. Wilson saw creating a unified political will and an efficient way of implementing that will as the prime task of students and actors in politics in the late nineteenth century. Yet—and this was Wilson's own dilemma—such a political will could not defy the democratic individualism sanctified by American traditions. Power and authority had in some way to be democratically accountable. And this would require both institutional changes *and* the emergence of a newly "rational" democratic citizenry. For both Ward and Wilson, building an American state within a cultural tradition opposed to the idea was a necessity and an outstanding dilemma.

Wilson's noted introspection and the genuine frustration and anguish of his presidency are conventionally attributed to the unrealistic hopes and values of an "idealist" confronted with the hard facts of political reality. But Wilson's disappointments stemmed less from any existential dilemma between his "values" and "necessity" than they did from the contradictory tasks inherent in the version of liberal progressivism he and others espoused.[34] Wilson's concerns as a scholar were practical indeed, concentrating on how a strong and efficient national state could be accommodated to an evolving capitalism and a tradition built on individualism. To Wilson, America's strengths at midcentury were Continental Europe's weaknesses—and vice versa. European political elites had long ago created powerful, expert, and efficient bureaucracies that were superlative instruments of executive command. But the monarchical origins of such states severely weakened them because they failed to evoke popular support and energies. Continental states were built on shifting sand, subject to continuous internal strife and popular challenges to their legitimacy. In contrast, American political culture was already thoroughly and wholly "democratic." The American opportunity and dilemma was to erect a national state as efficient as that of the Europeans but controlled by wise democratic majorities. Such a state would combine the best of bureaucracy and democracy and indeed allow America to "pilot the world."

Idealism aside, Wilson's work as a scholar pointed out the practical deficiencies of an American democracy that currently refused to create popular democratic majorities with the strength to support effective and firm public institutions and leaders. Leery if not hostile to protest movements of all sorts, Wilson nonetheless thought that national greatness and international power would be achieved only if the new American state might be backed by a political majority stretching from responsible businessmen to those whom Wilson referred to as "the little men."

The doubts of Wilson's scholarly pursuits and the oft-cited "tragedy" of his political career stem less from an idealist confronting reality than from his view that America might and must have it both ways. Global power and institutional control often clashed with the democratic demands of socialists, as well as the selfishness and corruption of immigrant political machines. Wilson doggedly insisted on the compatibility of man's loyalty to the state and individualism—of power and participation, industrial modernity and preindustrial tradition, administrative expertise, and popular accountability. In the process, Wilson, like Ward, would gain neither.[35]

From the classic "The Study of Administration" to his ode to British cabinet government, Woodrow Wilson's arguments are consistent about the urgency of the tasks facing both scholarship and the polity.[36] Wilson feared that the intellectual and economic conditions that had promoted America's uniquely organic and democratic growth no longer pertained by the end of the nineteenth century. Ironically, to restore organic harmony required strong organization, special leadership, and organizational reform. Yet such changes might "Europeanize" American democracy and subject it to the same fevers and political extremes as Continental European politics. In the *Character of Democracy in the United States*, Wilson set forth the major problem facing America at the century's end:

> Our democracy was not a body of doctrine; it was a stage of development. Our democratic state was not a piece of developed theory, but a piece of developed habit. . . .
>
> What was true of our early circumstances is not true of our present. . . (The new problems) may require as much political capacity for their proper solution as any that faced the architects of our government. Every added element of variety, particularly every added element of foreign variety, complicates even the simplest questions of politics. The dangers of that variety which is heterogeneity is so vast in an organism such as ours, of course, that there is the danger of disintegration. We are conscious of oneness as a nation, of vitality, of strength, of progress, but are we often conscious of common thought in the concrete things

of national policy? Are we not, rather, dimly conscious of being pulled in a score of crossing influences and contending forces?[37]

According to Wilson, the Founders had been fortunate in that the society for which they devised political institutions was characterized by a unique cultural sameness, an extant spirit of self-reliance and political restraint among the citizenry, and a pragmatic, problem-solving approach to the choices involved in self-government. Building on English foundations, the Founders effected evolution rather than causing a revolution. Old institutions and practices were failing because the vast forces provoking a political, economic, and social transformation undermined their founding assumptions. The diversity of America's regional cultures and traditions—once thought to be the source of republican virtue in an agrarian society—now was seen as an obstacle to the emergence of "leaders of men" so necessary to meet the new challenges posed by the frontier's eclipse, the world of steam and electricity, and the influx of immigrants with what Wilson called their "alien habits and ways." The simple government once adjusted to a people ingrained in habits of democratic self-sufficiency now was expanding haphazardly. It was the product of a thousand improvisations, and the result was a government at cross-purposes with itself. The "natural" mechanisms of the capitalist marketplace, whose results once provided their own moral justification, now spewed forth great corporations and oftentimes unethical monopolists who sought to destroy the "spontaneous" interplay of market forces from whence material progress itself had sprung.

For Wilson the study of politics thus had to consist of two closely related elements that together made a contribution to the understanding of both the "cultural tradition" of American democracy and the new dangers and opportunities it faced from its own centrifugal tendencies. If scholars concentrated on both, unraveling the diverse strands of the American democratic tradition while they sought ways by which points of organization, coherence, and purpose could be brought to bear on it, American uniqueness could be preserved and extended in novel conditions. To extend the continuity the Founding represented, new instruments that the Founders never would have thought of had to be put into place. The study of politics for Wilson thus had to evolve into a study of America's cultural uniqueness and European administration. Ways of adapting the forms of the latter to the spirit of the former had to be found. Without modification, the people's democratic habits might degenerate, and without "leaders of men" the social and economic assumptions of the early Republic might wane in the face of immigration, urbanization, and industrialization. But if new instruments of coherence, power, and control imported from Europe were simply transplanted, the values of the "cultural tradition" itself would be lost.[38]

Scholars thus had to be sensitive to both American cultural uniqueness and the necessity of altering that culture. This cultural approach to politics Wilson pioneered was thought to create a type of intellectual who viewed his craft as a "literary art." It would be of service to politicians who employed intuition and insight. And it would "scientize" the craft of building political institutions in order to communicate America's cultural-political superiority to nations with fewer democratic credentials. A science of public administration could only be grounded in a profound understanding of man in society as he "really was," something Wilson thought his purely "scientific" contemporaries had misunderstood: ". . . by turning its thoughts to becoming a science, politics, like political economy, has joined its literature to those books of natural science which boast a brief authority, and then make for what is latest. The science, proper to them, as distinguished from that which is proper to the company they now effect, is a science whose very exposition is as deathless as itself, it is the science of the life of man in society."[39]

Wilson was equally harsh on the older school of so-called formalist scholars. These were said to be "students of mere machinery" not "competent to understand and expound government" because such knowledge meant that "you must know men, to appreciate characters as radically unlike your own, to see into the heart of society and assess its notions, great and small. . . ." Wilson continued: "The needed reaction against orthodox methods should be a literary movement—a movement from formalism to life."[40]

Wilson rejected the short-sightedness of the social science of his day. Yet in print and action he allied himself with the vanguard of the new social science movement. He took active part in the founding convention of the AEA, served as president of the American Political Science Association (APSA), lent his writings to the journals of the new professions, and worked as one of the leaders of the movement to establish separate departments of political science, economics, sociology, and public administration in America's most prominent universities. But as a "literary politician," Wilson successfully carved out for himself what he hoped to be a general role for new scholars in politics. He purported to be a kind of mediator between the statesman and the citizen. Because the literary politician was to stand slightly aloof from politics, he had the skills to understand, protect, and adapt the national spirit and tradition. As such, new scholarship was the guardian against authoritarian intrusions and European importations. For the politician and statesman, the "literary politician" could offer his insights into the "real life" of society, from workshops to the apparently old machinations of modern legislative bodies. The new scholar was a source of detached self-reflection for citizens and statesmen alike. He was a firm supporter of traditions, and thus in America his very nature was a guardian of democratic values.

Wilson also maintained that a clear separation between the political actor and the student of politics was necessary, even if such a separation served the same liberal Progressive politics as Lester Ward's had. To the scholar belonged the preservation of the past and the delineation of future possibilities. To the politician acting in a world of power and change lay the task of creating coherence out of chaos and of adjusting the old to the new.[41] Yet as Wilson himself moved further from academics to politics, his assertion of a division between politicians and academics was increasingly qualified. In his early essay entitled "Leaders of Men," Wilson hammered home the exclusivity of the two roles, pointing out that the study of politics could have at best a distant relationship with the "practical" world. But by 1911, when Wilson himself was both governor of New Jersey and APSA president, he appeared more at ease with the direct links between "statesman of thought" and "statesman of action." Both were said to be engaged in a mutual and nationalistic effort. Each learned from the other about how democratic purpose could be implanted within the present, problematic American diversity. Still, the literary politician was a character different from Ward's sociocrat, for he would act in a world thankfully bereft of desires, values, and ambition:

> I do not mean that the statesman must have a body of experts at his elbow. He cannot have. There is no such thing as an expert in human relationships. I mean merely that a man who has the time, the discrimination, and the sagacity to collect and comprehend the principal facts and the man who must act upon them must draw near to one another and feel they are engaged in a common enterprise. The student must look upon his studies more like a human being, and the man of action

must look more upon his conclusions like that of the student.[42]

Wilson's call for the complementarity of academic and office-holding roles can be seen as an attempt to redefine America's political tradition. By doing so, Wilson hoped he was promoting the politician's capacity to adjust the tradition to industrial might and imperial pretensions. Wilson's book *Congressional Government* (1886) is perhaps the work most representative of this blending of organicism, empirical observation, evolutionary imagery, and resistance to the statist nationalism of some of his contemporaries. *Congressional Government* is the kind of study most useful to the statesman and to the public. It is prescriptive without being meddlesome. In it Wilson achieved the perspective of the detached but astute observer who conveyed the texture and richness of everyday congressional politics. At the same time, it provided a comparative historical perspective that linked everyday American reality to the experience of deliberative bodies in other democratic cultures.[43]

Wilson begins on a typically antiformalist note. The Articles of the Constitution are seen as poor guides to the modern Congress's actual powers and behavior. Like every other political or social institution, the life of Congress is characterized by growth and change within preestablished rules. If we seek to understand Congress's workings, Wilson avows, then congressional politics must be considered as the intersection of constitutional prescriptions and the requirements of a dynamic society. What Wilson calls the "paper picture" of the Congress known to every American is discarded in the effort "to escape from theories" and attach the reader to "the facts." The scholar of Congress "should not allow himself to be confused by a knowledge of what government was intended to be—but [should] strive to catch phrases and to photograph the delicate organism in all its delicate parts, exactly as it is today."[44]

This approach is not as "value-free" as it first might appear because like his other works on the British Cabinet and the American Constitution, Wilson makes deep forays into the "delicate organism." He shows why Congress is "out of step" with the polity's need for positive and clear policy directions, and much worse, why Congress might be considered to be largely incapable of overseeing an ever-growing system of public administration. Congress is fragmented into narrow and isolated compartments, which is symptomatic of the social dispersion and drift in American society itself. Wilson's account of the role of political parties, his lengthy descriptions of the machinations of congressional leaders, and the intricate workings of the committee system serve to subtly highlight the urgency of reform. Never far from the surface of *Congressional Government* is the impulse to reveal and unmask the modern Congress's inadequacies: "There is no similar legislature in existence which is so shut up to the one business of lawmaking as is our Congress," Wilson asserted. This preoccupation has prevented Congress from performing the essential functions of administrative oversight, such as "informing and alerting the citizenry" about pressing public policy questions and decisions, and how they ought to be implemented. Congress's disease stems from the fact that "legislation is a conglomerate." "Nobody stands sponsor for the policy of the government. A dozen men originate it; a dozen compromises twist and alter it; a dozen offices whose names are scarcely known outside of Washington put it into execution."

This fatal weakness portends confusion and drift in the face of the problems of industrial growth and concentration, forces that have already twisted the unseen hand of the marketplace beyond recognition. A democratic institution like the Congress trembles before economic forces beyond its control "because its powers are divided, [it] lacks promptness because its authorities are multiplied, lacks wieldiness because its processes are roundabout, lacks efficiency because its responsibility is indistinct and its action without competent direction." No wonder "public opinion" is a phantom. Political institutions do not recognize it, respond to it, or shape it. The unhappy result is that "the average citizen perceives government as at best a haphazard affair, upon which his vote and all his influence can have but little effect."[45]

Wilson must be congratulated for the remarkable durability of these observations. Yet he stops well short of fundamental criticism in his antidote to the disease he describes. The constitutional ideal in America is strong enough to accommodate the shock of the new. He calls for an attack on congressional committee power and for the creation of responsible, centralizing mass parties with "accountable" leaders capable of turning Congress to new and democratic purposes. As an example of a flexible institution governed by social forces, Congress can be adjusted to its new purposes. But first, responsible, centralized mass parties with strong leadership need to emerge to challenge the labyrinths of committee power and the presently obscure nature of congressional debate. The force of "responsible" parties will make Congress more than a legislative factory. In the future, it will also be a popularly accountable institution that heeds the voice of organized and disciplined parties. Rather than passing legislation piecemeal, a Congress organized by reformed parties might both oversee and interpret laws that it has made and publicize the problems and abuses in the implementation of its policies by the Executive Branch.[46]

Congressional Government is the prime example of an approach to political study that simultaneously attempts to be culturally sensitive, politically relevant, and methodologically sophisticated. The book provides a focus by which the proper rapport of continuity and change is clarified. To bring a radically altered American society and its institutions together again is to confirm the spirit of American constitutional democracy by subjecting old forms to new interpretations and helpful criticism. Democracy can only grow if its institutions and the people who support them are able to shape public opinion into a coherent force that will oversee government's new and essential tasks.

By showing why an old and uniquely American institution should be adapted to new purposes, Wilson did not explore how such a change might be generated out of the raw materials of the American politics of his time. Nonetheless, on the foundation of supposedly "culturally sensitive" works such as *Congressional Government*, Wilson proceeded to consider what he believed to be an equally imperative and complementary task, the creation of an American science of public administration as a foundation for sweeping alterations of America's antiquated attitudes toward state power. Wilson recognized that notions of "the state" were linked to traditions antithetical to Anglo-American constitutional democracy. He nonetheless held that the backwardness and corruption of the American civil service were preventing the nation from realizing its duty and opportunity to "pilot the world." The science of administration, Wilson avowed, "employs foreign tongues; it utters none but what to our minds are alien ideas." Yet it was now an absolute imperative that the United States adopt the only models of effective and businesslike administration available, those from Napoleonic France and Prussia.

For Wilson, this could and must be accomplished, but with no loss to the kind of democracy Wilson thought would emerge in an appropriately reformed congressional system of government: "If we would employ it [the European science of administration] we must Americanize it, and that not formally in language merely but radically in thought, principle and vision as well. It must learn our constitutions by heart, must get the bureaucratic fever out of its veins, must breathe free American air."[47]

Exactly what Wilson means by this remains unclear even in his most straightforward attempt to clarify the proper relationship between the growth in government functions and the diffuse, fragmented, and squabbling cliques of American politics. The reform proposals of *Congressional Government* become a given rather than a desideratum as Wilson imagines how the best in American democracy can hold democratically accountable the new generation of American experts. The Americanization of the science of administration assumes the national popular will that Wilson elsewhere finds sorely lacking in America's leaders, parties, and institutions. Wilson claims that the impulse to build a national state apparatus does not threaten our liberties but fulfills them because "administration lies outside the proper sphere of politics." A properly revised democratic politics still "sets the tasks for administration, but it should not be suffered to manipulate its offices." The separation from "politics"—the sphere of expertise, efficiency, and accountability—will allow America to "be both free in spirit and proficient in practice."[48]

According to Wilson, true democrats have rightly been fearful of bureaucracies because they crush the spirit of public discussion and debate that republican cultures are supposed to nurture. Since authoritarian bureaucracies have always arisen in monarchies or despotisms, American democrats have mistakenly identified bureaucratic efficiency with autocracy. Somehow, administrative expertise and efficiency have always been scorned in American politics, a culture where the public is "apt to think itself quite sufficiently instructed in the art of debate before hand." Because of this deeply embedded tissue of beliefs, American institutions are now threatened by the imperatives of the "industrial and trading age." A singular and dangerous ignorance concerning the barest facts of public finance, taxation, industrial and labor regulation, or the organization of military power pervades American politics, an ignorance all the more surprising because American innovation and invention are so linked to its administrative, economic, and social progress.

Oddly, according to Wilson, a weak administration composed of political hacks and untrained office seekers weakens the democratic state that the enemies of administrative science defend. A sounder view would seek to unclog the channels through which the policies of a democratic government are implemented, thereby releasing the "inventive spirit" in this all-essential endeavor. Wilson holds that the importation of European techniques into American culture poses no problem whatever for democracy as it exists. Almost by definition, "The administration in the United States must be at all points sensitive to public opinion. . . . The ideal for us is a civil service cultured and self-sufficient enough to act with sense and vigor, and yet so intimately connected with the popular thought, by means of elections and constant public counsel, as to find arbitrariness or class spirit out of the question."[49]

In Wilson's work, the study of politics as a "literary art" and the study of administration as a "science"—a kind of instrument of the greater literary art—balance each other. Similarly, the democratic heritage checks and "Americanizes" the principles of imported, monarchical, administrative techniques. Wilson prided himself on the practicality of such visions and methods, for they eminently suited his dual purpose of adapting American democratic culture and institutions to new functions, and vice versa. More sensitive than most American Progressives to the cultural implications for democracy involved in state-building, Wilson sought to awaken popular opinion to its new tasks through traditional democratic language. He sincerely refused to choose, or admit the validity of choice, between a state backed by responsible corporations or a politics of "responsible mass parties" and active public opinion.

Since Wilson's whole argument relies on the assumed vigor of democratic culture despite its weaknesses, it might be helpful to describe the nostrums by which the "democratic" control of bureaucracy might come about. In fact, Wilson speaks about American "democratic culture" not as he himself describes it in *Congressional Government*, but as if it were already transformed and matured. In *Congressional Government*, "democratic culture" is synonymous with fragmentation, drift, and selfishness. Yet in other works, "culture" becomes a good deal more abstract, defined in terms of its self-justifying principles rather than its actual practices. At once, the corruption and confusion highlighted in *Congressional Government* no longer appear as permanent characteristics of "democratic culture," but as an anomaly in an otherwise sound legislative body. With a little reeducation, American legislatures could transform themselves into the ideal of the British Parliament. In the quest for the national state apparatus so dear to Wilson, the notion of "culture" deemed suitable to control it becomes hopelessly abstract and reified. The realism of *Congressional*

Government fades into Wilson's ode to the flexibility of democratic government. In the process, the problem of whom or what would prompt reform in the way Wilson prescribes emerges as a puzzling dilemma.

Wilson seemed aware of the problem, and his proposed solution was strikingly like Ward's. Indeed, in the absence of desirable movements for popular reform, the professional movement in the new social sciences became an appropriate surrogate. Wilson turned to the new breed of scholars and social scientists and asked them to use their literary and scientific knowledge, their historical-comparative method and education in the European science of administration, in order to accomplish the two public tasks that American "democratic culture" by itself seemed incapable of performing. Academics were first charged with the duty of "instructing public opinion" to make it "efficient without suffering it to be meddlesome." The peculiar dispersal of political energies typical of American democratic life might be checked by an intellectual movement. Second, since "the time will soon come when no college of respectability can afford to do without a well-filled chair of political science," political scientists were supposed to use their new prominence to train "cultured and self-sufficient public servants . . . intimately connected with popular thought." A new generation of academics was singled out, since neither the American state nor the mass public were likely initiators of progress on their own. Intellectuals become the democratic guardians best able to smooth the adjustment of the culture to necessary change.[50]

To Wilson the formation of the political science profession itself became the first in a series of reforms designed to educate the public about its role as authoritative critic and to socialize future administrators about their "democratic" responsibilities. Academics, through their increasingly important graduate schools and departments of political science, occupied an ideal position by which to educate and lead reform movements to a knowledge of the "democratic tradition" itself. They could teach "the people what sort of administration to desire and demand and how to get what they demand." As adopted in America, the science of administration extended the "democratic heritage" by training administrators in the techniques of specialization and expertise. The new university could include courses and curricula designed to stress the "responsibility" of public officials to the democratic sovereign.[51]

If the American democratic tradition by itself could not generate the reforms Wilson contemplated, then the newborn disciplines of social science could provide a therapeutic role, evoking the better—if disguised—natures of American public opinion and institutions alike. Wilson's famous caution receded when it came to outlining the indispensable role of new intellectuals in American life. In effect, intellectuals not only could ease the adjustment from tradition to modernity, but they could also reinterpret the tradition itself to fit into modern imperatives.

What Wilson saw as a "natural" or "organic" extension of the bright past in reality required basic changes in the traditional modes of American political practice, even if Wilson himself was unwilling to admit it. The preservation of the habits of "rule by law," "public debate," and critical questioning—all attributes of the democratic tradition that Wilson so frequently urged his audience to retain—must first be created in order to be preserved. Perhaps this is why Wilson's work on administration is vague where precise definitions are required. The democratic tradition is reduced to empty phrases such as, "Democracy is a principle with us," or it is simply "a piece of developed habit." Only in such ambiguous and hopeful forms was Wilson able to balance the desire to "learn from Europe" with maintaining essentially intact his faith in American political culture.

It need not be suggested that Wilson's efforts to adjust existing American practices to the potency of the bureaucratic state were in any way "un-American." Indeed, Wilson's belief that the American political tradition presented few real obstacles to the growth of a national state has itself become an intellectual tradition. Yet it should be underscored that the changes Wilson thought to be necessary in the forms and goals of participation in politics and in the powers, functions, and capacities of the national state rested heavily, if not exclusively, on the new role of intellectuals in the polity. The dream of disciplined parliamentary parties presenting neat packages of policy alternatives to an informed electorate, and a Congress adept at overseeing the implementation of policies by an expert and accountable bureaucracy, became a cottage industry in political science. And no wonder that Wilson, among the first to lament American fragmentation, was also among the first to pinpoint the indispensable role of political scientists in providing positive alterations. Unlike Ward, Wilson kept his distance from claims about sociocracy. But through his call for an administrative science, Wilson helped to legitimate the role of professional research organizations, the political science discipline, and the transformation of American universities. With their independent status as teachers and researchers, the new professionals straddled worlds of public opinion and government rationalization and growth. No wonder Wilson served as both Princeton University president and APSA president. Both roles provided powerful platforms from which social science professionals might "educate" the new administrators and citizens to the ideal reconciliation of the political tradition and industrial modernity.

Yet Wilson's political career provides some instructive lessons about the limitations of this third tradition vision of reform. One might place the hopes for a democracy of the "little man" contained in Wilson's *The New Freedom* against the corporatist structures of Bernard Baruch's War Industries Board. Here are the embodiments of the contradictory character of Wilson's thought, visible in both his academic and political careers. On the one hand, the War Industries Board failed as the first experiment in American state planning. The would-be state was easily captured by the large corporations it was supposed to direct, and congressional support for this corporatist body met fatal opposition at World War I's end. The "little man" of Wilson's "New Freedom" fared little better in an age of increasing corporate monopolization. Wilson's vision of a responsible Congress organized by centralized mass-based parties was stillborn with Harding's "return to normalcy."[52] Wilson established the Federal Reserve System as an instrument of national economic policy, but it could hardly be claimed that the Fed represented a triumph of an autonomous, expert administrative order.

On other counts, Wilson was a success. He effectively blunted illiberal socialist tendencies that threatened his definition of what was to be included and excluded as part of the American political tradition. The growth of American socialism halted with his presidential tenure. The effective presentation of an image of reform might have stymied radical movements, even though the substantive accomplishments of Wilson's presidency did not go very far to implement his vision. In his own words: "If you want to oust socialism, you have got to propose something better. It is a case, if you will allow me to fall into the language of the vulgar, of 'put up or shut up.' It is by constructive purposes that you are going to govern and save the United States."[53]

The irony and tragedy of Wilson's career is that—by his own criteria—he was never able to "put up." Yet neither did he "shut up." Wanting the best in Europe and America, he could not give enough substance to the notion of the "democratic culture" of the latter to achieve the powerful national state he thought typical for the former. A professional study of politics and science of administration, which Wilson hailed as the dual approach to a democratic reform politics, resulted in neither a bureaucratic state nor a revived national democracy.

Woodrow Wilson aggressively asserted the claims of a new field of political study and an innovative science of administration as a means of effecting political reforms. The need for a science of administration was adopted as the conventional wisdom of political science. Without question, Wilson catalyzed the professional development of political science. Yet Wilson's efforts to unearth the supposed "democratic culture" unique to America did not get very far, even though future generations of political scientists would return to his historical and cultural approaches as an antidote to "behavioralism." Wilson's "critical" stances vis-à-vis the American democracy of his time might have mistaken American potential for American reality. Yet the notion that the "American democratic tradition" was entirely compatible with the growth of the corporate liberal state has persisted to our own time.

The professional organizations and language of the American science of politics carried on Wilson's concerns but would face the same obstacles that he did in realizing the required "adjustments." A species of state power appeared, but not in the form of a cadre of politically and scientifically informed administrators held accountable by the clear dictates and strong supervision of mass political parties. The linkages of ethnicity and partisanship became less relevant, yet the "rational" public appeared more and more as a fantasy of self-proclaimed realist intellectuals.

The American Crisis Formulated

In personal temperament, social origins, and intellectual style, Lester Ward and Woodrow Wilson could not be contrasted more sharply. These differences found their way into their works, for the two had distinct views on the methods that ought to be employed in social scientific and historical study, as well as divergent opinions on the proper rapport between intellectuals and the polity. Ward, by far the more reform-minded of the two, was a good deal more aggressive than Wilson in his belief that social scientists could provide the intellectual vanguard for a popular resurgence that recreated the conditions for an organic and harmonious radical republicanism. To be sure, the forms of his sociocratic populism sharply diverged from anything his radical democratic predecessors conceived. But to Ward, the possibilities posed by "creative evolution" in a mature industrial society required a break with the mentality and demands of modern republicans. The protests of populists and skilled laborers missed their proper targets. The cultural and political language they employed—often anti-industrial and anti-institutional in outlook—simply weakened them as a force for radical change. If "sociocracy" could achieve the deference of an equalitarian audience, then it might steer justified protest to its proper objects. Social science promised to ground mere "sentiment" in the firmer earth of a philosophy of natural and human history. It promised nothing less than a state that would be an expression of equalitarian strivings rather than their negation.

Woodrow Wilson was much less optimistic about the possibilities of republican fraternity. Consequently, he made fewer claims about the radical beliefs of social scientists. Scholars were guardians of conservative "democratic values," values interpreted in the main, though not wholly, as the preservation of individual liberty and equality of opportunity rather than in terms of substantive social or economic equality. Appropriately, Wilson's scholarship addresses potential "leaders of men" and the individual's moral sense. It says little to or about masses or social classes. Yet he urges them to submerge their own self-interest in the broader effort to create and then control distinguishable instruments of collective action. Public bureaucracies once thought foreign to American traditions were now necessities if public choices and purposes were to emerge from the fragmentation and narrow-mindedness of an older political philosophy.

Yet despite their differences, Ward and Wilson framed the problems and prospects of American politics in similar ways. Their similarities emerge when the two are compared with their intellectual opponents. The image of "Americanizing the Prussian State," of making accountable an apparatus that in Europe appeared remote from popular control, pervades the works of both scholars. Both stressed the urgency of this reconciliation of legitimacy and order. A world now rich with ceaseless change and flux had let loose historical forces challenging the artisan world of Lester Ward's childhood, as well as the assured status of the patrician in Wilson's Virginia. Both men welcomed the disappearance of this older world, yet they feared the consequences of a newer one, replete with contradictions where resolvable tensions had existed before. The dualisms of the American tradition present at the Founding had produced a republican order that could accommodate within its boundaries political variety, diversity, and richness. The new industrial order turned variety into fragmentation or conflicts that could not be accommodated in a republic based on conscious purposelessness.

Ward and Wilson could not accept the stark alternatives some of their contemporaries posed. *Staatstheorie*, the historical economists' utopian socialism, and Social Darwinism either sacrificed republican legitimacy to authoritarian order or order to class conflict, or simply counseled drift. But the two men also could no longer believe that the republic would survive without conscious intervention and profound adjustments in the conceptions and practices of American democracy. To achieve political order, the various sources of republican hostility to a powerful and purposeful state had to be convinced of the positive merits of national power. And to do that, the American state had to somehow depart in spirit, practice, and organization from its Continental European counterparts.

From this perspective, the maturation of a science of politics, society, and administration provided a new structure of intellectual authority that gained credibility through its capacity to reconcile seeming polarities. One might say that Ward's and Wilson's work and activity sought to achieve this aim through serious misinterpretations of the American past and present. The qualities of purpose, expertise, and authority both men admired in the British Parliament, French civil service, and German bureaucracy were subjected to so much "free American air" that the American state emerged in their writing as a forced and artificial fusion of apparent opposites. In both men's works, the new scholarship was mandated to perform quite incredible tasks indeed. Ward's "sociocrats" were ambitious institution builders ever eager to take on the "money-power," all the while remaining chastened and obedient servants of an informed and virtuous public will. And while they were expressions of public virtue, sociocrats nonetheless shaped it when it strayed into false paths. Ward's populism assumed a nearly perfect harmony achieved through creative "evolution." "Collective intelligence" emerged as the focal point of a nearly mystical republican community.

Wilson's attempt to "Americanize" the Continental European state forms to fit them into the American cultural tradition required no less a leap of the imagination. Somehow Congress was to become the institution of accountability, command, and purpose that in his own time and in his own studies it refused to be. Future administrative experts were lectured on the democratic tradition to which they must pay homage as the citizenry was educated about the positive benefits of administrative expertise. In the effort to specify how the "tradition" and the state might come together, Wilson finally placed his trust in the presidential office he himself eventually assumed. In response to the often conflicting demands of legitimacy and order, a strengthened presidency became the only instrument of national reconciliation. Not surprisingly, an academic as president doubly served a consensual reform politics because the fusion of leadership and knowledge would surely be a potent combination.[54]

These third tradition visions could be labeled utopian if it were not for the crucial role assigned to organized social science as a catalyst of social and political change. Social science provided the missing link between order and legitimacy in the sense that it created a kind of intellectual authority evoking the loyalty and deference of both sides of America's split traditions. To Ward, the "emotions" of the Populists were not obliterated by the successes of scientific knowledge. Rather they were completed in the unity and purpose of the positive state. To Wilson, a strict separation between the "art" of politics and a "science" of administration was an indispensable one because a strong administration was the necessary prelude to the revival of cohesive parties led by talented "literary politicians" such as Wilson himself.

How did Ward's and Wilson's common response to the great transformation fare in the 1880s and 1890s? It is perhaps unfair to detail too obvious a gap between Ward's hopes and predictions, and the actual course taken by the popular movements of his time. It is equally unjust to note that Wilson had to wait until far into the next century before his perspective became the "common sense" of the Progressive movement. But the advantage of hindsight also provides a perspective on the ways both men's work was seminal for twentieth-century third tradition scholars.

In the 1930s Ward's ideas were seen as the intellectual source for the New Deal's program of social reforms, as well as its blending of social science expertise with governmental policy making. Yet those who claimed Ward as an ancestor usually forgot to mention that "positive government" advised by social scientists was not his primary intention, but part of a much broader fusion of the scientific outlook with radical democratic movements and sentiments. The New Deal's fusion of executive power and expertise was a pale imitation of Ward's efforts to recreate a radical equality of ability in a conflict-free republic.

If anything, Woodrow Wilson's political career highlights the even more problem-ridden dilemmas provoked by third tradition assumptions. The images of a democratic regime embodying the best aspects of European administration and the American tradition resulted instead in the haphazard and zigzag expansion of federal power by the kind of fragmented Congress Wilson had always lamented.

Yet in the Progressive era, the political and scientific claims of third tradition scholars expanded as quickly as new and more sophisticated scientific methodologies made their appearance and as professional growth accelerated. At the very least, Ward and Wilson aided in the overall transformation of American academia into professions that pretended to speak to various reform audiences. At the most, the two scholars provided the founding hopes and characteristic instruments of third tradition politics. After 1900, Charles Beard and Arthur Bentley helped to further develop methods and approaches their predecessors pioneered and to create a variant of the third tradition better suited to the political hopes of liberal Progressives. But they were also plagued by the same assumptions as their predecessors. The notion of a modern republic of power, efficiency, and legitimacy to be achieved from thoroughly American materials informed the approaches of Beard and Bentley as much as Ward and Wilson. And they led to similar and continual frustrations.

3

Science as Muckraking

The Cult of Realism in the Progressive Era

From the election of Theodore Roosevelt to the end of World War I, American Progressivism and the new political science discipline existed in happy symbiosis. Progressivism's overall goals were complemented by the APSA's formation in 1903 and by political science's growth in the years thereafter. The effort to extend the powers and scope of governmental functions in the capitalist marketplace, establish the first tentative mechanisms of economic planning and regulation, build a military establishment, and rationalize the delivery of social services—all were spearheaded by commissions and bureaus that included the political scientists of the "new" variety. Obstacles were placed in the path of immigrant political machines, as the reins of city budgeting and finance were secured by newly competent city managers. The instruments of political party power were replaced with devices such as the referendum, recall, initiative, direct primary, and short ballot. Governmental assistance to temper the most "irresponsible" forces of the marketplace was now available to those corporations who sought regulation. The conservation movement's "gospel of efficiency" decried the waste and depletion of natural resources, and the first primitive forms of land management and conservation were assumed by federal and state governments.[1]

All such reforms required the growth of new state institutions inhabited by those trained in the techniques associated with the new social sciences, political science included. The creation of schools of public affairs and graduate departments of economics, statistics, sociology, and political science provided the pool of expertise needed in the expanding federal, state, and local governments. Indeed, the formation of American graduate schools in political science was a helpful tool in the Americanization of the concepts, methodology, and focus of Progressive political science. The early founders of American social science had been educated largely in France and Germany. In the Progressive era, the production of American

Ph.D.'s at Columbia, Johns Hopkins, Harvard, and the universities of Pennsylvania, Wisconsin, and Chicago produced a pool of U.S.-trained scholars who later fanned out and expanded graduate programs in political science to the recently formed universities in the Northeast, Midwest, and West.[2]

The spate of reforms that altered the rapport between government elites and capitalist industry at first glance would appear to have vindicated the claims and institutionalized the power of the new study of politics in the polity. Indeed, the growing group of political science professionals and professors were active in some of the most important "movements" characteristic of Progressivism. Frank Goodnow, the first APSA president, served on President Taft's Commission on Economy and Efficiency, led the New York Bureau of Municipal Research, and was active in the Institute of Government Research and in establishing many legislative reference bureaus designed to bring social science information to government officials. Frederick Cleveland, W. W. Willoughby, A. Lawrence Lowell, Henry Jones Ford, and other disciplinary leaders also extended the link between social science and government.[3] In fact, organized political science as it emerged in the early twentieth century self-consciously grafted itself onto the Progressive reform movements as helpmate. Goodnow's inaugural address to the APSA emphasized that the proper "area" of political science was the "realization of State will" and the "formulation of the substance" and the "administration of public policy," all key themes of Progressivism's right flank. The early discipline's journals were replete with articles examining contemporary American political and administrative practices. Everywhere, the muddled and confused state of American administrative law and public policies was linked to the power of party bosses, immigrant political machines, and the short-sightedness of the *nouveau riche*.[4]

The establishment of political science as an organized discipline, the accompanying growth of undergraduate and graduate curricula, and the increased importance of political scientists in the government reorganization schemes of the Progressive era all vindicated the claims for "relevance," which men such as Ward and Wilson had earlier set forth. Yet in a sense the emergence of a profession predated a common focus to political studies and the subject matter of political science. The early leaders of the organized discipline might have agreed that their predecessors had only been dilettantes and amateurs, but they were in some conflict about the proper grounding and methodology of a new science of politics. Most of them spoke of the need for "rigorous methods" and indeed saw refined methods as one of the distinguishing characteristics of the new science. But few embarked on broad-ranging investigations to help define "rigor."

The professional standards and trappings of political science that emerged with some vigor in the early part of the century surely preceded much disciplinary consensus or even concern about the scope and methods of political science. To be sure, professors no longer simply accused American society of moral turpitude or bemoaned the fate of the impoverished. Instead, they embarked on numerous empirical and historical studies that were intended to shed light on the complexity and interconnectedness of a rapidly changing American society. A keynote was the failure of government capacity in the face of growing needs for rationalization of the marketplace and planning of social services. The inability to locate a clear source of state authority capable of ordering the marketplace and its competition was—to say the least—a common lament. But the questions such investigations addressed, as well as the proper methods of carrying them out, were hardly a matter of consensus or even a subject of much specific discussion. In the early twentieth century, the Ph.D. was seen as a new and indispensable badge of ability and competence. Professors were now expected to conduct research, write, and publish in the discipline's growing list of journals. Initially, however, these new professional standards and expectations disguised a great deal of confusion and ambiguity about what it was that was properly "scientific" about the new research.[5]

Political science professionalism and a certain version of Progressive reform were thus coupled in a mutual effort to establish new and revised forms that expanded the role of the "expert" in public affairs as rapidly as they expanded the government's regulatory functions within monopoly capitalism. The very social composition of the early APSA revealed the hoped-for interchange between academics and the various new consumers of political science scholarship. In contrast to later days, the APSA's early membership was predominantly nonacademic. More than 60 percent of the association's 200 members were lawyers, businessmen, government officials, or participants in various "good government" movements dotting the nation.[6]

To note the new discipline's affinity with the increase and rationalization of state functions or the connection between this enterprise and the growth of monopolistic economic forms in America is hardly a novel observation. Wilson's well-known separation of the "art of politics" from the "science of administration" here manifested itself in the new discipline's effort to concentrate on the second half of the equation, systematizing and depoliticizing the functions of budgeting, finance, data gathering, and executive management in federal, state, and local governments. But despite the claims of political objectivity the administrative scientists dominant in the new profession asserted, no one would seriously assert today that the administrative mechanisms that fused "business" organizational principles into "government" were in any way "objective." Replacing the partisan, immigrant political machines with an institutional apparatus designed as a powerful means of social control manipulated by "expert" political and economic elites was politics pure and simple.[7]

While the potential power of the emerging governmental organizations of conservative American Progressivism attracted most of the discipline's leading lights, it did not attract them all because the conversion of the new discipline into a science of administration begged certain questions fundamental to many intellectuals in and out of the new discipline, just as these issues bothered Ward and Wilson in the two previous decades. A science of administration linked to Progressive governmental reorganization neglected to consider issues such as the distinctions between political science and other new disciplines, as well as the precise units through which political life ought to be studied. But most importantly, a political science at the service of Progressive governmental leaders neglected to address the increasingly germane debates about the aims of Progressivism and the movement's relation to the American political tradition. Conservative Progressives were busy replacing traditions of partisanship with what they hoped would be powerful national institutions based on "competence and expertise." But to whom—and through what means—should such institutions be accountable? Were such institutions a reflection of a convergence between corporations and government, or should their purposes stem from other, only formally democratic sources of legitimation? If the corrupted party machines were being replaced, then what about the excesses, abuses, and concentration of power of the ever larger monopolies? What ways would the population be organized once the rule of the old parties had been broken? What role, if any, should political science play in relation to the popular constituencies and demands of the early twentieth century? And most importantly, how might a reconciliation be effected between "collectivism" and "individualism," "capitalism" and "socialism," in order to create a uniquely American synthesis of "state and society"?

Such questions were frontally addressed by those political scientists— few in number but great in influence—who turned to a "science of politics" as a means of linking institutional reforms with what was sometimes called the "coming middle-class revolution." This chapter discusses Charles Beard and Arthur F. Bentley because they turned to political science in much the same way as Frank Norris, Lincoln Steffens, and Upton Sinclair turned to muckraking, or Thorstein Veblen and John R. Commons to critical histories of American capitalism. In political science, the radical-liberal strand of Progressivism was expressed in dual but complementary ways. First, in Bentley's words, it was "an attempt to fashion a tool" that students of politics and society could use in their quest for the raw and unadorned facts of social and political "reality." New scientific methods would replace the metaphysical and ideological dogmas that had once purported to "explain" social behavior. Discovering ways to capture the ceaseless change of modern social reality separated Bentley from others as the prime methodological radical of his time, a radicalism that eventually led him far afield from political science to treatises on the philosophy of the natural and social sciences. Moreover, radical Progressives such as Beard sought ways to employ Bentley's methodology as a tool of revisionist history. In Beard's work, the "raw facts" appear as a form of didactic history with the explicit purpose of catalyzing, educating, and politicizing the "great middle class." As Jacob Riis's photo essays captured the gritty moments of urban decay, so too did Beard's and Bentley's "photos" delve beneath the formal traits of American politics to reveal the seamier side of the political process.[8]

Beard and Bentley carry forward the concerns of Ward and Wilson in the different conditions of the new century. Ward had attempted to "refound" social and political thought in the United States by showing why a powerful state might become an instrument for the satisfaction of mass demands. Wilson had pointed to the ways by which America's democratic culture might be updated as a master to a powerful and skilled public administration. Beard and Bentley felt the same urgings as their predecessors, but they had reason to think this time there were listeners among institutional elites and the mass public alike. Each was ready to hear the messages of the new scholarship. Bentley's methods could provide a tool for the discernment of scientific truth about politics. Beard's writings, professional influence, and political activity employed Bentley's tool to further a vision of democracy as the fusion of new state powers with a revived, educated, informed, and activist public.

The "third tradition" scholarship of Beard and Bentley thus stands apart from the variety of Progressivism which fought solely for institutional reforms that rationalized and routinized the workings of the marketplace by establishing regulatory agencies and administrative experts to guide them. Beard and Bentley also rejected the socialist currents within the labor movements of the period. Institutional reformers and socialists alike were insufficiently "scientific." At base, both perspectives were thought to be informed by at best subjective and ideological notions and at worst by pseudoscientific interpretations of social and historical change. In a sense, the prominence in American life of these polar alternatives—working-class revolt or a convergence of powerful industrial and political elites—was to both scholars symptomatic of the crisis of knowledge. Both perspectives produced scholarship and activism that ignored primary epistemological and methodological questions. In contrast, a properly grounded science of society and history promised to reduce the power of mere ideology by transforming existing political opinions and conflicts into questions for scientific investigation. In their methodological extremism, Bentley and Beard ploughed the middle course. A union of expertise and power with social equality and popular democracy was seen as a sort of "potential" discoverable through scientific investigation. Such a union was the special mission of a truly professional science of politics and society in America. Investigations into the sources and causes of human behavior were the first step toward reform without revolution and toward popularly supported institutional changes.

To Beard and Bentley the growth of social science thus promised to ease the tensions that accompanied American modernity. Such tensions understandably arose, but they were resolvable. And the political climate of the Progressive era presented the optimum conditions for the success of Beard's and Bentley's brand of scientific reform. In the 1880s and 1890s, professional social science was in its infancy and lacked that assured audience that made the communication of scientific knowledge into popular politics possible. But by the new century, the social science disciplines were already in place, and a citizen audience receptive to leadership by intellectuals was certainly present. In fact, never again would the alignment of scholarly and political forces typical of Progressivism be so well-suited to the effort at refounding that union of purposive national institutions and an attentive and alert public that was the hope of third tradition proponents such as Beard and Bentley.

In the pages that follow, Beard's and Bentley's very distinct journeys from methodology to politics are traced. Bentley's interests led him from the classic *The Process of Government* to collaboration with John Dewey, with a brief interlude of political activity sandwiched between. His ultimate fate was to be revived in the 1950s as the first "group theorist," an epithet he would have neither deemed desirable nor termed accurate. Charles Beard's initial enthusiasm for a union of science and politics waned after Progressivism's post–World War I demise. Ultimately, Beard became frustrated by what he viewed as the intellectual sterility and political impotence of the profession he did so much to shape. Beard became skeptical of the political orientation of the science of politics and often appealed to his colleagues to remember the purposes for which political science had been created. In both men's lives and works, the confidence that had first inspired their efforts to fuse scientific rigor, professional growth, and political action in their attempt to resolve the contradictions of a modern America diminished with time. Their personal stories reflect the wider dilemmas of the intellectual project in which they were active. As with Ward and Wilson, their "sciences" failed to achieve the results for which they had been formed. The two scholars' audiences became increasingly limited to only the world of scholarship. Above all, the new middle class on which they pinned their hopes failed to be aroused as an agent of "scientific" reform. Beard's and Bentley's successors would devote much time and attention to the construction and analysis of the "garrison state" Bentley and Beard warned against. Yet before World War I, Beard's and Bentley's scholarly investigations could rightly be seen as the foundation for a "new democracy."

Arthur F. Bentley: The Objective Science of Middle-Class Revolution

Like Lester Ward, Arthur F. Bentley has only lately been accorded a prominent place in the political science pantheon. Nearly half a century passed before Bentley's *The Process of Government* was unearthed as the methodological progenitor of the movement to place the study of political behavior on a sound epistemological foundation. Almost another twenty years elapsed before anyone realized that Bentley's importance to political science might be overshadowed by his mature works in psychology, mathematics, and the epistemology of the social sciences. If Bentley's *The Process of Government* was once perceived as the first comprehensive statement of the "group theory of politics," the work's orientations and concerns are in reality far different than the orientation and concerns that revived it in the 1950s and 1960s.[9]

Unique among the figures discussed in this work, Bentley was not a professor, profession builder, or political scientist. A brilliant student of Georg Simmel, Bentley nonetheless rejected a teaching career, choosing journalism instead. The bulk of his adult life was spent managing a farm in Paoli, Indiana. Yet his lengthy correspondence with John Dewey, and the publication of five major works in the space of two and a half decades, reveals a person whose distaste for academia was more than balanced by his lonely confrontation with the major epistemological problem of American pragmatism, particularly with the idea of "process" and its relationship to the social and natural sciences.[10]

Bentley is considered here because he was the Progressive scholar most concerned with developing rigorous methods of social scientific investigation for the analysis of an American society in transformation. Ward and Wilson talked of social science or administrative science; students of politics in the Progressive era bandied about the word "science" with few precise ideas about what it meant beyond the collection of facts according to some vaguely defined standards of empirical verification. In the midst of this ambiguity, Arthur Bentley stands as the paradigmatic scientific radical of his time. In the search for standards of scientific objectivity, Bentley built a science of society that sought to remove feelings, sentiments, ideas, and emotions both from the minds of the observer and the observed. Bentley's *The Process of Government* is Progressive political science at its most self-consciously realistic and skeptical extreme. Other pioneers of the descriptive American science of politics had protested the "formalism" of past studies, but Bentley's antiformalism was complete and total. Bentley sought means by which to observe what he considered to be the ceaseless change and flux of social processes; his world is entirely devoid of laws, grand designs, or essences, and instead traces men's actions, not their purposes. In Robert Wiebe's words, Bentley "obliterated the inner man."[11]

Bentley has thus rightly been considered as the earliest proponent of the detached, objective, and scientistic strain in political science. To those who rediscovered Bentley in the 1950s, his appeal lay not only in his methodological sophistication, but also in the detachment of his science and his person from any direct involvement in the "culture-bound" activities and studies of many of his Progressive colleagues.[12]

Yet it is our intention to demonstrate that while Bentley did indeed try to create a social science that separated scholars from any direct role in politics, an important purpose of such scientistic objectivity and detachment was self-consciously to "fashion a tool" whereby the chief dilemmas and crises of American Progressive politics might be addressed. The scholar's task and duty was indeed to gather and present knowledge objectively and not—as Ward and Wilson had thought—to serve as a frank advocate of the virtues of positive government. But the very scientism and detachment Bentley hoped for was designed to ground the program, goals, and activities of radical political reformers in the raw and unadorned "truth" of American politics. While a strict division between social scientist and citizen might exist, the very character of the separation in Bentley's work suggests that it is a division of labor for the accomplishment of a greater political task. The revelation of the "real" and often uncomfortable facts about American political life might stimulate the public to reformist action. In this sense, Bentley stands in the third tradition with Ward and Wilson. The political changes necessary to revive American democracy depended first on the availability of objective knowledge. Only then might the radical middle class be stirred to political action.[13]

As we shall see, Bentley's work up to the mid-1920s expresses perfectly the complementary qualities of political science and radical political renewal. An objective science of politics was a means of unmasking the pretensions and lies of the powerful in the American polity, society, and economy. Bentley was in the vanguard of those who destroyed the evangelical and naturalistic schemes of pre-1880 scholarship. He even went beyond those who, like Ward and Wilson, saw "mind" evolving from the chaos of social evolutionary change. Bentley, the informalist par excellence, is at the same time the best representative of a tendency to link a radical liberal social science with an equalitarian politics.

The Fashioning of Scientific Politics

The late-nineteenth-century pioneers of American social science had been struck with what they perceived as the unreal "abstractions" of the scholarly discourse of their time. Extant scholarship based itself not on the empirical examination of the ways individuals, states, political parties, and governmental institutions actually behaved or operated, but on timeless assumptions of "economic" or "political" man, mystical conceptions of the "nation" or "state," and the "ideas" they purported to embody. Such notions might have made explanations easier, but they never led to an examination of the "real" activity of human beings in the marketplace, parliament, or society. Moreover, by assuming a rational world, the classical economists and natural law theorists and philosophers locked themselves within static categories that made them incapable of explaining historical changes of obvious and great importance.

Bentley's *The Process of Government* purged all such alleged abstractions from scholarly argument and rebuilt social science on new investigative units that purported to capture the ceaseless flux and interdependent activity of "real social life." Ward and Wilson had rejected formalism, but Bentley went much further than both of his scholarly predecessors. Ward's "positive state" and Wilson's concern to observe change within institutional boundaries were, for Bentley, as teleological as the evangelical utopianism of the Populists. If a true science of society was to be created, Bentley asserted, causation, historicism, and Christian historical conceptions alike had to be jettisoned. "Politics," "economics," and "morality" were not discrete realms, each with their own set of principles that shaped human behavior. To Bentley, such categories were artificial structures conjured up in the minds of the observer, barricades against the invasion of the messy and oozing processes of "real life."

Bentley's effort to make a radical break with all past sociology is evident from the beginning of *The Process of Government*, where he launched a comprehensive attack on thinkers as diverse as Georg Simmel, Karl Marx, Herbert Spencer, Lester Ward, and Albion Small. By the end of his remarkable diatribe, Bentley removed what he called the "ghosts" and "soul stuff" from their methods and approaches. All of these thinkers, Bentley claimed, had mistaken "abstractions" of their own making for causative elements of social change. While Marx, Simmel, Gumplowicz, and others were to be admired for their attempt to discover units of investigation that would promote the study of actual social process, all were also victims of a priori thinking. All were guilty of labeling as historical "causes" what were really mere assertions. Class consciousness, the urge to power, and the search for status were "ghosts" to Bentley.

Beginning with notions of the state, historical categories such as class, or "essences" disguised as motives, feelings, emotions, views, or interests, these would-be social scientists only succeeded in developing a tangle of explanations that artificially halted the movement of real social processes. To Bentley, all such terms and modes of analysis were fatally laden with normative content, and their use as explanations only led to tautology. Academics who employed them were proposing "causes" as starting points for the phenomena they observed. Bentley hardly denied that interests, feelings, ideas, classes, or institutions existed and that they shaped action, but he strongly objected to their use as units of analysis. An objective social science must concern itself with the complexity and ultimate intractability of social processes: "I have denied . . . that the separation of feelings and ideas, looked on as individual psychic content, (separated) from social institutions as from social activity, is a legitimate procedure in the scientific investigation of society. When built into a system of interpretation, such a separation collapses of its own defects, and brings down the whole system in a crash. I have insisted that such a separation in fact exists whenever feelings or ideas are given independent values as factors in interpretation even though the interpreters themselves enter a most vehement formal denial."[14]

Bentley's critique shares with Ward's and Wilson's a nearly total disdain for the utopian, antihistorical modes of thought characteristic of those who sought to maintain the America of small island communities and simple republicanism. Yet Bentley does not tarry long enough to even consider the static world of American utopian thinkers, but instead levels his guns at those, such as Ward, Spencer, Marx, Simmel, and others, who held views of science that replaced utopian moralism with a historicism that posited "progress" as the inevitable result of evolution. Bentley's brilliance, and his ultimate dilemma, was the mode by which a science might be established after all the "idols" of social investigators collapsed of their own analytical defects. In a radical departure from historicism and organicism in all their various forms, Bentley in *The Process of Government* attempts to erect the science of society in what he regards as the only truly observable phenomenon—"pure activity," unadorned by feelings, interests, ideas, or purposes. All the "soul stuff" of previous social science can be understood, if at all, only as it is manifested in *observable* social action. In place of the calculative rationality of classical political economy, of Marx's notion of class consciousness, of Ward's efforts to derive a collective mind from the "psychic factors" in civilization, Bentley asserts that the raw material is nothing if not "action, 'something' doing; the shunting by men of other's men's conduct along changed lines, the gathering of forces to overcome resistance to such alternatives, or the dispersing of one grouping or force by another grouping."[15]

Bentley's emphasis on pure activity collapses all traditional dualisms between subjective and objective, mind and material. For purposes of scientific observation, the social world is a homogeneous procession of movement, a continuous flow of action. An infinitely complex and changing process without discernible ends replaces the "moment of reason" represented by the American Founding as well as the world of changing but palpable evolutionary progression Ward and Wilson posited. Neither the attempt to create a political community frozen in time nor the effort to extract laws of historical movement are proper to a world in which all phenomena are momentary and without apparent connection with each other. To Bentley, society is ever-changing and at any given instance cannot be understood as bounded by "abstract" categories derived from some academic's rendering of events.

Such views might have led others to despair of any effort at social analysis at all. Yet Bentley stops just short of giving up the attempt to find categories that might give form to the amorphous raw material of social life. The problem Bentley consciously poses can be stated simply. By definition, the scientist cannot seek to "explain" pure activity since that would bring back all the "soul stuff." Yet social scientists might make the effort to *describe* all the manifestations of pure activity. A "complete description" to Bentley obviously implies that there must be boundaries to activity—that it would be possible to describe all activities. Bentley, if nothing but intellectually honest, retreats to the only position that might be held given these assumptions. Only one frame in the moving picture of social life might be "completely" described at a time. Such "descriptions" will tell us nothing about what came before or after the frame. Still, spatial and temporal boundaries might be constructed in order to momentarily halt the unbounded flow of activity in the interests of a descriptive science. But how?

In *The Process of Government*, Bentley elucidates the "group concept" as a tool for defining any given cross-section or frame of moving reality. He is careful to distinguish his "fluid" notion of "group" activity from the static categories of his sociological predecessors. "Groups" are not defined by their functions, structures, histories, goals, or culture, but are only mental constructs employed to describe numbers of individuals actively associating. The group *is* its activity; for the purposes of description, it is a momentary phenomenon, existing only insofar as the specific activity defining the specific actors exists. "Groups" such as the American Farm Bureau Federation, the Prohibition Party, or the Industrial Workers of the World exist only in terms of interactions of individuals or in a specific instance, not in terms of the "roles" social scientists have mistakenly assigned to them. Furthermore, if the group is its activity, a group's interest is only the evaluation of that activity in specific interaction with other groups, not as a predetermined "interest" aggregate based on class, faith, status, or whatever. To Bentley, a "group" exists neither subjectively in speech nor abstractly in permanent structures, but only concretely in observable activity vis-à-vis other groups.[16]

The new social science's prime task is thus to plot courses of activity resulting from patterns of group interaction. If patterns emerge through description, such patterns are only artificially halted processes, most definitely not historical "stages" of evolution or degeneration. "Government" at any given moment is seen as only the temporary balancing of patterns of activity described, the "organization of forces, or pressures." Drained of structure, intentions, and goals, the complete group description is a strictly empirical rendition of reality. As Bentley proclaims: "When the groups are stated, everything is stated. When I say everything, I mean everything. The complete description will mean the complete science, in the study of social phenomena, as in any other field. There will be no more room for animistic causes here than there."[17]

In emphasizing that the group concept is "merely" a "tool," Bentley declines to provide such a "complete" description. Hinting that such a description itself has to be a group activity, he nevertheless mentions the difficulty of capturing even a single moment of group interaction. As soon as such activity is observed, it is already "mere" history; social processes have already passed it by. In a jab at James Bryce's view that the American Constitution was the product of "reasonable and able men who listened to thoughtful arguments," Bentley describes the "real stuff" of which the "reasoners" are made: "In government we have to do [*sic*] with powerful group pressures which may perhaps at times adjust themselves through differentiated reasoning processes, but which likewise adjust themselves through many other processes, and which, through whatever processes they are working from the flesh and blood of all that is happening. It is these group pressures, indeed, that not only make but also maintain in value the very standards of justice, truth or what not that reason may claim to use as its guides."[18]

There is an obvious paradox to Arthur Bentley's methodological extremism. The employment of the "group" concept is intended to revolutionize social science by creating a unit of analysis capable of comprehending the "moving foundations" of social reality. But even as Bentley defines the term "group" as no more than a momentary and specific interaction pattern, it still introduces "soul stuff" and "spooks" by allowing the social scientist to artificially entrap the flux of social reality. Bentley realizes that he has to create new units of observation if a social science is to exist at all, but even in *The Process of Government* he appears ambivalent about whether the group concept reintroduces too much discretion and too many analytic traps into a social process that can never be adequately captured.

Realizing this problem, Bentley in later works abandoned group interpretation and political analysis altogether. Those who in the 1930s, 1940s, and 1950s reintroduced "the group theory of politics" into political studies did so largely by ignoring the methodological dilemmas and concerns that led Bentley to question the "group" approach of *The Process of Government*, which Paul Kress succinctly captures: "The entire purpose of group interpretation is to get behind the incidental characteristic of appearance, but in order to do so, the formal or structural unities must be reduced [by Bentley] to simple activity. When we have arrived at a conception of the social realm as homogeneous, continuous action, we must then find the differentiating principles, ways to introduce discreteness—in short, new units of investigation. But Bentley had by this time rejected so much, closed so many doors, that he was unable, within the confines of *The Process of Government*, to recreate them."[19]

By the end of *The Process*, Bentley himself appears to realize that his own work, if taken seriously, will put social science as adrift as the social process it is supposed to describe. In the first chapters, he takes polemical jabs at the alleged abstractions of Marx, Simmel, and Gumplowicz. By the book's end, the triad emerges as the most important proponents of "primitive" group theory. Marx "made classes too hard and fast; the particular groups which he called classes were abstractions." Simmel "has traced the group lines, and endeavored to make clear many of the typical forms in which group relations occur," and Gumplowicz puts "group activities" on "a much wider and firmer foundation" than Marx. If in all three thinkers' works "the idea and feeling factors are still largely an undigested mass and so the cause of scientific indigestion," Bentley nonetheless proclaims that "it is only necessary to push down below them and strengthen them out a little further to get the statements in terms in which one can depend upon [them]." And, most important of all, Bentley even concludes that perhaps the social scientist might want to—and can—do more than describe the snapshots of dynamic social process, even though Bentley remains skeptical of the methodological validity of the enterprise. From the conclusion to *The Process of Government*: "There have been forming underneath the various dressings of history a substantial backbone and skeleton of accepted relations. . . . We can easily conceive of a solid structure of group relations as they have developed in historic times becoming known to us, which must inevitably define the fundamental shapes which the history writing that varies with the generation must take."[20]

The ultimate irony of Arthur Bentley's work is that the radical criticisms he levels at the social science of his time logically place his own efforts at methodological reconstruction in grave doubt. In the attempt to refound a science of society upon a "truer" and less value-laden basis, Bentley throws into question the potential utility of the social scientific endeavor itself.

Progressive Science as Critical Unmasking

By his own admission, Bentley's concern with the specific subject matter of political science was momentary, a kind of way station on his journey from journalism to pure social theory. This is perhaps as it should be since the group concept in any case appears to reduce politics to sociology. The uniqueness of specifically "public" and "political" concerns, still very much present in the works of Lester Ward and Woodrow Wilson, disappears from a science that is self-consciously purged of such "soul stuff" as "the idea of positive government." If pure activity and group interactions are the primary units of political analysis, then public institutions and political speech and debate are no more than momentary expressions of specific interactions located far beneath the surface of what only appears to be "politics." A comparison between Woodrow Wilson's writings in the 1880s and Bentley's work twenty years later highlights how far the "revolt against formalism" in social science has proceeded by the Progressive era. Under fire from Bentley's radical scientific critique, Wilson appears much like the formalists he attacked. In Bentley, the claims of social science become totally removed from those concerns for "cultural sensitivity" and change within limits so important to Wilson.

In what sense, if at all, did Bentley's "radical" science address those issues that we have identified as central to the third tradition in political science? Although in different ways, Ward and Wilson made significant claims about the utility of a new social science to the political world and the proper relationship between would-be truth seekers and the polity and society they believed to be in need of fundamental reform. What about Bentley, whose scientism would appear to exclude or ignore altogether such questions in the single-minded search for proper methods of description?

There are hints in *The Process of Government* that Bentley himself was not only concerned with methodology, but also that he recognized that his science might have profound implications for the Progressive politics of the day. While Bentley's methodological radicalism did not point either to the direct political involvement Ward suggested or the counseling role Wilson suggested, his science of "complete description" did suggest a profoundly important role for an objective science of society.

Indeed, Bentley saw his brand of science not only as "realism," but also as a means of providing the raw data by which American politics might be stripped down to its essentials, its hidden conflicts revealed, its pretensions unmasked as mere ideological obfuscation. Considered in the broader context of the Progressive movement and its claims, Bentley's search for a new science of the objective and complete description meshes well with that strand of radical-liberal Progressivism that reveals the "dirty deals" of existing American reality in the form of objective descriptions of the cold, hard, and impersonal consequences of "social processes." No matter how political doctrines and ideas attempt to cover up such consequences, Bentley's objective scientific methodology serves as the instrument by which the platitudes of common sense are revealed as so much ideological obfuscation by the self-interested and powerful.

The very impersonality and mindless dynamism of the "process of government" stands in stark contrast to the system-building, mechanical imagery employed in the *Federalist Papers* and captured in the institutional order of the Constitution. The institutional apparatus deployed to fragment group combinations and tyrannical majorities, and perpetuate the rule of the politically wise—so important to James Madison—dissolves in Bentley's notion of a social process that engulfs all before it. If Bentley's "group concept" is taken seriously, then the mechanisms designed to channel social process and promote the creation of an unselfish political elite are themselves victims of the interactions of the factions they are supposed to control. The contrivances of the Constitution, so carefully fashioned to promote a semblance of political order and control, fall before the push and tug, and rise and fall of interest groups.

If Bentley's methodology dissolves institutional controls into social process, so too does it sever the belief of late-nineteenth-century social scientists in the reciprocity of science, progress, positive government, and democratic control. Ward's populist "sociocracy" and Wilson's "literary politicians" and "culturally sensitive administrators" hardly could employ languages and methods independent of the group struggle. Wilson's appeal to salvage the "best" from the American tradition as "democracy" creates new instruments that might appear to Bentley as just another series of fallacious efforts at circular reasoning. The discourse of intellectuals must be brought down from its pretentious heights, just as the language of politics must be purged of all its prattle about "ideas," political "wisdom," "emotions," and related "spooks."

But as Bentley pricks the balloon of established (or even not so established) dogma, *The Process of Government* hints about what might come out of scientific muckraking. Here, the examples Bentley used to elucidate the benefits of group analysis are instructive. He emphasizes that the group concept can be applied to any social configuration. Yet the activities described are usually manifestations of corruption in finance, commerce, government, or the electoral process. The "complete description" of the pure facts of social inquiry depicts a process in which only the powerful are active, and thus observable.[21]

How the methodology initiated in *The Process of Government* might be employed for overt political purposes is provided by a lesser-known work that Bentley penned in the aftermath of World War I. Despite Bentley's efforts, *Makers, Users and Masters* was never published. If it had been, it might have substantially altered the endeavors of those behavioralists who thought that Bentley studied American interest group pluralism in order to praise it.[22] The methodological tool developed in 1908 is here employed to reveal capitalist and landholding groups. Relying on "facts that can be quantitatively stated . . . in terms of groups, of their interests as related to one another," Bentley identifies, using curious language, "a quantitative differentiation between political and industrial citizens," locating "an industrial government already controlled by manufacturing and finance capital, threatening to invade our political government."[23]

In *Makers, Users and Masters*, Bentley avows that his aim is "a maximum coldness in examining and stating the facts." Yet such coldness results in the conclusion that present social tendencies, left unaltered, will lead to either "a proletarian or capitalist dictatorship" in the United States. The "complete description" of group behavior does not lead to encouraging findings about the consequences of Progressive legislation. The federal government's regulatory policies in railroads, drugs, meat packing, and currency control have only furthered the powers of finance and manufacture. The growth of the state has only provided "new tools and new techniques as profitable for their purposes as the complete freedom that has been taken from them." Beneath the formal appearance of liberty and process, Bentley finds domination and structure. His perusal of endless amounts of data on group behavior reveals the surprising fact that "the channels of information are dominated by motives of profit."[24]

The structure of *Makers, Users and Masters* clearly portrays an important strain in the radical Progressive reform mentality. While Bentley asserts the same political position of men such as Ward, he grounds his political prescription on mounds of facts. Forswearing moralism, Bentley dismembers the actual processes by which entrepreneurial capitalism maintains itself and explains why "revolution to the laboring classes depends not on the ignorance and evil of entrepreneurs but arises out of the very industrial organization in which men live and work."[25]

The book's second half details why the American "middle class" of small farmers, small businessmen, and the newly educated is most likely to lead a "counterrevolution" against capitalist or proletarian dictatorship in the name of a "cooperative economy." For Bentley, the middle class is the "one group" that does not "figure" in the processes of industrial and political government. Nor would it be likely to advocate the suspension of formal civil liberties, which Bentley believed the proletariat would if it seized power. Rather, the middle class, if jarred loose from existing interest-laden political parties, might lead a peaceful revolution of "consumers and producers" in an effort to form social and economic groups that would be islands of cooperation in a rapacious, competitive economy. It would fight for a redistribution of property and wealth, and seek to directly own the means of production by establishing its own industrial enterprises and consumer cooperatives.

Bentley's middle class is not a moral category. Rather, it is shown to be the group most likely to be receptive to the facts revealed by an objective social science. The discovery of facts and the activities of fact-gatherers were prerequisites to political activity by the public. While the scientist and science must be utterly objective, such objectivity might only politicize the "great middle class," that group most willing to act on knowledge. As Bentley puts it: "We have the most ignorant middle class in the world; but at the same time it is the most intelligent. It is ignorant because the facts are hidden from it; not because it cannot comprehend and use the facts when it gets them."[26]

Thus, the proper union of detached scholarship and radical-liberal political reform emerges in Bentley's dual enterprises. *The Process of Government* fashions a tool to study social process; *Makers, Users and Masters* uses that tool as a sort of scientific pamphleteering that will lead the people to take the proper action. In his belief in the power of scientific information to yield truth, evoke outrage, and stimulate reform, Bentley the "realist" nearly outshines Lester Ward the scientific utopian. Yet unlike his predecessors, Bentley does not even call for a new system of education to make citizens into amateur social scientists. The middle class does not need institutional guidance or control from the outside because it is a "people out of doors," a people rational enough to respond to disenchanting realities without intellectual leadership. Bentley's is not a politics of institutions, administrators, or experts, but one of reasoned action within the spontaneous undergrowth of uncontrolled and unmediated social process:

> Given its information, given knowledge of the digested and verified and well-analyzed facts that have been accumulated . . . the middle class will be able to act. But if it does act, it cannot act through palliatives; it must act through a counter-revolution of its own . . . one that strikes through the superficial appearance of equity to the substantial underlying inequities, one that avoids destruction and violence of whatever nature, one that is radical, not in attacking, destroying or assailing, but in searching out the heart of the trouble and in guiding every step, slow or fast, so as best to reach the heart. These steps need not be radical,

but the purpose—the direction of progress—inevitably must be radical if the end is to be attained.[27]

Bentley stresses rights, liberties, substantive social equality, and popular control in government and industry in opposition to the institutional power, administrative control, and planning that American Progressivism's conservative mainstream promoted. He claims that scholarly detachment and obsession with methodology need not preclude a direct and unmediated link to popular and spontaneously generated sources of reform in the polity at large. A "scientific" *versus* a "political" Arthur Bentley does not exist. Rather, Bentley epitomizes the reciprocity of "pure science" and radical progressivism, as his own anti-metaphor suggests:

Society is not like a bridge or a steel building in which an error in computing the structural strength of one member may lead to the collapse of the whole. Society is forever changing. We watch what happens, and we help or hinder the process here and there by putting in this element of guidance or taking out that other. We must trust in our own ability in action than to trust in to form a satisfactory plan complete in all details in advance of action. . . . It is not the tinkering with government and industry that fails, but blind tinkering; the tinkering that deals with incidental evil while it lets the essential evil raise new harvests of harm.[28]

Robert Wiebe has characterized Arthur Bentley as the only Progressive intellectual totally given over to what he labels "bureaucratic thought." In this mode of thinking, "only men's social behavior deserved analysis," and the state, so alive to thinkers like Ward and Wilson, "now acquired meaning only as a mode of human behavior." The "laws" of social evolution and change, the basis of an earlier social science, became contingent rules of social behavior because Bentley's process view saw a "society of ceaselessly interacting members." In Ward's and Wilson's sciences and before, political issues had been separated into discrete questions, such as "Race," "Labor," or "Immigration." Bentley and the bureaucratic mode of thought Wiebe believes he ushers in "pared all of these back to their human components and subdivided them into recognizable, everyday problems."[29]

Above all, Bentley ushered in a novel view of science, now divorced from its meaning as the search for the principles of fundamental harmony that the investigator could discover. In Bentley's work, science becomes less justified by its substance than by the method through which it describes contingent and changing processes. Since Bentley dismissed the individual as a unit for analysis, the inner man was obliterated and only observable social behavior might hold sway in scientific discourse. In his rejection of "soul stuff," of "essences," and of all the philosophic idealism of the notion of social science as evolution, laws, and would-be historical tendencies, Bentley indeed is political science's equivalent of the Frederick W. Taylor school of scientific management or the psychological behavioralism of John B. Watson. "Efficiency," frugality, and virtue were no longer qualities of individuals. Rather, they were consequences achieved by constant watchfulness and management of a complicated, fluid social process. In Bentley's world, the clear, discrete, and discernible cause-and-effect relationships between human motives, actions, and consequences became the confused, tangled, and changeable objects of would-be social engineers.

Yet, importantly, Bentley used his critique of "everything existing" in a less ideological way than social engineers such as Frederick Taylor. The hard-bitten "realism" of Bentley's thought did not lead to a cynical manipulation of the "facts," but rather to a curious combination of blind optimism and pure science. The establishment of a true science brings into being a "scientific public"—the middle class—now knowledgeable enough to correct the abuses inherent in the notion of the group process itself. Observers of social process and actors are distinct. Yet they are joined in their mutual rationalism and constructive radicalism, both political and scientific.

Bentley's integration of "science" and "politics" is the ultimate radical Progressive contribution to the solution of America's political dilemmas before World War I. While Bentley's interests ranged far beyond a science for politics, with the proper qualifications he represents an important example of the political scientist as unmasker, the bearer of scientific revelations to the Progressive public. Yet clearly only Bentley's methodology remains his most direct legacy to later generations of political scientists. As shall be seen, Bentley's methodology seemed suited to the radically different concerns of political scientists in the 1950s. But even in Bentley's own time, some attempted to use the tool he had fashioned for both a new history and a new politics. If Bentley asserted the most radical "scientific" claims of prewar political scientists, Charles Austin Beard was the scholar who attempted to put these claims into scientific and political practice with decidedly mixed results.

Between Science and Sentiment:
The Chastened Optimism of Charles Austin Beard

More than thirty years after his death, Charles Austin Beard still stands as the most renowned American social scientist of this century. His public fame is appropriate since perhaps more than any of his contemporaries, Beard aimed at public visibility in his scholarship and life. Beard's writing above all aimed to instruct and inform the thinking citizen of the lessons to be learned from the usable American past. The author of forty-nine books and countless articles in academic journals and mass circulation magazines, Beard's didactic histories of the United States have sold more than 4 million copies since he penned *The History of the American People* in 1918. His influence extends well beyond his written work. Unlike Bentley, Beard was a leader in the development of the history and political science professions and served as president of both associations in the 1920s. More important, Beard was active in numerous organizations designed to bridge the worlds of academia and Progressive political reformers. He led the influential New York Bureau of Municipal Research and the National Municipal Reform League, and wrote the monumental "Charter for the Social Sciences," which helped revise elementary and secondary school education in the United States. A vociferous opponent of Roosevelt's tilt toward intervention in Europe's struggles of the 1930s, Beard had also left his position at Columbia in 1918 in one of the classic academic freedom cases of the World War I period.[30]

Through his work and life, Charles Beard represented the aggressive claims of less renowned academics, journalists, and activists who saw the growth of American social science as the indispensable pivot around which a reconstitution of American democracy and institutions might occur. Like Ward and Bentley, Beard was a vocal critic of the particular mode of individualist capitalism that had developed in the United States. But Beard's concerns stemmed far beyond a critique of laissez-faire economics, a doctrine that in his own time was already dying in any case. Beard's major concerns were positive and extended to the formation of a cooperative, "efficient" democracy as a counterpoint to the alleged determinism of Soviet Russia and the authoritarian nihilism of fascist Italy. The failures of laissez-faire liberalism and the revolutionary responses to liberalism's collapse in Italy, Germany, and the USSR only spurred Beard to renewed reflection about "democratic values" and the role of social science in a modernized democratic state.

Like many in his scholarly generation, Beard saw the intellectual development and professional growth of the social sciences as prerequisites for the solution of the continuing American intellectual and political crisis. But to Beard, whose career began with the presidency of Theodore Roosevelt and ended only with the cold war's advent, the political and intellectual "crisis" could be addressed neither through faith in a benign sociocracy nor through Wilsonian administrative reforms alone. America's crisis was deep-rooted in the forces unleashed by the technological and industrial innovations American political genius itself had promoted, by a dynamism that forged far ahead of human capacities to comprehend its impact on the American political tradition. The mechanical contrivances the Constitution imposed might have been suited to America's Founding, but they were radically inadequate in the dawning epoch Beard called "industrial democracy." Like Bentley, Beard perceived an intractable American social reality. Social process and group interaction flowed in, around, and over the neat structures the Founders established. The Industrial Revolution further undermined earlier assumptions about individual autonomy, natural rights, and freedom of contract, doctrines suited only to capitalism's primitive beginnings in the fight against feudal privileges. As Beard asked in 1908: "To discourse on the liberty afforded by jury trial to a man who has never appeared in court but often suffers from unemployment is to overlook the potent fact that liberty has economic as well as legal elements."[31]

American institutions were crippled by their arcane effort to balance power in politics alone. In the modern period, political powerlessness only stimulated the concentration of economic power. Moreover to Beard as to Bentley, "formalism" was inherently conservative and antidemocratic because it disguised the real sources of power and influence immanent in group interaction and social process, confused cause and effect, and provided ready ideological justifications for doctrines of social and cultural superiority, laissez-faire capitalism, and unfettered capitalist domination. Like Bentley, Beard perceived a world in which the seamless web of social process was destroying human abilities to act on the firm knowledge that a changeless realm of "politics" or "economics" existed. Beard moved from the search for analytical anchors in social process by which the world could be understood again to a critical posture toward the claims of "pure science" and a return to a telic science that consciously reimposed "values," theories, and the "idea of civilization" on the topsy-turvy, swirling world of industrializing America. Always, Beard's moral fervor for a reconciliation of a new popular democracy with institutional efficiency informed the claims he would make concerning the potential and limitations of "science" and the study of history. Always, the objective methods of empiricism were self-consciously appropriated for service to a greater political and intellectual project. The description of reality beneath ideology in itself constituted and promoted change.[32]

The political and historical sciences of Charles Beard are efforts to employ the tool Bentley created to clarify questions that Beard regarded as central for the expansion of the arena of democratic choice. Questions of scientific method were of direct political relevance because how one cut into and described social processes involved crucial decisions about processes that were and were not controllable by citizens. Despite important switches in emphasis and his growing frustration, Beard's scholarship spanning forty years reveals an urgency—even an anxiety—about the survival and revival of liberal democracy in the United States. His scholarship also reveals his belief that both social science and the knowledge it produces are the path to responsible and possible reform. His concern for questions of scientific method, professional growth, and other matters seemingly distant from political struggle are subsumed under his persistent effort to form a social science that revives the democratic citizen as it builds purposive institutions that might direct and control the raw material of social process.[33]

The Paradox of Realism

Despite Beard's fifty-year–long career and his incredible scholarly productivity, more has probably been written about Beard than by him. Usually, Beard's writings have been understood as a series of seeming paradoxes. Castigated as an economic determinist for his early works linking the Founders' political thought to their property holdings, by the late 1920s Beard seemed to reverse field and began to talk of the "independent role of ideas" shaping history. A "realist" concerned with unmasking political thought as mere ideology, Beard nonetheless often made claims about the "objectivity" of social science as a new species of political thought. As a publicist and popular historian, Beard dealt in ideas that motivated citizens to political action, yet his more scholarly endeavors hammered home the notion that the struggle of economic classes and groups were at the source of supposedly principled "political debate." And as an observer who saw public policies as the outcome of interest-group conflict, Beard was nonetheless hopeful for the day when state actions would be made coherent through accountability to a wise, informed, and broad-minded national electorate capable of choosing between competing programs offered by responsible mass parties.

Beard's work can well be faulted for its numerous inconsistencies and vagueness regarding important questions of historical interpretation. Yet the apparently contradictory character of much of it dissolves when the consistencies of his concerns are revealed. Above all, Beard sought a social science closely linked to the popular reform movements of his time. Social science's claims to objectivity only would further its legitimacy and authority as a uniquely American public language. Ideally, social science was both a method of study and a tool of political reform.

Accordingly, Beard's views on the actual development of professional social science were conditioned by his sense of how well or poorly such developments contributed to the larger reform role he always sought to implant within it. Ultimately, American political science was judged not only according to standards that it set for itself, but also by its effectiveness in catalyzing institutional reforms and promoting a sort of scientific outlook among the mass public at large.

In this way, some of the seeming flip-flops and contradictions in Beard's views regarding the integrity of "facts" and "values" might be explained. In the years before World War I, Beard was at his most strident, castigating political philosophy and existing social science as "mere speculation." In particular, Beard leveled his sights on the neo-Hegelian worship of the state his teacher John Burgess represented and on all doctrines that posited some abstract destiny above human control and intervention.[34] Like Bentley, he urged his colleagues on to "objective methods," which apparently meant a rejection of idealism and historicism in favor of focused and detailed investigation of the "facts" of real human life. All those who pretended to have discovered meaning in history were said to have engaged in a kind of "telic" endeavor. Worse, whether knowing it or not, such scholars saw the march of ideas and ignored the practical, material interests behind them. Beard took more than a little pleasure in unmasking the real "play of forces" behind sacrosanct institutional doctrines and philosophies of history of all sorts. He brought down to earth the heavenly city of the eighteenth- and nineteenth-century philosophers by debunking their ideas as mere intellectual expressions of one faction of the bourgeoisie or another. Beard was as skeptical as Bentley about the grand schemes of philosophical or historical interpretation of Hegel, Marx, Simmel, and others. Yet such skepticism only underscored, just as it did for Bentley, a much deeper strain of confidence. In the heady climate of liberal Progressive politics, Beard assumed that the sordid facts dredged up by objective science would surely activate the great middle class to action. "Science" thus replaced "values" in scholarship, providing an arsenal of facts to an already rational public that would know how to interpret and act on the raw slabs of reality.

World War I's aftermath fractured this strain of confidence, and Beard modified his views on professional political science and its public orientation accordingly. In the age of Harding, Coolidge, and Hoover, of the newborn Soviet Union, fascist Italy, and a shaky Weimar Republic, "unmasking" was not enough because it falsely presumed a popular consensus about the political response to the crisis once the dirty facts were known. In America, the Progressive public had not acted in accordance with the spirit of its self-appointed intellectual vanguard, and in the complacent 1920s and strife-bound 1930s, Beard urgently went about the task of submitting his early "scientism" to discussions of why the historically evolved "values" of progressive liberal democracy might become palatable global alternatives to "totalitarianism." The "isms" of Europe, Beard believed, could be countered only by a value-centered, democratic science of society and politics. Such a science would define the appropriate scope of collective human freedom and choice against Stalinism and fascism alike.

In short, the steady supply of facts to an assumed rational public no longer guaranteed the survival and adaptation of American democracy. Social scientists could no longer base their claims to political knowledge and insight solely on muckraking because what Beard now called "mindless empiricism" clearly had not had much political effect. In the 1920s, Beard grew increasingly disillusioned with the public's seeming apathy and political science's growing scientism, advanced in the name of the professionalism Beard had once embraced. Beard pleaded with his colleagues to return to value discussions and bemoaned the political and intellectual sterility of a science-for-itself. He now urged more from political science than it had previously given. The public had to be taught that "human control" could be asserted on seemingly mindless social and historical processes. Democracies needed to know that choices existed, and political science ought to be concerned with the knowledge that they actually did exist.

Science, in short, had failed to live up to the expectations of Beard's reform vision. The political world and the profession had changed, not Beard. Yet through it all, Beard still insisted that popular democracy and a powerful state were complements. The failure to build a permanent basis of popular support for the exercise of state power endangered Beard's faith in the survival of the "democratic civilization." As with Bentley, a science based on realism often failed to meet the expectations and hopes of the realists themselves.[35] The chastened hopes of Charles Beard are worth exploring in some depth because they show how easily the "realism" informing American social science led to disenchantment, dissent, and despair.

Realism versus Reform: Beard's Confrontation with the American Political Tradition

In a series of controversial works written between 1908 and 1917, Charles Beard developed the thesis that was to garner both fame and infamy. Beard's *The Economic Interpretation of the Constitution of the United States* and its subsequent refinements have been variously perceived by its detractors as a fundamental attack on American institutions, a vulgar Marxist diatribe reducing the American Constitution to a product of the commercial and banking bourgeoisie, or a flawed and overly generalized reading of historical data. Beard's own formulation of the question in *Economic Interpretation* indicates that he was prone neither to smear nor to praise the Founders, but merely to assert the claims of "scientific" research and empirical methodology over the "formalism" of philosophical discourse. His most influential book began: "Did they [the Framers] represent distinct groups whose economic interests they understood and felt in concrete, definite form through their own personal experience with identical property rights, or were they working merely under the guidance of abstract principles of political science?"[36]

Beard's answer to the question forms the basis of his notion of political science. He makes clear that "economic factors" are not only germane to an understanding of the Constitution but also to an understanding of all political events and documents. Like Bentley, Beard viewed "group struggle" rather than the march of ideas as the key to political understanding: "This great fact stands out clearly, through the centuries . . . that group interests were recognized as forming the very essence of politics both in theory and practice. . . . Statesmen spoke not of abstract men and abstract rights, but of real men and of real rights."[37]

Unlike philosophers, "real" politicians and students of politics have not concerned themselves with abstractions such as "natural," "political," or even "economic" man, but have rather removed all of what Bentley would call "soul stuff" and Beard would call "utopias" from their thinking. Accordingly, to view the formation of the American Constitution as the product of group struggle and social process was not to degrade the work of statesmen, but rather to bring their work down to earth. As practical balancers of group interests, they mastered the inherent "disparity in the kinds and distribution of . . . property." The American Constitution of 1787 was hardly unique as an expression of property interests. While the relevant economic actors and their goals might change over time, Beard perceived the ruling constitutions of all great states—from the Athens of Pericles to Renaissance Florence to the English Constitution of 1688—as alike. All were created, formal political structures that corresponded to the configuration of certain economic processes and groups then dominant. In fact, if the Framers of the American Constitution stood out in any respect, it was in their praiseworthy practicality and honesty about the groups served—and not served—by the new structure of the American Republic. Political foundings before 1787 tended to be justified by political philosophies and ideologies that Beard saw as derivative from material interests and their interplay. Real history proved that human nature was flexible and changeable. But Aristotle, John Locke, Thomas Hobbes, and others put static concepts of human nature to work to justify what in reality was the way certain individuals and groups acted in a particular historical conjuncture. The authors of the *Federalist Papers* had also mistakenly based their arguments on an essentially static view of humankind's foibles. Yet more than past utopia builders, they had still seen institutions as flexible instruments of changing group alignments. Rightly, they had started from "political realities" rather than "moralisms," and had almost self-consciously recognized that "politics and constitutional law are inevitably reflexes of these contending interests."[38]

The interpretation of American political institutions and practices in terms of the changing economic processes and groups that gave rise to them was Beard's major contribution to the methodology and focus of Progressive scholarship and political science. Yet for Beard, this approach did more than shed light on contemporary history. Group interpretation was the foundation for a new science of politics, itself a radical break with the distorted and ideological language of political philosophy. Scientists saw the interplay of concrete interests based on class, race, and nation dominate behind the universalistic pretensions of thinkers from Aristotle to Herbert Spencer. Bentley too had seen "groups" as a tool with which to cut into the ceaseless flow of social process. Beard used this tool in a way that stirred political controversy and debate, just as it supposedly reconstituted political knowledge on the activity of "real"—as opposed to "abstract"—political action. Where the tradition of speculative political thought "might be understood as a series of gross and subtle religious, class and patriotic biases," Beard proclaimed that the "real student of government knows that there is no hope for knowledge except in descriptions of the bewildering types of society gathered from the past and from the four corners of the earth."[39]

The new science of politics, capturing as it did the rise and fall, and the ceaseless interactions of a succession of new and old economic and social interests, aimed at "objectivity" in its descriptions. Yet Beard thought of his science not as an end in itself, but as a preface and method to a science of reform. Beard's "objective," descriptive histories were didactic and instructive, designed to teach the thinking citizen to distinguish between ideological dogmas and "reality." Moreover, Beard's empirical approach, employing as it did economic statistics detailing the ever-changing sources of wealth and power in America, was considered a prelude to broader political changes that transformed the "mechanical" checks and balances system of eighteenth-century American government into a powerful, purposive, and efficacious national state. The simultaneous multiplication of government functions and the simplification of lines of policy implementation were thought to be complemented by the growth of popular majorities reflective of the demands and needs of the educated middle strata and skilled working class. These, Beard thought, were the groups most likely to support the kind of political transformation leading to reform.[40]

Far from unmasking the American Founders as money-grabbing commercial and plantation elites, Beard emphasized that the original conditions in which the Republic's institutions were forged were no longer relevant. Fear of political power may have motivated the Founders, but today such fear could be replaced by speculation about its use. To Beard, James Madison's anxiety about the consequences of factional strife had, in the context of the late eighteenth century, been well justified. Perhaps the limited and mechanical democracy the Constitution articulated was the best that any realistic democrat could have hoped for in the days of early capitalism. But as Madison himself had realized, the forms of institutional artifice should not be inscribed in stone tablets, but should be altered in accordance with the rise of new groups and the decline of old ones. Twentieth-century conditions made a reevaluation and an extension of its meaning both urgent and politically possible. The overly crafted mechanisms of the Founders intentionally entrapped political and social movements in the complex layers of the federal system. To Beard, federalism was an archaic remnant of a past era, now appropriated by the most unscrupulous groups in the economy for the perpetuation of the dual role played by political bossism and capitalist individualism: "[The Founders'] fear of democracy and the passion for democracy have led to the same result—the creation of a heavy and complicated mechanism yielding quickly enough to the operation of the political expert and blocking at every turn the attempts of the people to work it honestly and efficiently. Powerful private interests find their best shelter behind a multiplicity of barriers."[41]

Considering Beard's extreme skepticism—some might even say anti-intellectualism—regarding the role of "ideas" in history, his faith in even a new kind of political science is ironic. By describing the ebb and flow of social forces constantly in transition and by pointing to the less than ideal origins of political philosophizing in the rough-and-tumble of fluid group interaction, Beard uncovered extensive injustices that begged for correction and human intervention. Faith in the form of skeptical, fact-gathering scientific reason itself became a meaningful reform. This was the critical method to be adopted by reform groups intent on raiding the arsenal of "fighting facts" with which to overwhelm those powerful forces in the economy that resisted efforts to meld collectivism with progressive capitalism. If the "facts" of past and present history revealed that constitutions and institutions were more than likely to be expressions of group struggle, then the creation of new "groups" of organized workers and the enterprising and educated new middle class should and would in turn change what Beard believed to be the "drift" and "anarchy" of American economic and political life. The realism of Beard's political science dictated that the group struggle be accepted as a given. The utility of such a science would unmask existing politics for what they were—a struggle for power by groups with distinct interests, not the embodiment of an abstraction such as the "national public purpose." Consciousness of the group basis of politics would activate those who had been systematically excluded from American political life.

Like the work of other Progressive intellectuals, Beard's didactic histories self-consciously fused political hopes with pretensions to scientific objectivity. Beard's interpreters have often perceived a contradiction between his "reform" impulse and his drive for objectivity. But Beard's objectivity was the source and tool of political passion. It was the very basis of a kind of democratic political knowledge that provided citizens with the necessary information on which they would surely act in salutary and self-interested ways. But what precisely did the fusion of scientific objectivity and political passion mean for knowledge's role in the American Republic?

First, scholars in American universities must be accorded the time, resources, and autonomy to undertake independent critical research. Second, the study of politics must set itself the task of training individuals for public service, supplying "expert, skilled, and democratic" civil servants to fill the "number of government positions requiring special training." Third, professional social scientists must involve themselves with "training for democratic citizenship." "The awakening of a deep and abiding interest in government and its manifold relations to social and private welfare"[42] was a primary task of any objective political scientist. The potentially elitist implications of a division between expert and citizen were neatly resolved when people realized that administrative reforms designed to "simplify" and "clarify" policy making in turn promoted the emergence of "clear choices" for citizens. If the public was aware of the consequences of each choice, then it would be fully capable of making the "right" decisions in its own interests. In Beard's words: "Democracy does not merely mean periodic elections. It means a government held accountable to the people between elections. In order that the people may hold the government to account, they must have a government they can understand."[43]

The service of experts to citizens should ensure that the "group process" was free from bias and institutional barriers, and that it was allowed to operate freely and openly, thereby allowing American political dialogue to become a simpler replica of informed scholarly debates. Unlike many of his Progressive colleagues, Beard did not maintain that social conflicts were harmful, but only that they should be mediated by political institutions and structures designed to resolve them. Once choices were organized by structured and ideological political parties, once proportional representation destroyed the provincial biases and fragmented group demands encouraged by single-member districts, Beard believed providing firm and democratic guidance to public administrators would then be possible. But until and unless the linkages between citizen participation and state policies were simplified and clarified, meaningful popular direction would fail to function effectively. The sheer volume of political decisions required of the state in a closely-knit technological society would overwhelm democratic institutions and delegate decisions and power by default to those in the best position to manipulate institutions and ideas.

Like Woodrow Wilson, Beard held that American democrats falsely held republicanism to be antithetical to governmental power, efficiency, and size. In his view this was an antiquated perception that served only the presently powerful. Democracy might indeed be synonymous with "military precision and efficiency" when it was realized that the democratic spirit had unfortunately "originated in an age when such traits were not essential to its survival."[44] The authoritarian states had manifestly demonstrated that such traits now *were* indeed essential to political survival. Achievements in economic and social planning, militarization, and industrialization in these nations only underscored the necessity for a "democratic alternative" as powerful and purposeful as it was accountable to popular majorities. Beard's faith that the supply of constant streams of scientifically gathered evidence demonstrating needless waste, inefficiency, and corruption in "industrial civilization" would evoke citizen outrage came mightily close to equating social science with democracy. Properly informed citizens, once presented with the raw data collected by academics, could effectively judge the actions of politicians and administrators alike. Thereby, the myths that economic competition, class polarization, and individualism were inevitable accompaniments of democratic civilization might be countered by a vision of welfare, collectivism, economic cooperation, and political consensus entirely compatible with a planned democracy.

Indeed, the role Beard prescribed for political science was so fundamental that professional growth was seen as nearly identical with political and social reform. Social science promoted the prediction of historical tendencies and opportunities; it therefore clarified rather than muddied opportunities and prospects. Science revealed potential points of intervention by the public in politics by stripping bare the existing political process and revealing its internal workings. Science readily prescribed reforms in procedures or structures, be they in the form of administrative reorganization and expansion, electoral processes, or in the internal democratization of political parties. Beard's efforts to establish workers' education programs, research institutes linking academics, civil servants, and reformers, and legislative reference bureaus providing data to lawmakers are all testimony to his faith in the identity of science and reform.

Yet there was a real vagueness when it came to science's role in substantive, as opposed to procedural, reforms. Beard's perspective assumed that once processes were reformed, well-intentioned citizens and political actors would make the proper choices and would infuse beneficent and cooperative purposes into politics. There is a certain irony to Beard's pre–World War I views regarding the efficacy of scientific muckraking as a reform tool. A social science that revealed the powerful economic interests that manipulated public institutions wound up as peculiarly "formalist" in orientation. Institutional alterations designed to cleanse the political process—rather than struggle among social classes and groups—were thought to be the way in which powerful corruptions are dislodged. Upon hearing the real "facts" about the motivations of power, a benign but wise public would surely act on such knowledge and pilot positive government.

Like Bentley's more sophisticated effort to create a pure and scientific method of investigation, Beard's faith in the efficacy of objective descriptions of real human behavior mixed extreme cynicism with profound confidence and hope. The "complete description" of human behavior in society revealed the facts of domination beneath the myths of democracy. But a reform public eager to act would surely use these "dirty facts." This notion of "objective science" foundered when Progressivism's popular thrust withered in World War I. In the 1920s and 1930s, Beard began to question the utility of "objective science" to incite public action. The complementary task of constructing new state power and functions tied to a revived popular, democratic consensus had stood as the major assumption of "objective science." Yet Beard now realized the failure of "objective science" to achieve the aims he posited for it. For Beard, political science and its approaches had to be altered in order to fulfill their original purposes. Muckraking and factual descriptions were not enough because they neglected what Beard saw as the now-necessary discussion of "democratic values." In the 1920s and 1930s Beard thus became an important internal critic of the profession he had helped to form. While a new generation of scholars developed the professional structures and refined the methods of political study, Beard lamented the discipline's unwillingness and incapacity to reevaluate its growing irrelevance to democratic advance.[45]

The Return to "Values"

As a Progressive, Charles Beard envisioned the development of political science and its organization and objective methodology as an instrument by which American democracy could be reconstructed institutionally and politically. From the mid-1920s until his death in 1948, the urgency of such a reconstruction increased while Beard's perception of political science's usefulness in the effort faded. The change in Beard's views in the mid-1920s was dramatic. Strident attacks on economic "determinism" replaced the analysis of economic groups. The meticulous specialized research he had once urged on others became for him "mindless empiricism." Scientific "objectivity," once praised as the chief attribute of science over political theory, now became both impossible and undesirable. Sorely needed "values" could never arise from facts alone. The history and political science disciplines, once heralded as "revolutionary," were now accounted to be overly specialized, bureaucratized, and bereft of creative insight.[46]

Many commentators have noted Beard's transformation. They have accounted for it by discovering a cleavage between Beard's "objectivity" and his reform politics.[47] But less had changed about Beard than about the profession he had helped to form and the political context in which it now operated after World War I. The public had failed to exert the moral and political energy that made objective "facts" useful in a larger reform effort.

Worse, the profession itself seemed to have responded not by trying to reforge such a movement, but by denying the special connection between scholarship and reform.

Chapter 4 discusses the kind of political science Beard rejected. But it is worthwhile here to note that Beard believed that the equation of objectivity with professional growth was nothing more than complacency and a retreat from original purposes. By the 1920s and 1930s the discipline had largely departed from its reform origins, both because of design and circumstance. Professionals in political science now concentrated on studying the sources of irrationality in public opinion rather than assuming it did not exist. The easy mixture of research, teaching, and consultation with reform groups of the Progressive era largely perished when post–World War I professionals turned to a specialized language of science largely inaccessible to all but fellow professionals. Beard believed that the new professional standards were gradually sapping political science's critical qualities by wrongly concentrating on issues of concern to academics only, or on erudite studies excessively financed by corporate philanthropy. He complained in 1930: "Important as are the collection and observation of data to creative enterprises, this operation has been overemphasized in training students and making researchers. . . . One of the great things with us in America . . . is our passionate faith in doing something; we are always . . . getting out one more monograph, doing more 'research,' heaving up great piles of printed matter."[48]

Collecting and filing tomes of data without a political purpose in mind was one facet of Beard's disillusionment. But a related and more important concern was the crisis in "political values" besetting the nation, one that left it morally exhausted in the face of challenges from abroad and at home. Before World War I, Beard had assumed that the public itself was quite intent on revising such values in such a way as to shed antique prejudices and outmoded ideologies. By the 1920s and 1930s something had indeed gone very wrong, so wrong that Beard now lamented social science's objectivity and instead called on scholars to return to "ethics." In the face of authoritarian ideologies abroad and the moral vacuum presented by the Republican administrations of Harding, Coolidge, and Hoover, Beard now proclaimed to his colleagues: "Science never tells anyone what to do in any large human situation, what is most valuable, what is most worth doing. It never commands anyone to do anything. A light and superficial skepticism respecting all values is easy, perhaps it is the prevailing temper;

[but] without ethics, political science can have no more vital connection with life than have the tables of an adding machine."[49]

The growing preeminence of behavioral and quantitative approaches in political science did not give an adequate reckoning of historical growth, movement, and potential. Such approaches therefore provided an increasingly useless guide to positive choices that individuals should make to collectively control their destinies. The didactic and descriptive exposés for which Beard had become famous now were replaced by a leap of faith. The scholar, Beard now believed, had to draw specific conclusions from data. One could no longer assume that the consumers of social science themselves would draw the right conclusions, or that social science would be employed for benign purposes. The "realism" that had once hailed "the complete description" as the "complete science" now had to be accompanied by the humanist's ability to analyze and interpret the facts: "So the task before us is that of clarifying our conception of American society and our purposes in selecting, collecting and organizing knowledge and thought bearing on the tensions, conflicts and problems of American society."[50]

Beard now not only doubted the utility of most social scientific research, but also, and more important, he began to deny that an objective science of politics was possible. Even if it was, he was not sure it would be useful. Historians and political scientists were now subject to the same critiques as political philosophers and their interpreters. Whether or not they knew it, studies that purported to be "complete" and empirically grounded only reflected the concerns and prejudices of the observer. Objective research was no more than a selective interpretation of the facts. Social scientists only artificially inflated their fundamentally biased outlooks by disguising moral and political assumptions and judgments behind claims of scientific objectivity. Beard even held that social science's major claim to authority— its ability to "predict" on the basis of compilations of data—was a menace to the complexity, vitality, and creativity of democratic societies. Worse yet, the effort to predict implied a deterministic and even a fatalistic view of human history. Prediction ultimately might lead to totalitarianism. If social scientists predicted, it would only narrow democratic choice. Beard warned in 1929: "Should mankind discover the law of its total historical unfolding, then it would be imprisoned in its own fate and powerless to change it; the past, present and future would be revealed as fixed and beyond the reach of human choice and will."[51]

Beard's rebellion against the methods, intentions, and claims of the social science of the 1920s and 1930s reflected his awareness that the social sciences were an increasingly ill-suited vehicle of reform politics. But without such a "science," Beard and his particular brand of reform politics lost much of their intellectual and political influence, both in the scholarly professions and in the ways social scientists acted within the highest policy-making bodies of the New Deal. Intellectually, Beard left social science largely behind in a meandering and ultimately unfruitful quest to bring "values" back into scholarly and political discourse. This was a lonely and, for Beard, a frustrating and disappointing adventure indeed. By the New Deal's height, Beard's imprint on the political science discipline was fading. While the discipline turned to behavioralism and—through it—to links with the new bureaucracies established by the New Deal, Beard went in the other direction. Disenchanted with the course and character of reform in the New Deal, he called for "socialization of whole sectors of the capitalist system." Frightened by the New Deal's failures, he warned that domestic turmoil might lead to foreign adventures and American rearmament. Isolated by his gadfly role within the profession, Beard could only admonish his colleagues for their narrow-mindedness. Having abandoned so many of his previously held views regarding the primary role of social science in fusing a powerful state with a resurgent national democracy, Beard wound up radically limiting the claims of knowledge altogether. In a last article written before his death in 1948, Beard lamented: "As a result of much study and reflection, I have come to the conviction that political scientists have no justification whatever for regarding our universe as a unified process under law and hence reducible to an exact science, either physical or political; and still less justification for supposing that, given the nature of our minds, we can grasp the scheme of things entire in its fullness."[52]

Third tradition scholarship combined a uniquely American vision of reform with the powerful notion that social science had a special role and authority in promoting it. At least in Charles Beard's career, the original promise of political science faded when it failed to meet these expectations. The course of Beard's career, like that of the radical progressivism he consistently upheld, was thus touched by the most profound irony. The skeptical realism designed to promote political reform was transformed into its opposite—a search and a hope for "values" that would heal the great gulf in the American political tradition.

The Demise of Fact Gathering

By World War I's end, the claims of many of the progressive liberal reformers who helped build a professionalized science of politics as a means of transforming political thought and practice had been dashed. The promise of a critical political science armed with methods, organizations, and findings that addressed the emergent "crisis" of American democratic thought, institutions, and practice in an age of industrial expansion spurred on scholars such as Bentley and Beard. For these two and others scattered about the newly born academic disciplines, a revolution in social thought might lead to an efficacious union of knowledge, power, and democracy. Such a union purported to supply meaningful answers to the far from academic epistemological questions of the early twentieth century. Whatever else might be said about Progressive scholarship, it was most certainly imbued with a dual sense of urgency and hope. The urgency emanated from the knowledge that reality no longer corresponded to traditional beliefs and practices. The hope lay in the prospect that scientific descriptions might awaken man's political action and revive political thought.

This sense of a clean break with the political past distinguishes Beard's and Bentley's search for moral and intellectual foundations. Perhaps no greater testimony to the character of this revolution can be found than in their concentration on the development of a tool—a method—to replace what had been thought to be "pure speculation." If Bentley's trenchant "Once the groups are stated, then everything is stated" signifies anything in the history of American scholarship, it is the passage of American social thought well beyond the notion that the Republic could be refounded by a single, dramatic act that transcended the drift, discord, and decay of the American political present. Bentley's and Beard's works also signaled the definitive end of older religious and evangelical modes of comprehending modern history. The fulminations of utopian radicals such as Ignatius Donnelly or Edward Bellamy, as well as conservative natural rights philosophers, were banned from the new scholarship.

The world of complete descriptions, fact gathering, and material analysis demanded specialized training. Knowledge now could be "accumulated." Moreover, scholarly research could now be a collective enterprise with evident and precise boundaries between experts and nonexperts. In contrast to intellectual life in agrarian America, attached as it was to the social and religious institutions of the local community, the new academic professions promised to restore intellectual unity to a fragmented social and political universe.

Arthur Bentley provided the most sophisticated and thoroughgoing sketch of the claims and difficulties of the new science and politics. Charles Beard was one of the most important profession builders and users of the "scientistic" methods Bentley proposed. Yet they both stood apart from some of the discipline's dominant tendencies. While they both embraced critiques of the transhistorical utopianism of Populist thinkers, they appropriated much of their reform energies. But such energies were now supported by a scientific realism intent on linking modern democracy with the growth of state institutions. More than their fellows, Bentley's and Beard's descriptive sciences were concerned with the political effects of scientific revelations. Once the public had the facts, political harmony was imminent. Beard and Bentley assumed that the language, methods, and discoveries of political science in America were not only or even primarily professional discourses, or merely ways to link scholarship with a politics of administrative management. Rather, the discourse of political science was in itself a popular language of reform. Its skeptical and critical outlook, its mode of analyzing the "real," its muckraking exposés—all were guides to popular reform politics precisely because of science's claims to objectivity. An accompaniment and complement to the much vaunted "realism" of these Progressive scholars was the hope that science's findings might catalyze vast changes in the nexus of social, economic, and political power in America. The methodology that dissolved politics into social processes and the scholarship that stripped institutions and political actors of their pretenses shaded off into Bentley's middle-class counterrevolution and Beard's call for a fusion of collectivism and democratic choice. Objective observation and political passion were fused as weapons of political reconstruction.

It is far beyond this work's intent to discuss in detail why the "reform public" designated by Bentley and Beard failed to move in the directions they indicated. The Populists, too, had failed to heed the higher call of Lester Ward's "dynamic sociology." But perhaps Beard's and Bentley's ultimate frustration was that the political science profession grew and expanded despite the failure of its founding mission. It, too, envisioned a link between science and reform, but of a very different variety. Instead of a vehicle for the fusion of new institutional power with popular democracy, political scientists increasingly turned to powerful political elites and leaders as the natural audience of social science. The construction of a new state apparatus, emboldened by new links to the world of big corporations, armed by a standing military force, and supplied with regulatory powers over the American economy, was aided and abetted by the growing discipline. Beard and Bentley certainly might have welcomed such institutional vigor, but they were to regret that such new strength was not shaped, guided, and directed by a political process that put the "rational" public at the helm. As disciplinary gadfly in the 1920s and 1930s, Beard lectured his colleagues on the need to return to science's reform mission. Yet few listened to this message. The overt efforts to link the discipline with popularly based reform faded in favor of efforts to refine scientific theory, organize ever more sophisticated links between corporate philanthropy and social science, and solve administrative dilemmas the American state's new powers and functions posed during the New Deal. The critical and democratic science of liberal Progressivism met its ironic end as an enterprise built on faith rather than on fact. Beard's and Bentley's successors would reduce the claims of political science as a language of democratic reform, just as they would inflate political science's claims as an indispensable tool in the rationalization of state functions. Abandoning the liberal progressive effort at a balance between state power and democratic legitimacy, the discipline increasingly gave its attention and resources to the former at the expense of the latter. Yet, as the next chapter explains, there were many important exceptions.

4

Reform and Disillusionment in the New Deal

The first two generations of political scientists at least lived in times when nearly everyone agreed that political reforms of some kind were sorely needed. In the Progressive era, political scientists warned of impending dangers, but they were fairly confident that somebody was listening. To a limited degree, muckraking seemed to work, although almost never to the extent that its advocates hoped.

In stark contrast, the aftermath of World War I seemed to show that elites and masses had gone somewhat mad. No one wanted to listen to political science vanguards. To Progressives, the 1920s were times of betrayal, ignorance, and ominous complacency. Sinister forces reemerged and reform publics were noteworthy by their absence. Examples of stupidity were everywhere. Woodrow Wilson died a lonely and slow death after Congress gutted his League of Nations proposal. Party hacks catapulted a poker-playing puppet to the presidency in 1920. "Silent" Cal Coolidge might have been smarter than Warren Harding, but one was never sure. Progressives feared Bolsheviks and revolutionaries, but the Palmer Raids and the accompanying appeals to nativism were scarcely greeted by those with liberal values.

The prosecution of the war itself gave scarce reason for optimism about the depth of intelligence or democratic beliefs in America (or, for that matter, anywhere else either). Political scientists supported the war for the usual reasons—it was supposed to end European autocracy and thus end war. It would vindicate the legitimate claims of struggling nationalities throughout Europe. Yet dirty laundry was evident beneath these principled goals. Most ominous was the ease by which people everywhere were manipulated by hypernationalist slogans and symbols government propaganda machines created.

Some social scientists had served on the federal government's Committee on Public Information. Their experiences were interesting and unsettling because it seemed as though "public opinion," even in America, was hardly immune from manipulation. Our propaganda machine had of course whipped up popular sentiment for the "right" causes, but what if illiberal regimes effectively employed these same techniques? What if they could be used in peacetime? What if propaganda machinery was controlled by the wrong people?[1]

In the Progressive era, scholar-activists like Beard always assumed the common sense of ordinary Americans. During and after the war, social scientists began to have doubts. A battery of intelligence tests administered to army draftees during the war turned up disturbing bits of information. The unflattering portrait sketched by these path breaking psychological tests seemed to indicate that democratic beliefs and reasoning power were much weaker among the masses than had been expected. Obviously, Progressive social science and its message had not been getting through to the average citizen, or so the postwar academic generation concluded.

Depressed by the masses, social scientists after World War I were both fascinated and appalled by the powers and techniques of strong leaders. Harding's mediocrity and Wilson's failures contrasted with the obvious successes of fascists and communists. How could liberal democracies survive against Mussolinis and Lenins if they were led by men of little ability and vision? Yet how could firmly liberal leaders be generated? For at least a few years after the war, social scientists were even taken in by Mussolini's corporatism. After all, he brought a divided Italy together, even if at the expense of the working-class movement. Trains ran on time and bothersome strikes were quelled by the state and its official unions. Enchantment with Italy passed, however, as Mussolini abolished liberal institutions altogether. But Mussolini's obvious power still raised an interesting question: Could democratic leaders capture such powers of mobilization? It seemed that democracies were doomed by their own conflicts—the experiences of Spain, Germany, and France after the war were hardly comforting to liberal hopes.[2]

These kinds of questions and concerns were outside the scope of Progressive political science and its presumed symbiosis of good scholarship with democratic reform. The younger scholars of the 1920s began a now time-honored cycle in disciplinary history. One's immediate predecessors were faulted for their naiveté, methodological errors, and extreme amateurism. No one discarded the Progressive legacy, nor did everyone attack the looseness and informality of the prewar discipline.

But there was a collective sense that Progressive political science had not helped to achieve Progressive political goals. Moreover, scholars traced Progressive failures to overindulgence in direct political advocacy at the clear expense of scientific scholarship. The world clearly had not responded to the objective revelations of people like Beard and Bentley. They had only dirtied their hands with reform politics and had drawn overly hasty conclusions about the high levels of public and elite receptivity to reform proposals.

Some clear disciplinary and scholarly trends appeared in the 1920s, all the result of this disillusionment with the immediate past. First, most postwar political scientists self-consciously isolated themselves in university life to immerse themselves in reformulating the agenda of scholarly research. Second, quite different ideas about the audiences for political science accompanied withdrawal from political action. From eager consumers of social science messages, citizens now became objects of study and observation to be "educated" and controlled. Leaders, too, were stripped for a time of their essentially benign image. They became "elites," and the studies of the secrets of their trade began with hope that they too could be guided to responsible exercise of their awesome vocation. Third, prominent political scientists became self-consciously "scientistic" in orientation. The discipline's work was said to have fallen behind advances in the "harder" sciences of psychology, biology, and statistics. "Politics" as a science had to catch up with the objective, sophisticated methods of the physical sciences. Political scientists were urged to establish their own unique vocabulary and concepts. They had to discover, measure, and quantify the key facets of "political behavior," which was suddenly the most fashionable new term of the 1920s. Like chemists and physicists, political scientists had to collaborate in complex, multifaceted, and specialized experiments in a great laboratory—the polity itself. Fourth and finally, all these developments accelerated pleas for greater organization of the discipline itself. Money was not only the mother's milk of politics. Under Charles Merriam's leadership, organized corporate philanthropy began to play a prominent role in political research. The number of graduate students multiplied, as did curricular offerings. By the end of the 1920s, a majority of U.S. colleges had a department of political science.[3]

At first glance, these tendencies may seem to be a forthright flight from a "science of reform politics" altogether—or from any politics except that of objective science itself. The new political scientists were opposed to what they thought were mere political exposés. And a sizeable portion of the discipline's leaders did indeed ally themselves against reformist orientations and in favor of a political science as "pure" as they believed the natural sciences to be.

Such people, though, were in the philosophical minority even within the discipline's leadership. Widespread discontent with amateurism and advocacy was not fundamentally a rejection of reform, but was a new way of asserting its necessity and shaping its boundaries and agenda. A supposedly surer understanding of political behavior was not only desirable in and of itself, but contributed to understanding the forces that previously weakened the urge to reform in pre–World War I America. The behavioralism of Charles Merriam and Harold Lasswell, for instance, promised not only understanding but transformation of the "irrational" segment of American political behavior into a democratic civic culture.[4] They promised political science as a therapy for passion and as a teacher of civic values. By laying bare the multifaceted character of political beliefs, third tradition political scientists asserted their new and even more ambitious claims as doctors to a sick but not terminally ill polity.

The scientistic, seemingly antipolitical disenchantment of postwar political scientists fell short of cynicism about democracy. If publics were not provoked by factual exposés, then informed citizens could be created by scientific reeducation and democratic leaders and policies. New and expensive collaborative research became the symbol of the political science of the 1920s because it promised useful understanding. Barry Karl has commented: "As essential as the pursuit of science was to the increased utilization of social knowledge by mankind, if the increase took place at the expense of public understanding of and respect for social knowledge it could scarcely avoid defeating its own purposes. The relation between social knowledge and democracy required communication of that knowledge at a level capable of generating public support if democracy were to continue to work."[5]

With so many examples of democracy not working, no wonder the new political scientists rejected prewar optimism. Fears of popular depravity or a fateful lapse into dictatorship outweighed the earlier confidence in the ability of political truth to provoke popular outrage. But the disaffection behind the scientistic tendencies of the 1920s went only so far as a deep strain of anxiety with the political configuration of the decade. A more complete and scientifically grounded theory was needed to explain the causes and sources of "irrational behavior" by leaders and masses. But once understandings emerged, political scientists could reenter politics as behavioral therapists.

The new scientists thus still held to America's exceptionalism if only because in America intellectuals like themselves could still steer the polity away from disintegration into the political extremes found abroad. The methods of Progressive political science could be spurned, but only to sustain the movement's overall goals in new conditions.[6] How to establish a strong and purposive liberal state without collapsing into totalitarianism became the primary hope and central dilemma of the new intellectuals. How to transform public opinion and the mass mind into vital and energetic supports for such a state became the ultimate question the new scientists tried to answer. Third tradition political aspirations thus appear in new form in the claims of a regenerated science. Between Harding and Mussolini stood the prospect of strong, responsible, democratic executives. Between dumb and complacent citizens and the mass psychology of fascist and communist "mobs," political scientists promised active, skeptical, and thinking citizens.

All this was less a promise to lead reform than to create reform publics where none existed. Injecting rationality into the polity was far different than assisting already eager reformers, and it would require a far different organization of scholarship and agenda for reform. Progressive scholars had only burnt their fingers through their activity in reform groups. All the appeals for scientific rigor in the 1920s might disguise a radical shift in the audiences political scientists wanted to address and the forms by which they presented them to the polity. Henceforth, political scientists tried to gain credibility at the *summit* of the political system, among leaders, notables, and officeholders with the power to shape mass opinions and judge public policies. There was now to be a national political science with a highly sophisticated division of labor, promoting concentration on every variable shaping political behavior. There were also to be *national* sources of funding and coordination of research, freeing political scientists from enslavement to the whims of university administrators. So, too, the focus of reform had to be national as well. The findings of the new studies had to be communicated at those political levels where action could be comprehensive in scope and execution. More than ever, the new political science concentrated on direct influence on the federal government and its officials and leaders. Capturing the polity's summit went a long way to capturing its base. Building strong national institutions could also encourage citizens' attention and cooperation with them. Concentrating solely on government and its functions could lead one to believe that science was above mere partisan politics.

There was only one way to be serious about this kind of profession-building—find research money and control its uses from a central source.[7] In 1923 the Social Science Research Council (SSRC) was born from donations of the Laura Spelman Rockefeller Memorial Fund, the Carnegie Corporation, the Julius Rosenwald Fund, and the Russell Sage Foundation.[8] The entrance of corporate philanthropy into social science funding signaled yet another move away from the unmediated political advocacy of the Progressive years. The SSRC was devoted to scholarly collaboration around huge, long-term, and intertwined research projects. Although it may have been above partisanship, it was not, however, above politics. The major political scientist behind SSRC's birth—Charles Merriam—successfully convinced well-heeled contributors that research on political behavior would have enormous implications for the functions and organization of government, but that such research was somehow *not* explicitly political because it was nonpartisan. In the new lexicon, "politics" would be asserted through the "objective" language of scientific research, not muckraking. The more specialized the language of political science, the more complex and theoretically concentrated research became. The more scholars were encouraged to engage in cumulative research separate from explicit political advocacy, the more the new science also subjected the polity to scientific therapies. In the 1920s the legitimacy of social science was linked to the search for a new basis of legitimacy for political life itself.

The most revealing contrast between Progressive political science and its successor is seen in changing attitudes toward the presidency and the executive branch. The idea that the American president was the prime mover in American government—that he was the only "public man" in a world of selfishness and factionalism—certainly predated the 1920s. The idea of fusing knowledge with presidential power, popular mobilization with strong presidential leadership, has always been popular among political scientists. But radical progressives like Beard always conditioned such admiration for the office with concern lest its powers become insulated from popular control. The president was supposed to be a champion of the underrepresented, a popular tribune—not just an intelligent rationalizer of government functions and activities.

But with the SSRC's urging, this emphasis changed—the office became the focus for the expansion of "nonpolitical" expert approaches to bureaucratic growth and management, not the people's voice. The Hoover administration established the Committee on Recent Social Trends. Corresponding to the idea that experts and engineers were above dirty politics, the committee was to be a collection of counselors supposedly above political struggle—a kind of sociocracy without the populist trappings people like Lester Ward wanted to assign to such bodies. The committee represented the idea that social, economic, and political problems had "objective" solutions. Once data had been collected on ongoing social trends, the president could act independently to impose order on chaos. Here, in short, was an American institution that could be above influence by the powerful forces in society and economy that resisted expertise.

The committee surveyed an extraordinarily broad range of phenomena, compiling statistical data on unemployment, inflation, education, crime, emigration, natural resources, and urbanization. It was supposed to establish correlations between these social trends, suggesting the causes of each. In true apolitical fashion, the tools of social science were introduced into government as nonideological "suggestions." The committee "would refrain from expressions of approval and disapproval" and "report their findings uncolored by their personal likes and dislikes."[9]

Hoover's second term was stillborn and so were the voluminous findings of the committee. But there were much bigger things to come in the 1930s—or so political science experts believed and hoped.

The Great Depression, the New Deal, and Franklin Roosevelt provided the optimum setting for the revival of the explicit spirit of reform in political science, now armed with increased numbers, organization, money, and connections. Franklin Roosevelt's popularity, intelligence, and engrained democratic sensibilities were a trio of qualities nearly perfectly matched with the concerns of the new political science. Political scientists studied the "irrational" bases of popular opinion. Roosevelt was a great pragmatic, popular educator who awakened Americans to the need for cooperative effort as a means of escaping the Great Depression.

As a very important part of their approach to research, political scientists spurned fascist "nihilism" and communist "determinism." Roosevelt and the New Deal accepted neither while nonetheless calling for strong governmental action backed by reasoned popular approbation.

Political scientists mourned the rise of Mussolini and Stalin yet feared that American democracy could not generate their kind of power and loyalty. Roosevelt was a firm democrat, yet he seemed to recognize the need for a massive change in the structures of state power. Finally, political scientists had lamented the inefficiency and amateurism of U.S. public administration. Roosevelt, without losing for a moment his acute political sensibilities, seemed intent on breaking the equation of American democracy with drift, discord, and national weakness.

Here was the supreme opportunity for the realization of third tradition political claims. Roosevelt liked political scientists and put many of them in prominent places in his administration. Executive reorganization, national economic and resource planning, the federalization of social welfare and labor policies, civic education, even experiments in ownership like the Tennessee Valley Authority (TVA)—all seemed to finally activate the energies of the Great Community, fusing political power with an active democratic consensus.[10]

Yet by the beginning of World War II the kind of disenchantment reminiscent of 1919 returned. For the most active professional scientists and reformers, the New Deal fell short of its promises. Once again, reform was mangled by the reappearance of older ways of thinking about practicing politics. The New Deal surely created new functions for the federal government, but these functions were absorbed within an older government philosophy that resisted state control. Government now administered thousands of programs, but some people still equated planning with the "foreign" doctrines of socialism. Others even advocated socialism itself. Dependent on interest groups and fractions of business, government would plan—but only by accident and only with the cooperation of powerful groups in the political economy. Voters, supposedly reeducated as scientific citizens, provided only hesitant and instrumental support to their favorite programs. By 1938 a conservative Congress halted the state's growth and repudiated the philosophy of state planning. Once again, executive branch reorganization was being lumped with dictatorship, economic planning with hostility to capitalism, and state-building with a violation of the supposed "natural harmony" of the marketplace. Whatever else the New Deal did, it failed to dislodge older political traditions suspicious of state power.

To those who blended profession-building with support for the New Deal, the failures of structural reform once again raised disturbing questions. At the apparent height of the profession's power, the failure to build a coalition in support of planning and institutional reorganization was all too obvious. To men like Charles Merriam and Harold Lasswell, the polity remained intractable. Moreover, their professional colleagues remained stubbornly ignorant about the potential and urgency of transforming the polity.

Charles E. Merriam and the Crisis of American Democracy

Few would deny Charles E. Merriam's special contributions to the vast changes in methods, organization, and role of political science that occurred after World War I. Merriam's hand can be seen in virtually every facet of modern political science. With help, he was the architect and master builder of the modern science of politics in the United States. Organizer of the National Conference on the Science of Politics and author of *New Aspects of Politics*, Merriam symbolized the scientific, behavioral revolt of the early 1920s. Department chair at the University of Chicago, he brought together the era's most impressive young political scientists. A SSRC cofounder and APSA president, Merriam linked the study of politics with organized corporate philanthropy. Finally, Merriam did the most to bridge professional social science and the federal government. From the Hoover to the Roosevelt administrations, he served on the Committee on Recent Social Trends, the Committee on Administrative Management, the National Resources Planning Board, and as Franklin Roosevelt's adviser. Merriam's intellectual achievements were less impressive than his activism. But his books and articles are nonetheless important because they persuaded a whole generation of political scientists that the search for the causes of political behavior through methodological rigor was the primary characteristic of academic professionalism. By almost every standard, Charles Merriam was a successful man, yet a full account of his life and work only reveals the dilemmas and frustrations of the liberal Progressivism that prompted his lifelong zeal.[11]

To many of his students and to historians of the period alike, Charles Merriam is remembered as the founder of value-free behavioralism in political science. He was an advocate of behavioralism, even though he was often vague when he tried to define it. But the epithet "value-free" is almost certainly a mischaracterization of Merriam's approach to the science of politics. Rather, the techniques of behavioral science transmuted into political studies were primarily new ways of verifying the "promise of American democracy," as well as modernizing and adapting its values to the conditions Merriam saw as threats to modern democratic prospects. In sharp contrast to many of his own students, Merriam tried to combine political passion and "pure science." He was sure that social science was the language of scholarship and democratic rejuvenation. Merriam cannot be accused of confusing "science" and "reform" because the two were inextricably fused in his mind. To him, each complemented the other in a single project. Actual government practices and ignorant people would be "adjusted" and "guided" toward their democratic destiny. Merriam's hopes and visions do not stand separately from his work or activity as a scholar, but are bound together in a coherent—if flawed—set of notions and expectations about the rapport between science and America's allegedly democratic potential and uniqueness. The organized political science Merriam helped to establish flourished. Yet the paradox of his life can be found in the failure of the vision for which he saw political science only as an important instrument. Merriam built professional political science as we know it today. But he did not achieve the political reform that was professional political science's ultimate goal. As such, his career possesses at least two ironies.

The first concerns the rather peculiar relationship between Merriam and the scholars who did so much to enrich and embellish the behavioral science Merriam always exhorted them to practice. The behavioral revolution Merriam began aimed at the discovery of the psychological and social factors that shaped mass political behavior. Merriam's kind of scholar also searched for universal definitions of political power and tried to define its proper use and improper abuse. Merriam encouraged this dual emphasis with supreme confidence about what it would portend for the future of American democracy. At the very least, behavioralism was supposed to promote the sort of social control and democratic engineering capable of creating rational, knowledgeable, and active citizens friendly to government. At the most, behavioral political science pointed to pregnant possibilities for democratic life that had previously been disguised.

Yet the scientists Merriam educated rarely uncovered any reasons for optimism. Merriam, the man who more than any other sanctioned the move toward specialization and rigor in the conduct of social research, began to criticize the narrowness of the conclusions or simply ignore some of the pessimistic findings dredged up by a whole generation of new political scientists. By the late 1930s and World War II, his writings and public commentaries began to seriously diverge from those of his colleagues in concern, temperament, and tone. By his death in 1953 Merriam had already become something like a legendary great-grandfather, praised and admired by all for his past exploits, and ultimately excused for some of the eccentricities of his golden years.[12]

The second and more significant irony strikes at the very heart of the political claims Merriam equated with the mission of social science. Merriam pioneered the rapport between professional social science and New Deal policy-makers. Ties between social scientists and policy-makers surely outlived him and even expanded after his death. Yet many, if not most, of the assumptions and expectations that had catalyzed Merriam to action came unraveled even in his own lifetime. Characteristically, Merriam himself never became bitter over—and thus never frontally addressed the reasons for—the failure of some of his most cherished aims. Yet it was unquestionably clear to him by America's entry into World War II that the promise of social science as a teacher, adviser, and servant of a "rational" citizenry and its vigorous leaders had hardly come to pass. Until the end of his life, he vacillated between expressions of dread and urgency about the American present and hope and optimism about the future. Merriam himself might have deemed appropriate an analysis that examined his own thought and action in light of the very different ways "social forces" reinterpreted his beliefs for different purposes.

Behavioral Political Science and the Crisis of American Democracy

Charles Merriam's enthusiasm for both scientism and professionalism in political science was a clear response and reaction to the failures of an earlier generation of liberal Progressive academics. Impressed and obsessed by the effects of technology on politics and society, Merriam was concerned about the possible social and political consequences of the "age of science" in America. More than other peoples, Americans were said to have pioneered the spirit of invention and industry. With a few exceptions, the whole society willingly endured massive and frequent physical dislocations and uprooting. Yet for all their ingenuity, Americans were curiously primitive and tradition-bound in politics. Political attitudes remained oddly prescientific and preindustrial, dangerously ill-suited to confront the vast social, economic, and cultural transformations that had already rent asunder the simpler world of the early Republic. The agricultural population had become urbanized, the frontier was closed, and machine technology placed farmer, worker, and capitalist alike in an interdependent set of market links. Huge agglomerations of corporate and labor power replaced the personal ties between owners and workers of an earlier era.[13] But political institutions and beliefs remained strangely timeless despite these changes.

The revolution technology and industrialization wrought had still left behind antique political perceptions, practices, and structures unadapted to a world of rapid economic and social change. The citizenry and its leaders alike still acted as if political forms were immutable, divinely inspired givens, rather than instruments that could be appropriated for whatever purposes people wished to assign to them. "Democracy" was still equated with a weak national state and haphazard means of "regulating" society. Democratic common sense in America still equated bureaucracy with mysterious powers inherently distant and unaccountable to simple and understandable popular commands. Worse yet, "executive leadership" was still shunned as a synonym for autocracy, monarchy, or dictatorship. For Merriam as for other Progressives, the crisis of democracy could thus be found in its false equation of popular control with governmental weakness, ignorance with democratic accountability, and political legitimacy with the persistence of the outmoded weak governments of the nineteenth century.

These traditional beliefs and institutions produced conflicts and distortions that threatened the very survival of democracy. Individualism might have made sense in the self-regulating villages of preindustrial America, but the advent of industrialization had broken up past loyalties without yet providing an alternative means and spirit of social cohesion. Class, ethnic, and nationalistic hatreds sprouted and flourished in the political jungle while public institutions stood powerless. When politicians and institutions proved resistant to or incapable of change, Merriam held, the prospect of revolution and totalitarianism emerged. The crisis of democracy was above all a question of distorted perceptions and reactionary beliefs.

To be sure, omens of a "crisis of democracy" were not the same as news of democracy's downfall. It was not the given "values" of American democratic theory that Merriam worried about, but rather the disappearance of those values in modern conditions. Consonant with Merriam's persistent advocacy of scientific method is an almost metaphysical political theology that is helped along by science. "Deeper values" will always "progressively develop" as long as scientific method is employed to unlock the secret of democratic evolution. Without science, democracy would surely perish; with its aid, political and social control, and democratic choice would be linked together. Portents of the "democratic crisis" were always accompanied by prophecies such as these: "It is a long road out of slavery to inanimate nature, up to the mastery of the dark and fateful forces around us and within; but the race is on the way. The future belongs to those who fuse intelligence with faith, who grope their way forward . . . from blind adaptation to creative evolution."[14]

Merriam's odd fusion of faith in the future and faith in the facts never left him. But it had to receive some embellishment after World War I because the preconditions for the realization of a democratic, scientific utopia seemed in grave doubt. No longer could scholars maintain that the "scientific method" was not only a way of studying politics, but was also an outlook suited to the goals and temperament of "the greatest middle class in the world." Merriam always saw the practical, skeptical, and experimental temper of science as eminently communicable to the mass public. But in the 1920s, he worried that blind ignorance kept the scientific outlook separate from politics.

The major distinction between Charles E. Merriam's mature perceptions and those of his colleague and sometimes-critic Charles Beard stems from the former's realization that the moral and popular consensus that supposedly supported Progressivism had evaporated. Simply, it no longer tapped the popular mainsprings, nor should it or could it be tied to a political movement of precise definition. Beard, too, realized that the language of science and its connections to popular reform could no longer be taken for granted after the war. But, as noted, he turned away from science toward an unsuccessful and lonely effort to extract "values" from history. Merriam's overall political vision parallels that of Beard. But unlike him, Merriam sought a solution to the crisis of American democracy by reworking and reconstituting social science in the now-inhospitable terrain of post–World War I American politics. "Values" were not in crisis; they simply had to be made real.

Merriam's efforts bore fruit, but at the cost of altering and tempering the vision and faith of liberal Progressivism that once sustained it. He began the long quest for an organized science of politics after World War I with the knowledge that the assured role Progressive political scientists once assumed was at best a hope and at worst a delusion. Older Progressives had simply overestimated the ease by which science might inform and activate reform in the ways indicated, and had underestimated the obstacles to progress. With these humbling experiences in mind, Merriam started his efforts with the notion that Progressives had appeared too radical and antitraditional. If science was to be accepted—if its attitudes, outlook, and findings were to become unquestionably valid—then somehow it had to become a nonrevolutionary extension of democratic culture in America in order not to break with it.

In Merriam's science, the residues of Beard's and Bentley's political radicalism were removed from the mainstream of social science. Rather than transformation, Merriam sought modernization. What he called the "American cultural complex" was beyond criticism, analysis, or scrutiny.[15] Merriam intuited a kind of immanent destiny in the democratization of this cultural complex. In contrast to the fevers of European politics, Americans might establish a proper realm of political order and choice on the one hand, and maintain private freedom and rights on the other. In the past, this separation had led to the domination of the marketplace and had denigrated the emergence of public values, choice, and politics. But now, events had to inspire collective decisions and political controls, even as the private realm was preserved. The skepticism of Americans about political action made totalitarianism an impossibility here. In America, the purposive state could emerge from democratic dreams and popular consensus, just as the Industrial Revolution had transformed and expanded humankind's powers.

In Merriam's writings, a democratic science of politics replaced divine Providence and the invisible hand as a masterful guide to the unfolding future. Politics itself, however, was not replaced by scientific understanding. The latter merely shaped the limits and established the potential for political creativity. Political science in America demystified the opaque and complex world of interacting processes. It clarified the scope and range of public choices, drawing lines between individual freedom and collective choices and obligations. At the service of democracy, science "socialized" and trained citizens and leaders for the rational pursuit of benign ends. As the preferred attitude of political modernism, a science of politics reinstated and updated the democratic character so it could once again operate in America.

Merriam's scientific advocacy of dispassionate enthusiasm for the quantitative and the clinical has a paradoxical zeal. Today, political theorists doubt that there is such a thing as classical democratic theory. To Merriam, the ideal of the liberal citizen was, curiously enough, to be realized through behavioral science. The discovery of irrationality in human thought and action—its essential susceptibility to symbolism and psychological manipulation—was a likely finding of Merriam's behavioral research. But this is behavioralism with an important twist. Social science research also promised that citizens could be trained to be as dispassionate as the political scientists who studied them. If academics could absorb the scientific outlook, so could citizens.

Merriam's new science was the alternative to the simplistic hopes of Progressives. They had neglected to suggest remedies for the abuses they uncovered, trusting to the innate political wisdom of the public for the political sensibilities Merriam believed had to be instilled anew. Merriam's behavioral political science emerges as a cleanser of impure residues in American political thought. Merriam was not the slightest bit ambivalent about the rationalization of the world. To him, the iron cage of industrial society was a modern political community—a perfect union of democracy and bureaucracy.[16]

Merriam's vision of political science provided few precise definitions of its substantive content. What was "methodological rigor?" Could a science of politics develop units of analysis as precise as atoms or molecules were to chemists? In the early 1920s, Merriam helped to organize and chair three landmark Conferences on the Scientific Study of Politics. These meetings did more to create disciplinary uniformity than perhaps all the efforts that had preceded them. Virtually all the discipline's leaders—and their growing numbers of graduate students—were won over to a kind of common definition of the basic units of political science. "Attitudes"—defined in one conference report as "the sum total of a man's inclinations and feelings, prejudices or biases, preconceived rational ideas, fears and emotions about a scientific topic"—contributed to the discipline's emphasis on study of the present. These conferences also helped to pinpoint what political science decidedly was not. Just about everything that could not be subject to quantification or measurement was now suspect. Political theory, philosophy of history, formalist descriptions of institutions—all were thought to be mere speculation. Merriam himself informed the conference: "The historian . . . could distinguish genuine writing from the bogus, could scour the world with immense enthusiasm to uncover manuscripts or activities hitherto unknown. . . . Yet in his critical analysis, he relied on the activities of other social studies."[17]

Bentley and Beard, of course, had made the same criticisms of their predecessors; now Merriam was criticizing the critics. In *New Aspects of Politics* (1925), Merriam made clear how his ideas differed from theirs. A valid political science was said to be characterized not as an effort to strip "ideology" away from the exercise of power. By its nature, scientific scholarship avoided generalizations about the ubiquity of conflict in politics. Once political studies were stripped of "opinions," consensual political action became possible. Once political scientists began ". . . minute, thorough, patient, intensive studies of the detail of political phenomena, [they would] bridge the gap between art and science and bring us to more precise methods of political and social control than mankind has hitherto possessed."[18]

Merriam and his colleagues tended to define any form of political radicalism as a kind of political pathology that developed only in the absence of political science knowledge. Regional or ethnic prejudices, class conflicts and hatreds—all were merely symptoms of a popular misunderstanding of the possibilities of cooperation and consensus through collective action.

New Aspects promised that science could promote "social cohesion in the larger unit." Without a discipline that took rigorous methods seriously, public debate and politics would continue to be polluted by the emotions of the masses—easy prey to totalitarian leaders: "When the passions of the community are aroused, it may be too late for impartial inquiry to be made or to command any wide influence if conducted. . . . Where the facts cannot be found, a premium is placed upon dogmatic assertion rather than upon careful judgment, and the most reasonable is overwhelmed by the least reasonable and least scrupulous."[19]

New Aspects was an appeal designed to create the necessary conditions for "impartial inquiry." Impartiality, Merriam held, was necessary if political science was ever to achieve the deference prewar Progressives unsuccessfully sought. Scholars such as Beard sacrificed science to advocacy. In their zeal, Progressives lost intellectual credibility, and a new public would listen only if science and its outlook preceded advocacy. Direct identification with political causes had to be replaced by organizations that brought together academics around common research agendas. Only after refined research had been conducted could political impacts be made. After the mysteries of the polity had been revealed by specialized research, political reform itself could become objective and nonpartisan, accepted by all thinking citizens: "The democratic movement, the larger leisure of mankind, the broader education of humanity, the new forms of inter-communication, the larger resources available for scientific inquiry—these are factors which are likely to force a readjustment of the bases of the political order, and which require the development of techniques of government upon a wholly different plane from that upon which it has hitherto rested. . . . Politics as the art of the traditional advances to politics as the science of constructive, intelligent social control."[20]

Some rejected Merriam's claims about scientific reform. Charles Beard served as APSA president just a year after *New Aspects of Politics* appeared. Beard made it clear that he was hardly sympathetic to Merriam's appeal for a new social scientific orthodoxy. While Merriam pointed to the advantages of organizations such as the SSRC, Beard complained of the corrupting effects of corporate philanthropy on critical and original thinking. While Merriam's metaphors stressed the virtues of "political science" in finding a "social consensus" beneath the strife of world politics, Beard reminded APSA conventioneers that the world was naturally and fortuitously replete with conflicts between classes, groups, and nations. Political scientists, Beard thought, were inevitably as divided as the society in which they worked.[21] While Beard feared the separation of social research from humanistic concerns, Merriam never saw the possible tensions and regarded Beard's outlook as precisely the kind of view that reduced scientific respectability and public influence.

Still others grumbled that Merriam was not really interested in "pure" science at all, but in political reform disguised as science. Robert Crane, one of the organizers of the Conference on the Science of Politics, often locked horns with Merriam. Crane insisted that specialization and scientific rigor should take precedence over the public impact of political science research. To have political relevance only corrupted the scientific endeavor. Merriam was even something of a paradox to his students and colleagues at the University of Chicago. As he sermonized on the virtues of standardization of research techniques and methodological rigor, he still protested against overspecialization and immersion in professional jargon. Yet he was curiously vague and elusive when it came to how a balance between the two might be achieved. Merriam tended to scatter his advocacy of the need to study comparative political behavior, propaganda, psychology, and statistics like so many breadcrumbs. Each student took Merriam's exhortations seriously, but often found that by the time they had followed the methods prescribed, Merriam was already on to some new and supposedly urgent field of investigation.[22]

Not surprisingly, Merriam remained unimpressed and unchanged by his various critics because he always insisted on the compatibility and even identity of "pure" and "applied" political science. Typically, Merriam's *New Aspects of Politics* urged others on to the rigors of research, motivated by his insistence that political scientists will be "utopians in their prophetic views." The very different protests of Beard and Crane fell before words such as these, addressed to the 1925 ASPA meeting: "A freer spirit, a forward outlook, an emancipation from clinging categories now outgrown, a greater creativeness in technique, a quicker fertility of investigation, a more intimate touch with life, a balanced judgment, a more intense attack upon our problems, closer relations with other social sciences and with natural science—with these we may go on to the reconstruction of the 'purely political' into a more intelligent influence on the progress of the race toward conscious control over its own evolution."[23]

This important homily suggests the depth of attachment between the discourse of science and the reconstruction of that sense of the political so visibly eclipsed by the collapse of Progressive political hopes. Science as the precondition of—and not the replacement for—the realm of political choice and decision encouraged Merriam to seek new links between a developing scientific discourse and the polity in dire need of his message. And there was no better place to begin than in the schools and their curricula, where the science of social control might have a direct impact on the making of new citizens.

The Making of a Rational Public

Until the post–Civil War tide of immigration to these shores, the communication of political values to the younger generations was seen as a proper responsibility of the family, the church, and the local community. The Constitution, after all, said nothing about political education, trusting to institutions the task of checking political ambitions. Yet the social authority of local notables that had held preindustrial America together was now gone. Citizens were only sloppily taught the civic values of modern democracy if they were taught at all. To people such as Merriam, whose early lives had been led in America's small towns, the industrialization and urbanization he so admired also raised perplexing issues. How could America at one and the same time create functional substitutes for the intimacy of education in village democracy and prepare citizens to understand and act in the interdependent, technological present? With both the family and community ever weaker, what would take their place?

The assumption by thousands of independent American school districts of responsibilities once safely left to home and church presented both an opportunity and a dilemma. If schools insisted on reflecting the old values, the same kind of "drift" Merriam had always decried would persist. Yet if American education became an object of national policy making, might it not be subject to the dangers of propagandists of either the left or the right, or remain the prey of "village idiots" such as William Jennings Bryan? Or even if educational policy in America could somehow be standardized by the "right" people, might it nonetheless violate one of the desirable features of American democratic culture? Progressives such as Merriam hardly needed to be reminded of the sad state of what passed for civic education in American schools. One need look no further than the Scopes trial to provoke fear and trembling. Yet with a glance abroad, Merriam could observe the power and success of "civic education" in the totalitarian states. Russian and Italian experiments were both tempting and repugnant; they revealed not only the .power of civic education but also its seeming incompatibility with democratic values. Yet education in democratic values was still a necessity.

Merriam carried on the third tradition's concern for the education of citizens, and he was one of the few behavioralists to do so. He was convinced that the propagation of political science and its way of thinking provided a way out of the tension between too much and too little authority. Young minds ought not to be manipulated by propaganda, but rather taught how to think. In his view, "scientific method" might constitute not only a way for scholars to interpret the world, but also a way for future citizens to understand it as well. In this light, civic education was perhaps the most direct solution to the earlier Progressives' reliance on "facts" as natural catalysts for political action. To Merriam, citizens not only had to be given facts, but they also had to be educated in the proper ways to interpret them. In other words, citizens had to be carefully socialized and controlled, their passions tempered by healthy skepticism and informed optimism. Fearful that citizens expected either too much or too little from their leaders, Merriam sought the eclipse of political passion in favor of tempered moderation.

Merriam's concern with these matters typically resulted in a conscious effort to blend a new research agenda with political activism. He organized, served as editor, and wrote the concluding remarks for an ambitious cross-national study, *The Making of Citizens: A Comparative Study of Methods of Civic Training*. The monograph series began with the premise that civic education of some sort was a universal function of all states and societies, whether primitive or modern, socialist or capitalist, democratic or totalitarian. Through subtle or direct means, states and societies sought to instill loyalty in young minds. Those that did not succeed, such as the Hapsburg monarchy, were prone to overthrow by revolution. *The Making of Citizens* anticipates the structural-functional arguments of the 1950s. From the very beginning, behavioral research concentrated on the irrational and emotional bases of political beliefs and loyalty.[24]

Most of the countries examined in *The Making of Citizens* were said to suffer from immoderate extremism. Premodern countries neglected civic education altogether while Nazis and Stalinists inculcated loyalty and submission. But what about the United States? From *The Making of Citizens*, Merriam moved to research activity as one of sixteen members of the American Historical Association's (AHA) Commission on the Social Studies. The commission's tasks were far-reaching, extending to an examination of every facet of social studies education in American elementary and secondary schools. Its report ran to sixteen volumes, the sixth of which, *Civic Education in the United States*, Merriam penned. One of three social scientists on the committee, Merriam was the only one who might be said to represent a "behavioral" position, concerned as he was with linking "scientific" studies of behavior—the physical and mental constitution of the personality—with a political perspective that "would revolutionize the process of political and social training." Merriam's participation in the commission's work reaffirmed his faith in the communicability of the scientific method and its results to educational elites. *Civic Education* made frank appeals to school boards and officialdom: if democracy was to survive in America, then the techniques and goals of education in America needed to be seriously reevaluated.[25]

But *Civic Education* was also a work intent on distinguishing "democratic" civic education from what Merriam viewed as the evils of indoctrination as it appeared in the USSR, Germany, and Italy. Merriam began the work with a long survey of the passing of rural society in Europe and the United States. The technological and scientific spirit was particularly prominent in America, Merriam noted, but it also created new instrumentalities of political, social, and economic power that the average citizen could neither understand nor control. The rise of large corporations and labor union organizations, the interdependence of the world economy, and the urbanization of the American population were now seen as all part of the necessary and inevitable developments demanding political intervention. The scientific revolution created the imperative of transformation in governmental roles and functions. Yet to Merriam, most citizens and political leaders were still taught a form of distorted individualism and privatism radically incapable of facing the realities of the modern world. Government was still thought of as a "thing" by which one was either victimized or from which one escaped. Citizens were taught the scraps of a barren formalism; government was thought to be a mechanism whose essential features were frozen in time, its workings distant from the "real" lives of citizens. From this miseducation, citizens naturally but wrongly concluded that "our task is as simple as that of ridding the government of coarse graft, crude incompetence and distressing disorganization." The upshot of such an education, Merriam asserted, was that citizens were ignorant of "the new forms developing within the old," of the "reorganization of traditions in the light of science and invention," of the new "interpenetration of large social and economic units with government," and the positive and negative aspects of the "new techniques of social control developed by students of human behavior." Democratic citizens thereby became passive objects of the evil abuses of modern propaganda techniques.[26]

But the dismal present need not form the bright future, or so it seemed to Merriam. Informed by the findings and outlook of behavioral science, a new educational policy might be formulated that avoided instilling any orthodoxy regarding the substance of what government should be or do. If America was to admit the desirability of civic education while at the same time preserving and enhancing its democratic traditions, then *methods* of thinking and analyzing—rather than predigested ideas and values that political elites determined—must constitute democratic civic education. Here, the inculcation of the scientific method, developed first in the natural sciences and later on in the social sciences, was to be the answer to the puzzle of democratic education. The scientific method taught students to perceive the functions and structures of government not as unchangeable or distant. Rather, students were merely taught to accept "governmental modifications and choices . . . as easily as inventions in the patent office." Civic education in a democracy might instill the virtues of "a free development of a multitude of devices for institutional control."[27]

Moreover, scientific method by its nature avoided firm conclusions. It rather spoke of "contingencies." All democratic citizens, regardless of their values, might therefore evidence a spirit of inquiry, a willingness to invent, to experiment, and to change in the light of newly discovered facts and changing social and political processes. Merriam's notion of scientific method and knowledge as changing, pluralistic, and open to interpretation also well suited it to his idea of how democratic citizens might view the "method of modern governance." Democracy should— and must—be composed of citizens who applied the same realism and flexibility in their attitudes to politics as social scientists did. Scholars analyzed data they themselves had collected. Likewise, the future citizen should use the scientific outlook to analyze personal experiences as part of a wider range of events and forces that tied the individual to larger social, political, and economic relationships. Thereby: "Concrete information regarding political forms and processes may be woven into this general frame, and varied from time to time as specific problems change form and meaning, avoiding the difficulty which arises from the more narrowly descriptive treatments of politics and the *memoriter* method of acquiring learning in this field."[28]

At first glance, Merriam's critique of current educational practices and his proposals for reform may seem to be a subtle attack on American democracy itself. Uniform rationality imposed through education replaces the autonomous development of political sensibilities and beliefs in communities, groups, or classes. Yet Merriam was careful to distinguish between the idea of scientific method *replacing* "political" values and emotions, and a notion of science as an indispensable *prerequisite* for politics, emotion, and vision to emerge in a clearer light. The realism of science was an indispensable instrument of the democratic citizen and not a synonym for citizenship itself. The scientific method served democracy by clarifying and elucidating the moving social and economic processes that formed the context within which differing values, choices, and interests formed and emerged. Science would neither dictate nor deny that choices, political goals, or what Merriam called "emotions" or "vision," must have their day. But it would be the common language through which all conflicts and choices could be discussed in rational and informed ways. Merriam asserted: "There is no fundamental inconsistency in the long run between democracy and scientific rule, however much an effort may be made to create such a conclusion. . . . The new scientific orientation, the new drive to remake the world, in creative fashion, may rest upon the assumption of faith in the possibilities of common humanity. . . . Nor are great human values so precious to the spirit of man destroyed under scientific direction, but on the contrary they are recognized and placed in a more realistic setting than ever before."[29]

Merriam concluded with words soothing to those who might question the compatibility of scientific method with the historical evolution of American democracy: "The democratic way of life was always an ideal, and it might make the basis of a new orientation in organization and function without great shock to values or institutions. . . . The practical starting point of any system of civic education is the local cultural complex, which will be assumed as desirable and useful and worthy of attachment, and which will not be subjected to scientific analysis but accepted as a basis of action."[30]

Merriam did not see his views as relativistic or as attacks upon "politics" in favor of "science." Rather, civic education that concentrated on scientific *method* was only a *means* of modernizing democratic sensibilities. Civic education, in this sense, made real politics possible. According to Merriam's biographer, Barry Karl, he ". . . .separated responsibilities for reform. The politics of the whole community was the center of democratic reform, not the judgment of experts manipulating the attitudes of future adult generations through the indoctrination of the young."[31]

Science brought forward the values of America's given "cultural complex." It might help the citizen "to look around and to look forward, to appraise values, institutions, propaganda in the light of the changing world in which he lives, and above all to habituate himself to the constant restructuring of the ways of life in terms of new experience."[32]

This idea of civic education was an alternative to two views Merriam believed to be extreme. The first opposed civic education altogether as a legitimate area for national public policy. Distrustful of experts, American "provincials" saw democratic life as self-perpetuating and spontaneous.

Uniform values should not be taught in schools, for community values were by definition already democratic. Tampering with them was tantamount to totalitarianism. The second extreme has had many variations in America, but its essence is the use of the schools as laboratories for political and social change, and experimentation. Existing community values, in this scheme, should be questioned and often challenged by radicalized students and teachers. Schools taught not only "methods," as was Merriam's way, but also inevitably truths and values with defined and precise consequences for the polity itself.

But Merriam saw both of these as threats. The second challenged the cultural complex itself—clearly a sin. The first resisted adaptation and change as a violation of moral purity, thereby proving itself to be an anachronism. In Merriam's perpetually altering world, scientific method provided the only link between leaders and citizens, legitimacy and institutional order. Knowledge, acceptance, and diffusion of the method altered the "cultural complex" of community power in America, but in ways consonant with democratic processes. His brand of civic education created "a higher form of patriotism and loyalty," based "not on jingoism, but on intelligent understanding of the world . . . in the most realistic terms possible."[33]

Merriam's *Civic Education* demonstrated that the introduction of "scientific method" into public consciousness presented no radical challenge to the hallowed "values" of American democracy. Through this fundamental conservatism, Merriam distanced himself from his pre–World War I Progressive colleagues. He insisted that "civic education" was reformist only in its method, but not in its values. But his colleagues on the Commission on Social Studies had other ideas. Typically, it was his old nemesis Charles Beard, and the latter's friend, Columbia education professor George S. Counts, who threw down the challenge. The conflict between Merriam and his cautious optimism, and Counts and Beard with their more overtly radical style, well captures the contrast between pre- and post–World War I political science.

Merriam refused to sign the "Conclusions and Recommendations" of the final report to the AHA Commission on Social Studies. The author, George Counts, stressed precisely those points that Merriam wanted to divorce from civic education and from social science. Counts wrote that it was not the corruption of individualism that was the source of democracy's ills, but the culture of individualism that American capitalism inspired. The values of cooperation and collective action were systematically excluded from American culture by capitalists and their hegemony over the world of ideas. The goal was not to transmit better the cultural heritage through education in scientific method, but rather to use the school as a laboratory wherein a new culture might germinate, one opposed to the values of the powerful and the ethic of acquisition and consumption.[34]

Merriam was horrified by the report, but he might have been happier if he had remembered that Beard's and Count's influence was waning in the new social sciences. Skeptical of "valueless" social science, Beard and Counts were only marginal figures in the world Merriam and other were trying to build.

At the same time, Charles Merriam's effort to diffuse social scientific methods as an antidote to the crisis of American democracy raises some interesting questions about his faith in the recoverability of democracy, as well as the scientific means he chose to effect that revival. Ultimately, the validity of Merriam's views had to be vindicated in the political world itself, and not in debates with radicals such as Counts and Beard. But what if the "cultural complex" did not prove amenable to the kinds of governmental power and experimentation Merriam so cherished? And what if—Charles Beard and George Counts might have asked—this "local cultural complex" was reflective less of democratic sensibilities than it was a servant of a powerful structure and ethos, that of American capitalism? And what if the growing heaps of specialized research, which Merriam encouraged, uncovered a democratic culture systematically unable to control the new techniques developed by intellectual radicals and meddlers?

The effort to extract democratic citizens from the existing cultural complex could prove difficult. Merriam was to learn some even harder lessons when he cast his fate and that of the political science he espoused with the consummate democratic leader and educator, Franklin Delano Roosevelt.

Charles E. Merriam and the New Deal

The inauguration of a new president in March 1933 presented the optimum opportunities for the science for politics Charles Merriam had been building. By 1933 Merriam's efforts to organize the links between social researchers through the SSRC had largely succeeded. The behavioral revolution he had helped launch a decade before seemed to have carried the day, even over initially strong opposition. Individual academics in the most prestigious universities were no longer scholarly atoms but specialists in a joint enterprise in constant communication with one another. The claims of "applied science" had already been vindicated, even under Herbert Hoover.

Franklin Roosevelt's campaign and election in the midst of the Great Depression seemed to signal that political leaders were now going to be receptive to the advice of organized social science. Roosevelt himself embodied the pragmatic, inventive, and experimental democratic style that Merriam thought necessary as an approach to American government. Moreover, Roosevelt was most evidently not only open to experiment, but also a man capable of leading and educating the mass public in the same non-ideological, practical style that people like Merriam saw as the trademark of the ideal and adaptable democratic leader. And voters themselves seemed willing to be led and educated, perhaps not in any which way, but at least in ways different from that the mediocre presidents in the 1920s had prescribed. Whatever else the Great Depression had done, it seemed to crystallize the sense of crisis about which Merriam had long spoken. But at the same time, it seemed to provide the elements for a solution. Citizens and leaders now largely accepted as a given the expansion of governmental functions and controls, and put their faith in a popular and obviously rational president as the source of reform and cohesion. Franklin Roosevelt's election vindicated the workings of a new civic education. Citizens and their democratic leader both now embraced inventiveness. Merriam's variety of liberal Progressivism had always placed its trust in leadership even though neither he nor anyone else could say how the electorate might recognize true leaders or how the American political system might systematically generate "greatness." Roosevelt was clearly such a person; he could see the whole from his vantage point atop the political system. He might make politics possible once again, and he seemed eager to hear the suggestions of social scientists and translate them into clear political alternatives. The New Deal was the ideal climate for the introduction of reform science into real politics.

Merriam's major role in the New Deal was his participation in establishing the first economic and social planning bureaucracies created after the demise of the National Recovery Act. Through his friendship with Secretary Harold Ickes, Merriam served first on the National Planning Board in the Interior Department, and after 1939 on the rechristened National Resources Planning Board located in the Executive Office of the President. Given the normal practice of American government in peacetime, the board's mandate was far-reaching. The NRPB was supposed to coordinate all federally sponsored public works projects in an overall effort to meet national goals in the areas of natural resources and land use, and water management. Moreover, the board was mandated to create specific policy proposals that tied the growing federal government's policy proposals together. Such an effort to plan proved offensive to the tangle of political and economic interests that had previously dominated U.S. public works administration and land-use policies. But in the course of the board's work, "jungle" politics was once again revealed to have the upper hand. After a fitful history, the NRPB met its demise in 1943, the victim of a Congress that used the same old arguments equating planning with the autocratic state. Not even Roosevelt's power, which Merriam and the others had so trusted, could save the effort to legitimize economic planning as a permanent feature of federal authority.[35]

The NRPB's rise is a perfect example of what scientific reform was supposed to be all about. Its fall illustrates the difficulties of the whole scientific endeavor. Between socialist experiments like the French Popular Front and laissez-faire capitalism, American planning was supposed to be assertive but not meddlesome, authoritative but not autocratic. That not even a minimal planning program succeeded after nine years of struggle does much to undermine many of the political assumptions Merriam had about the nature of American democracy. And organized social science's role in that world suffered, too.

The NRPB members approached their mission with great delicacy, but the board met its ironic end amidst congressional charges that it had usurped powers better left—if used at all—to states and localities. By all accounts the board members did everything they could to adjust planning goals to both federalism and the needs of individual businesses. And more than anything else, Merriam tried to adjust the NRPB to the federal structure. Much in the way social science was introduced into civic education, resource planning NRPB–style was supposed to fulfill, not contest, extant democratic beliefs and practices.

For instance, Merriam made every effort to make the NRPB's membership nonpartisan and politically independent. Board members and their staffs were not a new technocracy in the permanent employ of the federal government. Rather, they were a group of free-floating intellectuals who maintained their university positions even as they advised the government. Roosevelt and other accountable officials were left to do the politics. They could reject or accept the advice of their "scientific" advisers. The NRPB's members supported economic planning, but their mission was to present as broad an array of choices for consideration by Congress and the president as was possible.

Second, Merriam and the NRPB were careful not to offend state and local prerogatives. They only suggested "guidelines" for resource use and indicated ways of coordinating industry and government needs. To impose directives would, after all, have violated the holy cultural complex and therefore democratic values. The NRPB's production and resource use targets were thus only experimental. National goals and local democracy might be blended together only through mutual consensus, not by commands and coercion from a federal center to a state and local periphery. Under the assumption that city, county, and state governments were the legitimate bearers and representatives of ethnic, cultural, regional, economic, and political diversity, Merriam and the NRPB proceeded to devise a national public works, land, water, and natural resources management plan that tied the dispersal of monies to the cooperation of state, county, and city governments. By encouraging lower governmental levels to form their own planning commissions, and by their extensive consultation with agents of the local governments, Merriam and his NRPB associates believed that the democratic character of American planning might be made palatable to otherwise hostile local elites.

Yet a third characteristic of the NRPB's approach bore Merriam's stamp, reflecting his consistent concern to distinguish between the advice of experts and social scientists on the one hand, and the decision-making power of a popularly accountable president and Congress on the other. While independent social scientists were supposed to assemble the data and propose policy alternatives, Merriam was careful to remove the NRPB from any directly political role either in lobbying Congress or, more importantly, in the implementation and administration of planning policies. As with civic education, science in government would not replace politics but aid in the formation of the public agenda. The idea and possibility of "planning" was to Merriam akin to the virtues of scientific method in the reform of civic education. But while the idea of planning itself was seen as nonpolitical, a kind of gift of science to politics, both the substance and implementation of particular plans were best left to leaders and citizens' organizations.

Why then did this first experiment in permanent peacetime planning fail? Why, despite all of Merriam's best efforts to depoliticize social science and its impact on government, did the old provincial hostility to planning destroy the NRPB? Politics stayed in command to such an extent that the NRPB was abolished by the kinds of political forces Merriam had hoped would come to sustain it. To a multitude of congressmen, to the Army Corps of Engineers, to ideological opponents of planning who saw it as anathema to the American "free enterprise" system and as an instrument of Roosevelt's thirst for power, the NRPB seemed an unwarranted intrusion into some hallowed American political practices. Worst of all, the NRPB by its nature required a sort of permanent melding of self-interest, rightly understood, with loyalty to a lofty national vision never clearly spelled out in the political vision of New Deal advocates. By resisting congressional pork barrel projects, the NRPB could not help but seem "political," despite the claims of apolitical expertise offered. After 1940, and especially after Pearl Harbor, planning appeared to be yet another Roosevelt plot to usurp power from Congress. While the war emergency justified a temporary mobilization of the private economy, permanent state planning was another thing entirely. Not even the consummate democratic leader— Franklin Roosevelt—could sell the scientific ideal to a suspicious Congress and a recalcitrant capitalist class.[36]

The NRPB's demise was a fatal blow to most of Merriam's assumptions and hopes about the flexibility of American politics. His science of happy prospects and realizable ideals still violated the political traditions that he saw as passé. After World War II, business absorption of government programs created interest-group liberal politics, but this seemed more like an extension of an older philosophy than a thrilling new departure. And the New Deal's social coalition hardly vindicated calls for a "Great Community." The loyalty of New Deal constituencies proved to be contingent on access to federal largesse, not public-spirited consent to a benign and authoritative democratic state.

Reform versus Science

Methodological refinement, the professionalization of research, the organization of a discipline, and scholarship's crucial role in an advancing democracy—such goals had catalyzed Charles Merriam's quite substantial energies. In the 1920s, Merriam had been sure that the fault of prewar liberal Progressives had not been in their faith or their politics. The appearance of outright political advocacy was to blame, and Merriam's remedy was to establish a profession so above politics that it would easily win the applause and the ear of the wise and powerful. Convinced that the scientific methods he had developed to study political behavior would turn up the facts and tendencies that gave new credence to his Progressive beliefs, Merriam spent a lifetime propagating his version of science as the handmaiden to modernizing reforms. Behavioral research, Merriam insisted, showed that man was both a sensate *and* a self-sacrificing, rational being. "Emotion" might never disappear from the polity altogether, nor should it, because when matched with scientific rationality it produced loyal, critical, participating, and open-minded citizens, not just passive responders to "stimuli." In this sense, Merriam himself became the model citizen. His own native optimism about America's destiny complemented and fueled his scholarly, professional, and political endeavors.

Claiming that Charles Merriam's career was a failure—or tragic—is an overstatement, however. After all, he did probably more than anyone to establish political science as a large, wealthy, and influential enterprise. Yet his career might also be told as a story of optimistic intentions that always had unintended consequences. Note, for example, Merriam's response late in life to his own activities and his reaction to the profession he had helped to construct. Merriam came to question (as Charles Beard had much earlier) the effectiveness, attitudes, and values of the political scientists he had done so much to train. Often this involved Merriam in somewhat nostalgic efforts to remind the new generation that, in the final analysis, faith and vision in the perfectibility of humankind had given rise to behavioral political science. The behavioral persuasion was not skeptical, cynical, or a flight from politics. Merriam had always believed that a properly reeducated public and a properly powerful national state might produce a rational, progressive American democracy. But Merriam's colleagues and students were instead turning out research that showed the American citizen to be a misinformed, apolitical "mass" person, susceptible to emotional appeals from cynical and manipulating economic and political elites. Worse yet, some of the basic standards of American democracy came under the social scientific microscope, only to be revealed as shams. In a sense, Merriam had come full circle. He was now seen as methodologically deficient, theoretically immature, and naively optimistic about democracy.

By the late 1940s, Merriam and his associates were already talking past each other. He always defended his science for the possibilities it would make manifest to rational voters and benign elites. But the post–World War II generation rejected futuristic claims of a democratic potential as unscientific wishes; still, Merriam insisted that a political science separate from reform possibilities was a rejection of the scientific spirit itself.[37]

In the few years between the end of the war and the long illness that would take his life in 1953, Merriam appeared as Charles Beard did in the 1920s—the respected but now irrelevant leader of a movement with no followers. *Systematic Politics*, Merriam's last work, repeats for the final time the essentials of this temperament. Gone, however, are the urgings to caution, quantification, and professionalism. What remains is a kind of scientific revivalism reminiscent of the Progressive forebears he once tried to discredit. Words like these must have made his loving students wince and his critics chuckle: "Deeper study requires attention to the evolutionary quality of political effort and achievement, of rise from lower to higher forms. . . . Governmental processes are not wormlike squirmings in which men are enslaved without gain or goals, but are parts of the transition from darkness to light, from slavery to freedom, from drift to mastery."[38]

If Merriam's colleagues employed the methods of science and saw only wormlike squirmings, then something was indeed awry: "For the first time in history utopias need not be woven from fancy and hope but may be constructed from a wealth of science and reason to show indisputable opportunities lying before mankind at this very hour."[39]

Until the end, Merriam never could bring himself to make an outright attack on the profession he had done so much to form. This was consistent with his beliefs since he also continued to affirm that it was not the findings of social science research that were disappointing. It was only the narrowness of perspective and pessimism that was brought to bear in the interpretation of findings that was to blame. The new generation seemed to reject outright—just as Merriam had done twenty-five years earlier—what they now saw as the partisanship and subjectivity of Merriam's reform science. But Merriam had rejected prewar Progressive political science only to bring back Progressivism in a sanitized form. Charles Merriam's career ended not in tragedy, but in irony. The discipline of political science he had built had triumphed over its original functions.

While Merriam seemed conscious of this irony, he never seriously grappled with the implications of the failure of his political vision. The political project and faith that had taken up the great bulk of Merriam's life were simply never realized. "Jungle politics" defeated capitalist planning without much uproar from citizens supposedly trained to be enthusiastic about governmental invention. Franklin Roosevelt, despite his own best efforts and Merriam's hopes, had forged a coalition of self-interested groups rather than the self-sacrificing, loyal, participating, and rational public Merriam deemed necessary and possible. World War II blighted all efforts at instituting democratic planning as a permanent function of the liberal capitalist state. The new powers of the American federal government reflected less scientific rationality than interest group access to the expanded federal trough. Apparently, Merriam had overestimated the flexibility of the "cultural complex," at least in the way he had always understood it. A kind of civic culture wherein relationships of power and domination were absent, intolerance abolished, and democratic habits of informed self-interest a matter of common sense did not seem to fit well into the cold war climate.

Merriam was not a circumspect man. Yet some of his students and colleagues who had taken up his exhortations to experiment with psychological and statistical approaches to the study of human behavior were more conscious than he was of the gap between their research and third tradition claims. Harold Lasswell, Merriam's student and colleague, conducted the kind of research Merriam had always encouraged. But his findings raised new difficulties in the effort to meld research, professionalism, and a "policy science" that brought together state power and popular consent.

The Reformer as Therapist: Harold D. Lasswell

No account of the fate of third tradition scholarship in political science can ignore the work of Harold D. Lasswell. More than any of the other young recruits to Merriam's University of Chicago department, Lasswell took his chairman's homilies about methodological sophistication to heart. It could even be said that Merriam built his kind of political science for people like Harold Lasswell. Virtually every orientation of behavioral research can somehow be traced to paths earlier taken by him. And

Lasswell was nothing if not prolific. His list of published writings alone requires twenty pages.[40]

Lasswell can also be credited (or blamed) with the internationalization of American political science vocabulary and concepts, albeit in sometimes peculiar ways. Lasswell introduced Marxian, Freudian, and Weberian terminology into the discipline. His research on propaganda, politics and personality, public opinion, the effect of technology on society, revolution, political symbols, and transactional analyses encompassed a remarkably wide range of scholarly concerns. Much of his vocabulary became the common discourse of future generations of specialized researchers. Lasswell's "developmental constructs," "value pyramids," "event manifolds," "policy science," and similar terms quickly entered disciplinary journals.

Our intent is not to describe, much less analyze, the course of Lasswell's rapidly moving interests. That task in itself would require a major study. Examining that segment of his work that directly addresses third tradition themes is worthwhile, however, because Lasswell bridges two periods in the discipline's history and in American life. And oddly, Lasswell was something of a maverick in both eras. In Merriam's time, he appeared as the radical advocate of "pure" versus applied science. Yet after World War II he returned to the themes of Merriam's reform science at precisely that point when most political scientists were rejecting them.

Like his third tradition predecessors, Lasswell equated a crisis in American politics with a crisis in American democratic thought. As Lasswell understood them, the political theories that had built the Constitution and prompted the opposition to it were nothing but a string of ill-defined moralisms, value preferences, and mere speculation thinly disguised as truth. In their present forms, political, economic, and religious doctrines were full of assumption-laden caricatures of human beings. Such dogmas were notoriously unquantifiable, poorly suited to empirical testing, and thus functional only to political elites interested in intellectual justifications for their own domination. As they stood, political doctrines of all varieties were useless as tools for understanding politics and dangerous as premises for political action.

This sort of critique was, of course, typical of most American political scientists. But these beliefs led Lasswell to go well beyond his teacher Merriam in his search for ways that "symbols and practices" such as "democracy," "consensus," and "power" could be broken down and translated into "testable hypotheses." Lasswell spurned the older penchant for fact gathering in favor of a new credo. The search for such "testable hypotheses" about "the political in relation to the social process" always for Lasswell *preceded* "the prosecution of empirical research by all available methods." If such a thing as political philosophy did indeed exist, then all its propositions, Lasswell insisted, "are looked upon as being confirmed as confirmable by data."[41]

Of interest here is not so much Lasswell's similarities to (and extension of) the behavioral movement that Charles Merriam led. Rather, Lasswell's continuous quest for "testable hypotheses" began to push his scholarship beyond the beliefs that Merriam had held as foundations on which a science of politics had to be based. Specifically, Lasswell dissolved the crucial distinctions Merriam always drew between "social science" and "politics." To Merriam social science provided the methods, outlook, and knowledge that served but did not replace politics. Political leaders and the "rational" public appropriated science, but they did so only to clarify political debate and choices, and delineate "creative possibilities." Some of the major frustrations of Merriam's career can be attributed to the continuous rebuffs and undemocratic uses to which social scientists were always subjected as they entered the political arena. But Merriam never went so far as to suggest the replacement of political language by a sort of "technology of politics" in which semidepraved citizens and leaders alike were adjusted to the commands of scientific knowledge and discoveries.

At least in his early career, Lasswell took the road that Merriam rejected. His studies of political power, the psychopathological origins of political ideologies, propaganda, and public opinion all revealed the dangerous neuroses lying behind the supposed "ideals" of politics. Personal insecurities wrought by the impersonal workings of industrial society negated any hope for rational political debate in mass society. Collective action by groups or classes might be understandable reactions to the claims technological civilization imposed, but the revolutionary utopias political leaders at the helm of such movements sketched out were just so many exercises in symbol manipulation.[42] Gone in Lasswell's early works is the inviolability of Merriam's cultural complex as a source of renewable political values, even in America. In its stead, a "politics of prevention" is recommended. Lasswell saw the political realm that Merriam hoped to rejuvenate by means of social science as no more than an arena where personal and collective anxieties and insecurities wind their way.

At least in the 1930s Lasswell's works represented a real departure in political science. Beard's and Bentley's fact-gathering sciences had stripped bare social process so that the rational public might act. Merriam's reform science had noted and discovered irrationality in politics only so that it could be corrected through civic education and democratic planning. Lasswell's public—and for that matter, political elites—did not require education, but rather shock treatments administered by dispassionate but skilled political therapists. The problem facing Lasswell's political science was of a different order than that of the third tradition scholars discussed thus far. The American political crisis could not be solved by finding newly democratic forms and implanting revised democratic beliefs. The very existence and survival of the democratic legacy itself was at stake. In Lasswell's world, the bleak imperatives of technological advance produced only generalized anxieties and maladjusted individuals. To readjust and restabilize could only have undemocratic consequences.

Lasswell never fully developed the political consequences of the works he wrote in the 1930s. His concerns appeared as strictly scientistic, removed from the "applied science" Merriam was intent on building. But World War II seemed to jar Lasswell; by the early 1940s, just as scientism was becoming the disciplinary norm, Lasswell returned to the democratic orthodoxy of Merriam. But he radically extended the claims of social science Merriam made. Lasswell henceforth spoke of "democratic values" as givens in America and turned his attention to the roles science should play in furthering their reappearance. But his return to the liberal Progressive values of the third tradition could not share the democratic optimism of the past. For one thing, just about all hope in the cultural complex was gone—not even civic education was a big enough antidote for American political diseases. In order to revive American democracy, Lasswell found it necessary to convince citizens that they were profoundly subject to their own worst natures. Second, the American people had to be convinced that they could not be saved through devices of their own making. Third, citizens had to accede to the only source of dispassionate political knowledge now available in a democracy. Ironically, "policy scientists" would save the polity from itself; they would "reduce the expectations" of democratic sentiment and institute "humane" mechanisms by which the excesses of democracy would be "curbed."

In the 1950s Lasswell swam against the "pure science" tide then sweeping the discipline. He called the discipline back to Merriam's reform vision of a pure and applied science that would prevent the "garrison state" and realize the "dignity of man." But these noble goals, while hearkening back to his third tradition predecessors, required a rejection of most of the premises of earlier third tradition thought. Social scientists no longer aided the Populists, whispered to politicians, ignited the public, or informed and reeducated. From participants in a greater reform mission, social scientists became therapists and political doctors. In a polity where masses were inevitably manipulated by elites, and both were victims of their own anxieties, political scientists might develop a democratic technology that healed both. In Lasswell's words: "It is indisputable that the world could be unified if enough people were impressed by this (or by any other) elite. The hope of the professors of social science, if not of the world, lies in the competitive strength of an elite based on vocabulary, footnotes, questionnaires, and conditioned responses, against an elite based on vocabulary, poison gas, property, and family prestige."[43] Indeed, the claims of social scientists in the polity vastly expanded as political depravity was quantified.

The Early Works

Harold Lasswell's two most famous writings introduced, respectively, a quasi-Freudian framework into the study of political behavior and a concentration on the definition and uses of political power as the central concern of any true science of politics. Both works hardly confirm his teacher Merriam's confidence in the fundamental if underlying rationality and order within the American political system. Beneath the veneer of patriotic sloganeering and the myths of collective national purpose, Lasswell found a snake pit of personal anxieties forming the political sensibility of political elites. Elite depravity enhanced their political skills because they were able to dominate simply by their ability to create symbolic utopias that held the irrational loyalty of their followers. Liberal parliamentary regimes and their enemies were held together by the same collective myths and symbols. The Marxian philosophy of history, Lasswell asserted, might be an empirically valid set of generalizations about the rise and spread of industrial capitalism. But its analytical power paled before its ideological determinism and its ability to inspire mass faith in an ersatz Communist millennium. A citizen or a worker stripped of collective identity seeks it in a Marxian dream world. He "senses . . . the necessity for associating himself with some symbol of collective aspiration. . . . He must obtain his safety, income and deference somewhat surreptitiously by attaching himself to a collective symbol. . . . The person is free to project his potency fantasies into the future, and to identify himself with this remodeled symbol."[44]

Nor were capitalist elites less prone to project "potency fantasies." Lasswell's interpretation of Freud rested heavily on seeing the ego repressed by all modern forms of political solidarity, liberalism and socialism included.[45] Indeed, the patterns of irrationality and psychopathology that underlay the individual's subjective political behavior were not removable through social or economic revolution. Instead, a science that concerned itself with the effects of personal insecurity as they were revealed in politics required political doctors concerned with the adjustment of individuals to the inevitability of growing political organization. And quantitative method directed students of society to the study of subjective perceptions that recur regularly in the individual, while the study of psychopathology led to an understanding and ultimately control over the political consequences of mass irrationality.

From this "scientific" perspective, both the demands of political movements and the leaders who created the relevant symbols and goals of political activity bore only scant resemblance to the real and actual sources of tension and conflicts in modern society. Nor were the niceties of liberal politics much superior to that of the class, mass politics of European socialism and fascism. It was "political methods" in general that Lasswell perceived as the source of "disease" since their sole purpose was to artificially displace "private" motives, desires, drives, and fantasies into "public causes" adorned with the classic rhetoric of "political values." The ruling doctrines and ideologies of modern politics—the "rights of man," equality, liberty, patriotism, fraternity—created only needless conflicts and raised dangerous expectations: "Discussion frequently complicates social difficulties, for the discussion by far-flung interests arouses a psychology of conflict which produces obstructive, fictitious and irrelevant values. The problem of politics is less to solve conflicts than to prevent them, less to serve as a safety valve for social protest than to apply social energy to the abolition of the recurrent sources of strain in society."[46]

Yet Lasswell did not accept any or all means of obviating conflicts. The scientific acceptance of democracy was deduced from the rejection of the alternatives. Dictatorship, for instance, was a more severe symptom of political disease since it only gave greater vent to "displaced anxiety" embodied in the mystical bonds between leaders and masses. Yet dictatorship triumphed over democracy if the latter's tendencies were left unchecked. But unchecked by what? Lasswell's *Psychopathology and Politics* and *Politics: Who Gets What, When, How* were equally critical of both liberal democracy and modern dictatorships. But at the least one could say that democracies "bring the irrational bases of politics out into the open." If personality studies revealed the masses to be poor judges of their own self-interest, elites and their manipulative abilities were symptoms, not solutions, to the problem of political irrationality.[47]

To Lasswell, the "politics of prevention" stood as the only realistic alternative to the tensions, conflicts, and dangers of liberal democratic politics and its illiberal alternatives. Elites might not be prevented from manipulation of symbols and from "getting the most of what there is to get." Yet Lasswell believed that one "developmental construct" (in his lexicon, "one likely possibility") might be to place in power those who were most knowledgeable "about the factors which contribute to the raising and lowering of the tension level [and] the process of symbolization."[48] Intellectuals who made it their business to discover patterns of personal anxieties displaced onto the political realm in the form of ideological conflict had the sort of self-awareness and knowledge least prone to politicize and exploit those anxieties. A "therapeutic politics" might flow from social scientists to those most able to "reorient minds" and control and contain unnecessary political pressures: "Our thinking has too long been misled by the threadbare terminology of democracy versus dictatorship, of democracy versus autocracy. Our problem is to be ruled by the truth about the social conditions of harmonious human relations, and the discovery of truth is an object of specialized research, it is no monopoly of people as people, and of the ruler as ruler. As our devices of accurate ascertainment are invented and spread, they are explained by many individuals in the social order."[49]

Happily, the extant political and social forms of American democracy might be easily accommodated to the influence of these "therapists" because the United States had not *yet* been subjected to the power of one distinct group of "symbol manipulators." The numerous points of political access in America combined with its diversity to mean that "the achievement of this ideal of preventive politics depend much less upon changes in social organization than upon improving the methods and the education of the social administrators."[50]

In the 1930s at least, Lasswell was careful to note that the era of preventive politics might indeed be a long time in coming since it depended on the development of a much more sophisticated science of society able to identify the flows and tendencies of collective psychopathology, as well as on the dynamics of the rise and fall of various forms of political power. Indeed, much of Lasswell's work tended to identify the precise effects of technological change on society. Yet while Lasswell was careful to plead for caution in the face of present ignorance, the notion of social science as a "therapeutic activity" represented a real if understandable departure from many of the claims, assumptions, and concepts of social scientists of the third tradition. Like the young Lasswell, Lester Ward advocated "sociocracy," but only if carried as the political standard of a popularly based reform movement. Woodrow Wilson located the source of reform in the evolution of historically legitimated institutions and practices of American democracy. Charles Beard and Arthur Bentley rejected Wilson's moralism and formalism, but only because they were confident that process was bendable and flexible to the "rational" middle class. And Charles Merriam's schemes for civic training and democratic planning pointed to social science's role as an aid in the modernization of a recoverable tradition, not as a replacement of it. Lasswell's claims about political science perhaps responded to the failures of Merriam's limited but still relatively aggressive claims about social science's reform role. Both men attempted to influence political life indirectly. Merriam advocated civic training and increased ties between science and political leaders. But in Lasswell's work, civic training was not geared to "allow" political choices, but to prevent them. And Merriam's popular and powerful leaders became "elites," legitimated if at all by their ability to manipulate symbols.

Lasswell's scientific relativism, pessimism, and distance from politics in the turbulent New Deal divided him from many of his colleagues. But he did not rest easily with the potentially undemocratic conclusions that might be drawn from his work in the 1930s. World War II and its aftermath sparked Lasswell to reinterpret his past works in the light of a new "value consciousness" that replaced "therapy" with a "developing science of democracy." Lasswell began to carry on Merriam's optimistic vision of "unfolding democratic potential" and embraced what he believed to be a "traditional American value—the dignity of man." But this return to a version of reform science still substantially departed from Merriam's notion of a "science for democracy," even as it asserted the continuing efficacy of the democratic creed. Lasswell continued to assert the primacy of scientific research over politics, but now in a way that aimed at the clarification of democratic morals. The brighter prospects of a democratic future replaced the stark images of power built on elite manipulation of mass fantasies. Now, social science would be indispensable to the furtherance of a nonrevolutionary tradition. Power might be firmly exercised, and at the same time rational popular consent could be achieved. But still, popular consent was won only by revealing to citizens their own limitations and ignorance; Lasswell's embrace of democracy squeezed out its essence.

Lasswell's conversion to democratic orthodoxy had much to do with his fear of a "garrison state," his synonym for the military-industrial complex. He correctly feared that the full coercive police and military powers of the American state would be unleashed to slay the Soviet dragon and imprison dissenters from the cold war. As manipulative as American politics had been before World War II, Lasswell apparently felt that it was preferable to the garrison alternative. And democratic values, institutions, leaders, and public opinion—once subjected to the searing analysis of the 1930s—now were deemed worthy of salvation and capable of reform.[51]

Lasswell wrote *Democracy through Public Opinion* in 1941. In temperament and method, the book stands in sharp contrast to his scientistic, cynical works of the 1930s.[52] The commitments of the "scientific" democrat replaced the skepticism of the outside observer. Therapists became "guardians" of democracy, enlightening public opinion about current problems and suggesting the procedures by which they might be addressed. In Lasswell's earlier work, the entrenched elites in all regimes were a fairly distinct group who "got what they wanted" by not-so-subtle force. But Lasswell now asked not only how power was exercised, but also "what ways people can control their rulers." Citizens, in sharp contrast with the irrationality they evidenced but a few years previously, could now act "openly and continually upon government," just as "democratic governments act[ed] upon public opinion." Elites remained in democratic society, but they were not an identifiable class. Rather, they were "society wide."[53]

A more polite lexicon replaced the language of domination and submission. Instead of preventive politics, Lasswell in 1941 talked about how "public opinion" had to be reeducated so it could recognize "moral mavericks." Those who were skeptical about human perfectibility achieved through collective therapy, those uncertain about the possibility of democracy, had to be weeded out of public life. Public opinion must now be trained—not for preventive politics—but to make "provisional, ever-changing demands for popular policies consistent with the permanent demands . . . to maintain the integrity of justice and of majority rule in society." Thankfully, this training was now seen as achievable and workable—if and only if a democratic science of society emerged as a subspecies of social science. Instead of eschewing moral questions, democratic social science assumed that these questions already had been answered. Lasswell now aggressively sought to give "eyes, ears, hands, and feet to morality." In his words: "We cannot specialize indefinitely upon the cry for justice divorced from the means appropriate to the end of increasing the frequency of just events."[54]

As Lasswell tried to show in other works, "just events" were quantifiable. Measurement provided the clarity to the morality he deemed essential in the determination of democracy's "vital signs" at any given moment. In *Democracy through Public Opinion*, the determination of who the "enemies" and "friends" of democracy really were could be plotted by the new social scientific guardians. Academics discovered the public interest and taught "proper methods of thought" to a confused—but nonetheless redeemable and educable—citizenry.[55] Rather than preventing politics, social scientists now formed public discussion by "clarifying" it. They alerted citizens and democratic elites to the real and potential sources of "poison." Since the "citizen of our day wonders if there are any facts or only frauds," the mere forms of democratic procedure were deemed insufficient to clarify political reality. But popular education was not enough either. Above all, democracy needed specialists in social research and political clarification if it was to survive: "The degree of intelligence in society is not only a matter of the level of thought and observation, but of the number and skill of all who specialize upon the discovery of truth, upon clarity and upon interest. If the flow of communication is to further the discovery of the public interest, there must be a proper relationship among every kind of specialist upon intelligence."[56]

In 1942 Lasswell was even interweaving "science" and "democracy" as complements, just as Merriam had been doing, but the priority had shifted to the primacy of scientific therapy: "This much at least is clear:

whether or not the methods of scientific observation contribute to the eventual completion of a systematic science of democracy, they are certain to contribute here and now to the practice of democratic morals. Without science, democracy is blind and weak. With science, democracy will not be blind and may be strong."[57]

Lasswell's new identity of "science" and "democracy" had profound consequences for the meaning accorded to each. Initially Lasswell seemingly had simply adopted Merriam's position. Yet Lasswell's real innovation was to substantially transform Merriam's careful if unsuccessful treatment of the relationship between the organized pursuit of systematic knowledge and the reform of the polity outside the discipline. Merriam's science sought to catalyze political activity among those citizens newly educated in the scientific method as well as among leaders capable of organizing consensus and clarifying political choices. "Science," in short, could only go so far. It ultimately depended for verification and power on the free choice and activity of well-informed citizens. In contrast, Lasswell's science radically expanded the role of "objective" truth seekers in the polity. Scientists no longer "whispered advice," but instead provided "the most thoughtful interpretations available in the body politic at a given moment in history." Unlike citizens, social scientists were now seen as uniquely capable of freeing themselves from the "displaced anxieties" imposed by a "meteoric expansion of science and technology."[58] The professional contribution of an objective, multifaceted, and specialized science of society extended well beyond Merriam's notion that proposals and political decisions were to be strictly separated. Lasswell, in Bernard Crick's words: ". . . is not interested in making research a tool of an existing politics, but rather in the creation of a new scientific world society. . . ."[59]

The definition of "democratic values" was left to an oddly small and uniquely knowledgeable circle indeed. The development of what Lasswell began to label a "policy science" suggested that the "politics of prevention" might be out of place in a democratic society. There would still be "politics," but most of the policy alternatives would be suggested by social scientific "guardians." In place of therapy, Lasswell assigned scientists the task of initiation.

The functions of Lasswell's democratic guardians suggested a significant change in the relationship between social science and the public. Merriam, with some energy, addressed the mass public through their political leaders. But in the democracy Lasswell now praised, "communication" to citizens resembled control of them. In the words of a sympathetic colleague, Lasswell's science was addressed to "the knowledgeable." His policy science was informed by the belief "that it is above all necessary to get the conceptions of preventive politics across to the educated and the influential. If that is done, they will reach the masses eventually, through popularizations, authorized educational politics and informational and educational materials."[60]

In contrast to the reliance on the "cultural complex" as the ultimate and necessary source of democratic change, Lasswell appeared to locate the definitions and policies of democracy within either the new scientific guardians or the elite once thought to be the architects of manipulation. They were now "opinion leaders" in a regime of inherent and unquestioned legitimacy. Sincerely committed to platitudes such as the "dignity of man," the "free man's commonwealth," and the American "tradition," Lasswell abandoned his earlier pessimism. But the conversion to "democratic values," whatever they were, paralleled a sanctification of whatever "values" and whatever elites happened to be dominant at a given moment.

Harold Lasswell's scholarship is paradoxical. In his early work, the discovery of the irrational basis of the political order appears to preclude positive alterations in the values, institutions, and practices of American democracy. Such alterations only served to disguise the "elite-mass" relationship typical of the political disease he wanted to cure. Yet a new if empty definition of democracy accompanied Lasswell's democratic conversion. More than any thinker dealt with in these pages, Lasswell blended a liberal Progressive notion of democracy with the realism and authority of science. Yet scientific cures were merely bandages over hemorrhages. In his effort to find empirical referents for existing democratic practices, Lasswell found only diseases in need of scientific cures. But this bleak reality was covered with a democratic veneer. Only two alternatives were possible: the first, democracy without social science, would crumble on its own. The second was to achieve a contradiction in terms, a "democratic" revolution from above that assigned to social scientists the virtue once thought to reside in the citizenry itself. In the end, Lasswell espoused a democracy without citizens.

For Lasswell, the promise of social science was embodied in creation of that unity, purpose, and value consensus that Merriam's leaders and citizens were able to achieve with only a little advice. In a world of manipulators and the manipulated, why not "win the respect" of the "puzzled people" by "transmitting fundamental expectations regarding the allocation and objects of power?"[61] In Lasswell's work, the claims for scientific methodology and research reached their zenith. From Lester Ward to Harold Lasswell, the aims of scientific study changed from that of a helpmate to Populism to the prevention of popular depravity. The hopes of the third tradition were preserved by inflating the claims of social science, so much so that scientists became the only source of democratic values. Yet this is a logical progression since Ward and Lasswell are held together by a common if dubious assumption about social science's promise as the great nonrevolutionary modernizer of the American tradition. For Lasswell, this modernization had become intellectually difficult but even more politically necessary. Science now had to manufacture the democratic purpose and cohesion that Lasswell's predecessors had only attempted to catalyze.

The Eclipse of Reform Science: Conclusions

The early pioneers of the American science of politics rooted their limited claims to authority in their unique ability to decipher the kind of complexity that menaced the doctrines and institutions of a simpler American past. The language of science succeeded insofar as it dispelled old myths about human "essences" and discovered and communicated new truths concerning human flexibility and perfectibility. And one sure truth was this: The ills that beset the American polity were serious enough to require a new mode of explanation and a new group of explainers to point out several simple facts. The American present was indeed replete with dangerous tendencies threatening the Republic's survival itself. A distorted individualism still reigned in an interdependent society that negated the doctrines and reality of individual autonomy. Conflicts unique to interdependent industrial societies were piling up on top of older and still unsolved dilemmas present since the Founding.

These were serious political diseases. But it was the contention of third tradition thinkers that they need not be fatal. In a sense, the ills were conceived as products of a collective miscalculation and misunderstanding, not of any *systematic* and irremediable feature of American modernity. Indeed, miscalculations were possible to reverse by appropriate acts of an informed will. Sources of degeneration could be isolated and attacked merely if people's understandings were altered.

The effort to provide an alternative understanding was the source of the third tradition scholar's critical and skeptical posture toward the dismal American present and vision of the Republic's happy future. The production of scientifically based knowledge revealed no irreversible degeneration. It rather was supposed to change the minds of those now victimized by their own ignorance. In this sense, third tradition political science only tapped a layer of public virtue that had long been submerged in American political life, fragmented by the mechanical apparatus of the Founders and diverted by the utopian and irrational posturing of Christian and secular radicals. To the originators of the third tradition, social science evoked a preexisting harmony and destiny that had been hidden for too long. Governmental weakness and purposelessness disappeared once it was thought that a positive state was a friend and not an enemy of American liberties. The narrow-minded greed found in civil society likewise declined as science uncovered the potential of a collective, democratic destiny.

By their very nature, therefore, the claims of third tradition political science had to be vindicated in the polity itself by the impact of these claims on the public mind and on those leaders of social classes and political institutions capable of "educating" citizens to their "proper" obligations, rights, and loyalties. In this sense, social science and its methods, findings, and organization had to enter the world as a language autonomous from any one set of partisan interests or particular social classes. Its pretensions to objectivity were thus also pretensions to universality. Social science stood above the divisions of class and region—as it was then constituted, social science transcended political and economic power. Science taught that such conflicts were unnecessary. Properly educated majorities and democratically accountable experts were capable of transcending any particular interest in the name of a scientifically derived public interest.

The major assumptions behind these premises were, to say the least, grandiose indeed. First and most important was the notion that political science would find an appropriate public audience. Not only political studies but also political life itself would be scientific. The growth of professionalism only improved the autonomy and credibility, and thus the effectiveness, of social science messages. It crystallized what everybody knew but could never articulate.

The third tradition concept of American political crisis thus also relied on the hope and belief that citizens would defer to the patriotic but objective views of political change and reform discovered by experts. Politics could once again become an enterprise free of the class inequalities accompanying laissez-faire capitalism. Issues such as capitalism or socialism faded before a political and scientific language that embraced all. Class struggle and clashing ideologies disappeared before a general deference to social scientists by the important political and economic elites who listened to them.

Charles Merriam and Harold Lasswell held fast to the political aspirations first set out by thinkers such as Ward, Wilson, Bentley, and Beard. But their work shows that the hopeful assumptions sustained by their third tradition predecessors could only be maintained by distorting beyond recognition the American political tradition they so often praised, as well as by substantially redefining the role of political science in American political life. Even with such intellectual and organizational alterations, the claims of Merriam's reform science and Lasswell's policy science were hardly vindicated in the world they studied.

Most noteworthy in their work was the decline of the democratic public as the ultimate source of political reconstruction and the consequent rise of the political science discipline as an association of surrogate citizens. Earlier third tradition scholars embraced the goals of reform movements, even as they sought to channel their emotions and energies. In Merriam's view, citizens became able political participants only after intensive civic education and only when led by reasonable leaders. With Lasswell, the democratic public receded altogether, even as the future source of wisdom. Both men dramatically altered science's rapport with the mass public. Science no longer revealed the facts to a public who would know how to use them. The introduction of science into the polity now was perceived as an urgent measure of social control. Merriam never lost his faith in the public's ultimate emergence from the cave, while to Lasswell the public had to be recreated altogether out of whole cloth. Both men refused to jettison their hopes in the ultimate perfectibility of citizens, but such faith could be justified only through recourse to quite drastic nostrums indeed. As faith in the present virtue of citizens diminished, the role of social science in defining "democracy" sped forward.

This crucial change in outlook provoked an even more noteworthy transformation of the discipline's research agenda, a transformation with consequences Merriam and Lasswell lamented. As Merriam urged his colleagues toward what he saw as sophisticated behavioral research, the bulk of the profession adopted such methods while abandoning the assumptions and hopes that sustained his energies. The behavioral movement was supposed to create that deferent audience that always had eluded Merriam's Progressive predecessors; deference was for him a prelude to reform. But Merriam's professional and public audiences did not defer. To his chagrin, political elites only used social science for ends that still fit into the jungle politics science was supposed to be eliminating. Later, Lasswell christened social scientists the "guardians of democracy." Yet if social scientists guarded anything or anybody, they did so only on the terms set forth by the politically powerful. And Merriam's and Lasswell's colleagues were increasingly content to accept and even embrace this subsidiary role.

The fate of this kind of thinking contains more than a little irony. As its political claims were dashed, the professional organizations designed to fulfill the claims expanded. Only as the hopes for this brand of liberal reform weakened, only as the critical focus of political science narrowed, only as the political aspirations of the discipline's intellectual leaders became strained—only then did the political science profession gain in numbers, prestige, and money.

After World War II, political scientists returned to the universities and shunned direct advocacy, just as Merriam had done in the wake of World War I. Yet another cycle in the story of political science's perpetual new beginnings was launched, this time under the guise of "the behavioral persuasion." In the era of the "great American celebration," few would carry forward the limited critical and reformist outlook of the third tradition. Some did, however, although now strictly and only within the confines of apologies which proclaimed how democratic America already was.

The Behavioral Era

The dreams of reform-minded political scientists were shattered in the years following World War II. While the reelection of Harry Truman dispelled fears that the planning institutions established during the Roosevelt years might be completely dismantled, the Fair Deal was a far cry from the New Deal. War had lifted the nation out of the Great Depression, but there was no return to normalcy. Heightened East-West tensions gave rise to the revival of a massive military budget in 1950. A permanent war economy emerged that enabled the government to intervene in the economy as never before in peacetime. While such intervention provided the foundation for the unexpected economic boom of the 1950s and 1960s, it did not further the democratic vistas of men such as Merriam or Lasswell. Postwar intervention was not geared to democratizing modern state institutions, but at centralizing and strengthening them so that America might impress its economic, political, and military will on an increasingly intransigent world.

Postwar prosperity ultimately built new tensions and new anxieties into the American political system that supplanted those of the 1930s. A rapidly growing white middle class in suburbia isolated itself from most political activity and focused its attention on a narrow set of individualistic economic concerns to strengthen its position in America's new industrial state. Occasionally efforts were made to tamper with existing state institutions and political processes. But for the most part, there was little support for a major reform movement grounded in a revived vision of America's democratic possibilities. Indeed, McCarthyism made such reform movements a practical impossibility. Political scientists gradually drifted away from New Deal activism in the years following the war. Throughout the late 1940s and 1950s a fear of both right-wing and left-wing political movements developed in academic circles. Political change itself was deemed dangerous. In the mass society literature, for example, intellectuals began to express a deep-seated concern over the willingness as well as the ability of individual citizens to be able to participate intelligently in a modern democratic political system. Some even began to question the wisdom of allowing the masses to intrude directly into the policy-making process. In the tense postwar world, international peace and domestic prosperity were seen to be balanced on a fine edge. It was dangerous at best, foolhardy at worst, to democratize modern political and economic institutions, as earlier reformers such as Merriam and Beard had desired. For rationality to triumph in a postwar America, there had to be an end to ideology.[1]

Certain intellectual and organizational developments within the discipline reinforced the anti-ideological impulse in postwar political science. The "behavioral revolution," as these developments have since been called, radically transformed the type of work being produced by political scientists, the standards by which such work was judged, and the institutional structure of the profession as a whole. It also provided the basis for a stunning critique of the political science of Merriam and Lasswell. Behavioralists argued that the optimistic assumptions on which earlier political science had been based were politically naïve and methodologically suspect. Explicit political concerns tended to undermine the scientific foundations on which any social science had to be based. Rather than envisioning a political role for the discipline in reviving democratic accountability through civic education and modern social and economic planning, behavioralists sought to transform political science into a pure science of the political process. In so doing they hoped to free themselves from the all too practically oriented, valued-biased science of their mentors and to develop an objective, empirically grounded understanding of the American political system.

Earlier chapters have traced the way in which certain individuals turned to a science of politics in order to resolve certain problems in American political life. As we have seen in these chapters, men such as Ward and Wilson, Bentley and Beard, and Merriam and Lasswell did not see in professional political science an escape from politics. They turned to political science in order to address the contemporary crises confronting American political life from a new perspective, one which transcended the limits inherent in the two traditions of thought that had dominated American politics since the Founding. This new perspective envisioned political science itself playing a major role in building and democratizing American state institutions throughout the twentieth century.

In order to understand how this tradition of thought was transformed from the late 1940s through the early 1960s, we need to reverse the general approach used in earlier chapters, which explained how individual political scientists articulated third tradition concerns in their work and how these concerns shaped their vision of the role political science could play in American political life. This chapter, in contrast, investigates how the discipline itself began to have an impact on the tradition. The reasons for this shift are twofold. First, individuals' professional and disciplinary concerns began to dominate their larger political interests for the first time in the behavioral era. Those scholars who made important contributions to the third tradition during the late 1940s, 1950s, and early 1960s were professional political scientists first and concerned political actors only afterward. Second, the political crises confronting third tradition writers during the behavioral era were in large part defined by the findings and conclusions of neopositivistic behavioral science. Indeed, the fundamental problem confronting third tradition political scientists following the war was not how to find a place for science in their politics, but how to carve out a place for a meaningful politics in their science.

Attempts at coming to any complete definition of behavioralism are probably futile given the diversity of those who followed its banner. As one commentator noted, "the term served as sort of an umbrella, capricious enough to provide a temporary shelter for heterogeneous groups united only by dissatisfaction with traditional political science."[2] It is possible, however, to identify certain key features to the behavioral perspective that swept political science after World War II.[3]

First, behavioralism was a research orientation that sought to explain the phenomena of government in terms of the observed and observable behavior of people. In contrast to traditional institutional approaches, behavioralism focused on the processes underlying government and politics. Second, behavioralism implied a systematic research orientation that was directed by "formal theory." Research for the behavioralist grew out of a precise statement of hypotheses and a rigorous ordering of evidence that allowed the identification of behavioral uniformities, the validation of findings through successive research, and the accumulation of knowledge through the development of concepts of increasing power and generality. Third, behavioralism implied research that placed primary emphasis on empirical methods. Much of behavioral research was aimed at developing new methods for studying the political process. Finally, behavioralism maintained a sharp distinction between empirical explanation and ethical evaluation.

Postwar behavioralism thus represented, in certain aspects, an intensification of the scientific imperative found in the work of earlier political scientists. Many of the leading behavioralists in the late 1940s and early 1950s were students of Merriam and Lasswell, and drew heavily on their mentors for inspiration and guidance. In other respects, a vast gulf separated behavioralism from prewar political science. Behavioralism was based on new scientific tools, techniques, and methods that were considerably more sophisticated than those prewar political scientists used. The most important of these innovations emerged out of a field that was largely undeveloped in prewar political science, survey research. Much of the behavioral revolution centered on the explosion in survey research work that took place following the war. Along with the rapid development of computer technology and the ability of individual researchers to collect, store, and analyze data, survey research raised the hope once again that political science might be placed, at last, on a firm scientific foundation.[4]

Postwar behavioralism also embodied a strikingly different orientation to the political world than was found in prewar political science. Prewar political scientists had shared a common faith that behavioralism and political reform were mutually compatible. They believed that the discoveries of a behaviorally oriented political science ultimately would provide the raw materials out of which reformers would construct a democratized American state. Empirical theory thus was regarded as an enrichment of normative theory because it provided the bases by which norms and values could change reality. Postwar behavioralists, on the other hand, believed that a sharp distinction had to be drawn between scientific theory and political action. Understanding and explaining political behavior necessarily preceded any attempt to apply scientific knowledge to pressing social problems. Premature attempts at tying together scientific knowledge with political action inevitably were doomed to failure and threatened to undermine the foundations on which all scientific knowledge was based. Empirical theory thus was not an enrichment of normative theory, but an autonomous enterprise derived from one's investigation of the data. Far from being a tool for building and democratizing

American political institutions, empirical theory was used to consolidate behavioralists' understanding and appreciation of democracy as it existed in the real world.

The scientific and political gulf that separated behavioralism from prewar political science was deepened by a series of organizational changes that swept the discipline in the late 1940s and early 1950s. Survey research specialists who built their careers in government service during the war turned to the university as a place to pursue their work. In 1946 several members of the Department of Agriculture's Division of Program Surveys left government service and founded the Survey Research Center (SRC) at the University of Michigan.[5] In 1948 the Research Center for Group Dynamics, originally established in 1945 at the Massachusetts Institute for Technology, was transferred to Michigan and joined the SRC to become the Institute for Social Research (ISR). Later, the ISR would be expanded to include three other major behavioral research programs: the Inter-University Consortium for Political Research (1962), the Center for Research in the Utilization of Scientific Knowledge (1964), and the Center for Political Studies (1970). Along with other university-affiliated organizations such as the National Opinion Research Center (NORC) at the University of Chicago and the SSRC's Committee on Political Behavior, such institutions played a major role in promoting a neopositivistic behavioral perspective in political science that was far removed from the reformist concerns of prewar political science.[6]

The influence of these behaviorally oriented research institutions was enhanced by a number of other important developments in postwar political science. Following the war, large philanthropic organizations such as the Ford Foundation, the Carnegie Foundation, and the Rockefeller Foundation began to underwrite political science research, particularly behavioral research, more than they had before. The NORC was founded through a grant from the Marshall Field Foundation, and the Rockefeller Foundation helped to finance the voting behavior studies conducted by Lazarfeld, Berelson, and Gaudet during the 1940 election and the election studies the SRC conducted throughout the 1950s. Among other enterprises, the Ford Foundation helped to found the Center for Advanced Study in the Behavioral Sciences.[7] While such foundations were not completely responsible for the behavioral direction of postwar political science, they nevertheless exerted an enormous influence in determining what problems would be investigated and how they would be studied.[8]

Another factor contributing to the triumph of behavioralism was the simple fact that political science grew rapidly in the two decades following the war. Between 1946 and 1966, membership in the APSA rose from 4,000 to 14,000. Increasingly, professional academics inside the university community dominated APSA membership. Many of these new members, not surprisingly, bore the imprint of postwar behavioral training. Indeed, a large part of the success of the behavioral movement in postwar political science can be attributed to the fact that it emerged on the academic scene at the very time that American higher education was undergoing its most rapid expansion.

By the late 1940s, changes introduced in political science by the behavioral revolution had begun to affect the actual organizational structure of the APSA itself. APSA members, particularly disgruntled behavioral members, were dissatisfied with the dismal state of the APSA's finances and the autonomy certain APSA research committees had assumed in their pursuit of certain reformist goals.[9] This discontent culminated in two important reforms in the association that radically transformed its structure and very reason for being. In 1949 a new constitution established a Washington secretariat, headed by an executive director responsible for developing the association's professional and research services. This reform was followed by another in 1951, when the council itself decided that the APSA would undertake "substantive research projects" only "when the nature or the immediacy of the problem, or the requirements of facilities is beyond the control of individuals and institutions. . . ." Behind this reform lay a bitter controversy over whether the APSA should continue to assign research projects, particularly politically sensitive research projects, to its committees. As Somit and Tanenhaus noted, "Underlying this dispute was the Executive Committee's opposition to any type of Association undertaking which it could not control and . . . a vivid recollection of the wide swath cut by previous research committees. The merits of the issue aside, the Executive Committee's position was immeasurably strengthened by a manifest foundation reluctance to support proposals submitted by Association committees."[10] The net effect of these reforms was to sever the weak linkages that some reform-oriented political scientists had forged between the APSA and the real world of politics through the association's research committees. By the early 1950s, these reforms had transformed the APSA from a relatively loosely knit, decentralized association with reformist political tendencies into a more centrally directed, nonpartisan professional interest group. Such an organization was much more attuned to the needs, concerns, and visions of the neopositivistic behavioral movement than was the prewar association.

Much of the discontent that behavioralists felt toward prewar political science can be found in the critique that was leveled against the APSA Committee on Political Parties' 1950 report, "Toward a More Responsible Two-Party System."[11] The publication, reception, and impact of the report revealed in starkest terms the failure of prewar political science and marked a major watershed in the movement of political science away from the reform-oriented science of Merriam and Lasswell to the behavioralism of the postwar era.

The report was one of the most publicized documents the APSA ever produced. Its thesis and reform proposals date to Woodrow Wilson's *Congressional Government.* The report showed how the two-party system in the United States had developed into two loose associations of state and local party organizations. The party in power consequently was ill-equipped to organize its members in the legislative and executive branches into a government held together by a party platform. There was, in short, little responsive or accountable party government in the United States largely because of the weak, decentralized two-party system. "This," the report noted, "is a very serious matter, for it affects the very heartbeat of American democracy. It also poses grave problems of domestic and foreign policy in an era when it is no longer safe for the nation to deal piecemeal with issues that can be disposed of only on the bases of coherent programs."[12] In its conclusion, the report suggested reforms that could strengthen party government and structure political campaigns more firmly around policy issues. Underlying these proposals was the fundamental belief that democratic government in the modern world inevitably was predicated upon "responsible" party government.

While the report claimed to be a "summation of professional knowledge," it also set out explicit political goals. "The purpose of this publication," the report stated, "is to bring about a fuller appreciation of a basic weakness in the American two-party system. . . . This is not a research document aimed at professional readers only. It seeks the attention of everyone interested in politics."[13] The report was self-consciously a document of reform political science par excellence. Critical analysis based on scientific research was to serve as an impetus to public debate and political action aimed at alleviating the legitimacy crisis confronting contemporary democratic institutions. Organizational reforms or procedural rearrangements could never adequately cope with the current crisis. As the report explained: "Remedy requires not only understanding of the ailment but also willingness to try a likely cure. Both understanding and willingness, in turn, must be fairly widespread. It is not enough for a people to know about ailment and cure. Before action has a chance, knowledge must first become sufficiently common. The character of this publication is explained by the conviction of its authors that the weakness of the American two-party system can be overcome as soon as a substantial part of the electorate wants it overcome."[14]

The reception of the report was hardly the kind foreseen by those who drafted it. Both the American public and American politicians ignored it. The only people who appeared to be interested in its findings and conclusions were political scientists themselves, particularly newly trained behavioral political scientists. Julius Turner's response to the report in an article the APSR published in 1951 was indicative of how the report would be treated over the next decade.[15] While noting that the report made a valuable contribution to our understanding of political parties in America, Turner warned that "its conclusions should be treated with caution." According to Turner, the committee had underestimated present party responsibility. Through a roll call analysis of voting in Congress, he showed that political parties actually played a considerably more significant and influential role than the report's crude impressionistic analysis implied. Simply because American political parties did not operate according to the idea of responsible party government did not mean that they failed to present alternative choices to the electorate, as the report's conclusions inferred. Moreover, Turner argued that some of the reforms the report proposed would actually accentuate present defects in the two-party system. An inadequate scientific understanding of the political world thus had culminated in a misguided call for action. "It would be unwise," Turner commented in a footnote, "to take political action based on the Committee's report until after much more debate and much more scientific study."[16]

The report's fate was in many respects the fate of the reform science Merriam and Lasswell championed. Few cared to listen to or act on the prescriptions professional political scientists offered. Furthermore, those few political scientists who did care to listen could come to no firm agreement among themselves over what scientific knowledge they actually possessed about political parties. Indeed, path-breaking studies by prominent behavioralists throughout the 1950s challenged many of the assumptions and findings of the report. A discussion that reform scientists had hoped would culminate in substantive political action soon degenerated into a narrow disciplinary debate over the meaning of the data on political parties that new behavioral tools and techniques were uncovering.

A similar orientation can be found in *Voting*, the path-breaking study of Berelson, Lazarfeld, and McPhee. Much like the authors of *The American Voter*, those of *Voting* discovered that individual voters appeared to be unable to satisfy the requirements for a democratic system as outlined by normative political theorists. Yet they believed that the political system found in the United States nevertheless met certain democratic requirements. As they so eloquently explained, "Where the rational citizen seems to abdicate, nevertheless angels seem to tread."[17] As in *The American Voter*, troubling empirical findings did not lead to a call for political reform. Behavioral data could be used to deepen an understanding of the nature of American democracy and the factors that enabled it to grow and prosper. *Voting* was based on the assumption that the problem of power and legitimacy effectively had been solved in the American political system. The task of political science was not to help build democratic institutions; it was to explain how the existing institutions were, in fact, democratic already.

This chapter discusses the transformation of the third tradition in the behavioral era by looking at the work of V. O. Key and David Truman. Key and Truman were leading spokesmen of the behavioral movement in political science following the war. They were personally responsible for many of the organizational and intellectual changes that the discipline underwent in the 1940s, 1950s, and 1960s. They both chaired the SSRC's Committee on Political Behavior during its most influential years, Key from 1949 to 1953, and Truman from 1953 to 1964. Each served as ASPA president. Their works were and still are cited as classic examples of behaviorally oriented research. Besides being the author of path-breaking studies on interest groups, Southern politics, state politics, public opinion, and voting behavior, Key penned one of the first primers on the use of statistical analysis in political science. Truman, for his part, was the author of *The Governmental Process*, the most important group interpretation of American political life since Bentley's *Process of Government*, as well as *The Congressional Party*, one of the first behavioral studies of Congress.

Key and Truman were behavioralists with a difference. While championing the new scientific imperative formed in postwar political science, they never lost sight of the larger questions that had been raised in the third tradition about the relationship between power and legitimacy in the American political system. Key and Truman used the findings and language of postwar behavioral political science to develop a new appreciation of the delicate balance which existed in America between expanding state power and the processes that provided for democratic control. As was the case with other behavioralists, the critical reformist thrust of prewar political science was absent from the work of Key and Truman. Both accepted the belief that the problem of reconciling the tension between power and legitimacy had been resolved by contemporary state institutions and political processes. Unlike many other behavioralists, however, they consciously recognized the political role political science assumed during the behavioral era. Both envisioned their writings as providing political elites with a sophisticated understanding of their role as well as an understanding of the actual function of things such as parties, elections, public opinion, and interest groups in modern democratic societies. The crisis of democracy that confronted Key and Truman essentially was a theoretical crisis with real world consequences. They feared that if the elites failed to understand the nature of the modern political system and their role in it, the very processes that had emerged to provide democratic input and legitimacy to the American state in the twentieth century could break down. For Key and Truman, the crisis of democracy in the postwar era could be confronted fully only with the assistance of a highly skilled, politically astute discipline of political science.

There were, of course, other political scientists in the behavioral era whose work was firmly grounded in the third tradition. Robert Dahl, for example, played a major role in reshaping the way in which political scientists discussed and studied American politics. His early works, such as *Preface to Democratic Theory* and *Who Governs?*, were classic examples of the behavioral persuasion in action. But the themes running through Dahl's early work tended to echo those articulated in the work of Key and Truman. "*Homo Civicus*," "*Homo Politicus*," "actual and potential resources," the "Democratic Creed"—all were analogs to ideas Key and Truman initially developed in their own path-breaking works. Whatever his contributions to the discipline, Dahl did little during the behavioral era to move the third tradition beyond the logic found in the work of Key and Truman.

Behavioralism helped to redefine the historical project confronting third tradition writers in the postwar years. But men such as Key and Truman were hardly more successful in accomplishing their larger political goals than their forebears had been. The reason for their failure might have surprised earlier third tradition writers.

It became increasingly apparent to political scientists in the postwar era that the only audiences they had to address were themselves and perhaps their students. In their endeavors to build a neopositivistic science of politics, behavioralists effectively had isolated themselves from any outside public. In the absence of such a public, Key's and Truman's attempts to balance a deeply held belief in the givenness of American democracy with the discoveries of behavioral political science and its role in the American political system had collapsed. Biting methodological and political critiques by self-ordained postbehavioralists uncovered the conservative bias built into the behavioral persuasion and reintroduced concerns over a real world crisis of democracy into the discipline. Far from resolving the tensions that had confronted the third tradition throughout the twentieth century, the behavioral era only reemphasized the difficulties built into the historical project as a whole.

V. O. and the Third Tradition

Valdimer Orlando Key was born on March 13, 1908, in Austin, Texas. He received his B.A. and M.A. from the University of Texas in 1929 and 1930, respectively, and his Ph.D. from the University of Chicago in 1934. In many ways, his career represented that envisioned by Charles Merriam for political scientists when he established the graduate program at the University of Chicago. Key was a faculty member at the University of California–Los Angeles, Johns Hopkins University, Yale University, and Harvard University. From these academic positions, he published a constant stream of articles and books with a clocklike regularity, including *The Administration of Federal Grants to States* (1937), *The Initiative and Referendum in California* with W. W. Crouch (1939), *Politics, Parties and Pressure Groups* (1942, 1947, 1952, 1958, 1964), *Southern Politics* (1946), *A Primer of Statistics for Political Scientists* (1954), *American State Politics* (1956), *Public Opinion and American Democracy* (1961), and *The Responsible*

Electorate (1966). He was a member of the SSRC board of directors and chaired two of its most important committees, the Committee on Political Behavior and the Committee on Problems and Policy. In 1958 he was elected APSA president. Besides these professional activities, Key also was involved in extensive activities in public service. At the national level, he served as a consultant to the Social Security board, worked as an NRPB research technician, was employed by the Bureau of the Budget, and served on President Kennedy's Committee on Campaign Costs. At the local level, he advised the Maryland State Planning Commission and the Baltimore Commission on Planning and Economy.[18]

In other ways, Key's career marked a qualitative break with prewar political science. Unlike his mentors at the University of Chicago, Key remained throughout his career primarily a professional political scientist dedicated to the scientific advancement of the discipline. His use of quantitative tools and techniques was far more sophisticated than Merriam's. Indeed, works such as *Politics, Parties, and Pressure Groups* and *Southern Politics* paved the way for later detailed empirical studies of the American political system. Similarly, *A Primer of Statistics for Political Scientists* was designed specifically to overcome resistance among political scientists to the use of quantitative techniques in the study of political behavior.

Key also rejected many of the political assumptions that earlier political scientists had built into their scientific work. In sharp contrast to Merriam, Key argued that distinctions had to be drawn between facts and values as well as between science and politics if the latter were not to undermine the former. Too many political scientists held an undeveloped understanding of the empirical nature of modern democracy. Moreover, too little attention had been paid to studying the actual patterns of behavior underlying American political processes. What postwar political science needed most was not a series of reform proposals based on an inadequate understanding of the American political system, but a hard-nosed scientific explanation of the way in which democracy actually operated in the real world.[19]

This intensified concern over scientific quantification, method, and explanation in turn led Key to look at professional organizations in a different light than did prewar reformers. He was a prime mover behind the APSA's organizational reforms in 1950. Along with other prominent behavioralists, Key maintained that the discipline had to be freed from the simplistic reform orientation found in prewar political science. For political science to become a true behavioral science, it was essential that APSA itself be transformed into a centrally directed, nonpartisan organization that represented the interests of the discipline as a whole and not the narrow political beliefs of a few select members.

The behavioralism of V. O. Key differed most radically from that of Merriam and Lasswell in its orientation to the postwar political world. All of Key's work was premised on a deeply held belief in the givenness of American democracy. While he rejected many of the common assumptions held about the nature of American democratic processes, he never doubted that America was a democratic society. Similarly, he never questioned the idea that a good scientific analysis of American politics would be able to uncover the linkages that existed between the institutions of power found in postwar America and acceptable democratic norms and values. In contrast to earlier third tradition writers, Key believed that the principal task of the discipline was to understand objectively the nature of these linkages. Significantly, for Key this task carried with it important implications for the political world. Behavioral empirical theory ultimately provided political leaders with insight into their role in modern democratic institutions. In addition, it enabled them to understand what had to be done to preserve the linkages that had emerged between power and legitimacy in postwar America.

Key thus came into contact with the problems of the third tradition in a manner that was strikingly different from his predecessors. The crisis of democracy for Key was confronted as a crisis in the theory of democracy. Helping to mediate between power and legitimacy was not conceived as an immediate practical problem, but as an intellectual problem defined by the discoveries of a rapidly developing behavioral science of politics. The political objective of the discipline was to provide political actors with a deeper scientific appreciation of the forms and procedures of twentieth-century American democracy that went beyond the assumptions of popular political thought and prewar political science. Failure to go beyond the disturbing facts about American political life uncovered by behavioralism, Key feared, could undermine the very forms and procedures that gave American democracy its life and vitality. If American democracy was to survive in the troubled postwar world, it needed a behavioral science capable of comprehending its true nature.

Behavioralism as Pure Science

Key's earliest writings reflected the orientation toward the behavioral study of politics found in the prewar science of Merriam and Lasswell. His Ph.D. dissertation, written under the direction of Charles Merriam, was on "The Techniques of Political Graft in the United States."[20] Like other Merriam students, Key was interested primarily in analyzing the political and administrative realities that shaped politics, rather than simply the institutional structures. Similarly, in his first book, *The Administration of Federal Grants to States*, Key looked at the behavioral reality underlying federal aid to states by studying the actual operation of jointly financed activities in more than half of the states.[21] In neither of these works did Key attempt to question the scientific or political assumptions that had been built into prewar political science.

Key's approach to the study of politics took a distinctive turn in his second book, coauthored with W. W. Crouch, *The Initiative and Referendum in California* (1939). [22] Here, Key grappled with a question to which he would return in different forms throughout his career: What was the larger political significance of the Progressive reforms that had been instituted throughout the twentieth century? As Key and Crouch explained: "The advocates of the initiative and the referendum were grappling with the fundamental problem of democracy. Their basic objective was to contrive procedures which would enable 'The People' to have a higher degree of influence over the course of public policy. Their task was essentially the implementation of the spirit of democracy. In a way their hope was that the governed might govern the governors and thereby solve the dilemma of democracy.[23]

Unfortunately, at least from the perspective of the reformers, reforms such as the initiative or the referendum did not significantly alter the composition, methods, or objectives of current public policy. As Key and Crouch carefully demonstrated, existing and newly established interests had successfully accommodated themselves to the procedures of Progressive democracy. For example, initiative measures did not originate with "The People," but with a relatively small group of men animated by some special interest. While the proposals such men presented may or may not have been in the public interest, they generally tended to be for the benefit of that special interest. More important, when a group representing the public actually did emerge to champion certain proposals, the odds against success were strong because the opposition generally was strong and the support usually weak.[24] This early case study of the initiative and referendum differed from studies on the same subject by other prewar political scientists in important ways. First, it showed how the findings of behavioral research could be used to criticize the naïve notions of democracy found in American political culture, particularly those Progressives and reform-oriented political scientists championed. Second, the case study led to pessimism about the possibility of introducing substantive democratic reforms into the existing system of power and privilege, a pessimism Merriam never would have shared. Third, it showed how a behavioral study of politics could be turned away from explicit involvement in the political world toward a purely scientific study of the political system. Scientific explanation of the behavioral reality underlying American politics, not partisan political reform, became the hallmark of Key's scholarly work for the next twenty-five years.

As Key pursued his study of American politics throughout the 1940s, he continued to move away from the scientific and political orientations of Merriam and Lasswell. His primary concern in early editions of *Politics, Parties and Pressure Groups*, for example, was to challenge many of the commonly held ideas about American politics by looking at the power influential interest groups actually wielded in the political system.[25] Similarly, in *Southern Politics* he sought to explain how the politics of race had undermined the two-party system in the South and left it with a system of factional politics that was unable to provide either the organization or the leadership to cope with contemporary political problems. Both works were major contributions to the development of postwar political science. Like his study of the initiative and the referendum, they eschewed any overt involvement in the political world. In the place of misguided reform proposals, the books provided students with a wealth of new data about American politics and relatively sophisticated frameworks for giving order and meaning to the data. From the perspective of an evolving neopositivistic science of the political process, both were noteworthy achievements.

Yet both studies had a darker side that was not lost on Key. As he peered deeper into the behavioral reality underlying American political life, he was forced to grapple with questions that had confronted earlier third tradition writers. What were the foundations of democratic government in America? What sort of democratic controls limited and directed the scope of political power in twentieth-century America? What was the nature of legitimacy in the modern democratic order? For earlier third tradition writers, such questions had been first and foremost political questions that called for political solutions. For Key, however, they were scientific questions that called for theoretical explanations. Facts and values, as well as the "is" and the "ought," had to be clearly distinguished from one another in order to secure the objectivity of one's science. From Key's perspective, a commitment to a pure science of politics did not undercut a commitment to democracy. On the contrary, he believed that it ultimately reinforced commitment to democracy. As he noted in the second edition of *Politics, Parties and Pressure Groups*, ". . . realistic analysis of the struggle for power within a great democracy need not destroy the faith of the democrat. Such an analysis may merely furnish a more sophisticated defense of the tenets of the democratic order for those who live by political faith."[26] That the discoveries of an objective, empirically grounded science could ever clash with the fundamental values on which American political life was based was unimaginable to Key. Even in *Southern Politics*, where his indictment of certain American political institutions was the most complete, Key held the hope that it was only a matter of time until racism was supplanted by the politics of economics and the South became an open two-party system like the rest of the country. For Key an inquiry into the reality of American politics inevitably was an inquiry into the nature of democratic reality as it existed in the actual world. If facts were uncovered that raised serious questions about conventional notions of democracy in America, democracy was not at fault, but, rather, our understanding of it was.

Empirical Democratic Theory

The best way to appreciate Key's contribution to the third tradition is to look at his ongoing treatment of the roles parties, elections, and public opinion played in maintaining responsible democratic government in the United States. He returned to these topics throughout his career as he sought to comprehend the larger meaning of the data postwar political science was uncovering. Indeed, they lie at the heart of much of his later empirical work and theoretical argument, particularly that found in *Public Opinion and American Democracy* (1961), *The Responsible Electorate* (1966), and the final edition of *Politics, Parties and Pressure Groups* (1967). Key's treatment of these topics ultimately represented his most sophisticated attempt to explain how contemporary political processes and institutions effectively solved the tensions between power and legitimacy.

Key's first significant attempt to grapple with the problems of the third tradition is found in the first edition of *Parties, Politics and Pressure Groups* (1942). Perhaps the most striking aspect of the book is the way he used an interest group perspective for reconsidering the nature and function of parties in the American political system. Key emphatically rejected the idea that a party was a group of people united by a sharply defined set of principles or that the two-party system in America was ever meant to provide voters with a choice between two distinct programs for public action. According to Key, the major parties in the United States were interested primarily in putting forward candidates for public office and in making appeals to all groups of society in order to create a coalition powerful enough to win elections and to govern. Their true function thus was not to provide voters with alternative choices at the polls, but to mediate between the claims of competing groups and to seek a common ground for political action in the public interest. "It is," noted Key, "incorrect to say that American parties have no principles or policies. They have; but their principles tend toward similarity . . . The programs of both parties change at about the same rate and generally in the same direction. Their policies are the policies of a capitalistic society modified as recurring internal crises demand."[27]

Along a similar line of thought, Key drew on the recent voting study literature to expose the myth that elections translated the popular will into governmental action. For example, he pointed out that recent studies showed that between 30 percent and 40 percent of the electorate voluntarily disenfranchised itself during national elections simply by not voting. Moreover, these voters tended to be women, less educated, poor, and younger than age forty. Far from being a vehicle of the popular will as a whole, elections thus translated the concerns of certain groups into power and influence much more effectively than others. The true meaning of elections in a democratic system was complicated further by the fact that individuals tended to maintain an allegiance to a particular party, an allegiance that generally lagged behind changes in the interests of the voter. This meant, argued Key, that "the small portion of the total population that shifts from one party to another really determines the outcome of elections. That group is in a position to wield great power and to wrest whatever concessions it wants from the parties and the government."[28] In light of the available literature on voting behavior, Key finally concluded that about all an election really decided was who should fill a particular office. Indeed, he suggested that elections in a democracy were perhaps nothing more than the occasional intervention of the electorate into government. But, as he was careful to add, "these occasional interventions of the electorate into the direction of government are in a sense the characteristic that differentiates democracies from other forms of government."[29]

The portrait of the American political system Key painted in early editions of *Politics, Parties and Pressure Groups* was, in many respects, a disturbing one. It implicitly raised serious questions about the processes and institutions that had come to define the American democratic experience in the twentieth century. Not surprisingly, many of the concerns earlier third tradition writers expressed echo throughout the book. For example, much like his predecessors, Key was afraid that the rise to power of pressure groups may have created a gap in America's representative machinery. Not all groups were equally organized in the American political system. Moreover, public officials tended to succumb to the demands of the organized, often at the expense of the unorganized or the public as a whole. In addition, Key was concerned that the existing mechanisms for ameliorating interest group conflict might be approaching their limits. The looseness of party policy, the weakness of party discipline, and the "illogical process" of trading between interest groups may have contributed to the solving of sectional and group conflicts in the past. "Yet," he warned, "if this trend in government responsibility for the guidance of the national economy continues and with it the necessity for a consistent and interrelated set of governmental policies increases, the necessity for an overhauling of governmental machinery and party customs to produce that kind of public policy may become serious."[30]

Unlike earlier third tradition writers, Key did not turn such critical insights into American democracy into a wholesale critique of the existing political system. On the contrary, in early editions of *Politics, Parties and Pressure Groups* these insights were left as the tentative speculations of an impartial observer of the political process. In the end, these critical insights remained only sidelights, albeit fascinating ones, to the general empirical study at hand. Interestingly, in the last two editions, published in 1958 and 1964, most of them had been displaced by an overriding drive to explain the democratic nature of such institutions as parties, elections, and pressure groups as they actually existed in the real world.

As more empirical data was integrated into later editions of *Politics, Parties and Pressure Groups*, significantly less attention was paid to the crises confronting political institutions in America and more attention was directed to the crisis confronting democratic theory. For Key behavioral data was not to be used to expose the limits of existing institutional arrangements or to raise the possibility of reform. It was to be used to reveal the inadequacies of traditional democratic theory and to provide the basis for a new interpretation of the linkages that actually existed between power and legitimacy in American society.

Key's reinterpretation of democratic theory in light of the discoveries of modern behavioral science can be seen vividly in the theory of critical elections, one of his most important contributions to political science. He initially developed the theory in a couple of seminal articles published in the mid-1950s and integrated it into the last two editions of *Politics, Parties and Pressure Groups.*[31] The central idea behind the theory of critical elections was that a category of elections existed in which the emergent depth and intensity of electoral participation was high and out of which there came a sharp rupture in the preexisting cleavage in the electorate. These elections culminated in the formation of new and durable electoral groupings and in a profound readjustment in the power relations in the community. On its face, the theory of critical elections was a relatively straightforward generalization derived from an inspection of elections in American history. It provided behaviorally oriented political scientists with a conceptual tool for understanding elections that was grounded firmly in empirical data. Yet beyond this scientific function, the theory of critical elections also helped Key resolve a larger question firmly rooted in the third tradition: How were those individuals in positions of power held accountable by the people through the electoral process?

As noted above, in early editions of *Politics, Parties and Pressure Groups*, Key had reached the disturbing conclusion that the electorate intervened only occasionally in government, and even then in a rather limited way. By expanding in later editions his typology of elections to include those which displayed a lack of confidence in government, a vote of confidence in it, a realignment toward another conception of it, or a critical realignment of the electorate away from the past, Key developed a framework for explaining how powerful and long-lasting that occasional intervention could be. For example, Key argued that landslides that marked a general withdrawal of popular confidence in the party in power revealed the might of the people in a democratic order "in a spectacular fashion. The people may not be able to govern themselves but they can through an electoral uprising throw the old crowd out and demand a new order, without necessarily being capable of specifying exactly what it shall be. An election of this type may amount, if not to revolution, to its functional equivalent." In essence, critical elections were the most striking instances of the intervention of the people into the governmental process. Ultimately, they paved the way for a broad new direction in public policy.[32]

Importantly, the election typology Key developed out of his theory of critical elections was considerably different from that Angus Campbell and his associates at the SRC proposed.[33] For Campbell and company, elections were differentiated according to their relation to the pattern of party identification within the electorate. Accordingly, their typology of elections included maintaining elections, deviating elections, reinstating elections, and realigning elections. "This system of pigeonholes" maintained Key, "had its utility in that it focuses attention on the relation of a particular election to the underlying and enduring pattern of partisan loyalties." But it did not capture fully enough, at least for Key, the actual role that elections assumed in the democratic process. On the other hand, his own typology, which categorized elections according to the nature of the popular decision, did. To be sure, Key's typology of elections came with costs, and he was fully aware of them. As he pointed out, "To place elections in such a scheme involved a degree of divination to estimate the meaning of the popular verdict."[34] But the solutions the categorization provided for larger theoretical questions about the empirical linkages between legitimacy and power in the American political system more than adequately compensated for these costs.

Key's criticism of the behavioral research political scientists at SRC conducted was not limited to his rejection of their election typology. He also was highly skeptical of the conclusions that could be drawn from their analyses of voting behavior, particularly those derived from the theoretical model used to explain voting behavior in *The American Voter*. The idea that the electorate was politically apathetic and moved largely by considerations of partisanship and candidate personality was anathema to Key. The implicit conclusion in *The American Voter* was that the electorate was not equipped to participate in issue-oriented politics.[35] Such a conclusion cut to the core of Key's third tradition concerns. Without an electorate capable of intervening intelligently in the governmental process at least periodically through elections, demonstrating that the people actually had a substantive role to play in a democratic political system would be all but impossible.

In his last two major works, *Public Opinion and American Democracy* (1961) and *The Responsible Electorate* (1966), Key cultivated an alternative conceptual framework for understanding why the act of voting was by no means devoid of policy content or intent. Unlike SRC researchers, Key focused systematic attention on the phenomenon of partisan defection. By dividing the voting electorate into three categories—standpatters, switchers, and new voters—and studying what motivated voters to switch parties, he sought to demonstrate that the electorate was not straitjacketed by party allegiance as *The American Voter* had argued. In sharp contrast to *The American Voter's* typecast of "independent" voters as ill-equipped to deal with the complications of politics and voting, Key discovered a group of independents who were fairly sophisticated in political matters. Key's independents not only appraised the actions of government and held their own policy preferences, but systematically related these to their voting choices. As Key put it in *The Responsible Electorate*:

> The perverse and unorthodox argument of this little book is that voters are not fools. To be sure, many believe the electorate behaves about as rationally and responsibly as we should expect, given the clarity of the alternatives presented to it and the character of the information available to it. In American presidential campaigns of recent decades the portrait of the American electorate that develops from the data is not one of an electorate straitjacketed by social determinants or moved by subconscious urges triggered by devilishly skillful propagandists. It is rather one of an electorate moved by concern about central and relevant questions of public policy, of governmental performance, and of executive personality.[36]

As was the case with his theory of critical elections, Key's theory of voting behavior explained how those in power were held accountable by the people through the electoral process. Once again, empirical theory had put to rest whatever questions the discoveries of behavioral science had raised about American democratic processes.

Legitimacy, Power, and the Political Subculture

Key's theories of critical elections and of voting behavior helped to explain the important role the electorate played in the democratic political system. They did not answer satisfactorily all the questions that behavioralist studies raised about modern democratic institutions and processes. Two questions, in particular, came to haunt Key in his later years. First, how could the findings of survey research studies be reconciled with a viable notion of democratic legitimacy? Second, what features of the American political system guaranteed that power would be wielded according to these democratic norms? Both questions came to lie at the heart of a book that was, in many respects, Key's most important contribution to the third tradition, *Public Opinion and American Democracy.*

On one level, *Public Opinion and American Democracy* was simply another addition to the evolving public opinion literature. In the book, Key reviewed some of the most important innovations survey research specialists developed over the past thirty years, including the attitudinal and structural distribution of opinion, the properties of public opinion, and the formation of public opinion by institutions such as the family, the school, and the mass media. On another level, Key took up concerns that went far beyond other public opinion studies and were rooted firmly in third tradition concerns. For example, in his discussion of the attitudinal and structural distribution of public opinion, Key examined the idea that an underlying consensus on political beliefs was a prerequisite for democratic government. He noted that survey data showed that no real fundamental consensus on political beliefs actually existed. As Key explained, "While the data suggest that certain attitudes widely distributed within the population may bear on the way the political system works, to call these beliefs a 'consensus on fundamentals' imputes to them a more explicit and ordered content than they seem to possess."[37] Despite these findings, Key did not want to abandon the idea that modern democracies were founded on some basic consensus. Much as he had argued about elections and voting behavior, Key maintained that the type of consensus found in real world democracies was far more complex than that envisioned in classical democratic theory. To understand the true nature of democratic consensus, theorists had to go beyond the actual survey data and make certain assumptions and estimates about the role and behavior of political elites in the political system as a whole. According to Key:

Within the population generally the dominant set of attitudes and expectations may be compatible with a government that operates as if a consensus on fundamentals existed. Yet to round out the explanation it is useful to assume that the circles of leadership, the political activists of the society, constitute what might be called a "political sub-culture." Perhaps within this group are to be found these beliefs, values, habits of action, and modes of political life that give the political system its distinctive characteristics. Politicians, lobbyists, officials, party leaders, and influentials may be carriers of the political culture or holders of the basic consensus on modes and styles of action, even though they may be sharply divided on the issues of the day.[38]

Key's conception of the political subculture in *Public Opinion and American Democracy* was his most explicit theoretical explanation of how democratic norms had been reconciled with the exercise of political power in the American political system. The idea was expanded in the concluding chapter of *Public Opinion and American Democracy* to explain the real role public opinion played in a modern democratic system. Public opinion, argued Key, was not something static that could be easily grasped by normal sample survey studies. It was the product of a complex interaction between elites and the masses that underwent constant change. "Mass opinion," concluded Key, "is not self-generating; on the main it is a response to the crisis, the proposals and the vision propagated by political activists."[39] Moreover, it was not an entity that initiated action or translated its purposes into governmental action. It was instead more like a series of dikes that channeled public action and defined the discretionary range within which governmental discussion and action took place. From Key's theoretical perspective, the success of democracy, and thus the reconciliation between political power and democratic legitimacy, ultimately rested on the beliefs, the standards, and the competence of America's political elite. Conversely, it would fail "not because of the cupidity of the masses, but because of the stupidity and self-seeking of leadership echelons." Democracy failed not because the people had become corrupt, but because they had been corrupted.[40]

What was particularly fascinating about Key's theoretical reconciliation of the problem of power and legitimacy through the concept of an elite political subculture was that it implicitly identified a new role for a behaviorally oriented political science. If, as Key believed, the success of democracy rested in the hands of its political elites, it was essential that they be made aware of the true function of mass opinion in the modern democratic order and the role they played in mediating between it and the specific policy outputs of the state. And what would be better able to teach them about these matters than the political science discipline?

This theme of the political role of a behaviorally oriented political science took on central importance in Key's last original work, *The Responsible Electorate*. Indeed, his entire argument about the rationality of the electorate was predicated on the belief that empirical theories of voting behavior raised fundamental questions about the nature of popular democracy, and consequently played a major role in shaping leaders' perceptions of themselves, of public opinion, and of the role each played in the American political system. For Key, theories of voting behavior were important not because of their effects on voters, who were rarely aware of them, but because of their effects "both politically and in reality" on the political elite. As Key explained: "If leaders believe the route to victory is by projection of images and cultivation of styles rather than by advocacy of policies to cope with the problems of the country, they will project images and cultivate styles to the neglect of the substance of politics. They will abdicate their prime function in a democratic system, which amounts in essence, to the assumption of the risk of trying to persuade us to lift ourselves by our bootstraps."[41] In essence, while the fate of democracy might rest in the hands of its democratically committed political elite, the fate of this elite was inextricably linked to that of an evolving behavioral science of politics.

Public Opinion and American Democracy and *The Responsible Electorate* were profound affirmations of Key's faith in democracy and his concern over the problems dealt with in the third tradition. Both works reflect his belief that the fundamental tension between power and legitimacy had been resolved in the existing political system. They also reveal his fear that the crisis of democratic theory brought about by the discoveries of advancing behavioral science could undermine the very institutions and processes that had made this reconciliation possible. Like his third tradition predecessors, Key believed that political science could now play an important role in maintaining an already existing American democratic state.

In many ways Key's work, particularly his later writings, reflects an optimism difficult to appreciate in retrospect. Despite the harsh realities behavioral science uncovered, Key never abandoned his belief in the givenness of American democracy. If the truth of American democracy was not readily accessible to the untrained eye, he believed that it could be revealed and explained by the highly skilled student of the political process. Key died in 1963, well before postbehavioral criticisms of behavioral political science and the existing political order had reached their zenith. He thus never came to question the political assumptions lying behind his empirical work or the fact that his empirical theories about American democracy might be as much an apology for the existing structure of power as they were an explanation of its democratic character. Unlike many of his successors, Key never broke faith with the political system he studied throughout his career, the system he sought to preserve and protect through an advancing behavioral science of politics.

The Behavioralism of David Truman

The career of David Truman paralleled that of V. O. Key. Truman was born on June 1, 1913, in Evanston, Illinois. He received his B.A. from the University of Massachusetts–Amherst in 1935 and his M.A. and Ph.D. from the University of Chicago in 1936 and 1939, respectively. During the war, he served as an analyst for the Foreign Broadcast Intelligence Service, as an assistant head for the Division of Program Surveys in the Department of Agriculture, and as the deputy chief of the Morale Division of the U.S. Strategic Bombing Survey in the Pacific. Truman was a faculty member at Bennington College, Cornell University, Harvard University, Williams College, and Columbia University. In addition, he served as dean of Columbia College from 1962 to 1967, as vice president and provost of Columbia University from 1967 to 1969, and as president of Mount Holyoke College in the early 1970s.

While Truman was not as prolific as Key, his impact on the development of postwar political science was enormous. Two of his works, *The Governmental Process* (1951) and *The Congressional Party* (1959), were major contributions to the behavioral literature that helped to redefine the way in which political scientists studied American political institutions in the 1950s. Just as important, Truman worked tirelessly through a host of professional activities to impress a behavioral perspective on the discipline as a whole. In the 1940s he served on the staff of the SSRC's Committee on the Analysis of Pre-election Polls and Forecasts. Throughout the 1950s he chaired the SSRC's Committee on Political Behavior. Finally, in the 1960s he was president of the APSA (1964–1965), a vice president of the American Association for the Advancement of Science (1967), and a member of the SSRC's board of directors

Truman was a paradigmatic example of the professionally oriented behavioral political scientist of the 1950s. Above all he was committed to the scientific advancement of the discipline. However, the scientific orientation and political concerns found in Truman's work differed sharply from those found in Merriam's and Lasswell's work. For Truman, as for Key, facts about political behavior were not the raw data on which a democratization of American institutions was to be based. They were instead the foundations on which a pure science of the political process was to be built. Similarly, Truman, like Key, believed that the political processes found in the United States effectively had resolved the tension between political power and democratic legitimacy. From Truman's perspective, the political role of behavioral science in the postwar world was not to build new political institutions or to reform old ones; rather, it was to provide political elites with an objective scientific understanding of the way American democracy actually worked. With such insight, elites would know how to maintain the system into the foreseeable future.

That similar scientific and political imperatives are found in the work of Truman and Key is not by chance. Both men were reacting to common disciplinary and political developments. They drew heavily on each other's work for information and inspiration. Truman's *The Governmental Process* owed a large intellectual debt to Key's *Politics, Parties and Pressure Groups* and *Southern Politics*. Conversely, the arguments that Key developed about an elite political subculture in *Public Opinion and American Democracy* were drawn directly from *The Governmental Process*. Whatever the similarities, however, the two men's work had one important difference: Underlying much of Truman's work was a pessimism about democracy's future foreign to most of Key's work. While Truman accepted the givenness of American democracy, he focused a considerable amount of attention on ominous tendencies that threatened to undermine the delicately structured political processes found in pluralist America. The cold war combined with a seeming exhaustion of energy to create worries about the future. Whether America's decision-making processes could continue to respond effectively and democratically to contemporary political and economic problems was questionable.

Truman's concern over the impending crisis of American democracy in the 1950s and 1960s did not cause him to lose faith in the existing political system. Nor did it lead him to abandon the scientific or political imperatives built into postwar behavioral political science. As his concern over the crisis of democracy increased in the late 1950s and early 1960s, his commitment to the behavioral study of politics and the political imperatives built into it only mounted. Like Key, Truman believed that for American democracy to survive, it would have to be understood first, defended—or perhaps reformed—only second. While the fate of the Republic might rest in the hands of its guardian elites, their political consciousness, and thus their ability to act decisively on behalf of democratic values, was tied directly to the teachings of a behavioral science of politics.

From Reformism to Behavioralism

The reformist orientation found in Merriam's and Lasswell's work heavily influenced Truman's early work. For the youthful Truman, as for Merriam and Lasswell, a behaviorally oriented political science was seen to be a practical vehicle through which the modern centralized state could democratize itself. His Ph.D. dissertation, published in 1940 under the title *Administrative Decentralization*, addressed a problem rooted firmly in the traditional concerns of prewar political science.[42] How could the gap that had emerged between the people and the centralized state be bridged without abandoning either popular control or administrative efficiency? According to Truman, the answer lay in the proper form of administrative organization. By studying the behavioral reality lying behind the Chicago field offices of the U.S. Department of Agriculture, he tried to show that the solution to the problem of popular control over the modern state did not lie in the rejection of concentrated power or centralized policy making. Echoing Merriam, Truman saw hope ". . . in complementing this concentration with an administrative decentralization which will keep the program sensitive to the demands and the criticisms of those whose consent is central to its success."[43]

A similar reformist orientation can be seen in Truman's 1945 article, "Public Opinion as a Tool of Public Administration." According to Truman, public opinion research potentially was a valuable means for bringing increasingly "generalized, centralized, and remote" governmental administration back into contact "with the wisdom and ingenuity of the ordinary citizen."[44] Not only could research give administrators a better understanding of what could be done, but it also could provide them with a better appreciation of what the people believed should be done. Public opinion research was, in short, an ideal vehicle for democratizing the state. Too bad that many public officials did not yet recognize it.

During the late 1940s, Truman's work underwent a distinct transformation. As he became more deeply involved in the SSRC and the burgeoning behavioral movement in the social sciences, he gradually abandoned his commitment to a political science geared toward political reform. Like other postwar behavioralists, Truman reached the conclusion that the reformist orientation found in earlier political science had prevented the emergence of a true science of the political process. By neglecting to develop empirical theory in any meaningful sense, earlier political scientists had failed to take their science beyond raw empiricism. Postwar behavioralism, on the other hand, represented to Truman an attempt to develop an objective science of politics based on the methods of inquiry found in the natural sciences. Its ultimate goal was not political reform, but ". . . the development of a science of the political process, logically complete within itself."[45]

Despite his commitment to the behavioral revolution, Truman's understanding of its significance to political science differed from other behavioralists in several important ways. Truman believed that the application to political science of developments in the behavioral sciences had intrinsic limits. The center of gravity for behavioral science was the individual. In contrast, political science was centered on the institution.[46] While behavioralism could lead to a reworking and an extension of all the conventional fields of political science in which the investigator was concerned with processes, it could never completely displace or replace political science per se. More important, Truman recognized that despite the neopositivistic thrust of behavioralism, political values continued to play an important role in systematic political research. To be sure, behavioralists were not particularly concerned with how citizens ought to act. But they were interested in how values affected individual behavior.[47] In addition, Truman recognized that the values of the investigator in political behavior research played an important role in the selection of topics and lines of inquiry even when the immediate object was to test an objectively stated hypothesis. Thus, much like Key,

Truman rejected the idea that a behaviorally oriented political science could or should be unconcerned about problems that confronted the body politic. "Presumably," argued Truman, "a major reason for any inquiry into political behavior is to discover uniformities, and through discovering them to be better able to indicate the consequences of such patterns and of public policy, existing or proposed, for the maintenance or development of a preferred system of political values."[48]

Truman's interest in using political science to maintain or develop "a preferred system of political values" was no passing concern. It informed both his major contributions to the political science literature in the 1950s, *The Governmental Process* and *The Congressional Party*. Like Key, Truman believed that the institutional mechanisms that had emerged in twentieth-century American politics had largely resolved the tension between the exercise of state power and the demands generated by political participation. But the rise of presidential government, the decline of Congress, the growth of bureaucratic government, and the emergence of powerful interest groups also had sparked a debate over whether something should be done to modernize (and, according to some, to democratize) existing decision-making arrangements. Should Congress be restored to a central role in the policy-making process? Should the political system be restructured along the lines laid down by advocates of responsible party government? Or, should nothing be done at all? From Truman's perspective, what was striking about this debate was that few participants understood how contemporary democratic institutions actually operated or what the real problems were that threatened to undermine either their efficiency or their democratic legitimacy. He noted in *The Congressional Party*: "Before one can arrive at a defensible judgment of the proper place of the Congress in the political scheme of things and before one can estimate with any degree of confidence the probable consequences of various proposals for change, a clear conception of the actual place of the legislature and of the roles of the congressional parties is essential. In the realm of politics, as in other complex phases of the society, what might be is inevitably, if only in part, a function of what is."[49]

The larger political concerns embodied in Truman's science echoed those found in Key's work. The political task of the discipline was to offer leaders an understanding of how existing political processes actually operated, to show them how such processes perpetuated traditional democratic values, and to provide them with an insight into the problems and crises that threatened the future stability of existing democratic arrangements. While behavioralism thus was not envisioned to be the cutting edge of a great middle-class rebellion or even the tool of institutional reformers who sought to build a democratic state, it was perceived to have an important political role to play in the troubled postwar world. For Truman, as for Key, behavioral science was to be the educator of a guardian elite who protected and preserved the values embodied in the existing democratic system.

Pluralist Democracy

Truman's most systematic attempt to use behavioralism to reorient the way in which political scientists and political elites thought about American democracy is found in *The Governmental Process*, first published in 1951. On one level, Truman's concern in *The Governmental Process* was to criticize formal institutional approaches to the study of American politics from a behavioral perspective. "Essentially," noted Truman, "the book is an effort to take the concept of group, especially the interest or 'pressure group,' as a primary unit of analysis, and to examine patterns of action on the governmental scene in such terms."[50] On another level, the book went beyond a mere description of the role of interest groups in American politics and attempted "to account for and to indicate the necessary conditions for the long-term survival of the system in the context of interest group conflict."[51] *The Governmental Process* thus tied together Truman's interest in explaining why existing political processes in America were democratic with his interest in understanding how such processes might survive in the threatening postwar world. As was the case with Key, Truman did not seek to use empirical theory as a way to criticize or expose contradictions and injustices in the liberal democratic order. By definition, empirical reality was democracy, and the task was to study the conditions for its preservation and survival.

The Governmental Process is widely remembered for its development of the group model Bentley supposedly originated in *The Process of Government*. What is remarkable about the book, however, is not the use it makes of Bentley's conceptions of group activity, but rather how far Truman departs from them. As noted in chapter 3, Bentley believed that the goal of scientific description was to rid itself of all "soul stuff." He sought to explain all social action in terms of the observable activities of interacting individuals at a certain moment in time. The group concept inevitably presented Bentley with enormous methodological difficulties. It was, at best, a halfway house on the road to true scientific description. Truman, on the other hand, was interested primarily in understanding political institutions in terms of the interaction among groups. Large corporate groups, such as the American Federation of Labor or the American Farm Bureau Federation, were not looked at in terms of the observable behavior of interacting individuals. They were analyzed in terms of their *representation* of the interests of individuals not directly involved in a specific interaction. Similarly, government institutions and procedures, such as formal congressional hearings, were conceptualized as representing largely unorganized interests or "the rules of the game" in a democratic system. In his attempt to explain the group basis of politics in America, Truman thus reintroduced much of the "soul stuff" which Bentley had sought to expunge from a scientific analysis.

We emphasize these differences between *The Process of Government* and *The Governmental Process* not because they highlight Truman's sloppy use of Bentley. One may well believe that the misuse of Bentley was not only inevitable, but virtuous. What is important is that by emphasizing how Truman reintroduced "soul stuff" into his work, one can appreciate the way in which his behavioralism went beyond the critical muckraking orientation found in Bentley's writings. Far from providing an objective and complete *description* of a corrupted politics of privilege, Truman painted in broad strokes an explanation of how the group process reconciled political tensions. Truman's reintroduction of "soul stuff" into the study of the governmental process represented the means by which Bentley's tool was reshaped into a scientific weapon in defense of the existing political order. His analysis showed why the rise of powerful interests in American society was not necessarily a threat to traditional democratic values, and it explained how the existing process of group politics was only the latest development in the evolution of America's democratic culture.

There was a close connection between the new techniques made available by the behavioral revolution in political science and the general line of argument taken up in Truman's empirical theory. Survey research enabled Truman to make such notions as "unorganized interests," "potential groups," "overlapping membership," "rules of the game," and "cross-cutting cleavages" into operational concepts central to his theory. The very concept of an interest group was given its substantive meaning in the empirical reality revealed by behavioral techniques. As Truman explained, an interest group "refers to any group that, on the basis of one or more shared attitudes, makes certain claims upon other groups in the society for the establishment, maintenance, or enhancement of forms of behavior that are implied by shared attitudes." Survey research techniques thus permitted:

> the identification of various potential as well as existing interest groups. That is, it invites examination of an interest whether or not it is found at the moment as one of the characteristics of a particular organized group. . . . It is possible to examine interests that are not at a particular point in time the basis of interactions among individuals, but that may become such. Without the modern techniques for the measurement of attitude and opinion, this position would indeed be risky, since it would invite the error of ascribing an interest to individuals quite apart from any overt behavior they might display.[52]

In short, survey research provided Truman with the raw material needed to reinterpret the democratic values embodied in the existing political system.

Behavioralism also enabled Truman to analyze the functions that interest groups served in a modern democratic system without questioning the vitality of basic cultural norms about democracy. For example, with regard to whether interest groups could be considered "selfish," Truman concluded:

> In the first place such judgments have no value for a scientific understanding of government or the operation of society. Schematically, they represent nothing more than the existence of a conflicting interest, possibly, but not necessarily involving another group or groups. Judgments of this kind are and must be made by all citizens in their everyday life, but they are not properly a part of the systematic analysis of the social process. Secondly, many such political interest groups are from almost any point of view highly altruistic. One need only recall those groups that have risen to defend the basic guarantees of the American constitution, to improve the lot of the underprivileged, or to diffuse advantages stemming from a scientific advance.[53]

From Truman's behavioral orientation, scientific objectivity neatly dovetailed into his concern over explaining why and how the modern variant of American democracy functioned as best as could be expected.

For Truman, as for Key, a scientific analysis of the process of government was not meant to be an apology for the vast multiplication of special interest and organized groups that had come to dominate American politics. It was meant to be an objective reinterpretation of the American democratic experience in light of the evidence uncovered by modern behavioral techniques. While scientific analysis refused to consider the vitality of those values underlying the governmental process, it did provide a perspective for recognizing how "the pursuit of organized interest groups may produce a situation of such chaos and indecision that representative government and its values may somehow be lost." [54]

The final chapter of *The Governmental Process* highlighted Truman's concern over the long-term survival of pluralist democracy in America. The success of the contemporary political system, argued Truman, testified to the effectiveness of interest group politics. But he cautioned that this success did not justify the projection of the present equilibrium into the future. Ominous developments in the existing political system potentially contributed to the growth of "morbific politics."[55] In the future, Truman explained:

The processes through which unorganized interests restrain the activities of organized groups may not become operative in time to avert serious crisis. Potential groups may remain latent as a result of deficiencies in the means of communication. The claims of both organized and unorganized interests may assume an explosive character as a result of restraints upon the ability to organize, in consequence of the rigidity in the established patterns of access, and as an outgrowth of delay and inaction made possible by the diffusion of lines of access to governmental decisions. The frustration of group claims may be dangerously prolonged and the bitterness of group conflict may be intensified through class interpretations of the "rules of the game." Similarly, the expectations of groups emerging out of the less privileged segments of society may be poorly represented or dangerously frustrated in consequence of the concentration of, and privileged access of, organized groups among persons of higher status.[56]

Significantly, Truman did not conclude this line of reasoning with a call for a general restructuring of the governmental or constitutional system. He was convinced that any changes that would take place in the basic relationships that characterized the American governmental process would be of necessity, "gradual, slight, and almost imperceptible."[57] The great political task facing the nation and, as a result, facing political science as well, was the perpetuation of a viable pluralist democracy by maintaining the conditions under which a widespread understanding and appreciation of the system as a whole could exist. Effectively what this meant was that "the 'rules of the game' had to remain meaningful guides to action, meaningful in the sense that acceptance of them is associated with some minimal recognition of group claims. In the loss of such meanings lies the seeds of the whirlwind."[58]

Truman's notion of "the rules of the game" rings of Alexis de Tocqueville's democratic morality, but with one vital distinction. Tocqueville spoke of substantive manners and morals as being the foundation of all democratic principles in American society. Truman, in contrast, conceptualized the rules of the game in largely procedural terms. Gone was the earlier concern for civic education as a means of instilling virtue in citizens. If the breakdown of pluralist democracy was to come, it would be a failure of procedures and not of people. In a sense, the only democratic virtue about which Truman was concerned was instrumental loyalty to procedures.[59]

Maintenance of procedures was not to be trusted to citizens, but to enlightened political elites that were capable of rising up and protecting the rules of the game when threatened by either inertia or by organized interests actively opposed to them. Elites, like other members of society, belonged to "potential interest groups." If they were inculcated with a true understanding of how pluralist democracy worked, Truman believed that they could be counted on to represent such interests, even if such interests failed to mobilize in response to a threat either to themselves or the system as a whole. An educated elite represented an element of dynamic stability within the pluralist system. Their guardianship of the rules of the game would guarantee a basic consensus over the rules governing the pluralist political system and enable the system to adapt itself gradually to meet the challenges and crises of the postwar era.

The Seeds of the Whirlwind

Truman's concern over the future of pluralist democracy mounted in the decade following the publication of *The Governmental Process*. In articles published in 1959 and 1962, he amplified his fear that unless the elite became aware of its role in the pluralist system, destruction was imminent.[60] According to Truman, the American political system had been subject to a series of recurrent, almost chronic challenges since World War II. Soviet expansionism, the fall of China, and the *Sputnik* crisis had raised questions about whether the American political system could respond effectively to international challenges. The recurrent problems of urban decay, racism, and class stratification, in turn, raised questions about whether pluralist democracy possessed the political capacity to solve inescapable, but ill-recognized domestic challenges. Despite the seriousness of these problems, Truman believed that the real dangers facing the system lay less in the challenges than in the system's responses to them. The fundamental danger confronting the system was that ". . . of self-destruction, the danger that our reactions to frustrating and unexpected events will be so inappropriate to reality and their consequences so inadequately perceived that . . . we may destroy the democratic system by which we live."[61]

The rise of McCarthyism was particularly illustrative of the crisis Truman believed had confronted American democracy since World War II. As Truman understood it, the immediate challenge of McCarthyism was not in the substance of its claims, but in its radical denial of due process of law. McCarthyism ultimately represented an "ominous and diagnostic example" of the failure by elites, particularly nongovernmental elites, to resist an assault on the rules of the game by antidemocratic forces.[62]

Despite his concern over the elite's failure to respond effectively to the challenges of McCarthyism, Truman refused to modify his understanding of the democratic nature of the pluralist system or the role that elites played in it. Much like Key, Truman remained convinced that the mass of ordinary citizens was incapable of responding to threats to the democratic system. The McCarthy episode only intensified his belief that only the actions of a politically conscious elite fully aware of its own strategic and essentially privileged position in the political system could save pluralist democracy from imminent destruction. In fact, McCarthyism was seen as a symptom of mass politics run amok, not a rejection of it, a foreboding of what would happen when elites became careless. The remedy: "Awareness," he reiterated, "could bring into the bargaining situation restraints going beyond the need to preserve independence of action and capable of containing the threats of fantasy politics. Simultaneously it could provide intelligent, informed support for central initiatives necessary to meet the challenges of the age."[63]

By the late 1960s Truman's hope that an enlightened elite would rise up to meet the challenges confronting America's pluralist system in an efficient yet democratic way had all but faded from view. The turmoil that accompanied the civil rights and antiwar movements confirmed his fears that America's representative institutions were neither infallible nor imperishable. In place of his call for elites to recognize the role that they played in a pluralist system, there emerged on Truman's part somber speculation on how different the character of American politics in the 1960s might have been had pluralist democracy been recognized for what it was. An "unacknowledged revolution" had taken place in the American political system since the New Deal. "Had it been acknowledged," lamented Truman, "and were it fully recognized even now, the likelihood of meeting contemporary challenges constructively and within the system might be greater, and general confidence in the adaptive capacities of the system might be stronger."[64] The failure of elites to understand the crucial role they played in a pluralist system was a direct indication of the failure of Truman's behavioral political science to meet its larger political objectives in the troubled postwar era.

Reality Destroys Realism

The behavioral era marked a major watershed in the history of the third tradition. For the first time, the professional and disciplinary concerns of third tradition writers came to dominate more explicitly political concerns. Behavioralists such as Key and Truman were dedicated before all else to the scientific advancement of the discipline. Their careers centered largely on an ongoing attempt to apply the methods and techniques of neopositivistic behavioral science to the study of politics. In spearheading the behavioral revolution in political science, behavioralists such as Key and Truman also were responsible for articulating a new political role for the discipline that differed strikingly from that found in the work of earlier third tradition writers. Behavioralists accepted the givenness of American democracy. Unlike their predecessors, they believed that the tension between state power and legitimacy had been resolved in large part by existing political arrangements. They feared, however, that few political elites fully understood the democratic nature of the modern pluralist system or the role that they played in it. This made pluralist democracy particularly vulnerable to challenges from within and without. For behavioralists such as Key and Truman, the political imperative confronting an objective science of politics was clear—educate elites about the secrets of the system they directed.

In retrospect, appreciating fully the optimism found in the behavioral literature of the 1950s and 1960s is difficult. Despite the harsh realities their science uncovered, behavioralists refused to abandon their beliefs that the American pluralist system was fundamentally democratic in nature. Much like their third tradition predecessors, behavioralists' faith in the redeeming role of science in politics remained unquestioned. Ultimately, the flaws of the pluralist heaven could be corrected, or at least made less severe, with the insights provided by a highly skilled discipline of political science.

By the mid-1960s, the behavioralist attempt to confront the crisis of pluralist democracy in the postwar world had run aground. As the discipline grew in numbers, and as the techniques and methods of behavioral science became more complex, men such as Key and Truman found themselves speaking to an isolated, professionalized discipline not always sympathetic to their larger political concerns. Ironically, as the concern over the failure of pluralist democracy mounted, the distance that separated behavioral political scientists from the real political world had increased enormously. American democracy continued to follow its own path of development whatever Key, Truman, or other behavioralists did or said.

The problem of audience was compounded by the fact that events in the real world began to raise serious questions about the validity as well as the usefulness of behavioralist interpretations of the American political experience. The civil rights and antiwar movements highlighted one basic fact about postwar politics that others, less committed than either Key or Truman to the givenness of American democracy, had recognized for years. The problem of reconciling the power of modern state institutions with democratic notions of legitimacy was far more than just a problem of democratic theory. It was ultimately a problem of democratic practice. People both inside and outside the university became painfully aware that pluralist democracy had failed to understand the true nature and workings of modern democracy in America because serious structural problems within the existing political order remained.

By the mid-1960s, the behavioral chapter in the history of the third tradition had drawn to a close. Younger political scientists launched a devastating methodological and political critique of the assumptions underlying behavioral political science. According to these postbehavioralists, people such as Key and Truman had failed to address the real problems built in to the American political system. Behavioralism had not provided an objective scientific understanding of the democratic nature of the American pluralist system. It only had provided a convoluted apology for an existing structure of power that was far from democratic. Out of their critique of the behavioral heaven, postbehavioralists forged a new chapter in the history of the third tradition, one in which many of the theories and concerns of prebehavioral political scientists returned with a vengeance.

6

The Eclipse of Unity

In hindsight, the quietism and complacency of much of behavioral political science appears as an anomaly in the discipline's history, an interlude rather abruptly ended by the rebirth of political conflicts and the rediscovery of the seamier aspects of American political life. Of course, there was always an undercurrent of anxiety in the writings of scholars who otherwise saw the "end of ideology" in an age of easy economic growth and assured political consensus. Lurking in the shadows were nameless and unpredictable "potential interest groups" whose entrance into the system might change the rules and substance of consensus politics. The specter of a garrison state also loomed, despite the faith men such as Truman and Key placed in benign elites. And even in the 1950s, scholars such as C. Wright Mills at least had to be addressed—did consensus mask coercion?

To mainstream political scientists of the 1950s, possible lapses from pluralism were much less disturbing than pluralists' political assumptions themselves. In a society of ceaseless change within boundaries, what if public purposes and choices had to be generated? Wasn't the very genius of American politics its singular ability to blunt fundamental conflicts? And couldn't this "genius" wind up as mindless drift? Didn't pluralism encourage too much skepticism about public authority since all "public policies" appeared as consequences of factional struggles among private interest groups?[1]

These fears were only undercurrents. For most political scientists, American pluralist democracy did seem to generate cohesion, strength, and power when it was necessary. In an otherwise dispersed and porous system, executive leadership from presidents to mayors seemingly could and did emerge and thrive at crucial moments. John Kennedy, with his call to "get America moving again," demonstrated that centrism need not be weakness and that dedication to public goals and the requirements of free world leadership could be met. Force of will, fused with technological mastery,

185

firm democratic sentiments, and compassion generated the appropriate public power to fend off real and imagined foes. Confrontations with the USSR in Cuba, plans to save Latin America, counterinsurgency in Vietnam, and American resolve to beat the Soviets to the moon were evidence that democratically sanctioned authority could and did have muscle. The New Frontier, the rediscovery of poverty as a remediable ill, and the sponsorship of civil rights showed how tolerant, judicious, and directed people such as Kennedy could be. The effective use of presidential power for a "government more energetic, a politics more viable," was the special province of the "president as expert."[2]

Pluralist understandings thus meshed dispersion and control, personal power and democracy, leaders and people. No wonder professionalism in political science came to mean the specialization that came with distance. The system was self-regulating, and scholarly distance became admiration from afar. As long as leaders maintained the formal means of access to the political system, the essential conditions of democratic life were said to be preserved.

Within a few short years in the mid-1960s, all the cherished virtues of American politics had become systematic vices. Racial riots in almost all major American cities seemed to show that "access" to the interest group system was not so easily obtained and that mere access was perhaps not all the "potential interest groups" sought. The presidency's virtues quickly had become that office's excesses. Sympathy for the "loneliness" of the "most powerful man in the world" somehow seemed out of place with secret bombings, growing body counts, and preemptive first strikes ordered from the situation room at the White House. The presidency as the power point of innovation and energy turned toward tyranny, and the governmental process seemed paralyzed in the fact of confrontation politics and daily revelations of the insulation and isolation of Johnson, Nixon, and their sycophant advisers. Odes to the limits of power in the pluralist state appeared more than ludicrous when confronted with Mayor Daley, Watergate plumbers, and a trigger-happy National Guard. Worse yet, the compassionate Great Society programs were backfiring. Granting access to new interest groups only seemed to politicize, enrage, and polarize, generating a white backlash to a kind of black radicalism that hardly could be encapsulated within the bureaucratic logic of federal programs.

The world now refused to act according to the descriptions and prescriptions of behavioral political science. The carefully studied and crafted complex of institutions and practices once deemed stable and just were now everywhere under challenge, and those challenges were almost never limited to the narrow issues that advocates of pluralism loved to study. Somewhat ominously, the crisis unleashed in the 1960s, 1970s, and 1980s was above all a crisis of authority, of morality, of fundamental purposes—a crisis that questioned cherished procedural definitions of democracy and the constitution of political authority.[3] And since the universities and their role in American life were a special focus of challenge and protest, it is hardly surprising that the nature of social and political science and their connections with the system of power and control became a particular focus of attack and criticism, both from students and from new dissenters in the academy itself.

The character of this intellectual turmoil within political science is the subject of this chapter. Extending roughly from the mid-1960s until the present, the "postbehavioral era" in political science is defined more by what it is against than by any common focus about the nature of political science or its relationship to the polity. Some would say that a healthy eclecticism now pervades the discipline and that such diversity is the accomplishment of the critics of pluralist theory. There is room enough for everyone in the discipline now, and there are seemingly enough "approaches," subfields, and ideologies to accommodate every possible endeavor, ranging from congressional roll call analysis to Marxian political economy, from descriptions of personnel decisions in suburban hospitals to studies of state building in the nineteenth century. In short, the response of political scientists to the collapse of pluralist theory in the polity has been to implement pluralist rules of the game within the discipline itself. Mathematical modelers, Soviet specialists, students of Hobbes, and a few radicals—each group possesses its own disciplinary interest groups, complete with journals, panels, and accommodating letters from friendly fellow specialists during tenure decisions. Complaints about the incomprehensibility of *American Political Science Review* articles are easily met through "legitimating access." Once in a while, an article on Hobbes, Marx, Machiavelli, or even Habermas still appears. To those moderns who write and work as political scientists in the 1970s and 1980s, the fragmentation of the discipline may be justifiable, even welcome, considering the alternatives. But understanding what this passage from intellectual unity to diversity and fragmentation signals, in light of the assumptions, concepts, and hopes that justified and informed political science's emergence and growth in America, is worthwhile.

First and foremost, the central assumption and basic hope of at least four generations of political scientists—the ability and capacity of the American polity to fuse the institutional logic of control and power with the conscious aspirations and participation of democratic citizens—have receded as a promise of political science and as a focus of political research. On the one hand, both the faith and the focus guiding the American science of politics have given way to hyperspecialization, resulting in the neglect of major political issues and questions. On the other hand, scholars have begun to explore questions and ideas that challenge the assumptions and political methods of third tradition political science. If the sciences of men such as Ward, Wilson, and Merriam meant anything, then they rested on the assumption that the systematic, organized pursuit of knowledge in America would help the polity realize their liberal-Progressive vision. Democracy and capitalism, state and society, political power and democratic participation were not contradictions, but potential complements in a polity informed by scientific knowledge. But the present eclecticism and fragmentation of postbehavioral political science symbolizes the collapse of one of the major intellectual supports for American liberal Progressivism. The optimism of the past can no longer legitimately be sustained.

Simultaneously, the outside audience for political science has narrowed and sometimes even disappeared, even though dissenters within political science call for "relevance." If the American science of politics formed and grew with the expectation and hope of winning the attention and deference of a mass public and enlightened, progressive elites, the present state of the discipline would indicate that the organization of intellectuals has, to paraphrase a recent work, "triumphed over its functions." Political science is now an institution, not a crusade.

If these observations are true for the postbehavioral present, they are even more ironic considering the political and intellectual approaches of the postbehavioral "movement" of the mid-1960s. Indeed, postbehavioral political science at its origins recalled just about all the themes that we have associated with third tradition political science. The search for new connections with reform publics, the demand for relevance in research, the critical yet hopeful orientation of a new science, the concern for crisis in the political system—all echoed bygone concerns. The postbehavioral period is not the first time intentions have diverged from results in the discipline's history, but it may be the last time that efforts to reform political science in the old ways are attempted at all. For in the journey from the mid-1960s to the present, the effort to bring the profession back to a science of and for politics has resulted in an ironic twist. Third tradition political scientists now constitute a subfield within a minority within a discipline increasingly engaged in talking to itself. These demands for relevance—for the revival of a critical political science—have seemingly only splintered the discipline, prompting a great deal of confusion about the common methods, purposes, and character of modern political science. This is an odd fate for an intellectual tendency whose major claims have been rooted in the utility of scientific explanations for political change. What happened?

We will not examine all, or even most, of the intellectual currents that have surfaced in political science since the mid-1960s, but rather the strange ways in which traditional concerns reemerged and then faded in the postbehavioral era. Two phases of this reemergence and collapse will be discussed. First, how did prominent postbehavioralists understand the American crisis of the 1960s and 1970s? Curiously, the postbehavioral analyses concentrated not so much on the polity's ills, but rather on the ills of behavioral methods in political science. Postbehavioral political thought replaced political analyses with analyses of political analysts, and transformed dissent into odd and sometimes arcane debates about the political science discipline itself. Second, what organizational form did the postbehavioral "mood" take? What new rapport between intellectuals and society was sought? Oddly, and in sharp contrast with earlier generations of third tradition thinkers, political science became relevant not by establishing a new relationship with political activists. Rather, most postbehavioralists sought an internal restructuring of the discipline itself. APSA reform came to be mistaken for political advocacy in the world at large. Agitation for a new politics was largely channeled into agitation for new professional identities and for a more extended discussion among political scientists of relevant political issues and themes. The Caucus for a New Political Science (CNPS), begun at the Chicago APSA meeting in 1967, was the organizational expression of this dissent. In their effort to reforge a new political science, CNPS members succeeded only in underscoring the contradictions between professional activity and political activism.

In the search for a "new" political science, many of the old political assumptions and hopes of pre–World War II political science returned. Claims about the necessity and utility of social scientific knowledge for the resolution of crises in the polity were once again heard, and in ways that echoed Ward's, Bentley's, and Beard's efforts. The works of Theodore Lowi and Walter Dean Burnham perhaps best crystallize the shift back to the hopes and assumptions of reform political science. But as the latter part of this chapter shows, Lowi and Burnham detail the continued elements of the polity's crisis only to highlight the impasse and stagnation of the American political system. Lowi and Burnham dash the hopes for a science of politics capable of providing the means for a reconciliation of a politics of institutional purpose, power, and republican virtue. This is so even as the two thinkers revive the intellectual categories and critical spirit of their third tradition predecessors. As the old assumptions and hopes, and constituencies, of liberal progressivism as a public philosophy recede, so have the intellectual supports for it eroded, perhaps beyond repair. Extended discussion of Lowi's and Burnham's intellectual endeavors is needed, but only after the more generalized temper of postbehavioralism is examined.[4]

Postbehavioralism and the Search for a New Politics

As its name suggests, postbehavioralism in political science represented a confession of the discipline's past sins, but displayed some confusion and not a little disagreement about the nature of the penance. In response to the tumultuous and unexpected events of the 1960s, postbehavioralism became a "dissenting" faction that included just about everybody.

Perhaps the clearest and most surprising shift in mood occurred among leading old-guard behavioralists themselves, although the "break" with the past has, in retrospect, not turned out to be as clean as it seemed at the time. Representative here is David Easton's 1969 APSA presidential address, "The New Revolution in Political Science," which singled out several characteristics of behavioralism for particular censure, while leaving unclear the route of revolutionary transformation. Once the spokesperson for political disengagement and the advocate of "systems theory," Easton now charged that the behavioral persuasion had served to "conceal the brute realities of politics." Worse, political science as usual had failed to predict—and thus had been caught unprepared for—the social and political upheavals of the 1960s. Easton's prospective "revolution" echoed the sentiments of Robert Lynd's tract of thirty years before, *Knowledge for What?*, which was the apparent source of Easton's mea culpa. According to Easton, political scientists now had to advance "outrageous hypotheses"; scientific knowledge had to be made more consumable for the purposes of informing political action by nonintellectuals.[5]

Others' moments of contrition followed Easton's lead. The problem was not the methods and approaches of behavioral political science, but rather the fact that scientists were not discussing issues of relevance to nonprofessionals. In 1974 APSA President Avery Leiserson informed his colleagues that the "new revolution" was perhaps best conceived as a counterreformation. Scientific behavioralists really had been revolutionaries, and the discipline had to return to its origins. The scientific orientation of Max Weber, Leiserson argued, had to be synthesized anew with the practical political orientation of Charles Merriam. Leiserson, however, lacked Weber's ambivalence and skepticism about the impact of social scientific knowledge on individual freedom. He remained true to the Progressive assumption that scientific revelations corresponded and ratified the "democratic will": "As we political scientists improve our professional habits and skills of analysis and communications with our fellow publicists, we help to increase the factual scientific component in public value controversies, and thereby the public's understanding of the reliance upon it. Upon that foundation may be built the road leading to that "politicizing of the masses" of our fellow citizens, upon which our collective capacity to clarify and exercise some choice over our common, human destiny depends."[6]

To others—generally younger scholars—the problems were not solely in the relevance or irrelevance of the science of politics. Theirs was an effort to rethink the link between the existing centers of political power and the dominant methods and modes of political science inquiry. Esoteric theories in themselves were not political science's problem, but rather the flawed epistemology and bias contained in the empiricist methods and fact-value dichotomies of behavioralist political science. This group of critics has been far more influential in the discipline's intellectual future because it tended at first to bridge the gap among students of comparative politics, political theory, and American politics. The essence of the critique provided enough

ammunition for all three, and even brought together, albeit only tempo-
rarily, a range of intellectuals with disparate interests and political views.[7]

Students of comparative politics, for instance, lamented the cultural
biases and engrained parochialism associated with the dominant literature on economic modernization in the Third World. Most if not all
literature in comparative politics falsely assumed that ideological politics and profound social and economic cleavages disappeared during
economic growth. Thereby this literature was said to ignore the political
conflicts accompanying capitalist industrialization and wrongly assumed
the exportability of pluralist-liberal conceptions of democracy to Third
World countries. In a world of national liberation struggles, class and
cultural protest in Western Europe, and potential Chiles, the cultural
biases of comparative political studies ensnared the discipline in sterile
and meaningless categories. Joseph LaPalombara, then as now hardly a
political radical, noted in 1966 that his field was plagued by an "excessive
empiricism" and an unquestioning belief in science, oblivious "to the extent
to which empirical observations can be colored by the very orientation of
values that one seeks to control in rigorous empirical research."[8]

Political theorists, long relegated to pariah status in a discipline gone
quantitative, attacked the behavioralists' reduction of political philosophy
to an ornament, a kind of avocation for those out of touch with reality.
Now, political theory was said to provide a needed explanation of the
eclipse of political consensus, precisely because behavioralists had
confused the practice of politics in the United States with the definition
of liberal democracy. In the pluralist heaven, the existing posed as the
only possible reality, and a narrow empiricism replaced critical reflection
on the defining qualities and dispositions of democratic life. Lane Davis
perhaps best captured this kind of general critique of apologetic behavioral
theory, proclaiming:

> The heart of classical democracy is moral purpose. It prescribes this
> purpose, then a general strategy for its fulfillment and finally various
> institutions through which this strategy can be carried into operation.
>
> Contemporary democracy begins with institutions—that set of
> institutions which realistically describe the essential features of the
> existing democratic political system. It moves from institutions to
> values, taking as democratic those values which are inherent in . . . or
> can be accommodated to . . . the given political institutions.[9]

But dissenting scholars of American politics were the most numerous and forthright in their attacks, reserving most of their criticisms for the behavioralist theory and American practice of pluralist democracy. Post-behavioralists generally began their case where David Truman's specter of "morbific politics" left off. The open and porous system pluralist thinkers described was now perceived as closed to the demands of political movements with broad constituencies and moral claims—the civil rights and antiwar movements became cases in point. Pluralist politics worked only insofar as it fragmented and compartmentalized demands for democracy and participation. It admitted into its circle only those willing to bargain around narrow, nonthreatening, usually material interests. It evaded questions of public purpose, law, and authority, and disguised the exercise of informal but real power by the narrowly based private governments of corporate America. Interest groups were successful only insofar as they were bureaucratically organized and dominated by elites.[10]

For many, the American political system thus was indeed pluralistic, but with results and consequences that only highlighted the exceptional, unique, and problem-ridden character of American political development. The very virtues of American pluralist practice had now become serious defects because pluralism's triumph eliminated necessary distinctions between public and private power. Pluralism justified the immersion of the American state in a swamp of narrow and self-interested factions, providing access to public resources and control over public policy to the very groups the American state was supposed to regulate. Pluralism, moreover, provided a flimsy and ultimately self-defeating basis for political legitimacy. Under its aegis, political parties became mere sums of limited interest groups, and citizenship was turned into a uniform and increasingly passive and cynical spectatorship of the "political game."[11]

Actually, this strain of postbehavioral thought shared much with the pluralist dogmas it questioned. Each agreed that the polity was indeed pluralist, but disagreed about pluralism's normative value. Some of the very attributes the behavioralist "theory" of democracy cherished—shifting, competing centers of power, the makeshift character of law and its implementation, the absence of ideological and class struggles in politics—became characteristics postbehavioralists regarded as ills. Competing centers of dispersed private and public power did not mean that power was not being exercised, only that the American state lacked a means by which to implement any overarching vision of the public interest.

Some postbehavioralist critics, recalling the work of Lester Ward, began to note the peculiarities of the American state in comparison to its European counterparts. Others, unconsciously recalling Arthur Bentley, uncovered the real "political process" only to show how it repressed and dispersed democratic energies. Once again, the absence of a common set of democratic values was linked to the decline of democratic citizenship. Wrenching social and economic inequalities were natural products of the absence of both.[12] The crisis of public authority in America, in this view, did not stem from the concentrated and centralized power elite at the top echelons of business, the state, and the military, but rather from the fragmentation and dispersal of power among private groups of all kinds.[13]

If this was the dominant critique postbehavioralists launched, still others disputed pluralism both as *datum* and as *desideratum*. The prosecution of the Vietnam War by the president and a small band of advisers—as well as the secret activities of the Central Intelligence Agency and the Federal Bureau of Investigation—seemed to indicate that state power was a bit more insulated and concentrated than either pluralist theory maintained or antipluralist studies lamented. If the state was but a "black box" that processed "social inputs" into "political outputs," how could the secret bombing of Cambodia be explained?

But for the most part, discovering the flaws in the pluralist heaven sufficed.[14] This critique of pluralist democracy seemed to carve out a political agenda and a sense of mission for reform political scientists. Discovering that pluralist democracy granted only limited access to the unorganized or unveiling the cozy relationship between bureaucracies and their corporate clienteles was hardly questioning the compatibility of capitalism and democracy as some political scientists would later do. Rather, the dominant postbehavioralist tracts were critical within boundaries. They seemed to revive the discipline's role as a shaper of political events and turned the discipline away from sophisticated justifications. As injustices were uncovered, the seamy side of American democracy explored, and an intellectual arsenal of critical studies compiled, political scientists hoped that abuses might be remedied, public power reconstructed, democratic citizenship revived. Muckraking once again might raise true democrats from their slumber.

Accompanying postbehavioral criticism was a firm belief that political science knowledge would show the way toward democratic redemption. Even as serious defects were revealed, no systematic "crisis" or "contradictions" beset the polity. Appeals to reason and informed political action made zero-sum choices unnecessary. Democratic life did not have to be constructed, but only rebuilt.

Indeed, as a form of critical consciousness returned in the 1960s and 1970s, so too did concerns about how the new political science might relate to the popular constituencies of reform politics. Recalling the halcyon days of the Progressive era, political scientists once again proclaimed their discipline to be the natural guide to responsible change. A reconstituted political science provided the basis for a revitalized democratic polity. Indeed, scholars such as Henry Kariel recalled Arthur Bentley's and John Dewey's process views to postulate "a new political scientist," a "literary artist" who would unveil the hitherto "hidden potentials" of political action in democratic society. Political scientists could unmask, just as Charles Beard did, in order to reveal an "open-ended process pregnant with potential and contingency," ready for active creation.[15]

Yet what did or could this concurrent search for new professional identities and political change actually mean? We have already seen that the designation of particular publics as carriers and consumers of political scientists' reform perspectives hardly originated with postbehavioralists such as Kariel. Indeed, the notion that science reveals abuses and potential sources for democratic revival is as old as the discipline itself. Ward had pinned his hopes on the Populists, Beard on the skilled working and middle classes, Merriam on democratically accountable experts, Truman on political subcultures and responsible elites.

What about the postbehavioralists? Again, a new professionalism desig- nated reform publics—the "unorganized" outside of the pluralist world. And this was, and is, a very wide section of the American population indeed. By the late 1960s, many had opted out of electoral politics or had taken to the streets. How, then, to communicate the "reform potential," the essen- tial flexibility of the democratic polity to those in the purgatory of pluralist heaven? The answers were not easy because every attempt to remold the polity seemed to wind up as an effort to reform the discipline itself. Postbe- havioralists, like their forebears, did not abandon professionalism for politics; rather, they asserted their politics through the profession, and in the process only reconfirmed their own insulation. The reform constituency of reform political science became other political scientists themselves. Reform politics became disciplinary politics, and the passion and energy of real politics raged through the discipline as if the APSA was the polity itself.[16]

This curious mode of professionalized dissent is best seen in the organizational expression of disciplinary rebellion, the Caucus for a New Political Science. Formed in 1967, the bylaws capture the aims and methods of politicized postbehavioralism: "Whereas the APSA . . . has consistently failed to study, in a radically critical spirit, either the great crises of the day or the inherent weakness of the American political system, be it resolved that this Caucus promote a new concern in the Association for our great social crisis. . . . Be it resolved that one of the primary concerns of the Caucus be to stimulate research in areas of political science that are of crucial importance and that have thus far been ignored."[17]

From its birth, the CNPS made great headway within the APSA, but notably not as a united intellectual movement or as a group of intellectuals seeking ties with a public outside the discipline itself. Indeed, CNPS's activities centered exclusively on the politics of political science itself. The hidden, and not so hidden, biases of the behavioralist-oriented APSA were rooted out, and calls for a "new" professionalism were heard. If behavioralists could not and did not explore the causes of war, poverty, and racism, then a new and broader objectivity would.[18]

With such limited goals, the CNPS could be judged a success. The CNPS succeeded in democratizing APSA procedures. It contested elections, established annual panels devoted to current issues, and established a new journal, *Politics and Society*, as an alternative to the often unreadable *American Political Science Review*.

But the very success of the CNPS in its quest for intradisciplinary reform in a way served to highlight the inherent weakness of the dominant strain in CNPS thinking. The disciplinary focus of reform unconsciously repeated some of the old dilemmas of political science history itself. Once again, revolt concerned with changing the modes by which intellectuals thought, acted, and communicated was converted into a debate about professional standards. Anger over the Vietnam War and social injustice was converted into debates about methodology, objectivity, and scholarly biases. In the words of one prestigious caucus member, by the late 1960s the CNPS was "converted into the Caucus for a New Political Science Association."[19]

In pluralist terminology, the CNPS might be said to have accepted the "rules of the game." In the process, the CNPS narrowed its goals to the concrete, material, and limited demands of an interest group within the discipline, trading the uncertainties of movement activity for a larger piece of the existing pie. And, just as in the political world, the rules of the game had a tendency to exclude or fragment broader demands and goals, or so dissenters from the caucus's piecemeal approach lamented. Absent from the caucus's efforts was the essential component of past efforts at political reform. Nowhere was a "reform public" designated. Seldom were bridges sought between intellectual inquiry and movement politics. Indeed, the bulk of the most prominent CNPS dissenters eschewed such connections between political science and active reform movements. In a peculiar way, the reform public singled out by third tradition political science became itself. Polemics, critiques, and political activity became an effort to educate and mobilize other professionals, or—at best—graduate and undergraduate students.

In the process, the dominant strain in CNPS thinking began to mistake debates about the organization of the political science profession for intellectual confrontations with the major sources of conflict and tension in the world outside. Alan Wolfe, one of the leading dissenters from this line in CNPS thinking, noted that those "who formed the Caucus cut themselves adrift from the dynamics of political change in America and thereby lost touch with reality."[20] The irony of postbehavioral dissent is thus in its fundamental self-deception, its essential obfuscation of the issues involved in making political science "relevant" again. Reform political science became relevant again, but only as a species of organizational revolt.[21]

The response of political science to a crisis in the polity thus became self-reflection on its own impotence in the polity. But could it have been otherwise?[22] Could the CNPS have transcended the disciplinary constraints that encapsulated it? In the 1970s, after all, political scientists became active again in a host of organizations that in some ways bridged the gap between scholarship and the polity. The American Enterprise Institute and the Institute for Policy Studies might serve as key, if ideologically opposite, models. Perhaps the CNPS's failing might be better understood as a failure of that variety of postbehavioralist thought that most closely repeated the constant preoccupations and assumptions of third tradition political science. The individual most closely linked to that fateful repetition is Theodore J. Lowi.

Theodore J. Lowi and the Science of Phantom Reform

The critical orientations of third tradition thinkers always stemmed from their assumption that the American political order was unique. Political life in America has been blessed by its avoidance of ideological extremes. The expansion of American state power had never provoked an insulated bureaucratic apparatus intent on repression and social control. Nor had popular democracy run amok and challenged liberal rules and procedures. But the American blessing was also its singular curse; the avoidance of nightmares is no excuse for the absence of visionary dreams. American fears of the state had led to the extreme dispersal and fragmentation of all forms of public authority. If private power in America was ubiquitous, state sovereignty decidedly was not. The practice of mass politics in America diluted popular energies that could and should generate definitive notions of the proper scope of public, as opposed to private, power. Madison's factions ruled, but hardly with benign results.

Theodore Lowi's work in a sense is yet another attempt to revive these older questions about the structure and ideology of public authority. Lowi punctures the myths that have disguised these structures in the behavioralist interlude. His break with the immediacy of the behavioralist past restates the third tradition's intellectual and political project, even as it extends that tradition's growing impasse. Yet Lowi's work deals with the failures of earlier generations of political scientists. Recapturing the orientation of prebehavioral political science now means confronting the evident failure of his political science forebears to obtain a fusion of state authority and popular power. This is a gigantic intellectual and political task because Lowi's work shares the hopes of his predecessors even as he confronts the intellectual limitations of a science of politics that continually disappointed those hopes.

The result has been a curious circularity in Lowi's work. He returns the discipline to the institutional formalism that his predecessors rejected in the hopes of building the modern democratic state that they so craved. This effort is informed by a political vision common to third tradition thought—Lowi's notion of "juridical democracy" well captures the sensibilities of four generations of political scientists. But there is only one problem with it. The more Lowi asserts the imperative and necessity of changes in the dominant public philosophy of modern American liberalism, the more Lowi's own descriptions appear to confirm the political system's fundamental incapacity to make such alterations. Lowi's research reveals intractability and rediscovers the nefarious consequences of America's retarded political development and dispersed and confused institutional arrangements. Yet within his science, the future transcendence of "interest group liberalism" cannot be envisioned—there are no "rational publics" to activate and Lowi's science discovers only the consequence of stasis rather than the fruitful elements of future productive change. Thus, Lowi's remedy—"juridical democracy"—appears as a utopian longing. Analysis and prescriptions are cleaved in a way that undermines the claims of either.

Lowi's work is striking for its continuity. Each successive study is an embellishment or an addition to a central and overriding indictment of interest group liberalism as theory and practice. Lowi's first book, *At the Pleasure of the Mayor*, explores a well-worn subject in American political science and sociology—the nature of political and economic power in the urban setting, in this instance, New York City.

Pluralist students of American politics always stressed the informality and accessibility of city governments to organized interest groups. No systematic impediments were said to stand in the way of those groups that organized. Only apathy prevented political efficacy.[23] Lowi reverses these pluralist assumptions. Governmental laws, policies, intentions, and institutions are said to structure the number and nature of interest group interactions. New York City government, for instance, is seen not just as an expression of an "equilibrium of forces." Governmental structures supply the access, incentives, and resources for the establishment of what Lowi calls "arenas of power." Autonomous tangles of interest groups and city bureaucracies are ceded the power and discretion to determine and implement so-called public policies. According to Lowi, New York City is governed not by a power elite of the wealthy, but rather by practices even more insidious because sanctified by a public philosophy stressing participation and accountability while denying them in practice. As practiced in New York City, interest group liberalism narrows eligible participants in politics to those with the material resources and limited demands of interest group organizations.

Lowi details how the actual practices of New York City government deny these very values. What he calls the sine qua non of city government—the collective responsibility of elected officeholders to the electorate—is disguised by a system that avoids authoritative public decisions and thus erodes democratic values themselves. There is a certain irony in the rise of this kind of interest group liberal politics because it worsens the disease it was designed to cure. To Lowi, pluralist politics arose to replace the "corruption" of the political machine, but in so doing only created a monster. The political machine was at least in some sense accountable to party organizations and their large numbers of disciplined, ethnic voters. The old parties at least organized voters around ethnic passions and patronage, even if they horrified liberal Progressives. Interest group politics, in contrast, dulls passion and controversy.

Yet if the days of party machines are gone, what chances remain for the formation of a mass party system in America? The rise of modern industrial capitalism in twentieth-century America tended to create the need for the concentration and even centralization of governmental powers and functions, and the requirements of democratic life demand that policy-making capacities be subject to the control of the electorate. Yet Lowi finds that the unique feature of American politics is precisely its unconscious yet resolute immaturity, its adherence to processes and political habits that cleave the electorate along antiquated regional and ethnic lines. Expressing outmoded "social identifications" with ethnicity, place, or religion hardly corresponds to the real divisions and issues of an advanced industrial society, and irretrievably eliminates all hopes for a European-style party system.

In "Party, Policy, and Constitution in America," Lowi pinpoints the unique and apparently permanent traits of American political life. Political parties, he asserts, historically perform an exclusively "constituent" function in the United States. They are decidedly not organizations devoted to policy making, nor do they reflect broad popular mandates for defined programs and ideologies. Political parties in America, Lowi notes, survive precisely because they cleave voter organizations from the actual processes by which political decisions are made. The result: American politics, unlike America's society and economy, are frozen into "political response patterns . . . long after the original and most self-conscious bases for these patterns have been broken down."[24]

In precisely the epoch where new forms of bureaucratic control and mass democracy arose in Western Europe, America's political development was notable for the absence of either control or democracy. To Lowi, American political parties are not institutions that make policies. Their function is to preserve the illusion of popular accountability while administrative discretion triumphs in fact. The paradoxical result is a society and economy in continuous transformation, contained within a polity systematically resistant to modern democratic forms and political thought. Liberal self-deception about the "primacy of modern government" hides the real mastery of numerous functional groups and private governments. The political system's ability to avoid the firm exercise of state sovereignty and its obfuscation of all public questions helps to depoliticize the stresses and strains associated with the societies of advanced capitalism. As a result of our "constituent" party system, the mass electorate is not divided along the lines appropriate to advanced capitalism, but is fragmented into autonomous fiefdoms. In Lowi's words: "Party in America continues to make possible a popularly-based policy making process without very much directing the policy outcomes themselves. . . . Parties are indicative of the old-fashioned notion of higher authority that limits sovereignty and checks in very important ways the centralization and rationalization of governmental power."[25]

Echoing Woodrow Wilson, Charles Merriam, and liberal Progressive political science luminaries of the past, Lowi pinpoints the backwardness of American mass political organizations as the central cause of the dispersal of public authority characteristic of the American polity. Yet unlike his predecessors, Lowi traces the oddities and deficiencies of American political parties not to point to the necessity and potential of changing them, but only to highlight the reality and permanence of stasis. After all, he notes, if American political parties refused to become responsible even under the immense pressures the rise of industrial capitalism generated, they are even less likely to change now: "Any attempt to reform the parties toward policy responsibility would do violence to history and the modern political institutions," Lowi holds. Moreover, the unintentional if fortuitous function of archaic political parties in the United States has been precisely their ability to separate questions of the regime's legitimacy from the actual policy-making process. America's constituent parties, precisely because they do not organize voters around class issues and ideologies germane to actual government-society relations, "prevent conflicts over specific policies from becoming challenges to the legitimacy of the political institutions themselves."[26]

Praise for the resolutely ineffectual party system in America—and frank recognition of the party system's immunity to reform efforts—distinguishes Lowi from past generations of "responsible party" advocates. Yet with the responsible party palliative deemed impossible, what sources of democratic participation and control remain, or could emerge, in the contemporary polity? Even America's constituent parties have weakened with the growth of the welfare state, and, at least since World War II, the dominant interest group, liberal philosophy has expanded governmental functions only at the expense of crippling public power entirely. The growth of liberalism has only multiplied confusion about the proper uses and definitions of public power in America. Interest group liberals have generally avoided confronting such questions. To them, public policies are just broad "sentiments."

The End of Liberalism, Lowi's major work, is the most sustained analysis of the rising costs and penalties now exacted by interest group liberalism. The book's subtitle, *Ideology, Policy and the Crisis of Public Authority*, succinctly captures the essence of Lowi's larger interests. Questions of political choice have been obscured in American politics and democratic legitimacy has been eroded in the process. As the dominant public philosophy, interest group liberalism has helped to buy time for American political life. But by the 1960s the chickens came home to roost. The philosophy had led to ersatz "democratic" practices in which the power and authority of the state were parceled out to all organized private claimants. The result has been new structures of privilege, control, and lawmaking that have eclipsed the power of formal structures such as Congress and the presidency. The people and their institutions have ceded sovereignty itself. As Lowi explains: "Liberalism promotes popular decision making but derogates from the decisions so made by misapplying the notion of the implementation as well as the formulation of the policy. It derogates from the processes by treating all values in the process as equivalent interests. . . . Liberal practices reveal a basic disrespect for democracy. Liberal leaders do not wield the authority of democratic government with the resoluteness of men certain of the legitimacy of their positions, the integrity of their institutions or the justness of the programs they serve."[27]

In case after policy case, Lowi reveals the counterproductive impact of the liberal state's hapless expansion and dispersion. The regulation of business, the expansion of social welfare expenditures, and the implementation of the Supreme Court's desegregation decisions all reveal the negative effects of interest group liberalism. Housing policy, for instance, has only exacerbated segregation by giving discretion to city mayors and the real estate and construction interest groups that surround urban bureaucracies. Regulatory agencies have ceded their appropriate powers to the groups they are supposed to regulate. In some cases, public policies actually shape the groups that later influence them; far from being spontaneously formed, the interest group structure is often the outcome of public policy decisions that erode public power.

To Lowi, interest group liberalism can be criticized intellectually with the hope of convincing those that operate the political machinery that they have been deceiving themselves. Well-meaning public officials and officeholders, interest group liberals all, have been engaged in unconscious self-deception. If interest group liberal philosophy is simply a mistake, it therefore can be reversed by convincing its advocates that some alternative understanding of democratic government is possible and appropriate. Interest group liberal ideology can be argued out of existence by attacking the premises of pluralist democratic theory itself. In this way, a revived political science becomes the handmaiden of necessary reforms. Everyone will agree about the failure of interest group liberal practices once the cases are described. Lowi returns third tradition political science to muckraking. Political abuses need only be unearthed to catalyze change from aware and reasonable publics.

Indeed, the final chapter of *The End of Liberalism* offers an "alternative public philosophy" in which the essential spirit and goals of liberalism are maintained, even as its ambivalence and ambiguity about public authority are jettisoned. Lowi calls for "juridical democracy" to end the impotent informality of interest group liberalism, replacing it with what Lowi calls a "majority rule democracy limited only by the absolute requirement that government be run as closely as possible according to the way it says it is run."[28]

In a juridical democracy, law becomes more than broad grants of public authority to administrators and their clienteles; laws are now clear commands that emanate from lawmaking bodies and are executed by strong presidents. In juridical democracy, a sense of the appropriate size and power of the state informs public officeholders. They are decisive, knowing that they act with the mark of democratic legitimacy achieved through elections. Instead of confusing the delegation of public authority with providing open access to private groups, juridical democrats instead take the forms of democratic procedures seriously. The electoral process and public debate are the sources of the government's right to decide, command, and coerce. The notion that a weak and confused government is somehow a democratic one is ended, and with it the peculiar penetration of private interest groups into every realm of American governmental administration. "In a juridical democracy," Lowi asserts "chaos is preferable to a bad program." And bad programs presently abound because political officeholders—interest group liberals all—falsely confuse the exercise of strong public authority with autocracy, democracy with the erosion of the ability of the state to defend the public interest.[29]

No accident, then, that Lowi's juridical democracy revives all the older hopes for "democratic planning" and the "middle class counter-revolution" because his is a critical view of the practices of American government, even as it stresses the reasons why "rational" people can still serve the country well before fundamental challenges topple the government. Interest group liberalism has merely submerged long-simmering tensions, conflicts, and questions about the role of public authority in America. Juridical democracy, in contrast, appears as a nonrevolutionary public philosophy to which all "true democrats" might adhere. But for how long, and why?[30]

Just as each successive generation of political science reformers called for a new revolution in methods of study, so too does Lowi train his sights on political science itself. Since pluralism has been the major intellectual and ideological cause of present maladies, the alternative, juridical democracy, heralds a new dawn, an independent political science profession intent on the fusion of facts and values. Lowi constantly asserts that changes in political science alone cannot resolve the crisis of public authority, but he does view such changes in intellectual orientation as necessary preconditions for juridical democracy's rise. In the absence of an intellectual turnaround, "liberalism will continue to be the enemy rather than the friend of democracy."[31]

This kind of restatement of past political science hopes is only an unintentional and implicit one in Lowi's work. Little consolation is to be drawn from political science history by those who seek to repeat its failures. If a new political science is the prelude to political reform, then we might think that once and for all it would be that language to which all reasonable people might defer, just as Ward, Wilson, Bentley, Beard, Merriam, Lasswell, Key, and Truman hoped it would become. All these scholars designated reform publics, those classes and strata in political life that would most likely be recipients of political science knowledge. And their political activity as scholars was closely linked to perceptions of where in the polity political science would be received. Yet each successive generation learned hard lessons about these reform publics, and the 1970s presented no new reasons for optimism. Here, Lowi's work is newly symptomatic of an old impasse, for "juridical democracy" is an unlikely program for any "reform public" to adopt. Who, then, is the audience of Lowi's appeal for democratic formalism?

In *The End of Liberalism*'s final chapter, the doomed interest group liberal state suddenly becomes its own best therapist. Legislators are asked to rein in their lost sovereignty by passing good laws. The complex and interlocking "arenas of power" that typify the liberal state in America are asked to bend to a "new formalism," and the managers of the liberal state are asked to realize that they are in error. It is almost as if liberalism in America is some large, accidental, and entirely unnecessary development whose managers will remove once they read of its failings.[32]

Strangely, Lowi's hope that liberals will engage in self-transformation is consistent with his pessimistic assessment of the publics that might exist outside the liberal world. There is quite simply nowhere else to turn. Political parties, as seen earlier, are locked into a historical pattern that provides supports, albeit weak ones, for interest group liberalism. The voting public, in turn, is increasingly managed by media, consultants, advertising agencies, and private power—the obvious enemies of juridical democracy. In the final analysis, juridical democracy emerges as a sort of categorical imperative, a defiance of historical tendencies far too long in motion and now too difficult to overturn. Political scientists of the third tradition always stressed how social science paved the way to reform. In Lowi's work, research traces the impasse, as juridical democracy becomes an intellectually satisfying if politically unachievable "solution."

The social turmoil and political protest of the late 1960s seemed to provide some initial hope, at least for Lowi, that juridical democracy might be something else besides a nice idea. In the *Politics of Disorder*, Lowi proposes that political scientists turn their attention away from organized interest groups and concentrate rather on "social movements" among those "unrepresented" within the liberal state. If interest groups are overwhelmingly committed to the status quo, Lowi holds that movements definitively are not. As he explains: "When movements act on the government or any of its parts, there tends to be action with very little interaction—that is, very little bargaining. . . . The demands and activities of a movement tend to activate the mechanisms of formal decision-making."[33]

To Lowi, social movements maintain their autonomy and identity separate from the purse strings and influence of government administrators. They force democratic governments to live up to their own pretensions and formalisms. But they are, nonetheless, not very viable advocates of juridical democracy. Social movements in America, Lowi quickly concedes, nearly always deteriorate into the bargaining channels of pluralist politics. Either that or they doom themselves to eventual impotence as broad popular support for them erodes. Lowi might have added that any long-lasting or effective social movement could contradict interest group liberal practice, but it would not do so in the name of restoring the formalism of juridical democracy.

With reform from either "below" or "above" unlikely, if not impossible, juridical democracy appears more as an intellectual construct than as a political program. Yet Lowi's work has never turned a thought to *why* the liberal state is so intractable. Is it just the result of bad thinking, or does interest group liberal practice remain so secure because it is functional to the sustenance of the patterns of work, consumption, and behavior characteristic of liberal capitalism? Moreover, Lowi's work stops well short of pinpointing the possibility of radical "breaks" and "crises" in the political and economic system of Western societies. Instead, in the face of the system's continued impasse, Lowi turned inward in the 1970s. If the outside world did not listen, perhaps fellow professionals and university colleagues would. Just as previous generations sought shelter in revitalized methodologies, so too would Lowi begin to view the reform of political science as a surrogate for reform of the polity.[34]

One reform proposal made Lowi famous within the discipline. In the absence of new public policies, political science could develop new ways of understanding extant ones. Lowi proposed a new "typology" of public policies, one designed to promote a new understanding of the effects of governmental actions on political conflicts.[35] Lowi's "four systems of policy, politics and choice" reversed pluralist paradigms and assumptions about the political process. Public policies, Lowi asserted, shape and form the contexts and participants of political struggles and debates. Characterizing policies in one way or another would allow political scientists to uncover previously obscure points of power and control written into the liberal state's structure, as well as areas of overdelegation and sloppiness. To Lowi, examination of the political consequences of types of public policies might thereby widen and sharpen political debates. In the absence of juridical democracy, the excesses of liberalism still could be dissected by a new research agenda.

Lowi's new policy science recalls those of Lasswell and Merriam. Each carves out a special privileged role for political science in the polity. Yet by the 1970s there was no structured role for political science in the polity. Postbehavioralist political science's political aspirations are realized only through scientific investigation, not direct influence. In Lowi's words: "It should be the expertise of the political scientist to specify these kinds of political consequences, and a policy framework would be necessary to do this. This is science, yet it reaches to the very foundations of democratic politics and the public interest."[36]

Joining a host of predecessors, Lowi's policy science allows political scientists to feel important and autonomous again; his is a plea for the fusion of expertise, science, and political reform. Much the same could be said of Lowi's conception of the modern university, whose place in the configuration of the American technostructure was central to the political turmoil of the 1960s and early 1970s. In postbehavioral reformist fashion, Lowi sided with the student critics of the multiversity. Quisling-like service to outside political and business elites only hampered the independence of intellectual inquiry. But Lowi also had harsh words for *all* "service" concepts of the university, including ones proposed by radicals. Lowi saw "problem solving," whether for the Black Panthers or the State Department, as an attempt to intrude on the intellectual integrity of the university and the academic disciplines within it. Even calls for student representation on university governing bodies were as meddlesome as conservative boards of trustees, for each unduly "politicized" the university.

To Lowi, all such "service" ideas subjected intellectual inquiry to technocratic concerns and as such were inherently conservative. The university's central mission was to put itself in "constructive alienation" with society at large. If the university's valid role was to educate the generalist, its real mission today was to train specialists in service to private organizations.[37]

Lowi held that an autonomous and independent university would free political science from its unquestioned service to the liberal status quo. If the prospects for "juridical democracy" were dim, if relevant publics were either quiescent or misdirected, then the alternative languages, approaches, and prescriptions developed within Lowi's autonomous university once again became the first step in a very large educational mission indeed. Independent political scientists might teach social movements how not to become mere interest groups. Reminiscent of Charles Beard, Lowi appealed for the kind of intellectual autonomy that linked social science and political change, a tie denied by interest group liberal politics. Because spontaneous reform tendencies in the polity never got anywhere, a new political science could explain why—and suggest how—reforms might now occur.

Lowi's urgings for an autonomous university and an independent political science within it have increased as the polity's crisis deepens. In the second edition of *The End of Liberalism*, Lowi includes a new subtitle— *The Second Republic of the United States*. Government in the United States, Lowi holds, had undergone a crisis of public authority in the 1960s, and its last pretensions to legitimacy had eroded beyond repair. The de facto practices of the interest group liberal state of the 1960s had become the de jure regime of the late 1970s.[38] Interest group liberalism's triumph is the source of the regime's failure to capture energetic popular support or to construct needed political and administrative capacities. Political alienation abounds as public authority collapses. The Second Republic is a regime of systematic drift.

This hopeless situation spurs Lowi to call for "juridical democracy" with renewed fervor, even as workings of policies and politics in the "Second Republic" appear to preclude such alternatives. To Lowi cosmetic reforms merely deepen the crisis because "only a radical, organized constitutional revolt will succeed now where a sustained intellectual attack might have been sufficient." And for the present, Lowi holds, the prospects for such a revolt are bleak indeed, for the reality of impasse deadens plans for escape. The solution? In the absence of organized and effective opponents to the Second Republic, hopes for a "Third Republic" rest in what Lowi calls a "withdrawal from action sufficient for analysis of the way out of the current plight."[39] How or when such a "withdrawal" might culminate in a reform movement dedicated to the ideals of the Third Republic—the juridical democracy reminiscent of the progressivism of Bentley, Beard, Merriam, and others—are questions that remain unanswered. They simply cannot be addressed within the logic of Lowi's thought.

Nor can urgings for withdrawal into the university be taken too seriously, despite the good intentions with which they are made. By the 1970s the political science profession had already imposed on itself the isolation Lowi recommended if in ways he might lament. A survey Walter Roettger conducted for the APSA's journal *PS* revealed the peculiar plight of postbehavioral political scientists. Roettger discovered that Lowi was among the most prominent and esteemed members of the profession. But whatever Lowi's reputation *within* the discipline, Roettger also found that political science's notables were in no case ranked among the most prominent individuals in the American intellectual community as a whole. In fact, Roettger discovered that political scientists were notable only by their absence from such lists: "Matters of method and modeling are less likely to stir the souls of men [*sic*]," Roettger observed. He concluded by noting that disciplinary insularity might be desirable because "political scientists have managed to avoid raising (or exhuming) those vexatious substantive questions that could conceivably threaten the stability of the APS Association and the professionalization of its members."[40]

This kind of conclusion can hardly be comforting because Roettger seems to make oblivion and impotence into praiseworthy professionalism. If questions of relevance, audience, and political change are central to postbehavioralists such as Lowi, the discipline's insulation helps to entrap them. In Lowi's work and that of other postbehavioralists, an unbridgeable gap thus emerges between the actual plight of liberalism and their own inability to do much about it. This gap brings to a conclusion reform political science's most sincere aspirations and carefully worded justifications. The system of power associated with interest group liberalism is asked to become rational, and independent intellectuals ask the polity to become so. This is so even though the interest group liberal system is described as a tangle of self-sustaining parts whose interrelationships preclude any substantial alterations. After descriptions of impasse, appeals for intellectual and political leaps of faith ensue, even though breaks in the social, economic, and political coalitions supporting liberalism are perceived as unlikely. Lowi's theories about the practices of interest group liberalism appear to preclude developments toward juridical democracy, categorical imperatives aside.

If juridical democracy stands as the new liberal ideal, "scientific analysis" only details the retrograde and declining influence of political parties and social movements. Yet are the political aspirations and hopes of postbehavioralism just impractical? Are third tradition hopes only to be faulted for their utopianism? More than the reliance on professionalism and the recourse to scientific scholarship hinder Lowi's return to the discipline's origins. Lowi and third tradition scholars are not simply frustrated by the polity's nagging habit of ignoring political science's democratic delusions. Third tradition reformers have always been impressed by the perfectibility of the political system created at the Founding, and their analyses have always assumed the easy reformability of the political system, on the condition that misguided elites and democrats realize the error of their present practices. If Americans lack that "sense of the State," it is only because political elites and democratic movements have not lived up to their pretensions or their responsibilities. If radicals demand full democratization in patterns of work, consumption, and political participation, and political and economic managers respond negatively, each could learn that strong public authority and democratic political participation are not mutually incompatible opposites, but "potentially fruitful fusions of seeming contradictions" in Kariel's terms.

Promised here is a utopian realism. Conflicts about power are deemed unnecessary, even as their presence is ubiquitous. In Lowi's work, social and political contradictions become mere confusions and mistakes on which intellectual order can be imposed by professional scholars. If the models of work, consumption, and production consonant with advanced capitalism create a new threat to liberal democracy, if social movements in turn challenge liberal democracy, then each can nonetheless be understood through the teleological lens of third tradition political science. Fundamental conflicts between classes and strata can be reduced to unnecessary battles among the politically ignorant, soon to be informed by a common education. With Lowi's work, the compatibility of reform science and reform politics became the forced intellectual fusion of the latter with the former. The impossibility of building a proper democratic state is underscored, even as closing chapters assert its necessity. With the end of liberalism, political science becomes existential defiance.

The Critical Pessimism of Walter Dean Burnham

The work of Walter Dean Burnham brings third tradition political science to an end, even as it still employs the concepts and categories that made the people discussed in this book hopeful yet critical. The dominant images of American political life sustained since Ward and Wilson are primarily and potentially positive ones. To Burnham, they become symptoms of imminent crisis and permanent impasse. The oddities and peculiarities of American democratic life—which earlier American liberal Progressives saw as the raw material for a unique fusion of state power and democratic vivacity—become for Burnham the source of ominous, retrograde, and ultimately reactionary and authoritarian tendencies. Burnham's political science traces the dismemberment of the American political system, a dismemberment professionals observe and lament, but are powerless to halt. The liberal progressive science of politics halts with Burnham because he traces the historical erosion of the political, social, and economic preconditions that once sustained it. The democratic delusions of four generations of political science reformers end with Burnham's trenchant perception that a critical political science must move beyond liberalism. The assumption that "juridical democracy," or any other third tradition prescription, is possible, insofar as political science becomes more sophisticated, ends with Burnham's glum prognostications of a liberalism gone sour.[41] Burnham frames the American political dilemma in ways identical to his predecessors, but his findings only confirm the poverty of what he begins to call "political capitalism." Where science used to provide a curative, in Burnham's work science can only trace the zero-sum choices in American life, null choices that the likes of Merriam, Ward, Lasswell, and Key sought to define out of American political life.

How can it be said that Burnham "ends" liberal Progressive political science? Burnham's work begins with the most legitimate, even timeworn, concerns of third tradition scholarship, concerns typically postbehavioralist in orientation. His major work, *Critical Elections and the Mainsprings of American Politics*, contains themes and modes of analysis that Woodrow Wilson, Harold Gosnell, or V. O. Key would most certainly recognize. In the past, however liberal Progressive political scientists always saw potential fits between governmental structures and the mass electorate. In contrast, Burnham demonstrates why elections are increasingly blunt instruments by which conflicts are expressed or resolved in American political institutions.

Burnham finds that the gap between voters' frustrations and desires and the actual operation of the American state is historically rooted, systematically generated, and fundamentally irremediable within the limits of American political debate and dialogue as it has developed in this century. Burnham's theory of critical elections reverses the priorities of Key, Gosnell, and Wilson. America's history is said to be a legacy of "political nonevolution," of a chronic, systematic failure to translate the divisions capitalist industrialization created into political choices concerning the direction and content of public policies. The biggest datum about American politics, Burnham claims, is that the "constitution-making role of the American voter" has declined almost beyond recourse or repair. If critical elections like those of 1896 and 1932 were the safety valves by which a severely undeveloped political system had been brought back into a tenuous balance with the requirements of an advancing capitalist society and economy, Burnham traces the reasons why today a "critical election" is now impossible or unlikely.[42]

To Burnham, political stability since 1932 has been achieved only at the cost of a creeping authoritarianism, declining mass political participation in elections, and pronounced and systematic political drift. The periodic occurrence of "critical elections" in U.S. politics since the Founding showed spasms of health, however short, in the structures of American political democracy. Yet these democratic spasms only reveal how exceptional, even limited, political democracy has been in modern America. In the twentieth century, one of the key elements of modern liberal democracy—strong and organized political parties—has disappeared, severing the last fragile links between citizens and the constitution of political and economic power. Such "insulation of elites" is itself the product of past critical elections. The New Deal only delayed the continuing deterioration of partisan attachments among the mass electorate. The post–World War II period, characterized by an apolitical consensus around economic growth, the empire, and the sustenance of conservative social and cultural values, served to leave the formal electoral processes intact while draining them of substance. From the political science heaven of the 1950s, Burnham drops to political science hell. The modern system is said to be plagued by its incapacity to have a critical election, even though the social tensions in America surely need to be politically released. The disjuncture between the political system's structuring of political demands and the social needs and aspirations of ordinary people was, by the 1960s, unbridgeable. The biggest group in modern American politics is the politically impotent and alienated "party of non-voters."[43] In third tradition political science's terms, the situation Burnham describes is worse than a nightmare, for even a revival of the forms of democratic politics (such as Lowi suggested) requires that American politics relive periods of political development long since passed. But in the absence of a time machine, Burnham argues that politically organized Americans are frozen into a "Lockean cultural monolith." In the twentieth century, an ideology stressing the virtues of property rights, religion, acquisition, and privacy no longer supports the dispositions and behavior necessary for republican government.[44]

In past electoral studies, the weakness of American political parties was viewed only as a "problem" in an otherwise democratic society. In

Burnham's work, the decline of the electorate is not simply a problem, but rather an epitaph for liberal democracy. By the late twentieth century, the imperatives of corporate capitalism simply cannot be challenged through the electoral process. This is so even though such imperatives increasingly generate social disintegration, wars, anomie, consumerism, and intensifying social conflicts. As these pressures are generated, corporate capital is strong enough to obstruct potential challenges, but only at the cost of depoliticizing and scattering the forces of democratic participation. To Burnham, the 1960s revolts were spurts of potential democratic renewal, which insulated political institutions effectively blocked and blunted. "The task confronting it [the polity]," Burnham suggested, "now may be no less than the construction of instrumentalities of domestic sovereignty to limit individual freedom in the name of collective necessity."[45]

Such calls for the creation of public authority to limit private power are at least a century old, and a consistent refrain of political science thinking since the 1880s. But Burnham's warning is different because an analysis that perceived democratic popular support for such "instrumentalities of domestic sovereignty" had always accompanied past pleas. Burnham, in contrast, doubts that such reforms can occur democratically. By the 1960s, any Bentleyan "middle-class counter-revolution" or an upsurge of a "responsible electorate" would likely form a sense of the state at the expense of both a growing, "technologically obsolescent" underclass and working class, and through the repression of cultural dissenters—feminists, gays, minorities, and anti-imperialist intellectuals.[46]

To Burnham, America long ago missed a crucial stage in democratic development. In other nations, capitalist industrialization had spawned the political organization of working-class voters and intellectuals into modern social-democratic or socialist parties. In the United States, the absence of such a development created numerous social strata competing for the minimal benefits corporate capitalism offered. Without unified ideological and political challenges to the corporate state, in the absence of that working-class collectivism typical of Western Europe, American politics has remained stagnant and retarded. The forms of democratic procedure have survived only at the expense of depoliticizing the great mass of potentially left-wing voters. By the late 1960s, the war of powerless strata against other powerless strata only furthered the drift toward forthright authoritarianism because to Burnham politicization this late in history has only led to dual and equally undemocratic alternatives.

The first may involve the continued consolidation of a state apparatus centered in the executive branch of the federal government, mandated to enforce the ideology and policies deemed essential by the managers of the private economy. With the major decisions removed from popular control, any bureaucratic-corporate alliance could safely leave the smaller decisions to Congress, preserving the façade but not the structures of democratic rule. A continual quantitative and qualitative decline in voter participation in elections would only reinforce the growing gap between state power and citizens.

Burnham's second prospective scenario is even more frightening—instead of statism and subtle repression, a new "critical election" could pit a reactionary white middle class against the technologically obsolescent underclass and its minimal "entitlements" under the welfare state. Whichever of these two paths would be taken, Burnham concludes ominously that the "American political system is not likely to emerge unchanged from its ordeal."[47] Notable by their absence in each scenario, of course, are the "democratic reform publics" always designated by third tradition scholars as the essential supports for the continuation of liberal democracy. By the late 1960s, "reform publics" were the weakened victims of repression, the voiceless and politically alienated, or the reactionary defenders of cultural conformity and Lockean individualism.

In the last decade, Burnham's views have undergone substantial embellishment and not a few changes in methods, focus, and approach. But before discussing Burnham's recent commentary, it is worthwhile to mention the impact of his book on the political science profession itself.

Burnham's arguments were certainly not ignored. Indeed, the amount of praise, blame, and research they have sparked is something close to a cottage industry itself. The interesting aspect of the high volume of commentary, however, is not the way critics and supporters of Burnham's work took to debating the immense consequences of his argument for conventional American views of democracy. As is perhaps now predictable, the debate centered instead on the methodology and specifics of Burnham's study. At its highest reaches, the "critical elections debate" even resulted in the establishment of yet another subfield, founded with the profound task of deciding whether the 1964, 1968, or 1972 presidential elections were indeed "critical," "normal," "realigning," or none of the above. The greatest parlor game has, of course, been devoted to the 1980 Republican victory. In these academic debates, arguments about the relative merits of survey data versus aggregate data, the exact character of the 1896 election, or the effect of legal versus behavioral factors in the decline of voting participation raged with all the intensity and skill that fervent professionals could muster. Of course, the process of methodological squabbling did little to address the freshness or breadth of Burnham's arguments. Indeed, the debate became so abstruse that it indirectly helped to highlight the insularity of contemporary political science. In search of relevance, political scientists seemed to turn political controversy into subfields.[48]

Burnham himself became partial prey to internecine warfare. But by the late 1970s, the deepening economic crisis, the rise and rapid fall of Jimmy Carter, the landslide election of Ronald Reagan, and the subsequent efforts to demolish the remains of Great Society programs all seem to have pushed Burnham even further away from the niceties of liberal-progressive political science as it has developed in this country. Indeed, it might even be remarked that Burnham's career itself represents the conclusive end of the assumptions, questions, hopes, and mode of discourse once central in political science.[49]

Critical Elections was in many ways a traditional political scientist's book; its methods were rigorous and its language was replete with professional terms and tentative conclusions. But in 1982, Burnham wrote two commentaries on the 1980 election, signaling his passage away from the dominant concerns of third tradition political science. The language and outlook of neo-Marxian political economy replaced the caution of *Critical Elections*.

Totally absent are any residual hopes that the American polity can somehow be patched back together through halfway measures. In fact, Burnham's articles read like an obituary for what he refers to as the project of "political capitalism," the project of the New Deal Democratic Party. Pretenses about state benevolence and rhetoric about social harmony are now useless. Without economic growth, liberal capitalism is reduced to imposing austerity on those whose lives are already austere with vague promises made about future economic growth. Political capitalism's efforts to buy social peace through public expenditures have foundered on the necessity to achieve capitalist growth through imposed hardship and sacrifice on the working class and underclass.

With political capitalism on the wane, Burnham perceives the kinds of alternatives that third tradition intellectuals have always dreaded. The present crisis, Burnham asserts, affects every pillar of contemporary

American life, including the nation's economy, the economic empire, the state, and the cultural norms of American life. And at first glance, the nature of the present impasse appears to preclude the emergence of viable changes in any political direction.[50] If conventional wisdom dictates that political capitalism is dying, few alternatives are available to take its place.

The 1980 Republican victories are a case in point. Finally ideologues have been elected to office, and their policies have begun to dismantle the structures of political capitalism. But Burnham holds that the Right's victory is far from a "mandate," much less a critical election. With only 28 percent of the potential electorate, the 1980 Republican surge is evidently another symptom of "dealignment" rather than "realignment." Survey data indicate that only a small portion of this 28 percent were supporters of the ideology of the Republican right. More clearly, Reagan's victory was a repudiation of an intellectually bankrupt Democratic Party directed by the hapless Jimmy Carter. The Right succeeds in America only because there is no Left, and the former's victory has only accelerated what Burnham calls a "regime crisis"—the Right has made a frank trade-off favoring capital accumulation over political legitimacy. Accepting class conflict as natural and inevitable, Reagan's program "amounts to a one-sided declaration of class war on most of the American people." The Right, unlike the Democratic non-Left, recognizes that "political capitalism has achieved bankruptcy."[51]

Here, American uniqueness returns to haunt. Burnham holds to the belief that it is not the Right that is victorious, but the absence of a Left that can mobilize the huge "party of non-voters." The Democratic Party, sustainer of the liberal-individualist tradition, can play no role in formulating the needed democratic or socialist alternative to Reaganism. The extent of Democratic Party decomposition is so intensive as to remove it as an agency of any potential, future political realignment. As the major sponsor of political capitalism, the Democrats flounder when the capitalist economy no longer generates the surpluses necessary to buy off its dwindling constituencies. The Democratic Party symbolizes the American impasse. The historical absence of a Left today destroys political capitalism, excludes collective solutions to political capitalism's woes, and defaults to the Right. Because the Democratic Party has never been a Left, it is unlikely to become so now. With its doctrines of social harmony shattered, and its economic policies reduced to incoherence, the price to be paid is huge: "The Democratic fraction of the potential electorate continues to decline," leaving the narrowed electoral field to conquest by "the true believers of the capitalist gospel." Third tradition hopes are shattered with Burnham's simple statement that "you cannot get there from here in American politics if the direction is leftward, since the basis for a collective energizing left consciousness and will does not exist in this country. But you can if you are headed to the right, at least when the established order is in crisis and when there is wide agreement that it is not replacement but revitalization."[52]

With these straightforward remarks, Burnham passes from the concerns, theories, and assumptions that have been central to successive generations of political scientists. His analysis shows that the political and economic forces presently struggling to bolster state power do so only by sacrificing the values of democracy to the imperatives of cultural orthodoxy and capitalist accumulation. And their victory, ironically, strengthens the state apparatus only at the expense of insulating the state from the aspirations of the vast majority of the American people.

Should the scattered, unorganized, and largely politically silent social classes naturally supportive of mass democracy somehow arise, their political program and aspirations would no doubt go well beyond the platitudes of liberal progressive "political capitalism." Something as tame as the philosophy of juridical democracy would be an unlikely trumpet call for America's nonvoters. Burnham imagines a future crisis in which the time-honored liberal verities of American politics are finally shattered and the vision of potential political harmony achieved through a guiding political science is eclipsed. When the Right fails, we can anticipate "either some form of dictatorship to cope with the debacle," or the rise of a "socialist political movement on the ruins of—and extending far beyond, the Democratic Party."[53]

In this image of inevitable breakdown, Burnham ends one hundred years of democratic delusions. You just cannot get there from here in American politics if the "there" is power and legitimacy within the confines of corporate capitalism. Charles Merriam, rest in peace.

The Irony of Postbehavioralism

Postbehavioralism in political science was less a break with the past than it was a return to the politicized sciences of the pre–World War II years. The quietism, complacency, conservatism, and hyperfactualization of behavioralism provided a kind of interlude in political science history. The subsequent reintroduction of values, criticism, and relevance into most political studies bears more than a little similarity in design and execution to the intellectual projects of Ward, Wilson, Bentley, Beard, Merriam, and even Lasswell.

Postbehavioralists tried to go back. But to go back also meant having to deal with the intellectual and political failures of their reform predecessors, and worsening through repetition some of their most egregious errors. This time, history was repeated once too often to be seen as tragedy because postbehavioralist political studies tended to reveal postbehavioral politics as farce. As scientists, postbehavioralists traced the erosion of reasonable hopes for liberal Progressive revival. Either that, or they increasingly turned to subfields, respectable political science cul-de-sacs in which the semblance of academic community could be rekindled through the avoidance of disturbing questions. As advocates, postbehavioralists either retreated into intradisciplinary disputes as surrogates for politics, asserted political hopes that their own studies contradicted, or, like Burnham, waited for the apocalypse.

The postbehavioral plight is disturbing, but it is comprehensible given the understanding of American life long characteristic of third tradition political science. In a sense, third tradition intellectuals have gradually painted themselves into a corner; postbehavioralists have only helped finish the job. In search of a cosmopolitan, autonomous realm of public authority in America, they now wonder aloud about why this is an impossibility. In search of a reform public that could supply energy, support, and legitimacy to state authority, they have found only decomposing political parties and declining political participation.

Lowi's and Burnham's works end a century of liberal Progressive justifications for political science with the assertion that American politics are quite simply intractable. Even with interest group liberalism dying, the prospects for juridical democracy look even worse. Intellectual honesty perhaps requires Lowi to see juridical democracy only as a kind of categorical imperative rather than an ongoing political tendency. In the absence of a reform public, juridical democracy might as well be kept alive as an idea in academic circles, just as monks in the Dark Ages preserved Aristotle. But if juridical democracy is kept alive as a "value," what is left of the intellectual tradition that once sought to ground such values in the language of "facts" and the discipline of reality?

This question is implicitly being answered in the 1980s. And the answer seems to be—not much. As the political basis for even the enfeebled welfare state erodes under the imperatives of the corporate economy, so too has political science drifted—sometimes leftward, sometimes rightward, and sometimes to nowhere at all. Political science has not perished, but its major claims, purposes, and justifications have.

Conclusion
The End of the Third Tradition

Generally ignorant of their own history, successive generations of political scientists have not been particularly self-conscious as they have repeated past errors. Discredited analyses, in fact, are often trumpeted as the latest new discoveries. Consistent in the belief that theirs has been a cumulative enterprise, political scientists and their history are actually more prone to the ups and downs that can be associated with the cyclical view of history. Political scientists remember their ancestors, but they conveniently forget that their predecessors often ended their careers in frustration and disappointment.

Yet there is good reason today to think that political science in America is not about to relive its past as if it is embarked on a new and ultimately fulfilling common enterprise. The continuity of concerns, visions, and identities that have characterized the century-long history now seems to have come to an end. This, of course, does not mean that political science itself has come to an end, but rather that the kind of tenuous harmony and common intentions of the past have slowly if steadily eroded. The irony, of course, is that older political science has perished with neither a bang nor a whimper, but has simply faded away without even much recognition of its passing. Not really knowing their past, political scientists have few instruments to construct a common, if radically different, future. That is not to say that there is not a future of any sort, for modern political science is most undeniably an ongoing enterprise of some kind. Political scientists have offices at universities and colleges. Seminars are held, graduate students are produced, research is conducted, journals are published, national and regional conventions are convened. But what Brian Barry has said of political philosophy within political science is perhaps true of the profession as a whole. Barry is bothered by the "nightmarish feeling that the literature has taken off as an independent life and now carries on like the broomstick bewitched by the sorcerer's apprentice."[1]

Barry's is an old lament, but it has special relevance now because it appears to be representative of a widespread sense that the discipline of political science, together with the growing multiplicity of research subfields within it, has lost its identity and a common focus. Of course, what John Gunnell has called the "dispersion" of political science may not be negative, since pluralism may be the result of just and reasoned uneasiness with the paradigms of the past. But perhaps this brand of pluralism is not altogether healthy either, for as Gunnell notes, dispersion in the main has not produced fertile and healthy debates, but a variety of academic cul-de-sacs and enclaves in which each method, each approach, and each paradigm is awarded with its own self-contained journals, conference groups, and subfields. This is the kind of dispersion that does not encourage much intellectual confrontation or introspection, but rather tends to obscure it for fear of opening up gnawing and uncomfortable questions about the nature, purposes, claims, and role of knowledge. Growing mounds of scholarship do not reflect wealth, but a glut. Ironically, political science's increasing crisis of identity may in fact be the result of the failure of earlier, self-conscious efforts by the people discussed in this book to create one. But the discipline's present status suggests a radical relativity altogether ignorant of, and even hostile to, past questions of identity and focus.

One may be tempted to argue that we can account for today's dispersion by runaway professionalism. After all, the urge to construct professional standards, identities, and organizations has been a continuous one in the activities of the scholars discussed in this book. Unfortunately, the crisis of American political science is far deeper, extending to its fundamental understanding of American political life and its own self-proclaimed role in the polity.

We have argued that professionalism in political science has been understood by its promoters as a means to an end, not an end in itself. Political science's autonomy and its insulation from political conflicts have not been intended to "objectify" the American polity solely as a field for scientific study. Rather, professionalism was a way of doing politics, of injecting objective "truth" into the polity in an age wherein political and social conflicts threatened to undermine all claims to intellectual authority and neutrality. Professional language, methods, and organization were said to create a distance necessary both to defend academics from the retribution too often visited on intellectuals in nineteenth-century America and to promote a powerful reform role for intellectuals in the polity. Political scientists would not just serve the polity; they would confront it, understand it, and act on it on their own terms. Professionalism was but the means to a new form of advocacy, one that stood apart from close ties to partisanship, even as it formed the contours and possibilities of political action in the polity.

Yet the organizational success of professionalism has continuously contradicted the intentions of the foremost profession builders. Professional growth brought either no deference or brought the kind of limited and practical influence that disappointed scholar-activists such as Charles Merriam. At the beginning of each period discussed in these chapters, energetic political science reformers viewed the solution to the problems of professionalism as more professionalism. The prominent representatives of each generation accused their predecessors of premature political advocacy, only to be disappointed in turn by the consequences of professional growth. As the claims of professional social science expanded, the polity's intractability seemed only to have increased. As professionalism grew, the justifications for its existence withered.

It is tempting to say that professionalism has turned into a bad strategy aimed at achieving worthwhile goals and that somehow American intellectual and political life would have evolved in ways far different if the "professional miscalculation" had somehow not been made. Indeed, historians of early American social science have begun to single out yet another way that American cultural and political history diverges from Western European developments in the same period. As the secular religion of the middle classes, professionalism prevented that cross-fertilization between intellectuals and the working class so instrumental to the rise of socialist and social democratic parties elsewhere ("The 29th reason for the lack of socialism in the United States," Gene Poschman has called it.).

Indeed, in the seminal period of American industrialization—the 1880s and 1890s—the growth of professionalism helped to flatten some of the early political and intellectual extremes. Men such as Richard Ely, Henry Carter Adams, or even Lester Ward, in this view, were quickly co-opted into the norms of professional respectability and security within the modern university, thereby "removing a good portion of potential or actual intellectual talent from the society and politically neutering it."[2]

Plausibly, then, one could maintain that the die was cast very early on in political science history. When left-leaning political scientists in the 1930s,

1960s, and 1970s sought to reconnect social science to ongoing political and social protest movements, they wound up carrying political debates into the discipline but failed to provide much intellectual leadership to dissident movements in politics. It was quite simply too late to change the oft-noted peculiarities of American political development. In America, professionalism imposed a false harmony on social science intellectuals precisely at the moment when political polarization was occurring in society. In the crucial period at the height of capitalist industrialization, America got neither the class-mass parties of the Left nor the conservative administrative, military, and economic planning bureaucracies characteristic of a strong state. The incomplete accomplishments of American liberal progressivism conditioned the future of American social science, even as they reflected its limited and far from autonomous impact. Disappointed by the publics they sought to guide, American political scientists—despite the best efforts of many of their numbers—became remarkable either for their splendid isolation or, like the scholars discussed here, became unwitting instruments of the dominant forces in the political world they sought to transform. Influence over public policies often meant providing services to political elites whose purposes were far different from those of the reformers. Political institutions, mass organizations, and political movements in the United States, in this view, remained strangely immune to the kind of expertise the professional social scientist offered. Each only repeated the archaic logic of nineteenth-century predecessors. Political life in the United States remained strangely frozen, even as American society, as well as the economy, became notable for the degree and depth of its transformation. As political scientists ran harder, each generation suffered the consequences of past failures. Too often, the shelter of professional life became a prison even to dissenters who sought to mold political life through reform of the profession.

Yet if the impasse of political science has been only, or even primarily, due to the unintended consequences of professionalism, then the continuing crises and cycles of political science history might be more resolvable than they in fact are. If professionalism has not worked as the objective instrument of reform, why not simply get rid of it and carry on with the tasks and political vision of third tradition liberalism with a different instrument? The professional treadmill continues and challenges to professional identities often wind up as subgroups or conference groups at the next annual APSA meeting for obvious and even profound reasons.

What was true for Richard Ely and Henry Carter Adams is even truer for the profession as it has grown. The discipline's leaders may often wonder why intentions so often diverge from results, but there is no doubting the fact that the structures and ethos of professionalism are stronger than they ever were if only because the rules for admission to and advance in the profession have stiffened. Long ago, at least three years of graduate education became the only admission ticket to the job market. Today, career success for new Ph.D.'s is often measured by the mere possession of those increasingly scarce "tenure track" positions achieved mainly by the lucky few "educated" at the right institutions, recommended by the right advisers, and engaged in the most popular subfields. "Publish or perish" may have been true fifteen or twenty years ago. Today, it is entirely possible to publish *and* perish if the publishing is not done in the right journals, with the right publishers, and to universally laudatory reviews. This is hardly a system designed to welcome pariahs. And if there are rebels, the forms of protest are not likely to be radical. By the time the lucky point-scorer receives the hard-won prize of tenure at a major institution, who could—or would—rock the boat? A few probably, but not many.[3]

But even assuming that the institutions, markets, and ideologies that sustain this kind of professionalism could be modified, this book's contention is that professionalism is decidedly *not* the primary source of the present impasse. Indeed, the impulse toward profession building of scholars such as Woodrow Wilson, Charles Beard, Charles Merriam, David Truman, and Theodore Lowi can hardly be separated from the political vision that always has accompanied it, and that always has failed the test of efficacy. Overprofessionalization is not just some "mistake" that can be corrected and after which all will be well, but it is a symptom of what happens to intellectual endeavor when its raison d'etre has been discredited by its impotence in front of an intractable reality.

If the problem is not just hyperprofessionalism, what is it? To its advocates, the organization of intellectuals into professions only reflected the unique possibilities inherent in American politics. "Uniqueness" was captured by the absence in America of the rightist authoritarianism that discredited the state's rise in Western Europe. "Uniqueness" also meant that the new class-based demands of the modern middle and working classes need not be threatening to "progressive" capitalism or public institutions. The great contrast between America and everywhere else was that in America choosing between conflicting, undemocratic versions of statism, one despotic and intrusive, the other authoritarian and elitist, was not necessary. The constant refrain of our scholars has been the assertion of an essential compatibility between the rise of the American state and the maturing American democracy. In America, statist and democratic excesses were simply not necessary.

This fortuitous uniqueness reduced the risks to democracy state-building posed. In other countries the efficiency and power of strong states came at the expense of perilous and persistent class stratification. European states were thought to be hapless or dangerous giants because their vaunted military and administrative apparatuses were rooted in sand or defied mass citizenship in both theory and practice. Insofar as democratic movements grew, polarization resulted and prospects of class warfare and even revolution increased. Intellectuals were forced to attach themselves to classes and their political expressions—either the state or the working classes were the given choices.

But not in America. Here the embrace of a neutral, nonpartisan social science was possible precisely because state-building and democracy could be complementary activities, not contradictory opposites. Objective investigation provided knowledge of the facts and tendencies endemic to modern economic and social development. The training of technically expert and democratically accountable civil servants was seen as reinforcing political harmony and interclass solidarity, not as their opposite. Modernity as a flawless meshing of state and society, leaders and led, institutional control and popular direction, the "technical" and "creative," public authority and popular democracy has been a recurrent image of the science of politics in America. Absent is the ambivalence of Max Weber about the routinization of an administered world. And totally absent are any kind of Marxian definitions—class struggles in America are dissolved into intergroup competition, softened by a great middle class that is the foundation of interclass harmony.

Without the least trace of insincerity, our political scientists could separate "politics" from "administration," holding that the scope of political choices would expand insofar as the expertise and instruments available to public servants did as well. Nor was there a trace of doubt that reforms that disabled the "antique" party system—the short ballot, the referendum, the voting machine, and the primary election—were instruments that increased the scope of democratic choice, even as they accelerated the role of administrative experts in politics and deflated the autonomy of political parties from the state. To scholars such as Charles Merriam—or even the radical Charles Beard—devices such as these were part of the larger war against "provincials," who falsely equated modern democracy with opposition to centralized and concentrated political power. After a little civic education, citizens of all classes would realize that the old political parties, the old practices, the old localisms only obfuscated the great choices that ought to be made by the masses and efficiently implemented by the professional experts at their service. Ironically, in works such as Lowi's, the same laments are still to be heard: What, after all, is fundamentally un-American about juridical democracy? The construction of a state worthy of the name will only increase—not diminish—the sphere of public choice and influence over the unconscious squirmings of the marketplace and the fragmented, dispersed drift of government and its agencies.

What is remarkable about political science is not that it served as a vanguard for succeeding generations of triumphant state builders, but rather that its major claims have not been vindicated either in the structures of the growing American state or in the forms that have passed for political democracy. Most scholars of the Progressive era have too easily mistaken the intellectual preeminence of third tradition thought for its political success in the cumulative reforms achieved in the administrations of Theodore Roosevelt, Woodrow Wilson, Franklin Roosevelt, and Lyndon Johnson. More often than not, our vanguard has been disappointed by the architecture of the liberal state in America. It has felt victimized and abused, or it has seen political reforms that have been achieved as palpably inadequate considering the depth of the problems they have addressed. Far from champions, sponsors, or ideologues for the political institutions associated with liberal reform, third tradition scholars have been either its occasional servants or its most dogged critics. Often, like Merriam, they have been both.

Instead of feelings of abuse and misuse, one would have thought that disappointment and frustration might have led to serious self-examination and intellectual turmoil. Why were political science's easy lessons so often ignored? Why did intelligent citizens refuse to act in the prescribed ways? Instead of asking such questions, damning indictments of the political system were launched as if the damned would realize and correct their failings. No systematic impediments to modern democracy existed—just unenlightened if educable people. Faced with the mindless dispersion of public authority, political scientists have sought the "centripetal presidency," only to recoil in horror when the executive turns out to be Johnson, Nixon, or Reagan. Even now, responsible political parties are held out as an alternative to interest group fragmentation. But the party system's logic continues to defy its own mandate to mobilize and concentrate public power. When "power" had been created against the interest groups, it often has appeared not as benign, but as malign.

This pattern of perpetual gap between analysis and prescription, actuality and disappointment, has existed too long to be classified and written off as yet another case of idealists chastened by reality. Political scientists are not latter-day mugwumps. But they have for too long thought about, defined, and looked for reform in all the wrong places. And in doing so they have misinterpreted the goals, intentions, and action of the publics political science has always sought to guide or catalyze to action.

Perhaps third tradition political science's most serious misinterpretation has been its overestimation of the ease by which broad interclass political support, consensus, and participation could be forged around the construction of new instruments of control and intervention in the American corporate economy. The essence of third tradition political science's claims rested on gaining the organized and conscious support of all social classes for the regulatory, planning, social welfare, and military instruments of the modern state. No social classes were said to lose in the creation of such public instruments; no fundamental interests of any class were violated by the creation of new instruments and purposes because the dynamism of the private economy would be guided toward democratic purposes. No one truly rational could doubt the desirability of this fusion of democratic purpose and industrialization via the neutral, technocratic state. In America, such a state would be as free of ideology as the professional academics that sponsored it; its claim to authority consisted of its promise to adjust America to the potential of the present without polluting the polity with the class and status polarities so typical of the Western European state.

But the problem with this vision is that it failed to account for the resilience of older American beliefs about the proper sphere of democracy and public life. The identity and autonomy of ethnic groups, villages, and localities might be seen as simple antiques, soon to be superseded by a technocratic, democratic future. In this sense, the very success political scientists achieved only underscored the problematic nature of their harmonious futurism. Third tradition political scientists got the expansion of governmental functions and roles they desired. They got experts in public administration. They got, albeit with many compromises, the state structures they always advocated. But they achieved the program at the expense of their vision because there was no fundamental break or rupture, no ideological reawakening that accompanied this so-called revolution in government functions. As the fact of government became ubiquitous, the authority of government appeared to decrease. Distinctions between the "public" and the "private" spheres became more difficult to make, even as the adoption of new governmental responsibilities multiplied. In the behavioral era, this "seamless web" of government—"the black box," the "parallelogram of forces"—turned a dilemma into a virtue.

But most third tradition political scientists sometime in their career would wind up reflecting on the new equilibrium as if it were a monster to their own Frankenstein. It was all somehow a mistake, and it could be corrected if all the strands in the "seamless web" came to their senses. As Merriam reflected on the demise of democratic planning in the New Deal, so would Lowi later urge "the liberal state" to change its own ways. The managers of the modern state simply did not know what they were doing and reasoned argument might convince them of the defects of their own public philosophy.

The growth of government in the United States has thus been accompanied by no sea change in its relationship to society. Succeeding generations of state builders have added to the old building without altering its foundations and basic design. The gulf between the plans of third tradition architects and the resulting rubble can perhaps best be accounted for in two ways.

First, third tradition scholars mistook the political proclivities and dispositions of twentieth-century American capitalism. Here was a form of capitalism unusually resistant to the well-intentioned efforts to politically modernize it, harmonize it, plan it, and organize it in accordance with politically designated goals. There has not been, of course, the slightest trace of anticapitalism in the century-long efforts of enlightened intellectuals and politicians to regulate and coordinate the exploitation of natural resources, the construction of public works, the enactment of taxation, the provision of military weapons and supplies in wartime and peacetime, or the imposition of production and distribution priorities on the private economy. But as Merriam learned and Lowi lamented, the state assumed these functions not through increasing its public authority to make binding decisions—not through nice and neat spheres of political choice and expert administration—but rather through ceding what sovereignty it did possess to thousands of satrapies, each with its own monopoly on public policies. If conscious, expert, publicly accountable economic planning failed with the NRPB, a form of planning did live on in philosophically unacceptable ways—as "interest group liberalism" and the morass of private-public relations it sustained. In the "victories" of the New Deal, the Fair Deal, the New Frontier, and the Great Society, third tradition political scientists achieved their greatest defeat. Instead of a reasonable, organized electorate making choices between clearly delineated and achievable political, social, and economic goals, the new state seemed to disguise choices, defy political control, and drain electoral and legislative debates of meaning. Talk about the "unique genius" of American politics has gradually turned to distant contemplation of the state's strange existence as a diffused body scattered about and attached to hundreds of groups and associations in the private economy. Third tradition political scientists have always seemed surprised that organized private groups would be perfectly willing to feed at the public trough, insofar as they could wander out of the barnyard to forage on the open range. While the kind of progressive, administered society seen by third tradition political scientists may not in the abstract be harmful to corporate capitalism, the political and ideological strength of modern American business has been great enough to dampen whatever statist tendencies that heretofore have arisen. American business has ruled, but only through the dispersed and porous apparatus of the creaking federal state.

Third tradition political scientists have misunderstood the political proclivities of American capitalism. Such a misunderstanding has often led to criticism of, and dismay and disdain for, the kind of state-building that has already occurred, even as such criticisms usually try to show why present reality could have been avoided. A parallel misunderstanding and puzzlement has beset our scholars when it has come to the comprehension of—and influence over—the forms, objects, and constituencies of political participation in modern America. As liberal progressives, political scientists have paid special attention to voting as the one most important political act in liberal capitalist democracies. But generating popular energy and support for the centralized, purposive state political scientists thought they were building has proven to be a more difficult task than originally envisioned. The "reform publics" political scientists designated have either failed to adopt the political program prescribed for them or they have taken paths far different than our scholars hoped or expected. Whatever else they have done, "reform publics" have not generated consistent support for third tradition political hopes. Neither the "responsible two-party system" Wilson and Merriam advocated, nor the "revolutionary middle class" of Bentley and Beard, nor the rational citizen groups and organizations dedicated to the discussion and resolution of national issues have risen above the antique parties or the interest group structure.

Mainstream and third tradition political science have variously praised and blamed nonvoting, apolitical attitudes, and interest group liberalism. Rarely, however, has lamentation extended beyond itself to question the essentials of the progressive-liberal project and why it has so seldom succeeded in building popular support for the rise of the positive state. The romance with Franklin Roosevelt was an initially important manifestation of hope. But behavioral studies discovered that the New Deal coalition was a fragile stockpile of interest groups—groups understandable in terms of Robert Michels's "iron law of oligarchy," rather than in the more glorious terms of a triumphant fusion of mass participation with state authority. As the state expanded, voters seemed less willing or able to control it, and the dwindling numbers of voters seemed more influenced by the media, by personalities, or by impressions, rather than by the seasoned elites of intelligent party democracy. Among those lower classes least likely to vote, ominous signs for liberalism appeared, especially in the 1960s.

Indeed, when citizenship was exercised, it seemed only to attack the liberal state rather than embrace it. As the War on Poverty fought its battles, it had the odd effect of generating either anger or apathy among both the constituencies it was supposed to serve as well as the middle class that was supposed to support it. Falling short of revitalizing the mass base of the Democratic Party, the Great Society only highlighted the ethnic and class contradictions and tensions within American life. Social movements and their moral claims all too quickly became interest groups and their clienteles. Predictably, of course, these "progressive" programs helped mobilize the white middle class against government "giveaway" programs and "bureaucracy," even as they crippled and co-opted political movements among the disenfranchised and poor. As always, there was a missing link. As government's responsibilities increased, its authority and efficacy declined. As efforts to stimulate more participation in electoral politics and alter representative institutions increased, the insulation of institutions like Congress and the presidency only seemed to expand. The quintessential political act by which liberal citizens speak—voting—further declined, and the mass character of political party organizations further atrophied. As the social, economic, and cultural tensions in America multiplied, scholars mused about the political system's inability to articulate these tensions, much less resolve them.

But who has failed whom, and why? Are the principles and organization of democratic citizenship prescribed by third tradition scholarship to be scored only for their impracticality, or rather for their substance? Perhaps, to echo a popular song, our scholars have usually looked for democratic life in all the wrong places, and have unwittingly helped to displace it with all the wrong forms. Third tradition political scientists have been part of a long and drawn-out effort to weaken the organizations, culture, and beliefs associated with republican life in preindustrial, nineteenth-century America. That movement has weakened in theory as well as in fact the ethos of laissez-faire capitalism. But it has not weakened it enough to make the modern state that arose in its place very authoritative. The United States has had the latest and weakest welfare state in the world—if it has had one at all.

Third tradition political science has suffered a similar fate as it has defined democratic legitimacy. The major vehicle for mass political participation in the nineteenth century—the undeniably corrupt party system—has been defeated, along with most of the ethnic and local loyalties that sustained it. Popular opposition to that party system— populism and various socialisms—shared with the older parties hostility to distant and centralized economic and political power. Those doctrines and movements too have yielded before the onslaught of political and institutional "modernization."

But this "success" has fatally underestimated the persistence of the political dispositions of the earlier epoch. American political beliefs still seem antique, even though these dispositions remain unorganized and subterranean, allowing social scientists to brand them as reactionary rubbish or political provincialism.

In the 1880s, Lester Ward was perhaps the first to begin this pattern of misunderstanding by labeling American populism as the future and potential bearer of "scientific sociocracy." In the 1920s, Arthur Bentley thought the virtues of humane moderation resided in the great middle class of skill and knowledge. In the 1930s, Merriam mistook the American "cultural complex" for a support of new types of efficient capitalist planning. And in the 1980s, scholars such as Walter Dean Burnham have urged leftists to once again put social democracy on the agenda, reasoning that the great mass of nonvoters in America is the very constituency that has supported social democratic regimes elsewhere. Consistent here is a flawed understanding of the consequences of the liberal progressive legacy. Christopher Lasch's comments on Burnham are probably equally valid for Burnham's predecessors:

> The political process is now so remote from the lives of ordinary citizens and participation so narrowly limited to those with access to the media or interest group bargaining that masses of people feel completely powerless. Under these conditions it is hard to see how another national party, even if it were social democratic in its ideology, would overcome the deeper sources of political alienation.
>
> Liberal elites believe in self-expression, non-binding commitments, abortion, gay rights and cosmopolitanism. Working people believe in family ties, neighborhoods and loyalty to your own kind. How would a social democratic movement put an end to this "cultural civil war" as it has been called?[4]

Lasch's comment suggests that third tradition political thought, successful as it has been as an organized enterprise, has hardly eliminated these diffuse and often contradictory yearnings for, and experiences of, democratic life. The America of island communities and ethnic loyalties has largely disappeared with the triumph of modern American capitalism, and the organizations and definitions of popular republican rule of the nineteenth century have been practically and intellectually undercut. But these preindustrial democratic forms have not been replaced by consistent, organized popular support for the agenda of third tradition political science. Suspicion of this kind of technological, administered, and centralized polity has remained if often only as an amorphous and diffuse bundle of sentiments, less often in the form of civil rights, labor, antiwar, and other forms of direct political protest. Sometimes, this strand of antique republicanism has taken forms that scare liberal progressives. Attachments to neighborhood, fundamentalist religion, ethnicity, and chauvinism have been part of the price paid for the failed politics of third tradition political science. But from Anti-Federalists to George Wallace, from populists to antinuclear protesters, a subterranean strain of political alienation continues to persist despite the understandings of third tradition political science.

A cultural civil war may still exist in America. The fact that such a civil war has infrequently lapped over into frontal political conflicts is perhaps the best testimony to the gradual weakening of the organizations of nineteenth-century democratic life and to the nonemergence of those responsible, bureaucratically organized, nationally oriented parties and associations of enlightened technological society.

To most third tradition scholars, this divergence between cosmopolitan aspirations and American reality has been understood as an unfortunate and entirely avoidable mistake. Reform publics have failed from lack of intelligence and will, not from any systematic failure of theory or understanding of democracy in America. Often frustration has led to soul-searching—"what we have here is a problem of communication." Our argument, however, has been that problems of academic communication with the public understate the substantive impasse of political science. What is evident is that its failed political claims go a bit beyond the predictive value of scholarship, while including it. Whatever roads have not been taken in American politics are due not only to a simple failure to communicate, to a miscalculation of strategy and tactics, but also to the much greater dilemma of the whole intellectual and political project of third tradition political science and the liberal progressivism for which it has been an important and consistent advocate.

Today we have evidence that political studies in the United States are dividing along precisely those lines that third tradition political scientists have always feared. This separation accompanies and follows a prospective transformation of the relationship between the crisis-ridden capitalist economy, the American state, and the forms and goals of the political organization of social classes in America.

If third tradition political science has always sought a union of its version of state power and political legitimacy, the current situation and political dialogue suggest that the prospects of such a happy union are very dim indeed—at least if this union is sought within the present structures and practices of the American political economy. Today, the advocates of state reconstruction abound, but all their analyses tend to move beneath or beyond the easy fusions of state power and popular democracy central to earlier generations of scholars. To the new "neoconservatives" in political science, any reconstructed American state must adopt principles that further insulate it from the supposed "overload" of political demands that are said to beset it. Challenges from new social and political movements among blacks, the poor, women, youth, environmentalists, and unions undermine the now apparently fragile social and political patterns and dispositions that sustain monopoly capitalism. According to the neoconservative scenario, what is now required is a concerted effort to create an "investment climate" and reinforce the political and social mores and dispositions consistent with the new imperatives of "austerity." The radical subjectivity of popular political ideals must now be adjusted to the grim necessities of political centralization, technological rationality, and economic concentration. Even in their weakened and imperfect present condition, the institutions of liberal democracy are not threatened by the dispersion or fragmentation of interest group liberalism, but by an "anti-power ethic" that promises disharmony and turns political life into "moralism." Samuel Huntington has stated this position most clearly:

> The widespread consensus on liberal democratic values provides the basis for challenging the legitimacy of American political practices. . . . If people try to make government more legitimate by bringing practice more into line with political principles, that will weaken rather than strengthen it. As a result of the IVI [Institutions vs. Ideals] gap, the perennial gap between the actuality of *institutional* practice and *ideal* standards, the legitimacy of American government varies inversely with belief in American ideals.[5]

Professor Huntington's work is representative of a new strain of neoconservative thought, wherein hard choices between liberal democracy and the requirements of institutional authority must be made. There is little doubt about which will be chosen. To Huntington, American political history is pockmarked by unfortunate "creedal passion periods"—upswellings of pathological challenges to the structures and imperatives of organized political and economic power. Democratic protest movements in American history are essentially emotional, irrational, and immature responses to what Huntington views as the inevitable "realities" all polities face. "Creedal passion" stands in the way of Huntington's locomotive of history, and his work is a forthright statement in favor of class stratification, economic concentration, and military glory. To the extent that mass political participation is expanded, institutional power is said to become limited and confined. To the extent that further curbs are placed on "democratic excesses," institutional power becomes "legitimate" in the sense that it is "freed" to perform its appropriate necessary and natural "functions."

This brand of contemporary conservatism is a significant departure from Woodrow Wilson's hope that "Prussian efficiency will breathe free American air" because each has continued to choke the other. Neoconservatives have shed the "democratic delusions" of third tradition political science, and in the process they have shed democratic hopes, beliefs, and thought as well. Unlike third tradition scholars, they cannot be accused of glossing over the political proclivities and tendencies of modern capitalism or of failure to locate and influence some kind of "public" outside the discipline. Today, neoconservatives have effectively mixed academic research with influence on an enlightened corporate and governmental elite. Journals such as *The Public Interest* and *Commentary* lend political legitimacy to ideas often thought, but not often so boldly expressed, in twentieth-century American political life. The current beautification of capitalism, Japanese-style, suggests that some among our elites are now prepared to leap enthusiastically into a brave new world in which social, economic, political, and cultural authority is enforced through a revolution from above. In place of interest group mindlessness, Japan, Inc., appears as an orderly model. To Huntington its strength lies "in its effectiveness for centralized communication and its capability of efficient and swift mobilization of the collective power of its members." Former Anglophiles, political scientists join with others in admiration for the traditional virtues—no longer of England—but of a country that has never had a democratic revolution.[6]

If the stakes were not so high, the neoconservative idea that we are presently living in some sort of "radicalized democracy"—that the 1960's protest movements actually succeeded—would be amusing. Neoconservatives could be told that the barbarians are not as close to the gate as they believe. But the frank admiration for power and control, submission and obedience, suggests that conscious state-building may still be on the agenda in America if only in ways that third tradition scholars would probably have deemed abhorrent and impossible.[7]

Thinkers on the Right have undermined liberal progressive political science's conflation of state power with democratic legitimacy in America. But third tradition hopes have also been eroded from the Left, and even among former doyens of liberalism themselves. Liberal scholars like Robert Lekachman and John Kenneth Galbraith—along with magazines like the *Nation* and the *Progressive*—have begun to find few solutions within the intellectual or political orientations of traditional American liberalism. Within political science itself, the language of "crisis" has often replaced that of potential pluralist consensus, at least if the recent works of Charles Lindblom, Robert Dahl, and Burnham himself are to be taken as examples. A growing number of the most influential scholars have adopted or reinvigorated the categories of neo-Marxian political economy. In so doing, many have moved beyond the muckraking orientation of past scholarship. Systematic contradictions between the imperatives of modern capitalism and the sustenance and growth of political and economic democracy now are postulated where cautious and gradual reforms of the capitalist economy sufficed before. Where neoconservatives perceive liberal democracy as working "too well," a growing Left within political science traces the increasing erosion of its already limited and confined existence in politics.[8]

To some, nothing less than a "regime crisis" is in the making because the authoritarian tendencies in late capitalism now appear to necessitate rule by force rather than persuasion and propaganda. The "welfare state" can no longer be afforded by late capitalism because the system is now gearing itself up for "reindustrialization" and capitalist accumulation that further stratifies classes and drains electoral "choices" of any substantive meaning. Caught between stagnant and unworkable welfare liberalism and an assertive and repressive Right, American democracy's present survival lies outside liberal capitalism in the mobilization of those people now effectively disenfranchised and politically victimized by capitalism. Any truly legitimate political order of the future, scholars such as Alan Wolfe contend, must transform presently "nonproductive citizenship into repoliticization"—"the attempt by people to seek genuine politics for themselves outside the political arena." And, Wolfe holds, "any repoliticized population is one that is subversive of the dominant tendencies associated with the late capitalist state."[9]

Without elaborating too much on the politically stimulating substance of many of these new works, this much can be noted here: The polarization reflected in the most prominent political science works today suggests the silent passing of the century-long political and intellectual efforts of the scholars described in this book. The prominent political scientists of today choose between the two traditions that past political scientists always sought to reconcile as scholars and political actors. Scientific therapy administered to universally deferent publics has become direct intellectual and political advocacy for conflicting movements and policies. Instead of overseeing a benign fusion of the liberal-capitalist state with new forms of mass democracy, today's observers assert the incompatibility of one with the other. Instead of calling on elite and mass audiences to reconcile their needless differences, contemporary scholars rather trace their irresolvable disputes.

In this sense, third tradition political science is dying at the same pace as liberal progressivism is faltering in the polity. There are few articulate defenders and little enthusiasm among anyone for the now-confused discourses and policies of progressive liberalism. To the Left, such policies have been bandages over hemorrhages because they have neglected the causes and sources of crisis in the investment priorities, imperial assumptions, and cultural beliefs associated with modern corporate capitalism. To neoconservatives, welfare liberalism is now too costly because it hinders capital accumulation and order, raising expectations that cannot any longer be satisfied. In the present climate, the practice of citizenship is either too narrow or too expansive. To left-wing democrats, the demise of political parties and the depoliticization of society represent the crucial withholding of political support from the alternatives presented by Democrats and Republicans. To right-wingers, institutions are beleaguered by a selfish, ignorant mass of cultural and economic protesters who resist the stark imperatives of corporate capitalism. Whatever the case, the language of assured consensus, so common in the past, is startlingly absent from contemporary political science.

Given this novel outpouring of real political and intellectual divisions among political scientists, concluding this work with an epitaph for political science as it has been practiced in the United States might be valid. With liberal centrism dying in the polity, so, too, might it be withering away in the academy, thereby freeing American political life to express and articulate long-deferred conflicts and alternatives. The nation and the academy together may finally get to live as an "ordinary country," experiencing all those realities long noted for their subterranean existence in American politics. For generations, American politics has been full of missing links. Advocates of democratic socialism and statist conservatism may finally form the contours of future American politics.

But these are possible tendencies, not inevitable developments. As political theory and practice, third tradition political science today has few defenders and a dwindling audience among outsiders. But its demise has its ironies because it leaves in its wake the professional structures, subfields, and mentalities that once were its instruments. The organization of modern political science may triumph over its original functions, becoming a mode of discourse of and for itself, heaving up great mounds of academic literature and specialized debate. Paradoxically, works like this one probably provoke interest only within the discipline they seek to criticize. So, too, may it be for the new advocacy of the first and second traditions—the Right and Left of present-day political science. The Right's much vaunted influence through think tanks and "committees on the present danger" is indeed bought at a high price because here is the kind of influence that comes from sycophantic justification and ratification of the new corporate agenda. For the political science Left, one hundred years of isolation from mass politics have left their imprint; writers such as Theda Skocpol, William Connolly, and Alan Wolfe try to draw links between new intellectual approaches and the future of mass politics in America. They hope to develop "a sense of public consciousness and virtue that transcends the mundanely political but is not confined to the academic world."

But for all these new departures by Left political science, such efforts may have more in common with those of Merriam than their politics might suggest. While the political science Left's concern "is with the transformation of society and the public consciousness . . . it remains firmly planted in the academic universe and in a fundamental sense is disjoined from politics as an existential activity."[10]

That so many now seek ways out of the professional impasse is a hopeful and encouraging sign, as is the break with a now-declining liberalism. When the new ways of thinking about and defining democratic life in America become more than a limited intellectual endeavor confined to reconfirming the givens of American life to an educated audience, then the iron cage in which political studies have entrapped themselves will be opened. When democracy becomes more than a set of forms and procedures that bolster the liberal state, but a practice whereby citizens make fundamental decisions in modern societies, then the democratic delusions of third tradition political science might become shared democratic aspirations.

Historically, political science professionalism has only obscured fundamental conflicts and choices in American public life because it has treated citizens as objects of study or clients of a benign political paternalism. The democratic delusions of American political science have always excluded and feared a future beyond liberalism. Until political scientists realize that their democratic politics cannot be realized through a barren professionalism, intellectual life will remain cleaved from the genuine if heretofore subterranean democratic dreams of American citizens. Political science history has confirmed this separation, even as it has tried to bridge it. Modern political science must bridge it if delusions are to be transformed into new democratic realities.

Afterword
A Science of Politics, A Science for Politics

James Farr
Northwestern University

When it first appeared nearly three decades ago, *Disenchanted Realists* helped inaugurate a new era in the historical and critical study of the discipline of political science in America.[1] Authored principally by Raymond Seidelman with the assistance of Edward J. Harpham,[2] it unleashed a critique of the discipline in 1985 on the basis of a tale of four generations of prominent liberal academics who wanted the science *of* politics also to be a science *for* politics. Alas, the discipline that for a century sought to bolster democratic politics and an energetic state by the methods of science was crashing under the weight of its own aspirations. As was the polity at large, political science was in crisis, and its proudest lineage was at an end.

No mere history, the book openly desired "at minimum" to "rekindle self-examination" (xix) for those very many political scientists who were "generally ignorant of their own history" (222). Seidelman introduced it as a "modest history of the intertwined fate of political liberalism and some of the major leaders of American political science." But if the history was modest, the contemporary judgment on the fate of the discipline was not because "our subject is the increasing insulation of political science from the realities of politics, power and protest in twentieth-century America" (xix). The subtitle—*Political Science and the American Crisis, 1884–1984*— announced the basic idea, which was graphically reinforced by the original cover art. Against a blood-red backdrop, a frayed white-and-blue postcard of a veritable hall of power, the U.S. Capitol building, was ripped apart from another white-and-blue postcard of a placid hall of learning, the Wren Building at the College of William and Mary.

Disenchanted Realists was not alone in the mid-1980s in sensing a discipline at sea about its declining prospects.[3] It was also not alone in attempting a critique of political science by historiographical means. A few months prior to its publication, there emerged in print *The Tragedy of Political Science* (1984) by David M. Ricci.[4] *Disenchanted Realists*, already a decade or so in gestation, did not mention Ricci's book, so fresh was it off the press. Readers, though, soon came to sense that something tragic and disenchanted was in the discipline's air for two such evocative titles to come out almost simultaneously. *Disenchanted Realists*, however, did look back to remember other historiographical precursors. One was *The Development of American Political Science: From Burgess to Behavioralism* (1967) by Albert Somit and Joseph Tanenhaus that, amid lots of disciplinary information, worried about a "scientism" that had overtaken the public ambitions of many political scientists.[5] Another, and most importantly, was Bernard Crick's *The American Science of Politics* (1959),[6] "the best and broadest work on the history of American political science" (242, n2). *Disenchanted Realists* shared Crick's critique of the discipline as a scientific knockoff of American liberalism. Yet another book loomed in the intellectual and political background as well—Theodore Lowi's *The End of Liberalism* (1969).[7] Lowi figured as one of the select political scientists featured in *Disenchanted Realists*. He also wrote the original foreword that ended with the line, "This book is either a preface or an epitaph" (xvii).

Despite some overlap with these other works, *Disenchanted Realists* was distinctive in the ways it rattled the iron cage of the discipline. First, it alleged that political scientists had profoundly misunderstood the basic structure of American politics that their science was ostensibly to be "of" and "for." They "conjured up an image of the State as a benign and conscious reflection of, and actor for, an interdependent society" (10). This was coherent enough since it did separate administration from politics, and suggested the countless intersections and overlaps of state and civil society. The real problem, though, was that corporate capitalism undermined at every turn the democratic state on which so many civic hopes had been invested. This dashed the aspirations of successive generations of political scientists that their vaunted realism could help administer the state while activating democratic participation in the citizenry. This failure of political imagination was tied to professionalism—even a "hyperprofessionalism" (227)—but it was more importantly tied to liberalism itself. Liberal political scientists, in short, "mistook the political proclivities and dispositions of twentieth-century

American capitalism. Here was a form of capitalism unusually resistant to the well-intentioned efforts to politically modernize it, harmonize it, plan it and organize it in accordance with politically designated goals" (231). Science was gambled and reform sought "in all the wrong places" (229).

Second, not *all* political scientists, historically, were implicated in this failure of political imagination, but only those associated with a "third tradition" in American political thought. The third tradition just *was* the tradition of liberalism, especially in the guise of reform liberalism or liberal progressivism. "Liberalism" was always capacious enough to cover many streams (and it turned out that many in the third tradition were quite different kinds of liberals, especially as the term and referents changed over the course of a century). The third tradition, moreover, jostled alongside two older traditions, namely, the institutionalist and radical democratic traditions associated originally with the Federalists and Anti-Federalists, respectively. The first was all about the mechanics of government, the second about the political spontaneity of the citizenry. Hereby, *Disenchanted Realists* rested on a historiography of traditions that, too, was a novel addition to the critical histories of the discipline. The fate of this third tradition, moreover, was narrated selectively in the life and works of ten major political scientists, a pair per generation and per chapter: Woodrow Wilson and Lester Ward; Charles Beard and Arthur Bentley; Charles Merriam and Harold Lasswell; David Truman and V. O. Key; Theodore Lowi and Walter Dean Burnham. This choice allowed for fairly detailed "case studies," as it were. Some case studies were—and remain in republication—quite arresting in the telling. The half-chapter on Lasswell, for example, was—and remains—especially convincing, given the thesis of the book, not to mention the sheer brilliance of Lasswell himself on power, propaganda, and the garrison state.

The "end of the third tradition" was nigh. Here was the prophetic voice—and third distinctive feature—of *Disenchanted Realists*. The "eclipse of unity" was evident in the 1980s, as documented in the postbehavioral scholarship of the last disenchanted pair. "Lowi's and Burnham's work end a century of liberal Progressive justifications for political science" (221). In a subsequent essay—"Political Scientists, Disenchanted Realists, and Disappearing Democrats" (1993)—Seidelman reiterated the prophecy that reform political science "is now very near at an end." He continued: "the residues of reform political science seem either irrelevant, quaint, despairing, or hopelessly out of touch with broader intellectual developments in American letters and the political climate in American society."[8] There was, however, a slight hesitation in the soothsaying, a counterfactual hint that political science could perhaps change itself to deliver on its century-old desire to improve democracy, not as elites or experts but as self-conscious left-oriented scholars working with fellow citizens on public problems. These were only "possible tendencies, not inevitable developments" (240), of course—and they could be nothing more than possibilities, given the prophetic vision and political critique that sustained the book to the end. But the last three words of *Disenchanted Realists* dared raise the prospect in the discipline and the polity of "new democratic realities" (241).

Finally, there was the *ethos* of the authors behind the book. Despite prophecy and criticism, they displayed considerable respect for the political scientists of the third tradition. As Seidelman and Harpham told their story, third tradition scholars proved themselves time and again to be sharp critics and earnest reformers who "blended scholarship and political advocacy" (2). They were least of all conservative apologists of a status quo, contrary to Bernard Crick's earlier assessment (242, n.2). As Seidelman put the point later, "reform political science had its nobler themes and moments. Among them was its penchant for criticism, its search for political clarity, and its ambition to have a transformative public role."[9] Seidelman and Harpham also wrote with great zest and arresting formulations. Readers found nothing dry or tedious about "the raw slabs of reality" (85) they encountered in its pages. Then, too, there was the frank confession about the potential irony or paradox in which they found themselves inevitably enmeshed. Not waiting for the accusatory *tu quoque* of their critics, the authors admitted it at the outset (xix): "There is an irony to this project: if political science is insulated, what is to be said about those who write about it?" And they did so again in conclusion: "Paradoxically, works like this one probably provoke interest only within the discipline they seek to criticize" (240). Notwithstanding, it was worth their effort.

The reception of *Disenchanted Realists* repaid the authors' efforts. The discipline took considerable notice of it (and one imagines renewed notice with this republication). The book figured in three APSA presidential addresses: Lucien Pye in 1989, Theodore Lowi in 1991, and Robert Putnam in 2002.[10] It drew the attention of prominent political scientists known for their broad reflections on the past and future of the discipline, including Albert Somit, Gabriel Almond, Heinz Eulau, and Walter Dean Burnham. It made the rounds in reviews by historians, political theorists, and social scientists, as well, among them Burton Bledstein, Eldon Eisenach, John Stanley, Stephen Whitfield, Charles Camic, Pippa Norris, Charles Helm, and William Lasser. Naturally, it was and continues to be discussed quite thoroughly by those who at the time counted (or now count) in "a new, small, and doubtless expanding pond of disciplinary historians,"[11] as Seidelman put it in a critical exchange of 1990, in broad reference to (by now) John Gunnell, David Ricci, Rogers Smith, James Farr, John Dryzek, Stephen Leonard, Terence Ball, Emily Hauptmann, Robert Adcock, Shannon Stimson, Mark Bevir, Arlene Saxonhouse, Ido Oren, Brian Schmidt, Erkki Berndtson, Michael Kenny, Michael Stein, Nicolas Guilhot, William Scheuerman, Timothy Kaufmann-Osborn, Mark C. Smith, and others. The dominating phrase of *Disenchanted Realists* that caught so much attention—"A Science of Politics and a Science for Politics"—figured as the topic and title of Bruce Miroff's 2008 keynote address to the New York State Political Science Association, delivered in memoriam of his close friend and coauthor.

"Provocative" was the term that governed the reception of *Disenchanted Realists*. Getting ahead of the trend, Seidelman and Harpham were unapologetic about their hopes: "If we have erred, we hope it is on the side of provocation rather than pedantry" (xix). Norman Jacobson, historian and critic of political science from the previous generation, agreed in the blurb on the back cover: the organization of the book around the theme of a "third tradition" was "interesting and provocative." In the foreword, Lowi hailed "this splendid and provocative book" for its reach and imagination (xv). Disciplinary historian emeritus Albert Somit half agreed with Lowi in his review in the APSA's leading journal: "provocative," yes, but "not splendid."[12] John Stanley shuffled similarly: the book was "recommended for the provocative questions it raises, not as an overall history of the discipline."[13] "Provocative" was clearly useful as a term that could go either way, positively or negatively. The reviews and commentaries thus varied in their summary judgments of the book's merits or demerits, usually depending on whether the reviewer or commentator thought his ox—or someone else's ox, more deservingly—was being gored. While Burnham, who was featured in the book, found in it "an interesting and wide-ranging discussion," Eulau, who was absent from its pages (save for a pair of bibliographic notes [260, n2 and 264, n50]), editorialized that it was simply "depressing."[14] On and on did it go, *Disenchanted Realists* provoking competing briefs.

Apart from the thumbs-up or thumbs-down briefs of the broad merits of *Disenchanted Realists*, some assessments and criticisms were of a more engaged and engaging kind that took on some of the real issues of the book, both politically and historiographically. One was its openly leftist critique of the discipline's failure of political imagination and of its counterfactual, postliberal prospects if any. Here was the political and historiographical legacy of Crick among disciplinary historians, as noted by some reviewers, not the least of whom was Gunnell, who called *Disenchanted Realists* "neo-Crickian."[15] The closing pages of the book, if not those all along, were anything but surreptitious about their political character. Seidelman, in particular, was always honest in referring to "leftists like myself."[16] This could hardly foreclose commentary or criticism, of course. One reviewer was wry about it all: "Written from a leftist perspective, *Disenchanted Realists* derives lip-smacking pleasure from the unmasking of the wrecked liberal programs and tarnished scientific claims that are among the monuments of political science."[17] Backhandedly, or so it sounded when considering the candidates for the distinction, was the observation by another reviewer that the book was "one of the better Left critiques of political science, including radical political science."[18] The distinguished historian of professionalism in education, Burton J. Bledstein, more simply appreciated Seidelman's "taking a deep breath of contemporary fresh air and calling things by their rightful political names," liberal or left.[19]

The political orientation of *Disenchanted Realists* provoked a more serious if accusatory assessment from Gabriel Almond in his now-famous essay, "Separate Tables: Schools and Sects in Political Science."[20] The essay hit a chord in the discipline for ostensibly bemoaning the fact that political scientists as a whole had hived off into separate cliques with whom to dine, never moving about the other tables. In short, to most readers this seemed to be an account of a fragmented and divided discipline all the way around. This was true even of the literature here considered, for example, Pye's presidential observation that "Almond used the vivid metaphor of 'separate tables' to warn us that our cliquishness in methodology and ideology has become a major obstacle in the advancement of knowledge."[21] But any closer reading showed that it was a complaint about the cliques that Almond thought formed at the margins of the discipline as he defined them. *They* refused to come to the "great cafeteria of the center, from which most of us select our intellectual food, and where we are seated at large tables with mixed and changing table companions." The contrast with the cliques was abundantly clear because "the overwhelming majority of political scientists are somewhere in the center—liberal and moderate in ideology, and eclectic and open to conviction in methodology."[22]

With the "center" defined this way, Almond sorted the side-tabled cliques with their "extreme views" into one or another of four cells as constructed in a rudimentary two-by-two matrix. They were either soft or hard (methodologically) and left or right (ideologically), although "reality, of course, is not quite this neat." *Disenchanted Realists*, like *The Tragedy of Political Science*, was deemed "soft-left," with Seidelman's "a more sharply radical treatment of the history of American political science" than Ricci's. It remains unclear why, for example, Seidelman's treatment of Lasswell was in any way "soft," save that it was historical and textual. If Seidelman's orientation toward the discipline's prospects was indeed "left," why, in Almond's view, all leftists were "in the Marxist tradition"[23] remains unclear. Seidelman, at any rate, could fault historians of the capitalist state for "awkwardly wheeling into position . . . some heavy-duty neo-Marxist artillery" when Charles Beard would do just fine.[24] Apart from castigating disciplinary historiographers who leaned left, Almond tendentiously insisted on "getting our professional history straight" (where straight *somehow* "does not lead to any of these separate tables" that, yet, *somehow* are "strongly lit and visible, while the large center lies in shade" under the lamps of Almond's disciplinary cafeteria). Before concluding with a breathtaking and detail-less sketch of "the historically correct version of our disciplinary history" that began with the ancient Greeks, Almond pronounced the Orwellian point of his disciplinary centrism, paraphrasing a line out of *1984*: "Whoever controls the interpretation of the past in our professional history has gone a long way toward controlling the future."[25] What a threat *Disenchanted Realists* posed to the very future of political science![26]

Less futuristic or threatened were the scholarly reactions to the disciplinary historiography of *Disenchanted Realists*. The book certainly raised key questions about how to organize and narrate a history of a discipline as storied and complex as political science. There was considerable turbulence at the time about the so-called third tradition. *Who* counted in it? *What* was its relation to the other two traditions? *When*

did it start? *Where* did it go? *Why* think it was actually a tradition? The
skepticism behind such questions often accompanied praise for the book's
many accomplishments, not the least of which was the close attention it
paid to the actual writings of the featured ten. Nonetheless, Somit was
not alone in thinking that *Disenchanted Realists* was "sketchy" on the first
two traditions, without proper identification of any political scientists
associated with them. He was, however, rather more barbed than others
when noting how "dubious" it was to call the main figures "disenchanted
realists" or claim "that they represent a truly separate third tradition."[27]
In an important article, Dryzek and Leonard asked more generally if
rhetorically: "In what sense do we have a real tradition here?" Members
were unaware of it; and the alleged third tradition "lacked even a name
until Seidelman and Harpham came along."[28] One reviewer thought it
was just "a fancy name for mainstream political science."[29] Another, who
thought the discussion of the main figures "quite good," nonetheless
pointed out that "there is little effort to justify a *coherent* tradition these
figures *belong* to." Similarly, the authors "fail to adequately clarify their
choice of individual scholars or the importance of the 'third tradition'
within political science."[30] Other reviewers shared his noticing the absence
of Robert Dahl in particular.[31]

These criticisms and challenges raised a final concern about the
prophetic voice of *Disenchanted Realists*. If Dahl was still around, or the
third tradition did not really exist, or the mainstream flowed on, how
could one prophesize "the end" of it? Dryzek located an author's new
book on democracy "solidly within . . . the 'third tradition,'" suggesting
that "this tradition has not expired in the custody of Theodore Lowi and
Walter Dean Burnham, after all."[32] Somit opined that "the alleged demise
of liberalism" was perhaps as premature as "the end of ideology" or even
"God is dead."[33] Bledstein was skeptical but genuinely challenged by the
prophecy: "Seidelman has written a thoughtful epitaph for *the* academic
enterprise and those who disagree with his prophetic judgment (and I am
one) are challenged to explain why."[34]

These were matters of real significance raised in reaction to the
historiographical and political challenge of *Disenchanted Realists*.
Seidelman and Harpham were not inattentive to their import from the
very beginning. Seidelman in particular took notice. Within a year of
publication of *Disenchanted Realists* and before most reviews came out,
he allowed in public that readers would not be wrong to debate the three

traditions or the prophecy that liberalism was at an end. He did so at a summer institute on "new approaches" to disciplinary history at the Center for Advanced Study in the Behavioral Sciences in 1986, organized by the historians of anthropology, George W. Stocking and David Leary.[35] In that context, Seidelman also admitted that a fuller study would have to better explain the nineteenth-century origins, if not the late-twentieth-century demise, of the third tradition. He stated that *Disenchanted Realists* already admitted in its introduction that "possibly liberalism will not be eclipsed" if it proved to be less singularly prominent than it was thought to be in the 1980s (2). Later, in print, he furthermore admitted that he had indeed used a "makeshift name" for the "disenchanted realists" of the "third tradition." He insisted, nonetheless, that there *were* identifiable traditions in political science, however many there might be, only that they are not exhaustively defined "from the inside" as traditions of "research" alone, since they concerned questions about "the public role" of political science. He therefore hoped that "the history of our discipline should, in some small way, prompt us to raise these questions again."[36] This hope was not in vain, to judge by Robert Putnam's subsequent APSA presidential address that cited *Disenchanted Realists* and relied on its sketch of the discipline's history to ground its forward-looking plea for "the public role of political science." On a short list with Rogers Smith and Larry Diamond, Seidelman was praised for being one of the "eloquent voices . . . raised in recent years in defense of the public responsibilities of the profession." Political scientists needed "to engage with our fellow citizens in deliberation about their political concerns, broadly defined. Political science must have a greater public presence."[37] The questions about liberalism, a third tradition, or the discipline's public role may never be answered to every reader's satisfaction. But it still seems fair to say of *Disenchanted Realists*:

> If it were to turn out that the beginning and the end of the so-called "third tradition" were but literary events of a book, nothing much would hang on it as regards the history of political science or the power of *Disenchanted Realists*. Liberal reform helped frame much of the *political* identity of American political science, and the disillusionment, which its perceived and real failures helped bring on, is part of the history of political science since the late nineteenth century, "traditions" notwithstanding. If liberalism, like capitalism, proves more resilient in the face of the future than some have suggested and others feared, it

will require a shot of optimism presently absent from political science. As Seidelman and Harpham rightly note—and in fact help to bring about—we do need more "self-examination within the political science discipline" (xix), the rekindling of which can find its air, if not its heat, in the history of political science itself.[38]

We may leave to others to debate whether the discipline has, in the last few years, received its shot of optimism, given the resilience and crises of a more globalized capitalist economy. But to do so will require commenting on the discipline's present in light of its past, which is the fundamental historiographical message of *Disenchanted Realists*.

In light of its republication and the appearance of kindred works of disciplinary history, one may ask how *Disenchanted Realists* may yet help us understand the history of political science beyond the temporal boundaries it set for itself. How, in short, does it instruct or reposition inquiries into our disciplinary past before 1884 and our present after 1984? Where did those disenchanted realists come from and where did they go?

Granting the conceptual fuzziness about traditions—as well as the population of the first and second—there *is* a brief to be made that American political science in fact dates to the debates between Federalists and Anti-Federalists. Those debates featured an ongoing discourse about "the science of politics" and "the science of government" in exactly those terms. The concepts behind the terms were not uniquely American since there were countless European equivalents. But they were deployed in such a way as to chart new and competing visions of "state," "nation," and "democracy," as well as "citizens" who were no longer "subjects." An emergent "commercial society" shaped the policies and positions of a "political economy" configured for a new world. Federalists carved their arguments out of this broader discourse, honing the constituent terms into wordy weapons. The Anti-Federalists did the same. "Institutionalist" and "radical democratic" are apt labels that capture features of what distinguished them, although Anti-Federalists were also interested in the shape of institutions but not always particularly democratic. Other labels would serve as well. In any case, this broader discourse of "the science of politics" persisted well after the monumental debates over the fate of the Constitution. One finds this discourse and its constituent terms in writings as varied as those by Nathaniel Chipman, James Kent, Joseph Story,

Thomas Grimke, and John C. Calhoun, well into the early national and antebellum periods. Indeed, the discourse would persist amid conceptual change for the rest of the nineteenth century to allow increasingly self-conscious "liberals" and nascent "Progressives" to think anew about how an academic "profession" of "political science" could "reform" itself along with the "economics" of a "democratic state" in the 1880s and 1890s.

Crucial linchpins in the transformation of the discourse of "the science of politics" into a decidedly reformist and Progressive one—as well as in the first steps toward a scientific disciplinary infrastructure—can be identified in the person of Francis Lieber and in the institution of the American Social Science Association (ASSA).

Francis Lieber was the first officially named professor of history and political science in the United States, at Columbia in 1857. His inaugural hailed "the very science for nascent citizens of a republic." Lieber's chair would be subsequently filled by John W. Burgess, whose School of Political Science was the first in the nation and whose groundwork was laid by Lieber's academic efforts. Prior to Columbia, when at South Carolina College, Lieber gained his academic fame for having written two of the signal "textbooks" of nineteenth-century political science, *Manual of Political Ethics* (1838) and *Civil Liberty and Self-Government* (1853). He called the former his "book on the State" and, in it, the terms of its discourse were explicitly tied to an American "nationalism." In these texts he also consciously bridged the ideals of a strong national state with the basic vision he praised in the papers of *The Federalist*. Federalist-minded, Lieber was obsessed with reform and offered novel schema for the transformation of schools, prisons, legal institutions, and the New York State Constitution. Proud to be identified with a science that demanded obligations of a public role, he accepted the solicitation by President Lincoln and General Halleck to write a code of war that, in turn, proved influential for the development of international law. He served in many other public capacities, as well. After the Civil War, still at Columbia, he helped found the ASSA. His dedication to scholarly research along with reformist advocacy was broadly influential for his ASSA compatriots, as well as for later nineteenth-century academics that were associated with social sciences in the new research universities. Not the least of these were Woodrow Wilson and Lester Ward, the first pair featured in *Disenchanted Realists*. Lieber's later biographer rightly hailed him as a prototypical "nineteenth century liberal."[39] We might imagine him as a prototypical "disenchanted realist," as well, whose statist reformism was buffeted by waves of disenchantment with slavery, protectionism, draft riots, and labor organizers. Near the end of his life he worried about politicians "surrendering to the Democracy."[40] Lieber would in any case be a likely candidate to be paired with another—say, Burgess or Richard Ely or William Graham Sumner, who (unlike Lieber) get brief notice in *Disenchanted Realists* (23–25)—as those who most helped to fashion and then pass the baton to the third tradition.

The ASSA—noted briefly in *Disenchanted Realists*—was the paradigmatic nineteenth-century institution dedicated to reform.[41] Created in 1866 in the wake of the brutal hostilities of the Civil War (originally as the American Association for the Promotion of Social Science of 1865), it directly modeled its mission on the British National Association for the Promotion of Social Science. "Social science" was about inquiry into social problems for the purpose of reform. Consistent with the purposes of its British model and immediate American predecessor, its constituted purpose was "to collect all facts, diffuse all knowledge, and stimulate all inquiry, which have a bearing on social welfare." Its membership included evangelicals and religious reformers who did their work through "the social gospel," as well as academics and political figures. The ASSA published its own *Journal of Social Science*. Its five departments commissioned research into finance, social economy, health, education, and jurisprudence (to which Lieber contributed, mainly). It inaugurated annual meetings in 1868, becoming more prominent and visible in its research and reform work in the 1870s and 1880s. It persisted until the very early twentieth century. In the closing years of the nineteenth century, its membership broke up in stages. The splintered remains, in turn, created the principal academic associations that are still with us: AHA, AEA, ASA, and APSA. *Disenchanted Realists* underscores the evangelical, moralistic, and amateurish element of ASSA members. For them, "a science of society was no more than the application of Christian morality to the solution of practical problems" (22). This captures an important dimension of the ASSA. But there was more than that. The ASSA counted among its leading lights Lieber (Columbia), Andrew Dickson White (Cornell), Francis Wayland (Brown), Theodore Dwight Woolsey (Yale), and Daniel Coit Gilman (University of California at Berkeley and Johns Hopkins), among others. In short, it had prominent academics from elite institutions of higher learning that were in the process of shedding a denominational college image and embracing elements of a more secular, nondenominational research university. While its slow-motion breakup signaled the tensions and contradictions between its evangelical and secular wings—its religious and liberal membership—the ASSA was nonetheless, for all its contradictory tendencies, a crucial spawning ground for the "third tradition" whose story *Disenchanted Realists* dramatically traces until its "end" in 1984.

But *did* it end? Are there no more realists to disenchant or liberals to reform? Have all the democrats disappeared? Or, are there successors, as there were predecessors like Lieber, Burgess, and Ely, giving the third tradition—or, if not tradition, at least the storied line of reforming scholars in the discipline—a longer lifespan?

In the spirit and format of *Disenchanted Realists*, I think we can identify a pair of contemporary political scientists who are public-oriented leaders of the discipline, as well as realist-minded reformers committed to a democratic citizenry and a participatory civil society supported by the state. There are other candidates for nomination, but the pair that stands out in my mind is Robert D. Putnam and Jane J. Mansbridge. With greater emphasis on the groups, networks, and volunteers of civil society when compared to previous pairs in the "third tradition," both nonetheless have achieved great success as scholars who have repeatedly stressed the importance of reform and civic engagement as part of what it is to *be* a political scientist. Indeed, they would have the discipline do more by way of education and encouragement to revitalize the civic life identified with the third tradition of *Disenchanted Realists*. Here it is only possible to provide a thumbnail sketch of each, guided by the categories and historiography of *Disenchanted Realists*. Of course, the venture is hypothetical and speculative, given the prophetic voice and apparent finality thirty years ago about "the eclipse" of a third tradition. But if the venture is suggestive and the pair convincing, then *Disenchanted Realists* was not only largely correct about an important lineage in the discipline's past but also about the ongoing presence of reform scholars who believe by their words and deeds that a science *of* politics can also be a science *for* politics.

The scholarly and popular reaction to the work of Robert Putnam in the last dozen years—especially *Bowling Alone* (2000)—has been nothing short of remarkable. A national best-seller, *Bowling Alone* has been cited in academic journals more than 25,000 times and featured in popular magazines such as *People* and *Cooking Light*. It surely counters the 1985 diagnosis in *Disenchanted Realists* that "third tradition political science today has few defenders and a dwindling audience among outsiders" (240). A Yale-educated scholar of comparative political elites, Putnam was already a highly regarded political scientist when he moved to Harvard in 1979. His interest in "democratic theory and practice," as embodied in "civic traditions," came to fruition in *Making Democracy Work: Civic Traditions in Modern Italy* (1993), an important treatise in which he introduced the concept of "social capital." Derived principally from the work of James Coleman, social capital laid claim to considerable explanatory power, but also proved to be highly value-laden. Putnam defined social capital in terms of the "features of social organization, such as trust, norms, and networks, that can improve the efficiency of society by facilitating coordinated actions." The networks that were of greatest importance, democratically, consisted of individuals, groups, and organizations in state and civil society involved in "civic engagement."[42] Following quickly on the heels of *Making Democracy Work*, Putnam found further place for social capital in a surprisingly well-received article in a new academic journal with a catchy title, "Bowling Alone: America's Declining Social Capital" (1995).[43] Among countless others, Seidelman himself took note: "I like to quote an article called "Bowling Alone" by Robert Putnam. In it he says there are more people bowling than ever, but there are fewer people in bowling leagues. He argues that bowling is not just entertainment, it was a way for people to associate with people who would otherwise be strangers."[44] There was the nub of it. Americans, with their social capital veering into the gutters, were individually hitting the lanes, but not in leagues. This matter of bowling was symbolic of a wider ranging decline in American civic and political life, measured in all imaginable ways. Buoyed by the reception of this article—or just persistent in his diagnosis of America—Putnam deepened and broadened his research, eventually publishing the huge and hugely successful tome, *Bowling Alone: The Collapse and Revival of American Community* (2000).[45]

The subtitle of *Bowling Alone* held out the promise of a revival of America's civic prospects. The concluding chapter even itemized "an agenda for social capitalists."[46] But it did so only after hundreds of pages documented the collapse of public life in the second half of the twentieth century. Indeed, after distinguishing between "bridging" and "bonding capital"—the one crossing over to different groups, the other cementing given networks—Putnam's realism and honesty led him to "The Dark Side of Social Capital."[47] He concluded the chapter bearing that ominous title by noting "some kinds of bonding social capital may discourage the formation of bridging social capital and vice versa. That's what happened in the case of busing" to achieve educational equity in the face of racial discrimination in the United States at midcentury.[48] More generally, bonding social capital could be at war with the liberal values of equality, fraternity, and toleration. The dark side got darker in some subsequent research into the hardening of community groups and the plummeting of trust when faced with racial or ethnic diversity.[49] This important research agenda on social capital continued through the first decade of the twenty-first century, and it shows no sign of abating today.[50] In any case, this prolific agenda was the basis for many awards, as well as Putnam's election as APSA president.

Only the few hardened political scientists wed to pursuing "pure" research or fingering the beads of ancient "truths" would be indifferent to the despair conveyed in such findings about America's modern civic life. But Putnam not only conveyed them, he *inveighed against* them as one might expect from a reform-minded liberal with an agenda for civic education and engagement. He ended *Bowling Alone* with a (Leninist–tongue-in-cheek?) section on "What Is To Be Done?" His original article earned him audiences with President Bill Clinton and Prime Minister Tony Blair, who were then organizing several civic initiatives and, in Blair's case, a "social capital unit" in his cabinet. As already noted, Putnam devoted his APSA presidential address—in which he praised the "eloquent voice" of Ray Seidelman—to the "public role of political science." He created and has sustained for more than fifteen years the Saguaro Seminar on Civic Engagement that brings together academics, clergy, activists, and political leaders to discuss actionable ways to build social capital in diverse communities and changing environments. In its early years, the seminar included the then–civil rights lawyer Barack Obama. It created a popular website for broad dissemination of information, BetterTo-gether.org.[51] It insinuated "social capital" into the lexicon of the World Bank and the United Nations. It also, quite realistically, recognized the scope of the problems Putnam had identified. The prospects of building or restoring social capital were not guaranteed given the mountains of data presented in *Bowling Alone*; and indeed the internal tension between bridging and bonding capital suggested something like permanent struggle. But Putnam and his Saguaro colleagues have shown their reform commitments in word and deed. There's still time for the onset of disenchantment, some might say. And the whole enterprise has not wanted for leftist critics, not least because of the casual use of the terminology of "capital" and "capitalist."[52] But, for now, Putnam's dedication to political science and reform advocacy as twin activities bears all the signs of a living third tradition—or its morphed inheritor.

Putnam's colleague at Harvard's Kennedy School of Government— Jane J. Mansbridge—has an equally strong claim to the inherited mantle of the third tradition. The 2012–2013 APSA president, Mansbridge has long been an influential scholar of democratic theory and practice. Raised within earshot of (and often hearing) the voices of New England town meetings, she took their democratic spirit with her to Harvard in the 1960s, when it was still very much a bastion of white male academia. She emerged with her Ph.D. and a deep commitment to participatory democracy and feminist politics as complementary "causes" that informed her subsequent scholarship.[53] In her major book, a decade in the making— *Beyond Adversary Democracy* (1980)—she made clear these commitments, emphasizing how hers was an "'empirical' approach to doing theory." This entailed listening to "ordinary people" (in interviews or discussion groups) about their problems and interests, as well as how they "think about normative issues."[54] In the course of her intensively researched and incredibly detailed study of a town meeting government ("Selby") and a participatory workplace ("Helpline"), Mansbridge discovered and brought to the fore "the centrality of interests" for determining forms of democratic governance. While "interests" (in term and concept) had been a staple of political thought since at least the eighteenth century and were very prominent in pluralist democratic theory of the twentieth century, she pried apart "common" interests from "conflicting" ones and then forged their respective connections to what she innovatively called "unitary" versus "adversary" democracy. Common interests were not only possible but also discoverable in deliberation, allowing at least small polities and aspects of larger ones to move "beyond" an adversarial politics of conflicting interests. Mansbridge also solved an important theoretical puzzle at the same time, namely, in democratic governance structures constituted by common interests, there need not be complete "equality of power," an alleged ideal of democracy since the ancient *polis*. Not only did these theoretical interventions play a prominent role in debates over democratic theory at the time of their publication, they reinforced Mansbridge's long-term interest in "self-interest," which too could be gotten "beyond."[55] Moreover, with the emphasis on talking with ordinary citizens and finding in unitary democracy the centrality of deliberation,

Mansbridge proved to be an early and influential theorist of what has become known as "deliberative democracy."

The national controversy over the Equal Rights Amendment (ERA)—the subject of Mansbridge's next major study, *Why We Lost the ERA* (1986)— proved that adversarial politics still ruled the fifty states in America. After ten years of debate in living rooms, classrooms, and state legislatures—between 1972 and 1982—the proposed amendment to the U.S. Constitution that called for equal rights for women failed to reach the threshold for ratification. Published shortly after *Disenchanted Realists*, *Why We Lost the ERA* shared its mood. The ERA's "defeat was a major setback for equality between men and women." "As a political scientist," Mansbridge was not only a scholarly witness to the struggles for the ERA, but also an advocate and activist in Illinois. One of the signal lessons to be learned "from defeat" shed light on the public interest, the dynamics of organizations, and the politics of volunteers: "organizations that depend on volunteers to promote the common interest seem to have an inherent tendency toward ideological purity and polarized perceptions." "Ironically, the greatest cost in organizing for the public interest may be the distortion, in the course of organizing, of that interest itself." Attention to irony of this kind was a supplementary lesson for democratic theory and practice, as well. And though there was a mood of defeat and disenchantment, Mansbridge concluded by deeming the ratification effort worthwhile. It "raised consciousness, helped women organize politically, and stimulated legislative and judicial action." Its "political death" even corresponded to "a flowering of feminist thought."[56]

The principle of equal rights that animated the ERA was a liberal one, and liberals were its supporters. One might say—in the categories of *Disenchanted Realists*—that in her major works, Mansbridge embraces a strain of liberalism, say, reform liberalism or radical liberalism. She might balk at such labels, preferring simply feminist and democrat.[57] But, then, some of the major figures in the lineage Seidelman identified burst their confining labels.[58] Of greater import, however, is the commitment to reform, the combining of scholarship and advocacy. Mansbridge exemplifies this combination in her career and life's work *as* a political scientist. When in graduate school, she helped draft the chapter on sexuality for the feminist manifesto *Our Bodies, Our Selves*. Looking back on her work, she admitted that there was "a manual for practice embedded in the ERA book, just as there was in the book on participatory democracy."[59] An adviser to the National Commission on Civic Renewal,

Mansbridge combines the defining characteristics of what Seidelman articulated as the third tradition. This is nicely captured in an award created in her name after she left Northwestern University after sixteen years of teaching—the Jane Mansbridge Scholar-Activist Award.

Disenchanted Realists struck a nerve in the discipline of political science when it appeared thirty years ago. It may do so again. Perhaps this time it may be less the deck-clearing criticism of the discipline that so riled some establishment political scientists than the more inspiring image of scholars actively committed to democracy and reform. A healthy skepticism would still have to attend this; the political times are hardly improved since 1985. Certainly no enchanted idealism lies in the wings. But with models like Mansbridge, Putnam, others—and Ray Seidelman himself—political scientists may still aspire to active citizenship and sophisticated scholarship. The principal author of *Disenchanted Realists* "was himself a 'disenchanted realist,'" Bruce Miroff said in memoriam, "but he never gave in to cynicism or retreated into quietism." What was "more important to him" than even his *own* advocacy and activism "was inspiring his students to take what they learned in political science and bring it to bear in democratic activism."[60] This inspiration has now taken legislative form in a 2012 New York State Senate bill—"put forth in the memory of the late Dr. Ray Seidelman"—that mandates the provision of voter registration forms to students by colleges, universities, and public high schools. "Sharing his belief in the electoral process and grass roots democracy," the preamble notes, "he inspired his students to actively participate in elections at all levels." It continues: "Dr. Seidelman's definition of democracy, 'Democracy is not what we have, it is what we aspire to be. So dare to aspire to it, for in the process you become a democratic citizen. It takes courage to live as a democratic citizen, and that's why we fight for it; this will involve you in great risks, but it's worth it because it will make you free.'"[61] This is what animates *Disenchanted Realists* and is its fundamental political message. Its critical historiography is in the service of a living democratic history of political science.

Notes

Chapter 1: Introduction

1. The retreat from what has been taken to be New Deal liberalism is particularly acute among the advocates of various reindustrialization schemes. The most prominent examples are, for the supply-side position, George Gilder, *Wealth and Poverty* (New York: Bantam Books, 1981); for the "Atari" Democrats, Robert Reich and Ira Magaziner, *Minding America's Business* (New York: Vintage, 1982); Paul Tsongas, *The Road from Here* (New York: Vintage, 1981); Lester Thurow, *Dangerous Currents: The State of Economics* (New York: Random House, 1982); for corporatist Democrats, Felix Rohatyn, "Reconstructing America," *New York Review of Books*, March 5, 1981, p. 16f. On the democratic socialist left, see Alan Wolfe, *America's Impasse* (New York: Pantheon, 1982), and Samuel Bowles, David Gordon, and Thomas Weisskopf, *Beyond the Wasteland* (New York: Doubleday, 1983).

2. The best and broadest work on the history of American political science is Bernard Crick, *The American Science of Politics* (Berkeley: University of California Press, 1959.) Crick emphasizes the essential "conservatism" of American political scientists; they are said to accept the "givenness" of American institutions. In contrast, we contend that prominent political scientists have often been critical of American political institutions because theirs is a brand of political thought designed to replace "premodern" American modes of political thinking. Other disciplinary histories emphasize the developmental character of the discipline. See Albert Somit and Joseph Tanenhaus, *American Political Science* (New York: Atherton Press, 1964). This book contends that political science is hardly a cumulative or evolving enterprise of ever more sophisticated methods and findings. Political science history is, rather, cyclical: succeeding generations always "rediscover" and then abandon ideas and goals of their predecessors.

3. See Norman Jacobson, "Political Science and Political Education," *American Political Science Review* 57 (1963): 561–69.

4. Adams quote from Gordon Wood, *The Creation of the American Republic, 1776–1787* (New York: Norton, 1969), p. 571.

5. Wood, *Creation*, pp. 593, 492, 610. Wood's argument differs from Jacobson's in several important ways, especially regarding the character and strength of the anti-Federalist position.

6. See Madison's famous argument in Federalist No. 10.

7. Paine is only one among many opponents of the institutionalist position. His support for the Constitution is rooted in ideas far different from those of other supporters. See Nelson Adkins, ed. *Thomas Paine: Common Sense and Other Political Writings* (Indianapolis: Bobbs-Merrill, 1953).

8. Wood, *Creation*, p. 317.

9. Jacobson, "Political Science," p. 561. See also Sheldon Wolin, "The Peoples' Two Bodies," *democracy* I, no. I (January 1981): 9–24.

10. Stephen Skowronek's *Building a New American State: The Expansion of National Administrative Capacities: 1877–1920* (New York: Cambridge University Press, 1982) traces the pitfalls of state-building in nineteenth- and twentieth-century America. Skowronek points out that would-be modernizers faced a strong and entrenched premodern state of courts and parties that continually thwarted efforts to build modern instruments of state power through the military, economic regulation, and civil service reform.

11. The best accounts of these cultural definitions of science are: Robert Wiebe, *The Search for Order* (New York: Hill and Wang, 1967); Crick, *American Science;* Haskell, *Emergence.*

12. Walter Lippmann, *Drift and Mastery: An Attempt to Diagnose the Current Unrest* (Englewood Cliffs, NJ: Prentice Hall, 1961), p. 61. Lippmann is not a political scientist, but his political philosophy is nearly identical to that of the political scientists discussed in this work. For further discussion of the idea of science, see Ronald Steel's excellent *Walter Lippmann and the American* Century (Boston: Little, Brown, 1981).

13. This essential optimism of political science modernists perhaps explains why they have largely ignored, or seriously misinterpreted, the alternative ideas of social science of Marx, Weber, and others. See Marshall Berman, *All That Is Solid Melts into Air* (New York: Simon and Schuster, 1982).

14. Dwight Waldo's *The Administrative State: A Study of the Political Theory of Public Administration* (New York: Ronald Press, 1948) is still an excellent account of American admiration for bureaucracy.

15. See Martin Shefter, "Party, Bureaucracy and Political Change in the United States," in *Political Parties: Development and Decay*, ed. Louis Maisel and Joseph Cooper (Beverly Hills, CA: Sage, 1978), pp. 211–65.

16. The fervor for the creation of "new citizens" is a little-noticed leitmotif of political science history. Usually, such advocacy is contained in the final chapters of works critical of this or that facet of American political culture. For a comprehensive statement, see Charles Merriam, *Civic Education in the United States* (New York: Scribner's, 1939).

17. See Mary Furner, *Advocacy and Objectivity* (Lexington: University of Kentucky Press, 1975); Haskell, *Emergence;* and Dorothy Ross, "The Development of the Social Sciences," in *The Organization of Knowledge in Modern America*, ed. Alexandra Oleson and John Voss, (Baltimore, MD: Johns Hopkins University Press, 1979), pp. 107–38.

18. For excellent accounts of the "professionalism" movement, see Lawrence

Veysey, *The Emergence of the American University* (Chicago: University of Chicago Press, 1965); Burton Bledstein, *The Culture of Professionalism: The Middle Class and the Development of Higher Education in America* (New York: Norton, 1976); John Higham, "The Matrix of Specialization" and Edward Shils, "The Order of Learning in the United States," in Oleson and Voss., eds., *Organization of Knowledge.*

Chapter 2: The Impulse toward a Science of Politics, 1880–1900

1. Until recently, the literature on this formative period of American social science tended to be divided roughly into two groups. The first and dominant strain comprehends early social science as a harbinger of the liberal, progressive (and benign) welfare state. Revisionist historians such as Mary O. Furner or James Weinstein, in contrast, have stressed early social science's ties with "corporate liberalism." If the first strain stresses the thankful continuity with the liberal tradition expressed in social science, the second appropriately notes its ties with corporate philanthropy, its resistance to social movements, and its applause for imperialism as part of an overall "moral and intellectual rehabilitation of the ruling class."

For the former position, see especially Richard Hofstadter, *Social Darwinism in American Thought* (Boston: Beacon Press, 1965); Henry Steele Commager, *Lester Ward and the Welfare State* (Indianapolis, IN: Bobbs-Merrill, 1967), and *The American Mind: An Interpretation of American Thought and Character since the 1880s* (New Haven, CT: Yale University Press, 1950); Eric Goldman, *Rendezvous with Destiny* (New York: Vintage Books, 1956); and Sidney Fine, *Laissez-Faire and the General Welfare State* (Ann Arbor: University of Michigan Press, 1956). The latter position is perhaps best represented by David Eakins, "The Development of Corporate Liberal Policy Research in the United States, 1885–1965" (Ph.D. diss., University of Wisconsin, 1966); Mary O. Furner, *Advocacy and Objectivity: The Professionalization of Social Science* (Lexington: University of Kentucky Press, 1974); and Christopher Lasch, "The Moral and Intellectual Rehabilitation of the Ruling Class," in *The World of Nations* (New York: Vintage Books, 1974). Furner, however, is careful to detail how social science's early diversity was integrated into corporate liberalism with the help of the professional ethic.

2. Haskell, *Emergence*, p. 65. See also Bledstein, *Culture*, chaps. 6–8.

3. See Edward Bellamy, *Looking Backward* (New York: Modern Library, 1942); Ignatius Donnelly and his incredible *Caesar's Column* (Cambridge, MA: Belknap Press of Harvard University Press, 1960); and William "Coin" Harvey, *Coin's Financial School* (Cambridge, MA: Harvard University Press, 1963). Henry Adams's disgruntled works also went against the grain of social scientists since his "Virgin and the Dynamo" metaphors in *The Education* fundamentally undermined their belief in progress. The new social scientists welcomed the technological changes Adams and Donnelly lamented, even as they worried about their political consequences. See Henry Adams, *The Education of Henry Adams* (New York: Holmes and Meier, 1963).

4. See Furner, *Advocacy and Objectivity*, and Haskell, *Emergence*, chap. 5, pp. 91–121.

5. In a series of brilliant articles, Dorothy Ross demonstrates that early social science cannot be viewed solely as an effort to transform the liberal tradition from *within*. Early social science contained a wide variety of social thinkers not easily captured by either liberalism or by the two perspectives cited earlier in note 1. See her "Socialism and American Liberalism: Academic Social Thought in the 1880s," in *Perspectives in American History*, no. 12 (Cambridge, MA: Harvard University Press, 1977–1978), and "The Development of the Social Sciences," in Oleson and Voss, eds., *Organization of Knowledge*.

Ross's notions about the complexity and richness of social thought in the 1880s draw heavily on J. G. A. Pocock's arguments regarding the importance of "civic humanism" as a variant of liberal republican thought in America. See his "Civic Humanism and Its Role in Anglo-American Thought," in *Politics, Language and Time: Essays on Political Thought and History* (New York: Atheneum, 1971), and Ross's excellent "The Liberal Tradition Revisited and the Republican Tradition Addressed," in *New Directions in American Intellectual History*, ed. John Higham and Paul K. Conkin (Baltimore, MD: Johns Hopkins University Press, 1979), pp. 116–31.

6. Basic works by the three include Richard Ely, *The Labor Movement in America* (New York: Macmillan, 1886), and *An Introduction to Political Economy* (New York: Macmillan, 1889); John Bates Clark, *The Philosophy of Wealth* (Boston: Ginn, 1889) and "The Scholar's Political Opportunity," *Political Science Quarterly* 12 (December 1897): 589–602; and Henry Carter Adams, "The Position of Science in the Historical Development of Political Economy," *Penn Monthly* 10 (April 1879): 15–22.

As Dorothy Ross points out, however, the three were almost totally unfamiliar with the secular democratic radicalism of Paine, Jefferson, and the Locofoco tradition. All three were rather skeptical about the "native" sources of socialist development. See Ross, "Socialism," pp. 11–15, 32–33. Yet this strain of thinking had deep roots in the "second," anti-institutional strain of American politics discussed in Norman Jacobson, "Political Science and Political Education," *American Political Science Review* 57 (1963): 561–69. All three broke with the tradition of civic humanism of the previous generation. "Stages" of historical development replaced the earlier concept of cycles of founding, maturity, and inevitable decline of republics.

7. Mary Furner makes a similar case with scholars even less radical than these socialists; see *Advocacy and Objectivity*, chap. 11. Dorothy Ross tries to explain why a kind of American Fabianism did not emerge out of these early stirrings. She attributes it to the temptations of social mobility among this generation of scholars, temptations not present in Great Britain, where the first generation of socialist intellectuals already held patrician status regardless of their politics and were thus less subject to the intimidations and constraints of professionalism and its standards of conduct.

8. See Seymour Martin Lipset's essay on the early Sociology Department at Columbia University, part of Burgess's Faculty of Political Science, in Gordon

Hoxie, *The Faculty of Political Science at Columbia University* (New York: Columbia University Press, 1955), and John Burgess, *Reminiscences of an American Scholar* (New York: Columbia University Press, 1934), esp. pp. 150–60.

9. See A. D. White's *History of the Warfare of Science with Theology in Christendom* (New York: Dover, 1960) and his rabidly statist and nationalist "Education in Political Science," an address delivered at the third anniversary of Johns Hopkins University, February 22, 1879 (Baltimore, MD: Johns Hopkins University Studies in Historical and Political Science, 1879). For an attack on laissez-faire policies and an ode to the German-French conceptions of state authority, see T. K. Worthington's "Recent Impressions of the Ecole Libre," in the same series as White's.

10. See Hofstadter, *Social Darwinism*, chap. 1; and Haskell, *Emergence*, p. 262.

11. Given Wilson's later penchant for red-baiting, his youthful assertions that "in fundamental theory socialism and democracy are almost if not quite one and the same," and "the individual rights which the democracy of our century has actually observed were suggested to it by a political philosophy morally individualistic, but not necessarily democratic," are surprising. Wilson, as everyone knows, did not rest easily with this unpublished essay on "Socialism and Democracy" of his youthful days. Such vigor was readily absorbed into the progressive, liberal, individualistic dream of *The New Freedom* (Princeton, NJ: Princeton University Press, 1956).

12. From Woodrow Wilson's classic, "The Study of Administration," *Political Science Quarterly* 2, no. 2 (June 1887): 197–222.

13. Quoted in Henry Steele Commager, *The American Mind: An Interpretation of American Thought and Character Since the 1880's* (New Haven, CT: Yale University Press, 1950), pp. 234–35. For the debates about the AEA's "politicization" and its quick change into a "neutral" profession open only to those with academic credentials, see Furner, *Advocacy and Objectivity*, pp. 59–60. Joseph Dorfman, *The Economic Mind in American Civilization*, 5 vols. (New York: Viking, 1949); and Richard Ely, *Ground under Our Feet: An Autobiography* (New York: Macmillan, 1938) provide more general analyses of the rise of the economics profession.

14. See Samuel Chugerman, *Lester F. Ward, The American Aristotle: A Summary and Interpretation of His Sociology* (Durham, NC: Duke University Press, 1939).

15. Concise treatments of Ward are found in Hofstadter, *Social Darwinism*, and Commager, *Lester Ward*. The most direct statement of Ward's position is his "False Notions of Government," *Forum* 3 (June 1887): 16–23.

16. See Ross, "Socialism," p. 28, and Chugerman, *Lester F. Ward*, pp. 24–30.

17. See Samuel P. Hays, *Conservation and the Gospel of Efficiency* (New York: Atheneum, 1975), for an account of the social science linkage to the conservation movement. Ward's life perhaps epitomizes such ties, as he was an accomplished natural scientist before he turned his guns on the "waste and profligacy" in the human world. State management of natural resources was one of Ward's chief concerns in *Dynamic Sociology* (New York: Appleton, 1883), p. 14.

18. See Lester Ward, *Psychic Factors in Civilization* (Boston: Ginn, 1893), p. 295.

19. In this sense, Spenserian doctrine provides a theory of historical progression that had been missing from the cyclical views of the "civic humanist" tradition into

which Ward was born. Ward's absorption of Social Darwinism into a Comtean scheme of prediction and control of evolution thereby signals a characteristic break third tradition thinkers made. Degeneration from republican origins was not inevitable, especially with the creation of a "science of sciences" such as sociology. See Lester Ward, "Broadening the Way to Success," *Forum* 2 (December 1886): 12–17, for evidence of this move away from the cyclical notion of historical time.

20. From Lester Ward, "Plutocracy and Paternalism," *Forum* 20 (November 1895): 303.

21. This is the leitmotif of Ward's "Plutocracy and Paternalism." Ward believed that such a positive state would recreate the conditions for a kind of "natural equality of abilities" that had been perverted and corrupted by the "artificial" overlay of laissez-faire ideas.

22. See Ward, *Psychic Factors*, p. 325.

23. Ward, *Psychic Factors*, p. 295, and *Dynamic Sociology*, p. 11.

24. Ward, *Dynamic Sociology*, p. 21.

25. Quote is from Commager, *American Mind*, pp. 212–13. Ward's perception of agrarian and labor protest as the necessary but limited "emotional" component of a much broader "scientific" movement is characteristic of third tradition scholarship. One might wonder, though, if Ward's views are any less "emotional" than those of the political movements his science sought to educate. Moreover, Ward seemed to misunderstand completely the source of "emotional protest"—the Populists sought not only new policies, but also disputed the idea that citizens' powers could be delegated to distant (even if benign) authority. See Laurence Goodwyn, *Democratic Promise: The Populist Movement in America* (New York: Oxford University Press, 1976), and Bruce Palmer, *"Man over Money," The Southern Populist Critique of American Capitalism* (Chapel Hill: University of North Caroline Press, 1980).

26. Ward, *Dynamic Sociology*, p. 21.

27. Ward's "False Notions of Government" tried to separate justified hostility to the present, "corrupted" state from unjustified distrust of a future, regenerated, republican state. See also "Broadening the Way to Success" for Ward's vision of a state administration drawn from individuals of all classes. Ward never seems to draw distinctions between reducing the obstacles for individual "advancement" versus the quite different goal of promoting the advancement of groups, strata, or classes as a whole. He seems to suggest the "natural" process of "selective breeding," supplemented by the new state's guarantee of a universal standard of education and conditions of life, would invalidate such distinctions.

28. Ward's views on political science as simply one department of "applied sociology" are put forth in three essays in his massive six-volume work on sociology as the "queen" of all other sciences, natural and physical as well as social. The quote is from "The Claims of Political Science" in *Glimpses into the Cosmos*, vol. 3, p. 334. But see also "An Example in Political Science" and "The Science and the Art of Government" in vol. 4 of *Glimpses into the Cosmos*. (New York: Putnam, 1913).

29. Ward, *Dynamic Sociology*, p. 37.

30. Lester Ward, "Scientific Legislation," in *Glimpses into the Cosmos*, vol. 4, p. 170.

Ward proposed a "national academy of social sciences" as the central "clearinghouse" of data-gathering indispensable for planning. Compare Ward's ideas to those of Theodore J. Lowi, *The End of Liberalism* (New York: Norton, 1979), final chapter.

31 Commager sees Ward's position vindicated by the growth of organizations that bridge academia and the political world; see his *American Mind*, pp. 216–26.

32. Hays explores the connection between Ward and the conservation movement in *Conservation and the Gospel of Efficiency*, p. 215.

33. See Ward, *Dynamic Sociology*, p. 19, for this recourse to faith in the midst of "applied sociology."

34. The material relevant to these preliminary observations will be cited below. Still the most comprehensive biography of the "academic" Wilson is Arthur S. Link, *Wilson: The Road to the White House* (Princeton, NJ: Princeton University Press, 1957). For insights into Wilson's "moral affirmation of capitalism" and the Puritan, Smithian, and Burkean sources of this affirmation, see William Diamond, *The Economic Thought of Woodrow Wilson* (Baltimore, MD: Johns Hopkins University Press, 1943).

Martin Sklar has shown why and how Wilson's alleged "moralisms" do not contradict his supposedly "amoral commercialism," but are together components of a liberal capitalist ideology, rooted in the political economy of Adam Smith and the historicism of Burke. Both are combined in a view that emphasizes the organic continuity of social and cultural systems. See "Woodrow Wilson and the Political Economy of Modern United States Liberalism," in *For a New America: Essays on History and Politics from Studies on the Left*, ed. James Weinstein and David Eakins (New York: Random House, 1970), pp. 48–49.

35. In this sense, Wilson is linked to Ward. In Sklar's words, "It was that mixture of classical nineteenth century liberalism with conservative historicism that made Wilson the Progressive he was: rational adjustments, determined by enlightened men concerned with the general welfare, were made to irrational processes, that is, to processes not determined by men by evolving irresistibly in accordance with super-human natural law or predetermination"; see Sklar, "Woodrow Wilson," p. 54.

36. See *Congressional Government* (Boston: Houghton-Mifflin, 1885), hereafter referred to as *CG*; *Constitutional Government in the United States* (New York: Columbia University Press, 1908); and *The State: Elements of Historical and Practical Politics* (Boston: Heath, 1918).

37. Woodrow Wilson, "Character of Democracy in the United States," *Atlantic Monthly* 64 (November 1889): 585. Wilson's brief identification with a quasi-socialist notion of history was probably due to the influence of his Johns Hopkins professor, Richard Ely. In "Character," he has already returned to a Progressive view of history, that "mankind must adjust itself to new circumstances in the light of past customs and traditions and new experiences." Among these "circumstances" were large "economic combinations." See "Politics 1857–1907," *Atlantic Monthly* 100 (November 1907): 635–46.

38. See Wilson, "Character of Democracy," and "Democracy and Efficiency," *Atlantic Monthly* 87 (March 1901): 289–99.

39. Like many other Progressives, Wilson tended to juxtapose "science" and "leadership." The former was said to be deterministic, the latter "creative." See "The Study of Politics," in *An Old Master and Other Political Essays* (New York: Scribner, 1893), pp. 44–57.

40. See "A Literary Politician," in *Mere Literature and Other Essays* (Boston: Houghton-Mifflin, 1897), p. 74.

41. See Wilson's *Leaders of Men* (Princeton, NJ: Princeton University Press, 1952), p. 171, for an extended discussion of these distinctions.

42. Woodrow Wilson, "The Law and the Facts," APSA presidential address, *American Political Science Review* 9 (1911): 11.

43. To Wilson, studies of formal organization and the law could not capture the organic growth and change in institutions and the society in which they were embedded. See *CG*, p. 29. Arthur Bentley (see chap. 3 of this work) was to make a much more complete break with formalism.

44. Wilson, *CG*, p. 31.

45. Wilson, *CG*, pp. 206, 207, 214.

46. See Wilson, *CG*, "Conclusion," pp. 193–215, for these reformist suggestions.

47. Wilson, "The Study of Administration," *Political Science Quarterly* 2, no. 2 (June 1887), which might be said to be the founding manifesto of the modern American public administration movement. See Dwight Waldo, *The Administrative State: A Study of the Political Theory of American Public Administration* (New York: Ronald Press, 1948), for evidence of Wilson's influence on an "Americanized" conception of public administration through the idea of the separation of politics and administration.

48. Wilson, "Study," p. 210.

49. Ibid., pp. 215, 217.

50. Ibid., pp. 214–15.

51. Carl Friedrich addresses a similar solution to the problem of accountability. See the Friedrich–Samuel Finer debate in *Bureaucratic Power in National Politics*, ed. Francis Rourke (Boston: Little, Brown, 1965), pp. 165–87. See also Dwight Waldo's treatment in *The Administrative State*, p. 90. Indeed, this whole notion of accountability is typical of the third tradition thinking of Beard, Merriam, Lasswell, and others, since it interposes social scientists between the state and society. Quotes from Wilson, "Study," pp. 214–15.

52. See Robert Cuff, *The War Industries Board* (Baltimore, MD: Johns Hopkins University Press, 1973), on the questionable success of the administrative ideal.

53. Quote in Sklar, "Woodrow Wilson," p. 92.

54. The view that a "strong" executive might combine the qualities of popular leadership, national purpose, and bureaucratic rationality in a system otherwise plagued by a multiplicity of "private interests" has been a consistent strand of thinking in the social sciences from Woodrow Wilson to the present. For the New Deal period, see Barry Karl, *Executive Reorganization and the New Deal* (Cambridge, MA: Harvard University Press, 1963). Such images are strong even in the pluralist heaven of New Haven, Connecticut. See Robert Dahl, *Who Governs?* (New Haven,

CT: Yale University Press, 1961). Such images are equally vivid in antipluralist critiques. See the final chapter in Grant McConnell, *Private Power and American Democracy* (New York: Vintage, 1969). For an analysis of this strand of thought in Progressive thinking, see Wiebe, *Search*, pp. 155–62.

Chapter 3: Science as Muckraking:
The Cult of Realism in the Progressive Era

1. The literature on Progressivism's institutional reforms is immense. Here we cite only those works most germane to this study: Robert Wiebe, *Businessmen and Reform* (Chicago: Quadrangle Books, 1968); Samuel P. Hays, *Conservation and the Gospel of Efficiency* (New York: Atheneum, 1975); Richard Hofstadter, *The Age of Reform* (New York: Vintage Books, 1959); Gabriel Kolko, *The Triumph of Conservatism* (Chicago: Quadrangle Books, 1963); James Weinstein, *The Corporate Ideal in the Liberal State* (Boston: Beacon Press, 1968); Stephen Skowronek, *Building a New American State* (New York: Cambridge University Press, 1982); and William Appleman Williams, *Contours of American History* (Cleveland, OH: World Publishing, 1961).

2. See Somit and Tanenhaus, *Development of American Political Science* (Boston: Allyn and Bacon, 1967); Crick, *American Science*; Ross, "The Development of the Social Sciences," in *Organization of Knowledge,* ed. Voss and Oleson.

3. A self-congratulatory history of these ties is found in *Institute for Government Research: An Account of Research Achievements* (Washington, DC: Brookings Institution, 1956), and Gene Lyons, *The Uneasy Partnership: Social Science and the Federal Government in the Twentieth Century* (New York: Sage Foundation, 1969). Most of the growing ties between local, state, and federal governments and individual academics might be seen as part of what Weinstein has called "corporate liberalism." Distinct from Beard's and Bentley's orientation, corporate liberals forged "interlocking directorates" of business, labor, government, and academe, and excluded criticism of American capitalism. In contrast, Beard and Bentley were hardly socialists, but unlike their counterparts they wanted to extend the scope and range of collectivist-style reforms. In contrast, Willoughby, Lowell, Ford, and others were hardly concerned at all with the redistributive components of reform. See *Institute*, p. 15.

4. Frank Goodnow, "The Work of the American Political Science Association," *Proceedings of the APSA* 1 (1904): 1–17. *The Political Science Quarterly*, founded in 1886, was the major journal of political science in the 1890s and early 1900s. See Somit and Tanenhaus, *Development*, pp. 44–45. Somit and Tanenhaus found that the majority of articles between 1888 and 1904 dealt with "contemporaneous events."

5. Crick, *American Science*, pp. 95–113; Somit and Tanenhaus, *Development*, pp. 63–79.

6. Somit and Tanenhaus, *Development*, p. 55.

7. This, of course, is one of the central themes of Gabriel Kolko's and James

Weinstein's books. Our work does not contest their central premises. The dominant strand of Progressivism, represented in the politics of Theodore Roosevelt, William Howard Taft, and Woodrow Wilson as presidents, and in various corporate-dominated good government groups such as the National Civic Federation, was hardly designed to "curb" big business power, but to consolidate it in a new and powerful way through politics. Yet it must be asked: Did these conservative Progressives succeed in creating state structures that had the "autonomy" and "power" central to such a rationalizing mission? Moreover, distinctions must be made between conservative Progressive scholarship such as Herbert Croly's and the strain of thought we have characterized as the "third tradition." The latter was much more concerned about the popular roots of state autonomy, and even while third tradition thinkers were not opposed, in the main, to a system based on classes, they saw state-building as a counterpoint to the political power of big business. Perhaps, despite Kolko and Weinstein, conservative Progressives were not as successful in their "rationalization" efforts as they might have been. And perhaps third tradition scholarship provided a popular alternative within liberalism whose success might also be questioned.

8. The relationship between methodological refinements and the kind of muckraking scholarship that "teaches a lesson" has been explored by Wiebe, *Search*, pp. 134–61, and Crick, *American Science*, pp. 123–25.

9. The 1908 publication of *The Process of Government* was not greeted with much enthusiasm by anyone in the profession, except perhaps by Charles Beard and Albion Small (see Small's review of *The Process of Government* in the *American Journal of Sociology* 13 [1908]: 698–706). A more typical view might be that of *APSR* reviewer James W. Garner, who commented: "A hasty reading of some of these chapters fails to impress the reviewer with their value as a contribution to the literature of political science," *APSR* 2 (1907): 457.

Bentley was reincarnated as a founder of the group theory of politics in the 1950s. See especially David Truman, *The Governmental Process* (New York: Knopf, 1951). Chap. 5 of this work deals with Truman's reinterpretations at length.

Paul Kress has written an excellent intellectual biography of Bentley that challenges the mode by which political scientists have perceived Bentley's concerns. See *Social Science and the Idea of Process* (Urbana: University of Illinois Press, 1970).

10. See Sidney Ratner's introduction to Bentley's *Makers, Users and Masters* (Syracuse, NY: Syracuse University Press, 1969), and Ratner's obituary of Bentley in the *Journal of Philosophy* LX, no. 14 (July 3, 1958): 573–78.

11. Wiebe, *Search*, p. 148. Wiebe contends that "bureaucratic" thought such as Bentley's moves beyond the historicist notions of Ward, Wilson, and others, removing all "human purposes" or historical stages from social scientific investigation.

12. See Harry Eckstein, "Group Theory and the Comparative Study of Pressure Groups," in his coedited work with David Apter, *Comparative Politics: A Reader* (New York: Free Press, 1963). Eckstein contends that David Truman's modifications

of Bentley's methodology were entirely appropriate because as it stood, "no one would want to use it." Yet Eckstein, like Truman, largely ignored the connection between Bentley's methods and the muckraking tradition, instead emphasizing the "scientistic" strain in Bentley's work.

13. Bernard Crick has explored such a perspective without, however, consideration of Bentley's *Makers, Users and Masters*. In Crick's view, "not merely must the warm zeal of his appeal to facts against soul stuff be explained but also his obvious optimism that political problems could be solved by mere investigation. . . . A journalist himself for several years, he must, at heart, have shared the belief of actual journalists like Tarbell and Steffens . . . [that] in America the original and natural democratic virtue was being corrupted, and [that this] was due to the vast speed and complexity of industrial and urban growth, and could only be cured by getting more of the facts before the people and more government under popular control." See Crick, *American Science*, p. 124.

14. Arthur F. Bentley, *The Process of Government* (Evanston, IL: Principia Press, 1935).

15. Bentley, *Process*, p. 176.

16. Bentley's discussion of the group concept—and the distinctions he makes between his notion of it and those of Gumplowicz, Small, and Marx—are found in *Process*, pp. 208–18. See also the discussion by Kress, *Social Science*, chaps. 1–3, and Ross, "The Liberal Tradition Revisited," in *New Directions*, ed. Higham and Conkin.

17. Bentley, *Process*, p. 208.

18. Ibid., p. 447.

19. Kress, *Social Science*, p. 71.

20. Quotes from pp. 468, 475, and 481–82 in Bentley, *Process*.

21. In the Appendix to *The Process of Government*, Bentley analyzes several "cases" of group interaction in the "political process," carefully detailing the complex constituent elements at work in a seemingly simple "governmental decision." While Bentley's "complete descriptions" are tedious in their thoroughness, a kind of moral outrage emerges from these descriptions that is strikingly similar to Ida Tarbell's, Upton Sinclair's, or Lincoln Steffen's investigative journalism.

22. See Sidney Ratner's edition of Arthur Bentley's *Makers, Users and Masters*.

23. Ratner, *Makers*, p. 3.

24. Ibid., pp. 6, 69.

25. See Ratner, "The Middle Class Counter-Revolution," in *Makers*, pp. 221–52.

26. Ratner, *Makers*, p. 226.

27. Ibid., p. 223.

28. Ibid., p. 240.

29. Wiebe, *Search*, pp. 145, 148.

30. For a complete bibliography of Beard's works and much of the older secondary literature on him, see Bernard Borning, *The Political and Social Thought of Charles A. Beard* (Seattle: University of Washington Press, 1962). Borning's biography remains the comprehensive account. See the *festschrift* to Beard edited by Howard Beale, *Charles A. Beard: An Appraisal* (Lexington: University of Kentucky Press, 1954),

especially essays by Luther Gulick, Howard Beale, and George S. Counts in that volume.

31. Charles Beard, "Politics," an essay published by Columbia University Press (New York, 1908), p. 28. Written the same year as *The Process of Government*, Beard's essay seeks to reconstitute the fundamental units of social science through comprehensive criticisms of the whole tradition of "political" or "economic" theorizing. Beard claims that political philosophy artificially divides human activity into discrete and separate compartments.

32. Indeed, Beard's unification of moral fervor and realism in his portrayal of human emotions never seemed to him to be a contradiction. Like Bentley, the revelation of the dirty and sordid motives behind political actions did not contradict faith in the pristine qualities of reform constituencies.

33. David Marcell's *Progress and Pragmatism* (Westport, CT: Greenwood Press, 1974), pp. 258–322, is an excellent account of the changes and continuities in Beard's intellectual career.

34. See Max Lerner, "Charles Beard's Political Theory," in Beale, *Beard*, pp. 25–47.

35. Marcell, *Progress*, pp. 304–19, traces Beard's return to "values" as the heart and soul of an American science of politics. Perhaps the starkest contrasts between Beard's early and later careers can be found in the images conveyed by the Columbia essay "Politics" and the qualifications of Beard's "Time, Technology and the Creative Spirit in Political Science," APSR presidential address, *American Political Science Review* 21 (February 1927): 11, and "Limitations to the Application of Social Science Implied in Recent Social Trends," *Social Forces* II (May 1933): 505–10. Beard also tended to equate natural and social sciences' efforts at prediction with determinism. They were both said to imprison humankind within an unchangeable future. See Charles Beard, "Political Science," in *Research in the Social Sciences*, ed. Wilson Gee (New York: Macmillan, 1929), pp. 269–91.

36. This quote is from Charles Beard, *The Economic Interpretation of the Constitution of the United States* (New York: Macmillan, 1913), p. 73. Other works that debunk "abstract ideas" as the major source of American political debate and instead link events to economic events are *The Economic Basis of Politics* (New York: Knopf, 1934), *The Economic Origins of Jeffersonian Democracy* (New York: Macmillan, 1915), and the important and later much revised textbook *American Government and Politics* (New York: Macmillan, 1914).

37. See Beard, *Economic Basis*, p. 44.

38. In works later in life, Beard qualified the "economic interpretation" to such a degree that it became only one "variable" among many others that might be said to be active in human history. But even in *The Economic Interpretation of the Constitution of the United States*, Beard's analysis did not appear to be intended as a criticism of the Founders. All it demonstrated was the essential causes and sources of a political behavior, as present in the United States as it was elsewhere. Beard, in fact, praised the Founders for their frank appraisal of human motivation. Quote from Beard, *Economic Interpretation*, p. 15.

39. Beard, "Politics," p. 9.

40. The concern that American political and administrative practices were not yet suitable to the complex tasks required of them by industrial modernity linked Beard to Wilson. See "Training for Efficient Public Service," *Annals of the American Academy of Political and Social Science* LXIV (March 1916): 215–26, and "The Study and Teaching of Politics," *Columbia University Quarterly* 12 (June 1910): 268–74.

41. The attack on "complicated mechanisms" was a leitmotif in Beard's popular textbooks. To academics and public officials, Beard tended to stress obstacles presented to experts by such mechanisms. Yet when Beard wrote for a mass audience, the political defects of America's limited government became the basis for polemics against "private interests" that had wormed their way into the structures. Quote from Beard, *American Government*, p. 479.

42. See Beard, "The Study and Teaching of Politics," pp. 271–74, and "Training for Efficient Public Service," as well as Charles Beard and James Harvey Robinson, *The Development of Modern Europe* (Boston: Ginn, 1907).

43. "Report of Reconstruction Commission to Governor Alfred E. Smith," Albany, October 10, 1919, p. 4–5.

44. See Charles A. Beard, "Congress under Fire," *Yale Review* 42 (September 1932): 42. Importantly, Beard was not a believer in simple majoritarianism. The "group" basis of political behavior still stirred appropriate political conflicts among citizens. But if public questions were presented in clear ways, Beard thought, the fragmentation of group conflict might give way to a kind of tempering of group egotism. The public-spirited citizen emerged when choices and consequences were presented simply and directly, and not dispersed and sullied as they were in the American present.

45. David Marcell has dated Beard's disillusionment from 1926 and the publication of *The Rise of American Civilization* (New York: Macmillan, 1927). His skepticism took two forms. Beard, who had equated "social science" with the search for causes and effects in social and historical inquiry and the primacy of economic motivations as a cause for political behavior, now seemed to feel that historical evaluation was a more complicated phenomenon. By 1927 the "independent role of ideas" and "acquisitiveness" were seen as complementary, not contradictory, causes of political behavior. Second, Beard came to doubt the validity of specialization and professionalism because both qualities tended to create "small minds" unable to discern the complexity and contingent character of modern history. See Marcell, *Progress*, pp. 276–81.

46. Beard's "Time, Technology and the Creative Spirit in Political Science," his 1926 APSA presidential address, *APSR* 21 (February 1927): 1–11, is doubtless the most critical address an APSA president ever delivered. Hinting that political scientists had become supine servants of corporate philanthropists and water carriers for politicians, Beard's address is a blistering attack on specialization as a symptom of conservatism and intellectually sterile scholarship. Beard's attacks continued in the 1930s because he saw political science and related disciplines as "value-neutral" enterprises that in reality covered up the huge changes, dislocations, and inequalities

of modern capitalist societies. See also "Conditions Favorable to Creative Work in Political Science," *American Political Science Review* XXIV Suppl. (February 1930): 25–32. For Beard's ideas about the proper role of a newly politicized social science, see his contributions to the *National Report of the Committee on the Social Studies, A Charter for the Social Sciences*, and *The Nature of the Social Sciences in Relation to Objectives of Instruction* (New York: Scribner's, 1932 and 1934, respectively). Chap. 4 of this book contrasts Beard's views with those of Charles Merriam.

47. See Borning, *Political and Social Thought*, chap. 8; Marcell, *Progress*, 278–81. Beard's contemporaries were also quick to note a seeming contradiction in his work. See Henry Elmer Barnes's critical review of *The Nature of the Social Sciences* in the *American Historical Review* 40 (October 1934): 97–99.

48. Beard, "Conditions," p. 28.

49. Ibid., p. 29.

50. Charles Beard, "The Task before Us," *Social Studies* 25 (May 1, 1934): 217.

51. Beard in *Research*, ed. Gee, pp. 273–75.

52. Charles Beard, "Neglected Aspects of Political Science," *APSR* XLII (April 1948): 221.

Chapter 4: Reform and Disillusionment in the New Deal

1. For the involvement of Progressives on the Committee on Public Information, see J. R. Mack and Cedric Larsen, *Words that Won the War* (Princeton, NJ: Princeton University Press, 1939). See Richard Hofstadter's discussion of the Progressive intellectuals and World War I in *Anti-Intellectualism in American Life* (New York: Vintage Books, 1973), pp. 197–214. The Committee on Public Information was not the only agency that involved academics. The War Industries Board and military intelligence agencies, Hofstadter reports, "swarmed with academics." See Hofstadter, *Anti-Intellectualism*, p. 199. For the disillusionment of Progressive intellectuals, see Charles Forcey, *The Crossroads of Liberalism, 1900–1926* (New York: Oxford University Press, 1961).

2. John P. Diggins's *Mussolini and Fascism: The View from America* (Princeton, NJ: Princeton University Press, 1972) is a thorough account of the mixed reactions of Progressives to Corporatist ideology.

3. For surveys of this period, see Somit and Tanenhaus, *Development*, pp. 110–134; Lyons, *The Uneasy Partnership*, pp. 31–46; Richard Jensen, "History and the Political Scientist" in *Politics and the Social Sciences*, ed. Seymour Martin Lipset, (New York: Oxford University Press, 1969), pp. 1–29; Crick, *American Science*, chap. 3–5.

4. Somit and Tanenhaus, *Development*, pp. 87–97, summarizes these debates, as does Barry Karl's *Charles E. Merriam and the Study of Politics* (Chicago: University of Chicago Press, 1974), pp. 103–17. Our account of Charles Merriam's activities owes much to this interesting biography.

5. Karl, *Charles Merriam*, p. 113.

6. Concentration on the psychology of power and leadership only echoes

previous efforts to develop points of expertise, efficiency, and order in a Jeffersonian America perceived as naturally distrustful of such qualities. See Herbert Croly, *The Promise of American Life* (Indianapolis, IN: Bobbs-Merrill, 1965). Robert Wiebe has seen the quest for leaders as a fundamental characteristic of the search for order. Yet the paeans to executive leadership by early Progressives only revealed contradictions that would later emerge in political science in the 1920s and 1930s. In Wiebe's words: "How could the electorate recognize a public man? Not only was government inoperative without its public men, but with false leaders the whole system turned into a nightmare. . . . In the end, the public man remained a mystical, self-evident truth, and countless Americans simply made it an article of faith that at the right time he would materialize and lead." See Wiebe, *Search*, p. 162.

7. See Lyons, *Uneasy Partnership*, pp. 17–49; Louis Wirth, ed., *A Decade of Social Science Research* (Chicago: University of Chicago Press, 1940); and Charles B. Saunders, *The Brookings Institution* (Washington, D.C.: Brookings Institution, 1966). All of these accounts are laudatory and largely ignore the political consequences of ties between philanthropy and social science.

8. The SSRC's ostensible purpose seemed indeed, in Lyon's words, to replace "reform with research." "Its purpose was not to undertake research but rather to stimulate greater interaction among the various disciplines, to improve the conditions for research, and to increase general understanding of the nature of the social sciences," *Uneasy Partnership*, p. 43. For the role of corporate philanthropy in the funding of the SSRC and the Brookings Institution, see Raymond Fosdick, *The Story of the Rockefeller Foundation* (New York: Harper, 1952), pp. 192–202.

9. See the two thick volumes delivered to President Roosevelt in 1933, *Recent Social Trends in the United States* (New York: McGraw Hill, 1933).

10. The most perceptive work on the influence of social scientists in the management and planning organs of the New Deal is that of Barry Karl, *Executive Reorganization and the New Deal* (Cambridge, MA: Harvard University Press, 1963). See also Lyons, *Uneasy Partnership*, pp. 50–79, and Otis Graham, *Towards a Planned Society: from Roosevelt to Nixon* (New York: Oxford University Press, 1976).

11. Karl's *Charles E. Merriam* is the definitive biography. For a nearly complete bibliography of Merriam's work, see Leonard D. White, *The Future of Government in the United States: Essays in Honor of Charles E. Merriam* (Chicago: University of Chicago Press, 1959), pp. 133–55.

12. Merriam's last book, *Systematic Politics* (1945), is notable for his unease about the discipline's course. He scored his colleagues' research for its singular and consistent reluctance to "paint a picture of the attainable . . . showing what the gains of civilization are likely to be and holding out definite hope to man." Indirectly, Merriam criticized his own students for the pessimism and cynicism in their judgments of their own research findings. The glum findings political scientists made about the voters' ignorance and irrational allegiances violated Merriam's lifelong penchant to outline the possibilities of a benign and scientifically verifiable future. He did not dispute the findings, but he did berate his colleagues for their reluctance to provide remedies. David Easton's *The Political System* (Chicago:

University of Chicago Press, 1952) perhaps best represents the unease of later behavioralists with Merriam's concern for "values."

13. Virtually every major work Merriam wrote repeats these simple beliefs in a titanic battle between Hamiltonianism and Jeffersonianism in American life, now to be won by the realization by both sides of the benefits of "science applied to the vastly important forces of political and social control." Merriam's most prominent statements of the positions distilled in these pages are his famed *New Aspects of Politics* (Chicago: University of Chicago Press, 1925); *Political Power* (New York: Whittesley House, McGraw Hill, 1934); *Prologue to Politics* (Chicago: University of Chicago Press, 1939); and his summary of "Committee Findings" in *Recent Social Trends*, vol. 1.

14. Charles Merriam, "The Education of Charles E. Merriam," in *Future of Government*, ed. White, p. 59.

15. See Charles Merriam, *Civic Education in the United States* (New York: Scribner's, 1934), esp. chap. 3, "The Goal," pp. 33–51.

16. A fascinating treatment of this theme in Woodrow Wilson's and Max Weber's thought is Michael Rogin's "Max Weber and Woodrow Wilson: The Iron Cage in Germany and America," *Polity* (December 1971): 557–75.

17. Quoted in Jensen, "History and the Political Scientist," in Lipset, *Politics*, p. 22.

18. Merriam, *New Aspects of Politics*, p. 237.

19. Ibid., p. 169.

20. Ibid., pp. 5–6, 18.

21. Beard, "Time, Technology and Creative Spirit," 6–24.

22. See the discussions by Somit and Tanenhaus in *Development*, pp. 110–22, and Karl, *Merriam*, pp. 121–26.

23. Charles E. Merriam, "Presidential Address to the American Political Science Association," *American Political Science Review* 20 (January, 1926): 16.

24. Charles E. Merriam, *The Making of Citizens: A Comparative Study of Methods of Civic Training* (Chicago: University of Chicago Press, 1931).

25. Quote from Merriam, *Making of Citizens*, p. 356, and Merriam, *Civic Education*, p. 112. See note 34 following for Merriam's critique of Charles Beard's and George Counts's approaches.

26. Merriam, *Civic Education*, p. 37.

27. Ibid., p. 11.

28. Ibid., p. 48.

29. Ibid., p. 44.

30. Ibid., p. 48.

31. Karl, *Merriam*, pp. 191–92.

32. Merriam, *Civic Education*, p. 49.

33. Ibid., pp. 146–50.

34. See "Conclusions and Recommendations" of the *American Historical Association's Commission on Social Studies* (New York: Scribner's, 1933).

35. Karl, *Executive Reorganization*, pp. 211–65.

36. Karl, *Merriam*, p. 255.

37. See Karl's analysis of Merriam's distress with the "new realism" of the post–World War II period in *Merriam*, pp. 290–303. Many of the works by Merriam's own students and associates appeared to question not only the efficacy of the "third tradition," but the desirability of reforms, even given the fact that they might be possible. In the early 1950s this "behavioral" realism became the dominant current in political science. See chap. 5 following for an account.

38. Charles Merriam, *Systematic Politics* (Chicago: University of Chicago Press, 1946), p. ix.

39. Ibid., p. 339.

40. For a complete bibliography of Lasswell's work, see Duane Marvick, ed., *Harold D. Lasswell on Political Sociology* (Chicago: University of Chicago Press, 1977), pp. 425–43. Marvick's introduction (pp. 1–72) is also a comprehensive, if uncritical, intellectual biography.

41. Harold Lasswell, *The Analysis of Political Behavior: An Empirical Approach* (London: Routledge and Kegan Paul, 1948), p. 92.

42. The works that best capture Lasswell's departures from the more optimistic assumptions were all written in the 1930s. See Harold Lasswell, *Psychopathology and Politics* (Chicago: University of Chicago Press, 1930); *World Politics and Personal Insecurity* (New York: McGraw Hill, 1936); Lasswell and D. B. Jones, *World Revolutionary Propaganda* (New York: Knopf, 1939).

43. Lasswell, *World Politics*, p. 20.

44. Harold Lasswell, "The Strategy of Revolutionary and War Propaganda," in *Public Opinion and World Politics*, ed. Quincy Wright (Chicago: University of Chicago Press, 1933), pp. 187–221. This is essentially an extension of Lasswell's argument in *Psychopathology*.

45. See Herbert Marcuse, *Eros and Civilization* (Boston: Beacon Press, 1955), and the fine biography by Morton Schoolman, *Herbert Marcuse: The Imaginary Witness* (Glencoe: Free Press, 1981) for an alternative account of the political consequences of Freud's work.

46. Lasswell, *Psychopathology*, pp. 196–97.

47. Ibid., pp. 184–86.

48. Ibid., p. 186.

49. Ibid., p. 198.

50. Ibid., p. 265. A similar concern with how the administrative elite ought to be perceived is found in Lasswell, *Politics: Who Gets What, When, How* (Cleveland, OH: Meridian Books, 1951). In both books, the "therapeutic" role of social science is promoted as an antidote to popular psychopathology.

51. See "The Garrison State," in Lasswell, *Analysis*, pp. 156–72. For an account of Lasswell's turnaround, see David Easton, "Harold Lasswell: Political Scientist for a Democratic Society," *Journal of Politics* 12 (1950): 450–477.

52. Harold Lasswell, *Democracy through Public Opinion* (New York: Bantam, 1941).

53. Ibid., p. 15.

54. Ibid., pp. 16, 70.

55. Ibid., p. 35, and Lasswell, "The Developing Science of Democracy" in his *Analysis.*

56. Lasswell, *Democracy*, p. 28. The emphasis placed on the problem of communication transformed Lasswell's preceding thoughts concerning propaganda. Propaganda was no longer just a generalized attempt by elites to influence the masses; its content was now essential. With democratic content, it could be productive.

57. Lasswell, *Democracy*, p. 12.

58. Harold Lasswell, "Political Power and Democratic Values," in *Problems of Power in American Democracy*, ed. William Kornhauser (Detroit, MI: Wayne State University Press, 1951), p. 57.

59. Crick, *American Science*, p. 194.

60. See Bruce Lannes Smith, "The Mystifying Intellectual History of Harold D. Lasswell," in *Politics, Personality and Social Science in the Twentieth Century*, ed. Arnold Rogow (Chicago: University of Chicago Press, 1969).

61. Harold Lasswell, *The Future of Political Science* (New York: Atherton Press, 1963), p. 22, and Crick, *American Science*, p. 199.

Chapter 5: The Behavioral Era

1. See Daniel Bell, *The End of Ideology: On the Exhaustion of Political Ideas in the Fifties*, rev. ed. (New York: Free Press, 1962); Chaim I. Waxman, ed., *The End of Ideology Debate* (New York: Simon and Schuster, 1968).

2. Evron M. Kirkpatrick, "The Impact of the Behavioral Movement on Traditional Political Science," in *Essays in the Behavioral Study of Politics*, ed. Austin Ranney (Urbana: University of Illinois, 1962), p. 12; see also Somit and Tanenhaus, *Development*, pp. 176–77; Robert Dahl, "The Behavioral Approach in Political Science: Epitaph for a Movement to a Successful Protest," in *Behavioralism in Political Science*, ed. Heinz Eulau (New York: Atherton Press, 1960), pp. 68–92.

3. David Truman, "The Implications of Political Behavior Research," *Items* 5 (December 1951): 37–39; see also Somit and Tanenhaus, *Development*, pp. 177–79; Mario J. Falco, *Truth and Meaning in Political Science* (Columbus, OH: Merriam, 1973), pp. 93–94.

4. See David E. Leege, "The Development and Use of Sample Surveys," Phase II Report for the National Science Board, Twelfth Board Report (June 1979); Richard W. Boyd and Herbert H. Hyman, "Survey Research," in *Handbook of Political Science*, vol. 7, ed. Frederick I. Greenstein and Nelson Polsby, pp. 265–350 (Reading, MA: Addison-Wesley, 1975).

5. These individuals included Renis Likert, Angus Campbell, George Katuris, and Leslie Kish.

6. See Institute for Social Research, *A Quarter Century of Social Research* (Ann Arbor, MI: Institute for Social Research, 1971); Austin Ranney, "The Committee on Political Behavior, 1949–64, and the Committee on Government and Legal

Processes, 1964–72," *Items* 28 (September 1974): 37–41. For brief discussions of the programs sponsored by the Committee on Political Behavior, see "Research on State Politics: A New Program of Grants in Aid," *Items* 9 (September 1955): 25–27, and "Grants for Research on American Government Processes: A New Program of the Committee on Political Behavior," *Items* 10 (March 1956): 16–17.

7. See Somit and Tanenhaus, *Development*, pp. 167–70; Leege, *Surveys*, p. 28; Dahl, "Behavioral," pp. 74–75.

8. Robert Dahl has noted, "If the foundations had been hostile to the behavioral approach there can be no doubt that it would have been very rough sledding indeed. For characteristically, behavioral research costs a good deal more than that needed by the single scholar in the library—and sometimes, as with the studies in presidential years, behavioral research is enormously expensive" (Dahl, "Behavioral," p. 74).

9. Members were particularly concerned over the activities of the Committee on Policy in the 1930s and those of the Committee on Research and Committee on the Advancement of Teaching in the late 1940s. As Somit and Tanenhaus noted, the reports published by the latter two committees "enhanced neither the public image nor the self-respect of the profession . . ." (*Development*, p. 150).

10. Somit and Tanenhaus, *Development*, pp. 152–53.

11. American Political Science Association, "Toward a More Responsible Two-Party System: A Report of the Committee on Political Parties," *American Political Science Review* 44, Suppl. pt. 2 (September 1950): 37–84. Hereafter referred to as Toward.

12. APSA, "Toward," p. v.

13. Ibid.

14. Ibid.

15. Julius Turner, "Responsible Parties: A Dissent from the Floor," *American Political Science Review* 45 (March 1951): 143–52. See also Evron M. Kirkpatrick, "Toward a More Responsible Two-Party System: Political Science, Policy Science, or Pseudo Science," *American Political Science Review* 65 (December 1971): 968; Alan Wolfe and Marvin Surkin, "The Political Dimensions of American Political Science," *Acta Politica* (October 1973): 46; Austin Ranney, *The Doctrine of Responsible Party Government* (Urbana: University of Illinois Press, 1962).

16. Turner, "Responsible Parties," p. 143.

17. Bernard Berelson, Paul F. Lazarfeld, and William N. McPhee, *Voting* (Chicago: University of Chicago Press), p. 312.

18. "In Memoriam: V. O. Key, Jr.," *American Political Science Review* 58 (March 1964): 204–05.

19. See V. O. Key Jr., *Politics, Parties and Pressure Groups*, 2nd ed. (New York: Crowell, 1947), pp. 11–12; "The State of the Discipline," *American Political Science Review* 52 (December 1958): 961–71.

20. V. O. Key Jr., "The Techniques of Graft in the United States" (Ph.D. diss., University of Chicago, 1934).

21. V. O. Key Jr., *The Administration of Federal Grants to States* (Chicago: University of Chicago Press, 1937).

22. V. O. Key Jr. and W. W. Crouch, *The Initiative and Referendum in California* (Berkeley: University of California Press, 1939).

23. Ibid., pp. 571–72.

24. Ibid., p. 572.

25. In the preface to the first edition, Key noted, "A basic assumption of the book is that a student cannot gain an adequate comprehension of politics by concentration of attention narrowly on political parties." V. O. Key Jr., *Politics, Parties and Pressure Groups*, 1st ed. (New York: Crowell, 1942), p. vii.

26. Key, *Politics*, 2nd ed., p. 9.

27. Key, *Politics*, 1st ed., p. 256.

28. Ibid., p. 622.

29. Ibid., p. 637.

30. Ibid., p. 521.

31. See V. O. Key Jr., "A Theory of Critical Elections," *Journal of Politics* 17 (February 1955): 3–18; "Secular Realignment and the Party System," *Journal of Politics* 21 (May 1959): 198–210; *Politics, Parties and Pressure Groups*, 5th ed. (New York: Crowell, 1964), p. 436.

32. Key, *Politics*, 5th ed., pp. 522–23, 535.

33. See Angus Campbell, Philip E. Converse, Warren E. Miller, and Donald E. Stokes, *The American Voter* (New York: Wiley, 1960). For Key's discussion of the *American Voter*'s alternative categorization of elections, see Key, *Politics*, 5th ed., p. 536.

34. Key, *Politics*, 5th ed., p. 536.

35. See David B. Hill and Norman R. Luttbeg, *Trends in American Electoral Behavior* (Itasca, IL: Peacock, 1950), pp. 21–23.

36. V. O. Key Jr., *The Responsible Electorate: Rationality in Presidential Voting, 1936–1960*, with the assistance of Milton C. Cummings Jr., foreword by Arthur Maass (New York: Vintage Books, 1966), pp. 7–8.

37. V. O. Key Jr., *Public Opinion and American Democracy* (New York: Knopf, 1961), p. 49.

38. Ibid., p. 51.

39. Ibid., p. 557.

40. In a striking footnote to the last sentence of the book, Key writes, "This analysis and its implications should be pondered well by those young gentlemen in whose education the Republic has invested considerable sums" (ibid., p. 448).

41. Key, *Responsible Electorate*, p. 6.

42. In a 1981 interview, Truman claimed that despite the fact that he studied with Merriam, he was not really a Merriam product. However, even the most cursory reading of his *Administrative Decentralization: A Study of the Chicago Field Offices of the United States Department of Agriculture* (Chicago: University of Chicago Press, 1940) or "Public Opinion Research Is a Tool of Public Administration," *Public Administration Review* 3 (1945): 52–72, will reveal a close affinity between Truman's early work and Merriam's. See "Interview with David B. Truman," by Donald E. Stokes, *News for Teachers of Political Science* (Winter 1982): 7.

43. Truman, *Administrative Decentralization*, p. 7.

44. Truman, "Public Opinion Research Is a Tool of Public Administration," p. 67.

45. Truman, "Implications of Political Behavior Research," p. 38. See also "The Impact on Political Science of the Revolution in the Behavioral Sciences," in Eulau, ed., *Behavioralism*, pp. 38–67; "Disillusion and Regeneration: The Quest for a Discipline," *American Political Science Review* 59 (December 1965): 865–73.

46. "The political scientist cares little . . . about what a judge does to the Supreme Court—unless he is the instrument of a major redirection of its activities—and still less about the effect on him of the membership of the Court. He cares rather about the role of the Court in the society, its functioning in the process of societal adjustment and on the allocation of values. This involves, perhaps, the analysis of individual behavior, but the generalizations sought are about the institution, not about the individual actor" (Truman, "Impact," pp. 60–61).

47. Truman, "Implications," p. 39.

48. Ibid.

49. David B. Truman, *The Congressional Party: A Case Study* (New York: Wiley, 1959), p. 9.

50. David B. Truman, *The Governmental Process: Public Interests and Public Opinion*, 2nd ed. (New York: Knopf, 1971), p. xix.

51. Ibid., p. xxxviii.

52. Ibid., p. 34.

53. Ibid., p. 38.

54. Ibid., p. 503.

55. Ibid., p. 516.

56. Ibid., p. 523.

57. Ibid., p. 534.

58. Ibid., p. 524.

59. "These widely held but unorganized interests are what we have called the 'rules of the game.' . . . Each of these interests (attitudes) may be wide or narrow, general or detailed. For the mass of the population they may be loose and ambiguous, though more precise and articulated at the leadership level. In any case the 'rules of the game' are interests the serious disturbance of which will result in organized interaction and the assertion of fairly explicit claims for uniformity" (ibid., p. 512).

60. David B. Truman, "The American System in Crisis," *Political Science Quarterly* 74 (December 1959): 481–97; "The Politics of the New Collectivism," in *Trends in American Society*, ed. Clarence Morris (Philadelphia: University of Pennsylvania Press, 1962), pp. 115–42.

61. Truman, "American System," p. 482.

62. Ibid., pp. 493–96.

63. Truman, "Politics," p. 135.

64. Truman, "Introduction to the Second Edition," *Governmental Process*, p. xlviii.

Chapter 6: The Eclipse of Unity

1. These fears are present in the prominent works of pluralists themselves. See Daniel Bell, *The Coming of Post-Industrial Society* (New York: Basic Books, 1973); Daniel Boorstin, *The Genius of American Politics* (Chicago: University of Chicago Press, 1953).

2. See Richard Neustadt, *Presidential Power* (New York: Wiley, 1960), for the most notable ode to presidential authority. See also the celebratory *A Thousand Days* by Arthur Schlesinger (Boston: Houghton Mifflin, 1965). See also Robert Dahl's praise of strong leaders in *Who Governs?* (New Haven, CT: Yale University Press, 1961).

3. See Michael Lipsky, *Protest in City Politics* (Chicago: Rand McNally, 1970); Frances Fox Piven and Richard Cloward, *Regulating the Poor* (New York; Random House, 1971); and John Schaar, "Legitimacy in the Modern State," in *Power and Community*, ed. S. Levinson and P. Green (New York: Vintage, 1970), pp. 276–327.

4. Lowi's and Burnham's works will be discussed following.

5. David Easton, "The New Revolution in Political Science," *American Political Science Review* 63 (December 1969): 1051–61. Robert Lynd's *Knowledge for What?* (Princeton, NJ: Princeton University Press, 1939) was a more forthright attack on the growing insularity of social science from political reform movements.

6. Avery Leiserson, "Charles Merriam, Max Weber and the Search for Synthesis in Political Science," *American Political Science Review* 69 (March 1975): 175–85, and Samuel Paterson, "Introduction to Avery Leiserson" in the same volume, pp. 173–75.

7. See, for example, the collected essays in Charles McCoy and John Playford, eds., *Apolitical Politics* (New York: Crowell, 1967); William Connolly, ed., *The Bias of Pluralism* (New York: Atherton Press, 1969); and Levinson and Green, *Power and Community*.

8. Joseph LaPalombara, "Decline of Ideology: A Dissent and an Interpretation," *American Political Science Review* 60 (March 1966): 5.

9. See Lane Davis, "The Cost of Realism: Contemporary Restatements of Democracy," *Western Political Quarterly* 18 (March 1964): 37–46. See also Sheldon Wolin, "Political Theory as a Vocation," *American Political Science Review* 63 (December 1969): 1062–82; Robert Pranger *The Eclipse of Citizenship* (New York: Holt, Rinehart and Winston, 1968).

10. The best examples of this strand of postbehavioral thought are Henry Kariel, *The Decline of American Pluralism* (Stanford, CA: Stanford University Press, 1961); Grant McConnell, *Private Power and American Democracy* (New York: Knopf, 1966); and Theodore Lowi, *The End of Liberalism* (New York: Norton, 1969).

11. See Peter Bachrach and Morton Baratz, *The Theory of Democratic Elitism* (Boston: Little, Brown, 1967).

12. Pranger, *Eclipse;* Michael Rogin, "Non-Partisanship and the Group Interest," in *Power and Community*, ed. Levinson and Green, pp. 112–41; J. David Greenstone, *Labor in American Politics* (New York: Knopf, 1969).

13. This is made explicit in McConnell, *Private Power.*

14. Postbehavioralists are divided on the question of whether the system was

indeed pluralist at all. Contrast sociologist G. William Domhoff's *The Higher Circles* (New York: Random House, 1970) with the works cited in note 10 earlier.

15. See Henry Kariel, *Saving Appearances* (Belmont, CA: Duxbury Press, 1972); *The Promise of Politics* (Englewood Cliffs, NJ: Prentice Hall, 1966); *In Search of Authority* (New York: Free Press, 1964).

16. For evidence supporting this point of view, see Alan Wolfe, "The Professional Mystique," in *An End to Political Science*, ed. Alan Wolfe and Marvin Surkin (New York: Basic Books, 1970), pp. 288–309; and Alan Wolfe, "The Myth of the Free Scholar," *The Center Magazine* (July 1969): 72–77.

17. From Theodore Lowi, "The Politicization of Political Science," *American Politics Quarterly* (January 1973): 43–44.

18. Lowi, "Politicization," pp. 44–49, and Alan Wolfe, "Unthinking about the Thinkable: Reflections on the Failure of the Caucus for a New Political Science," *Politics and Society* (May 1971): 393–44.

19. Lowi, "Politicization," p. 52.

20. Wolfe, "Unthinking," p. 393.

21. See also Wolfe and Surkin, "Political Dimensions of Political Science," *Acta Sociologica* (October 1969): 45.

22. Indeed, some would have had it otherwise, and not only from a radical perspective that the Caucus prescribed. For the thoughts of an unreconstructed behaviorist, see Heinz Eulau, "Communication to *PS*," *Political Science and Politics* (Fall 1974): 450.

23. See Theodore J. Lowi, *At the Pleasure of the* Mayor (Glencoe, IL: Free Press, 1964). Lowi's study of power in New York City stands in marked contrast to pluralist community studies. See, for examples, Wallace Sayre and Herbert Kaufman, *Governing New York City* (New York: Sage, 1960); Nelson Polsby, *Community Power and Political Theory* (New Haven, CT: Yale University Press, 1963); and the classic by Robert Dahl, *Who Governs?* (New Haven, CT: Yale University Press, 1961).

24. See Theodore Lowi, "Power, Policy and Constitution in America," in *The American Party Systems*, ed. William Chambers and Walter Dean Burnham (New York: Oxford University Press, 1975), pp. 238–76.

25. Lowi, "Power, Policy," pp. 276–77.

26. Ibid. Lowi's work is a departure from many of his third tradition predecessors in the sense that he recognizes that it is too late to talk of developing "responsible parties." Contrast his chapter cited above with the APSA's "Toward a More Responsible Two-Party System."

27. See Theodore Lowi, *The End of Liberalism: Ideology, Policy and the Crisis of Public Authority*, 1st ed. (New York: Norton, 1969), p. 288.

28. See also, for another statement of the juridical democracy proposal, Theodore Lowi, *The Politics of Disorder* (New York: Norton, 1971), pp. xvii–xviii, and the final chapter, "Toward Juridical Democracy," pp. 287–314.

29. Ibid., p. xviii.

30. See the discussion of Arthur Bentley in this book's third chapter.

31. Lowi, *The End of Liberalism*, p. 297.

32. Ibid., p. ix.

33. Lowi, *The Politics of Disorder*, pp. 55–57. For an alternative view of social movements and their fate, see Frances Fox Piven and Richard Cloward, *Regulating the Poor* (New York: Random House, 1971), and *Poor Peoples' Movements* (New York: Vintage Books, 1979).

34. Lowi explicitly rejects the organizational focus of the Caucus for a New Political Science, calling instead for an "intellectual revolt." But he does seem to view increasing university independence from services to specific groups outside as an indispensable ingredient of "intellectual revolt." And, as we contend, the role Lowi prescribes for political science necessitates an inward, organizational orientation.

35. Lowi developed the "policy framework" in several articles. See his "Decision Making vs. Policy Making: Toward an Antidote for Technocracy," *Public Administration Review* (May/June 1970): 314–25, and "Four Systems of Policy, Politics and Choice," *Public Administration Review* (July/August 1972): 298–310. An example of this theory at work is Theodore Lowi and Benjamin Ginsberg, ed., *Poliscide* (New York: Macmillan, 1976).

36. Lowi, "Four Systems," p. 300.

37. See Lowi, *The Politics of Disorder*, chaps. 6 and 7.

38. See Theodore Lowi, *The End of Liberalism: The Second Republic of the United States*, 2nd ed. (New York: Norton, 1979).

39. Ibid., p. 91.

40. Walter Roettger, "Strata and Stability: Reputation of American Political Scientists," *Political Science and Politics* (Winter 1979): 6–12.

41. The essentials of Burnham's position are set out in two path-breaking works: "The Changing Shape of the American Political Universe," *American Political Science Review* 59 (March 1965): 7–28, and *Critical Elections and the Mainsprings of American Politics* (New York: Norton, 1970).

42. Burnham, *Critical Elections*, pp. 181ff.

43. Ibid., last chapter.

44. Ibid., p. 193.

45. Ibid., p. 188.

46. At least in *Critical Elections*, Burnham suggested that the "middle-class counter-revolution" would be against the "permissive society"—it would oppose the upper-class liberalism of politicians such as New York Mayor John Lindsay as well as the gains made by the poor and the underclass.

47. Burnham, *Critical Elections*, p. 193.

48. See the symposiums on "Issue Voting" in *American Political Science Review* 64 (June 1972): 415–67, and "Political Change in America" in *American Political Science Review* 66 (September 1974): 1002–57, for just a few examples of this academic debate.

49. Walter Dean Burnham, "The Eclipse of the Democratic Party," *democracy* 2, no. 3 (July 1982): 7–17. This article is hardly a bolt from the blue, but the culmination of a decade-long passage from traditional political science language and assumptions

to the approach of radical political economy. See, in order, "The Constitution, Capitalism and the Need for Rationalized Regulation," in *How Capitalistic Is the Constitution?*, ed. R. Goldwin and W. Schambra (Washington, DC: American Enterprise Institute, 1972), pp. 75–105; "The Disappearance of the American Voter," in *Electoral Participation: A Comparative Analysis*, ed. Richard Rose (Beverly Hills, CA: Sage, 1980), pp. 35–73; and "The 1980 Earthquake: Realignment, Reaction or What?" in *The Hidden Election*, ed. T. Ferguson and J. Rogers (New York: Pantheon, 1981), pp. 98–140.

50. Burnham, "Eclipse," *democracy*, p. 15.

51. Ibid., pp. 16–17.

52. Ibid., p. 16.

53. Ibid., p. 17.

Chapter 7: Conclusion: The End of the Third Tradition

1. Quoted in John Gunnell, "Political Theory: The Evolution of a Subfield" (unpublished manuscript, 1983), p. 283.

2. See Gene Poschman, "Emerging American Social Science and Political Relevance: Extractions from a Less than Classic American Literature" (paper delivered at the 1982 APSA Annual Meeting, Denver, CO, September 2–5, 1982), p. 11.

3. Reliable if anonymous sources report that some schools have established "point" systems for tenure. Journals and book publishers are ranked according to their "distinction." In these schemes, four articles in *Polity* may equal one article in the *APSR*. *PS* has even sponsored a lively debate about whether the "reputational" or "citational" approach ought to be used to assess the status of individual political scientists. See John Robey, "Reputations of Political Scientists," *Political Science and Politics* (Spring 1982): 199–200.

4. See Christopher Lasch, "The Prospects for Social Democracy," *democracy* 2, no. 3 (July 1982): 31.

5. See Samuel P. Huntington, *American Politics: The Promise of Disharmony* (Cambridge, MA: Harvard University Press, 1981). Quoted in John Wallach, "The Fearful Establishment," *democracy* 3 (1983): 117–29.

6. See Raymond Seidelman, "Pluralist Heaven's Dissenting Angels: Corporatism in the American Political Economy," in *The Political Economy of Public Policy*, ed. Alan Stone and Edward J. Harpham (Beverly Hills, CA: Sage 1982). See also Barry Bluestone and Bennett Harrison, *The Deindustrialization of America* (New York: Basic Books, 1982), chap. 5, for further reviews of this strain of thought.

7. A still good selection is Samuel P. Huntington et al., *The Crisis of Democracy* (New York: New York University Press, 1976).

8. See Charles Lindblom, *Politics and Markets* (New York: Basic Books, 1977). For examples of left criticism, see William Connolly and Michael Best, *The Politicized Economy*, 2nd ed. (Lexington, MA: Heath, 1982); Frances Fox Piven and Richard

Cloward, *The New Class War* (New York: Random House, 1982); Alan Wolfe, *America's Impasse* (Boston: South End Press, 1982).

9. See Alan Wolfe, *The Limits of Legitimacy* (New York: Macmillan, 1977), p. 345. There are, of course, substantive differences within Left scholarship itself. For a survey of these differences, see the symposium on the Democratic Party in *democracy* 2 (1982).

10. Gunnell, "Political Theory," p. 117.

Afterword

1. Raymond Seidelman with the assistance of Edward J. Harpham, *Disenchanted Realists: Political Science and the American Crisis, 1884–1984* (Albany, NY: SUNY Press, 1985). All page references in the text are to the original edition. All other references appear in these notes.

2. The project originated in a reading group that also included Stephen Skowronek when the three were graduate students at Cornell. Seidelman wrote "the bulk" (xxi) of *Disenchanted Realists*, while Harpham penned the important chapter on the behavioral era (and contributed to other chapters). As principal author, Seidelman went on to write more about the history of political science, as noted in this Afterword.

3. See James Farr, "The History of Political Science," *American Journal of Political Science* 32 (1988): 1175–95, in which figures an assessment of *Disenchanted Realists*.

4. David M. Ricci, *The Tragedy of Political Science* (New Haven, CT: Yale University Press, 1984).

5. Albert Somit and Joseph Tanenhaus, *The Development of American Political Science: From Burgess to Behavioralism* (Boston: Allyn and Bacon, 1967).

6. Crick, *American Science*.

7. Theodore J. Lowi, *The End of Liberalism* (New York: Norton, 1969).

8. Raymond Seidelman, "Political Scientists, Disenchanted Realists, and Disappearing Democrats," in *Discipline and History: Political Science in the United States*, ed. James Farr and Raymond Seidelman (Ann Arbor: University of Michigan Press, 1993), p. 323.

9. Seidelman, "Political Scientists," p. 324, when criticizing, by contrast, "the postbehavioral present."

10. Lucien W. Pye, "Political Science and the Crisis of Authoritarianism," *American Political Science Review* 84 (1990): 3–19; Theodore J. Lowi, "The State in Political Science: How We Become What We Study," *American Political Science Review* 86 (1992): 1–7 (reprinted in *Discipline and History*, ed. Farr and Seidelman); and Robert D. Putnam, "The Public Role of Political Science," *Perspectives on Politics* 1 (2003): 249–55. Seidelman was also named as a historical source in Matthew Holden Jr.'s presidential address, "The Competence of Political Science: 'Progress in Political Research' Revisited,'" *American Political Science Review* 94 (2000): 1–19.

11. See Seidelman's contribution to James Farr, John Gunnell, Raymond

Seidelman, John S. Dryzek, and Stephen T. Leonard, "Can the History of Political Science Be Neutral?" *American Political Science Review* 84 (1990): 587–607, at p. 596.

12. Albert Somit, Review, *American Political Science Review* 81 (1987): 1377.

13. John Stanley, Review, *Contemporary Sociology* 15 (1986): 623.

14. Walter Dean Burnham, "Those High Nineteenth Century American Voting Turnouts: Fact or Fiction?" *Journal of Interdisciplinary History* 16 (1986): 613; Heinz Eulau, Editor's note, *Political Behavior* 7 (1985): 307. Eulau's absence was noted by, among others, Charles J. Helm, Review, *Ethics* 98 (1988): 590, and Stephen J. Whitfield, "Disciplinary Problems," *Reviews in American History* 14 (1986): 47.

15. John G. Gunnell, "Handbooks and History: Is it Still the *American* Science of Politics?" *International Political Science Review* 23 (2002): 347.

16. In Farr et al., "Can the History of Political Science Be Neutral?," p. 598.

17. Whitfield, "Disciplinary Problems," p. 47.

18. Stanley, Review, *Contemporary Sociology*, p. 623.

19. Burton J. Bledstein, Review, *Journal of American History* 72 (1986): 969.

20. Gabriel A. Almond, "Separate Tables: Schools and Sects in Political Science," *Political Science and Politics* 21 (1988): 828–42. This essay was later included in Gabriel A. Almond, *A Discipline Divided: Schools and Sects in Political Science* (Thousand Oaks, CA: Sage, 1989).

21. Pye, "Political Science and the Crisis of Authoritarianism," pp. 3–4.

22. Almond, "Separate Tables," p. 830

23. Ibid., pp. 829, 830, 831.

24. Raymond Seidelman, Review of Clyde Barrow, *Universities and the Capitalist State*, *Journal of Politics* 53 (1991): 567.

25. Almond, "Separate Tables," pp. 830, 835, 836, 840.

26. In a later handbook chapter, Almond returned to Seidelman and company, as well as to his synopsis of the "curve of scientific progress" since antiquity. See Gabriel A. Almond, "Political Science: The History of the Discipline," in *A New Handbook of Political Science*, ed. Robert E. Goodin and Hans-Dieter Klingemann (Oxford, UK: Oxford University Press, 1998), pp. 50–96. For a critical review of this "rhetorical and one-dimensional history of the field," see Gunnell, "Handbooks and History," pp. 347–352.

27. Somit, Review, p. 1376.

28. John S. Dryzek and Stephen T. Leonard, "History and Discipline in Political Science," *American Political Science Review* 82 (1988): 1251.

29. Stanley, Review, p. 622.

30. Helm, Review, pp. 591, 592.

31. Whitfield, Review, p. 47; and Farr, "History of Political Science," p. 1192.

32. John S. Dryzek, Review of James Morone *The Democratic Wish*, *American Political Science Review* 85 (1991): 1036.

33. Somit, Review, p. 1376.

34. Bledstein, Review, p. 970.

35. It was in this context that I met Ray Seidelman and came to admire his intelligence, humor, and deep commitment to students and political principle.

36. In Farr et al., "Can the History of Political Science Be Neutral?," pp. 597, 599, 600.

37. Putnam, "The Public Role of Political Science," pp. 249, 250.

38. Farr, "History of Political Science," p. 1194.

39. Frank Freidel, *Francis Lieber: Nineteenth-Century Liberal* (Baton Rouge: Louisiana State University Press, 1947).

40. Ibid., p. 411.

41. See Haskell, *Emergence*.

42. Robert D. Putnam, with Robert Leonardi and Raffaella Y. Nanetti, *Making Democracy Work: Civic Traditions in Modern Italy* (Princeton, NJ: Princeton University Press, 1993), pp. xiii, 167, 171.

43. Robert D. Putnam, "Bowling Alone: America's Declining Social Capital," *Journal of Democracy* 6 (1995): 65–78.

44. Donna Greene, "Westchester Q and A: Ray Seidelman; How Nonvoters Affect Government," *New York Times*, January 7, 1996. Seidelman said in the interview: "I try to make the case that it's not people who have left the political system, but that the political system has left them."

45. Robert D. Putnam, *Bowling Alone: The Collapse and Revival of American Community* (New York: Simon and Schuster, 2000).

46. Ibid., pp. 402–14.

47. Ibid., pp. 22–24, 350ff.

48. Ibid., p. 362.

49. Robert D. Putnam, "*E Pluribus Unum*: Diversity and Community in the Twenty-First Century," *Scandinavian Political Studies* 30 (2007): 137–74.

50. Robert D. Putnam and David E. Campbell, *American Grace: How Religion Divides and Unites Us* (New York: Simon and Schuster, 2010), pp. 526–32.

51. See also Robert D. Putnam and Lewis M. Feldstein, *Better Together: Restoring the American Community* (New York: Simon and Schuster, 2003), being "a book of stories about social capital," p. 5.

52. For example, Ben Fine, *Theories of Social Capital: Researchers Behaving Badly* (New York: Pluto Press, 2010). When addressing the "lessons of history" from the Gilded Age, *Bowling Alone* (p. 381) recognized: "Then, as now, new concentrations of wealth and corporate power raised questions about the real meaning of democracy."

53. Jane J. Mansbridge, "Writing as a Democrat and a Feminist," in *Our Studies, Ourselves: Sociologists' Lives and Works*, ed. Barry Glassner and Rosanna Hertz (Oxford, UK: Oxford University Press, 2003), pp. 127–38, at p. 127.

54. Jane J. Mansbridge, *Beyond Adversary Democracy* (New York: Basic Books, 1980), p. xii.

55. Jane J. Mansbridge, ed., *Beyond Self-Interest* (Chicago: University of Chicago Press, 1990).

56. Jane J. Mansbridge, *Why We Lost the ERA* (Chicago: University of Chicago Press, 1986), pp. x, xi, 2, 6, 188, 197.

57. See the treatment of ideological labels in Jane J. Mansbridge, "Carole Pateman: Radical Liberal?," in *Illusion of Consent: Engaging with Carole Pateman,*

ed. Daniel I. O'Neill, Mary Lyndon Shanley, and Iris Marion Young (University Park: Pennsylvania State University Press, 2008), pp. 17–30.

58. Lester Ward, for example, is credited with "radical democratic aspirations" in *Disenchanted Realists*, p. 38.

59. Mansbridge, "Writing as a Democrat and a Feminist," p. 136.

60. Bruce Miroff, "A Science of Politics and a Science for Politics" (keynote address, New York State Political Science Association, Albany, NY, April 2008), p. 10.

61. New York Senate Bill S542A-2011 (April 11, 2012).

Bibliography

Author's note: The list below includes the most pertinent works consulted during the preparation of this book. It is intended to guide the interested reader who may wish to consult the primary and secondary sources concerning the periods and people discussed here. Accordingly, all the works cited in the text are not included here, while works of general interest that are not cited in the text have been added. Some of the broadest works are also listed more than once if they are germane to more than one of the chapters. In order to ease the reader's effort to investigate any specific time period discussed in this book, we have arranged the bibliography by chapter.

Chapter 1: Introduction

Adams, Henry. *The Education of Henry Adams.* Cambridge, MA: Houghton-Mifflin, 1961.

Barber, Benjamin. "The Compromised Republic: Public Purposelessness in America." In *The Moral Foundations of the American Republic*, ed. Robert Horwitz. Charlottesville: University Press of Virginia, 1979.

Bledstein, Burton. *The Culture of Professionalism: The Middle Class and the Development of Higher Education in America.* New York: Norton, 1976.

Bowen, Norman. "The Language of Science and Politics: Theoretical and Institutional Transformation in Social Science during the Progressive Era." Ph.D. diss., Graduate School of Public Affairs, State University of New York at Albany, 1979.

Brown, Bernard E. *American Conservatives: The Political Thought of Francis Lieber and John Burgess.* New York: Columbia University Press, 1951.

Crick, Bernard. *The American Science of Politics.* Berkeley: University of California Press, 1959.

de Jouvenal, Bertrand. "On the Nature of Political Science." *American Political Science Review* (1961).

———. "Political Science and Precision." *American Political Science Review* (1965).

Eakins, David. "The Development of Corporate Liberal Policy Research in the United States, 1885–1965." Ph.D. diss., University of Wisconsin, 1966.

Ekirch, Arthur. *Progressivism in America: A Study of the Era from Theodore Roosevelt to Woodrow Wilson.* New York: New View Points, 1974.

Fine, Sidney. *Laissez Faire and the General Welfare State.* Ann Arbor: University of Michigan Press, 1956.

Fries, Sylvia D. "Staatstheorie and the New American Science of Politics." *Journal of the History of Ideas* 24 (1964).

Furner, Mary. *Advocacy and Objectivity.* Lexington: University Press of Kentucky, 1975.

Gilbert, James. *Designing the Industrial State: The Intellectual Pursuit of Collectivism in America, 1880–1940.* Chicago: Quadrangle Books, 1975.

Habermas, Jurgen. *Legitimation Crisis.* Boston: Beacon Press, 1976.

Haddow, Anna. *Political Science in American Colleges and Universities, 1636–1900.* New York: Appleton-Century, 1939.

Hartz, Louis. *The Liberal Tradition in America.* New York: Harcourt, Brace and World, 1955.

Haskell, Thomas. *The Emergence of Professional Social Science.* Urbana: University of Illinois Press, 1977.

Heimert, Alan. *Religion and the American Mind.* Cambridge, MA: Harvard University Press, 1966.

Higham, John. "The Matrix of Specialization." In *The Organization of Knowledge in America,* ed. A. Oleson and J. Voss. Baltimore, MD: Johns Hopkins University Press, 1979.

Higham, John, and Paul K. Conkin, ed. *New Directions in American Intellectual History.* Baltimore, MD: Johns Hopkins University Press, 1979.

Hofstadter, Richard. *The Age of Reform.* New York: Random House, Vintage Books, 1959.

———. *Anti-Intellectualism in American Life.* New York: Random House, 1963.

———. *Social Darwinism in American Thought.* Boston: Beacon Press, 1965.

Irish, Marian D. *Political Science: Advance of the Discipline.* Englewood Cliffs, NJ: Prentice-Hall, 1968.

Jacobson, Norman. "Political Science and Political Education." *American Political Science Review* 57 (1963).

Jensen, Richard. "History and the Political Scientist." In *Politics and the Social Sciences,* ed. Seymour Martin Lipset. New York: Oxford University Press, 1963.

Josephson, Matthew. *The President Makers: The Culture of Politics and Leadership in the Age of Enlightenment, 1896–1919.* New York: Harcourt, Brace and World, 1940.

Landau, Martin. *Political Theory and Political Science.* New York: Macmillan, 1972.

Lawson, Alan. *The Failure of Independent Liberalism (1930–1941).* New York: Capricorn Books, 1971.

Lippmann, Walter. *Drift and Mastery: An Attempt to Diagnose the Current Unrest.* Englewood Cliffs, NJ: Prentice Hall, 1961.

Lasch, Christopher. "The Moral and Intellectual Rehabilitation of the Ruling Class." In *The World of Nations.* New York: Vintage Books, 1974.

Marcell, David. *Progress and Pragmatism*. Westport, CT: Greenwood Press, 1974.

Odum, Howard, ed. *American Masters of Social Science*. New York: Holt, 1927.

Oleson, Alexandra, and John Voss, eds. *The Organization of Knowledge in Modern America, 1860–1920*. Baltimore, MD: Johns Hopkins University Press, 1979.

Paine, Thomas. In *Common Sense and Other Political Writings*, ed. Nelson Adkins. Indianapolis, IN: Bobbs-Merrill, 1953.

Pocock, J. G. A. "Civic Humanism and Its Role in Anglo-American Thought." In *Politics, Language and Time: Essays on Political Thought and History*. New York: Atheneum, 1971.

Rogin, Michael. "Max Weber and Woodrow Wilson: The Iron Cage in Germany and America." *Polity* 3 (1971).

Ross, Dorothy, J. "The Development of the Social Sciences." In *The Organization of Knowledge in Modern America*, ed. A. Oleson and J. Voss. Baltimore, MD: Johns Hopkins University Press, 1979.

———. "The Liberal Tradition Revisited and the Republican Tradition Addressed." In *New Directions in American Intellectual History*, ed. John Higham. Baltimore, MD: Johns Hopkins University Press, 1979.

———. "Socialism and American Liberalism: Academic Social Thought in the 1880's." In *Perspectives in American History*, No. 12. Cambridge: Harvard University Press, 1977–1978.

Russett, Cynthia. *The Concept of Equilibrium in American Social Thought*. New Haven, CT: Yale University Press, 1966.

Shefter, Martin. "Party, Bureaucracy and Political Change in the United States." In *Political Parties: Development and* Decay, ed. Louis Maisel and Joseph Cooper. Beverly Hills, CA: Sage, 1978.

Shils, Edward. "The Order of Learning in the United States." In *The Organization of Knowledge in Modern America*, ed. A. Oleson and J. Voss. Baltimore, MD: Johns Hopkins University Press, 1979.

Skowronek, Stephen. *Building a New American State: The Expansion of National Administrative Capacities*. New York: Cambridge University Press, 1982.

———. "National Railroad Regulation and the Problem of State Building." *Politics and Society* 11 (1981).

Somit, Albert, and Joseph Tanenhaus. *American Political Science*. New York: Atherton Press, 1964.

———. *The Development of American Political Science*. Boston: Allyn and Bacon, 1967.

Steel, Ronald. *Walter Lippmann and the American Century*. Boston: Little, Brown, 1981.

Veysey, Laurence. *The Emergence of the American University*. Chicago: University of Chicago Press, 1965.

Waldo, Dwight. *The Administrative State: A Study of the Political Theory of American Public Administration*. New York: Ronald Press, 1948.

Weinstein, James. *The Corporate Ideal in the Liberal State*. Boston: Beacon Press, 1968.

White, Morton. *Science and Sentiment in American Thought.* New York: Oxford University Press, 1972.

——. *Social Thought in America: The Revolt against Formalism.* Boston: Beacon Press, 1957.

Wiebe, Robert. *Businessmen and Reform.* Chicago: Quadrangle Books, 1968.

——. *The Search for Order.* New York: Hill and Wang, 1967.

——. *The Segmented Society: An Introduction to the Meaning of America.* New York: Oxford University Press, 1975.

Wills, Gary. *Inventing America.* Garden City, NY: Doubleday, 1975.

Wolin, Sheldon. "The People's Two Bodies." *democracy* 1 (1981).

Wood, Gordon. *The Creation of the American Republic, 1776–1787.* New York: Norton, 1969.

Chapter 2: The Impulse toward a Science of Politics, 1880–1900

Brown, Bernard E. *American Conservatives: Lieber and Burgess.* New York: Columbia University Press, 1951.

Burgess, John. *Reminiscences of an American Scholar.* New York: Columbia University Press, 1934.

Burnham, John. *Lester Frank Ward in American Thought.* Washington, DC: Annals of American Sociology, Public Affairs Press, 1956.

Chugerman, Samuel. *Lester Ward: An American Aristotle.* Durham, NC: Duke University Press, 1939.

Clark, John Bates. *The Philosophy of Wealth.* Boston: Ginn, 1889.

——. "The Position of Science in the Historical Development of Political Economy." *Penn Monthly* 10 (1879).

——. "The Scholar's Political Opportunity." *Political Science Quarterly* 12 (1897).

Commager, Henry Steele. *The American Mind: An Interpretation of American Thought and* Character *since the 1880's.* New Haven, CT: Yale University Press, 1950.

——, ed. *Lester Ward and the Welfare State.* Indianapolis, IN: Bobbs-Merrill, 1967.

Cuff, Robert. *The War Industries Board.* Baltimore, MD: Johns Hopkins University Press, 1973.

Diamond, William. *The Economic Thought of Woodrow Wilson.* Baltimore, MD: Johns Hopkins University Press, 1943.

Donnelly, Ignatius. *Caesar's Column.* Cambridge, MA: Belknap Press of Harvard University Press, 1960.

Dorfman, Joseph. *The Economic Mind in American Civilization.* 5 vols. New York: Viking Press, 1949.

Eakins, David. "The Development of Corporate Liberal Policy Research in the United States, 1885–1965." Ph.D. diss., University of Wisconsin, 1966.

Ely, Richard. *Ground under Our Feet: An Autobiography.* New York: Macmillan, 1938.

——. *An Introduction to Political Economy.* New York: Macmillan, 1889.

——. *The Labor Movement in America.* New York: Macmillan, 1886.

Fine, Sidney. *Laissez Faire and the General Welfare State.* Ann Arbor: University of Michigan Press, 1956.

Goldman, Eric. *Rendezvous with Destiny.* New York: Vintage Books, 1956.

Goodwyn, Lawrence. *Democratic Promise: The Populist Movement in America.* New York: Oxford University Press, 1976.

Hays, Samuel P. *Conservation and the Gospel of Efficiency.* New York: Atheneum, 1959.

Hofstadter, Richard. *Social Darwinism in American Thought.* Boston: Beacon Press, 1965.

Hoxie, Gordon. *The Faculty of Political Science at Columbia University.* New York: Columbia University Press, 1955.

Huntington, Samuel, et al. *The Crisis of Democracy.* New York: New York University Press, 1979.

Jacobson, Norman. "Causality and Time in Political Process." *American Political Science Review* 58 (1964).

Larson, Margoli Sarfatti. *The Rise of Professionalism: A Sociological Analysis.* Berkeley: University of California Press, 1978.

Link, Arthur S. *Wilson: The Road to the White House.* Princeton, NJ: Princeton University Press, 1957.

Palmer, Bruce. *"Man over Money": The Southern Populist Critique of American Capitalism.* Chapel Hill: University of North Carolina Press, 1980.

Purcell, Edward A. *The Crisis of Democratic Theory.* Lexington: University of Kentucky Press, 1973.

Ross, Dorothy. "The Development of the Social Sciences." In *Knowledge in American Society, 1870–1920,* ed. A. Oleson and J. Voss. Baltimore, MD: Johns Hopkins University Press, 1979.

——. "Socialism and American Liberalism: Academic Social Thought in the 1880's." In *Perspectives in American History,* No. 12. Cambridge, MA: Harvard University Press, 1977–1978.

Rourke, Francis, ed. *Bureaucratic Power in National Politics.* Boston: Little, Brown, 1965.

Sklar, Martin. "Woodrow Wilson and the Political Economy of Modern United States Liberalism." In *For a New America: Essays on History and Politics from Studies on the Left,* ed. James Weinstein and David Eakins. New York: Random House, 1970.

Sumner, William Graham. *What Social Classes Owe to Each Other.* New York: Harper, 1883.

Ward, Lester. "Broadening the Way to Success." *Forum* 2 (1886).

——. *Dynamic Sociology or Applied Social Science.* New York: Appleton, 1883.

——. "False Notions of Government." *Forum* 3 (1887).

——. *Glimpses into the Cosmos.* 6 vols. New York: Putnam's, 1913.

——. "Plutocracy and Paternalism." *Forum* 20 (1895).

——. *Psychic Factors in Civilization.* Boston: Ginn, 1893.

White, Andrew Dickson. "Education in Political Science." Address delivered at third anniversary of Johns Hopkins University, Baltimore, MD, February 22, 1879.

———. *History of the Warfare of Science with Theology in Christendom.* New York: Dover Publications, 1960.

Wiebe, Robert. *The Search for Order.* New York: Hill and Wang, 1967.

Wilson, Woodrow. "The Character of Democracy in the United States." *Atlantic Monthly* 64 (1889).

———. *Congressional Government.* Boston: Houghton Mifflin, 1885.

———. *Constitutional Government in the United States.* New York: Columbia University Press, 1908.

———. "Democracy and Efficiency." *Atlantic Monthly* 87 (1901).

———. *Division and Reunion, 1829–1889.* New York: Longman's Green, 1898.

———. "The Ideals of America." *Atlantic Monthly* 90 (1902).

———. "The Laws and the Facts." President's Address, *American Political Science Review* 5 (1911).

———. *Leaders of Men.* Princeton, NJ: Princeton University Press, 1952.

———. *Mere Literature and Other Essays.* Boston: Houghton Mifflin, 1897.

———. *The New Freedom.* Princeton, NJ: Princeton University Press, 1956.

———. *An Old Master and Other Political Essays.* New York: Scribner, 1893.

———. "Politics 1857–1907." *Atlantic Monthly* 100 (1907).

———. *The State: Elements of Historical and Practical Politics.* Boston: Heath, 1898.

———. "The Study of Administration." *Political Science Quarterly* 2 (1887).

Wolfe, A. B. *Conservatism, Radicalism and Scientific Method.* New York: Macmillan, 1923.

Worthington, T. K. "Recent Impressions of the Ecole Libre." In *Studies in Historical and Political Science*, ed. Herbert Baxter Adams. Baltimore, MD: Johns Hopkins University Press, 1879.

**Chapter 3: Science as Muckraking:
The Cult of Realism in the Progressive Era**

Barnes, Henry Elmer. "Review of *The Nature of the Social Sciences.*" *American Historical Review* 40 (1934).

Beale, Howard, ed. *Charles A. Beard: An Appraisal.* Lexington: University of Kentucky Press, 1954.

Beard, Charles. *American Government and Politics.* New York: Macmillan, 1914.

———. *The American Party Battle.* New York: Macmillan, 1928.

———. Presidential Address. *American Political Science Review* 21 (1927).

———. *A Charter for the Social Sciences.* New York: Scribner's, 1932.

———. "Conditions Favorable to Creative Work in Political Science," *American Political Science Review* 24 (1930).

———. "Congress under Fire." *Yale Review* 42 (1932).

———. *The Economic Basis of Politics.* New York: Knopf, 1923.

———. *An Economic Interpretation of the Constitution of the United States*. New York: Macmillan, 1913.

———. *The Economic Origins of Jeffersonian Democracy*. New York: Macmillan, 1915.

———. "Government by Technologists." *New Republic* (1930): 115–20.

———. "Grounds for a Reconsideration of Historiography." In *Theory and Practice in Historical Study*, ed. Merle Curti. Social Science Research Council Bulletin, no. 54, 1946.

———. "Limitations to the Application of Social Science Implied in Recent Social Trends." *Social Forces* 11 (1933).

———. "The Myth of Rugged American Individualism." *Harpers*, December 1931.

———. *Nature of the Social Sciences*. New York: Scribner's, 1934.

———. "Neglected Aspects of Political Science." *American Political Science Review* 42 (1948).

———. "Political Science." In *Research in the Social Sciences*, ed. Wilson Gee. New York: Macmillan, 1929.

———. "Politics." Lecture, Columbia University, New York, 1908.

———. "Study and Teaching of Politics." *Columbia University Quarterly* 12 (1910).

———. "The Task before Us." *Social Studies* 25 (1934).

———. "Time, Technology and the Creative Spirit in Political Science." *American Political Science Review* 21 (1927).

———. "Training in Efficient Public Service." *Annals of the American Academy of Political and Social Science* 64 (1916).

———. *The Unique Function of Education in American Democracy*. Washington, DC: National Education Association, 1937.

Beard, Charles A., et al. "Report of Reconstruction Commission to Governor Alfred E. Smith." Albany, NY, 1919.

Beard, Charles A., and Mary Beard. *The Rise of American Civilization*. New York: Macmillan, 1927.

Beard, Charles A., and J. H. Robinson. *The Development of Modern Europe*. Boston: Ginn, 1907.

Beard, Charles A., with George H. E. Smith. *The Future Comes*. New York: Macmillan, 1933.

———. *The Open Door at Home*. New York: Macmillan, 1934.

Bentley, Arthur. *Inquiry into Inquiries*. Boston: Beacon Press, 1954.

———. "Kinds of Investigation in the Social Sciences." *Annals of the American Academy of Political and Social Science* 5 (1895).

———. *Makers, Users* and *Masters*, ed. Sidney Ratner. Syracuse, NY: Syracuse University Press, 1969.

———. *The Process of Government*. Evanston, IL: Principia Press, 1935.

Borning, Bernard. *The Political and Social Thought of Charles A. Beard*. Seattle: University of Washington Press, 1962.

Corwin, Edward S. "Democratic Dogma and the Future of Political Science." *American Political Science Review* 23 (1929).

———. "The Crisis of Democracy," *Annals of the American Academy of Political and Social Sciences* (1933).

Croly, Herbert. *The Promise of American Life*. New York: Bobbs-Merrill, 1965.

Eckstein, Harry. "Group Theory and the Comparative Study of Pressure Groups," In *Comparative Politics: A Reader*, ed. D. Apter and H. Eckstein. New York: Free Press, 1963.

Forcey, Charles. *The Crossroads of Liberalism, 1900–1925*. New York: Oxford University Press, 1961.

Garner, James. "Review of *The Process of Government*." *American Political Science Review* 2 (1907).

Goodnow, Frank. "The Work of the American Political Science Association." *Proceedings of the American Political Science Association* 1 (1904).

Hays, Samuel P. *Conservation and the Gospel of Efficiency*. New York: Atheneum, 1959.

Hofstadter, Richard. *The Age of Reform*. New York: Vintage Books, 1959.

Kariel, Henry. "Political Science in the United States: Reflections on One of Its Trends." *Political Studies* 4 (1956).

Kolko, Gabriel. *The Triumph of Conservatism*. Chicago: Quadrangle Books, 1963.

Kress, Paul F. *Social Science and the Idea of Process: The Ambiguous Legacy of Arthur F. Bentley*. Urbana: University of Illinois Press, 1973.

Landau, Martin. "The Myth of Hyperfactualism in Political Science." *Political Science Quarterly* 83 (1968).

Skowronek, Stephen. *Building a New American State*. New York: Cambridge University Press, 1982.

Small, A. W. "Review of *The Process of Government*." *American Journal of Sociology* 13 (1908).

Taylor, Richard W. "Arthur Bentley's Political Science." *Western Political Quarterly* 5 (1952).

———. *Life, Language and Law: Essays in Honor of Arthur F. Bentley*. Yellow Springs, OH: Antioch Press, 1957.

Weinstein, James. *The Corporate Ideal in the Liberal State*. Boston: Beacon Press, 1968.

Wiebe, Robert. *Businessmen and Reform*. Chicago: Quadrangle Books, 1968.

———. *The Search for Order*. New York: Hill and Wang, 1967.

Chapter 4: Reform and Disillusionment in the New Deal

American Historical Association. "Conclusions and Recommendations." In *American Historical Association Commission on Social Studies*. New York: Scribner's, 1933.

Committee on Recent Social Trends. *Recent Social Trends in the United States*. New York: McGraw Hill, 1933.

Crick, Bernard. *The American Science of Politics*. Berkeley: University of California Press, 1959.

Dewey, John. *Liberalism and Social Action.* New York: Capricorn Books, 1963.

———. "Social Science and Social Control." *New Republic* 67 (1931).

Diggins, John P. *Mussolini and Fascism: The View from America.* Princeton, NJ: Princeton University Press, 1972.

Easton, David. *The Political System.* Chicago: University of Chicago Press, 1952.

Forcey, Charles. *The Crossroads of Liberalism, 1920–1925.* New York: Oxford University Press, 1961.

Fosdick, Raymond. *The Story of the Rockefeller Foundation.* New York: Harper, 1952.

Graham, Otis. *Toward a Planned Society.* New York: Oxford University Press, 1976.

Institute for Government Research. *An Account of Research Achievements.* Washington, DC: Brookings Institution, 1956.

Jensen, Richard. "History and the Political Scientist." In *Politics and the Social Sciences,* ed. Seymour Martin Lipset. New York: Oxford University Press, 1969.

Karl, Barry. "Charles Merriam." In *International Encyclopedia of the Social Sciences,* vol. 10. New York: Macmillan, 1968.

———. *Charles Merriam and the Study of Politics.* Chicago: University of Chicago Press, 1974.

———. *Executive Reorganization and Reform in the New Deal.* Cambridge, MA: Harvard University Press, 1963.

Lasswell, Harold. *The Analysis of Political Behavior.* London: Routledge and Kegan Paul, 1948.

———. "Civic Education in the Technoscientific Age." In *Approaches to Education for Character,* ed. Clarence H. Faust and Jessica Feingold. New York: Harper and Row, 1967.

———. *Democracy through Public Opinion.* New York: Bantam Publishing, 1941.

———. *The Future of Political Science.* New York: Atherton Press, 1963.

———. "Immediate Future of Research Policy and Method in Political Science." *American Political Science Review* 45 (1951).

———. "Policy Sciences." In *International Encyclopedia of the Social Sciences,* vol. 12, New York: Macmillan, 1968.

———. "Political Power and Democratic Values." In *Problems of Power in American Democracy,* ed. William Kornhauser. Detroit, MI: Wayne State University Press, 1957.

———. "The Political Science of Science." *American Political Science Review* 50 (1956).

———. *Political Writings.* New York: Free Press, 1951.

———. *Politics: Who Gets What, When, How.* Cleveland, OH: Meridian Books, 1951.

———. *Power and Personality.* New York: Norton, 1948.

———. *Psychopathology and Politics.* New York: Viking Press, 1930.

———. "The Strategy of Revolutionary and War Propaganda." In *Public Opinion and World Politics,* ed. Quincy Wright. Chicago: University of Chicago Press, 1933.

———. *World Politics and Personal Insecurity.* New York: McGraw Hill, 1935.

Lasswell, Harold, and D. B. Jones. *World Revolutionary Propaganda.* New York: Knopf, 1939.

Lasswell, Harold, and Abraham Kaplan. *Power and Society: A Framework for Political Inquiry.* New Haven, CT: Yale University Press, 1950.

Lasswell, Harold, and Nathan Leites. *Language of Politics.* Cambridge, MA: MIT Press, 1949.

Lawson, Alan. *The Failure of Independent Liberalism, 1930–1941.* New York: Capricorn Books, 1971.

Lynd, Robert. *Knowledge for What? The Place of Social Science in American Culture.* Princeton, NJ: Princeton University Press, 1939.

Lyons, Gene. *The Uneasy Partnership: Social Science and the Federal Government in the Twentieth Century.* New York: Sage Foundation, 1969.

Mack, J. R., and Cedric Larsen. *Words that Won the* War. Princeton, NJ: Princeton University Press, 1939.

Marcuse, Herbert. *Eros and Civilization.* Boston: Beacon Press, 1955.

Marvick, Duane, ed. *Harold D. Lasswell on Political Sociology.* Chicago: University of Chicago Press, 1977.

Merriam, Charles E. *American Political Ideas: 1867–1917.* New York: Macmillan, 1920.

——. "The Assumptions of Democracy." *Political Science* Quarterly 53 (1938).

——. *Civic Education in the United States.* New York: Scribner's, 1939.

——. "The Education of Charles Merriam." In *The Future of Government in the U. S.,* ed. Leonard White. Chicago: University of Chicago Press, 1942.

——. *The Making of Citizens: A Comparative Study of Methods of Civic Training.* Chicago: University of Chicago Press, 1931.

——. *New Aspects of Politics.* Chicago: University of Chicago Press, 1925.

——. *The New Democracy and the New Despotism.* New York: McGraw Hill, 1939.

——. *Political Power.* New York: Collier Books, 1964.

——. "Present State of the Study of Politics." *American Political Science Review* 15 (1921).

——. "Presidential Address to the American Political Science Association." *American Political Science Review* 20 (1926).

——. *Prologue to Politics.* Chicago: University of Chicago Press, 1939.

——. *Public and Private Government.* New Haven, CT: Yale University Press, 1944.

——. *Role of Politics in Social Change.* New York: New York University Press, 1936.

——. *Systematic Politics.* Chicago: University of Chicago Press, 1945.

Odegard, Peter. "Political Scientists and the Democratic Service State." *Journal of Politics* 2 (1940).

Polenberg, Richard. *Reorganizing Roosevelt's Government.* Cambridge, MA: Harvard University Press, 1966.

"Report of the President's Committee on Recent Social Trends." New York: McGraw Hill, 1933.

Saunders, Charles B. *The Brookings Institution.* Washington, DC: Brookings Institution, 1966.

Schoolman, Morton. *Herbert Marcuse: The Imaginary Witness.* New York: Free Press, 1981.

Smith, Bruce Lannes. "The Mystifying Intellectual History of Harold Lasswell." In

Politics, Personality and Social Science in the Twentieth Century, ed. Arnold Rogow. Chicago: University of Chicago Press, 1969.

Social Science Research Council (USA). *The Fifth Annual Report of the Social Research Council, 1928–1929.* New York: Social Science Research Council, 1929.

Waldo, Dwight. *The Administrative State: A Study of the Political Theory of American Public Administration.* New York: Ronald Press, 1948.

White, Leonard D., ed. *The Future of Government in the United States: Essays in Honor of Charles E. Merriam.* Chicago: University of Chicago Press, 1942.

White, Morton. *Social Thought in America: The Revolt against Formalism.* Boston: Beacon Press, 1957

Wirth, Louis, ed. *A Decade of Social Science Research.* Chicago: University of Chicago Press, 1940.

Wright, Quincy, ed. *Public Opinion and World Politics.* Chicago: University of Chicago Press, 1933.

Chapter 5: The Behavioral Era

Almond, Gabriel. "Politics and Ethics: A Symposium." *American Political Science Review* 41 (1946).

American Political Science Association. *Toward a More Responsible Two-Party System. A Report of the Committee on Political Parties. American Political Science Review* 44 (1950).

———. *Goals for Political Science.* New York: William Sloane, 1951.

Appleby, Paul. "Political Science: The Next Twenty-Five Years." *American Political Science Review* 44 (1950).

Banfield, Edward. *Political Influence.* New York: Free Press, 1961.

Bell, Daniel. *The End of Ideology: On the Exhaustion of Political Ideas in the Fifties,* rev. ed. New York: Free Press, 1962.

Berelson, Bernard R., Paul F. Lazarfeld, and William McPhee. *Voting.* Chicago: University of Chicago Press, 1954.

Boyd, Richard W., and Herbert H. Hyman. "Survey Research." In *Handbook of Political Science,* vol. 7, ed. Frederick I. Greenstein and Nelson Polsby. Reading, MA: Addison Wesley, 1975.

Campbell, Angus, Philip E. Converse, Warren E. Miller, and Donald E. Stokes. *The American Voter.* New York: Wiley, 1960.

Campbell, Angus, Philip E. Converse, and Donald E. Stokes. *Elections and the Political Order.* New York: Wiley, 1967.

Charlesworth, James C., ed. *The Limits of Behavioralism in Political Science.* Philadelphia: American Academy of Political Science, 1962.

Dahl, Robert A. *After the Revolution?* New Haven, CT: Yale University Press, 1970.

———. "The Behavioral Approach to Political Science: Epitaph for a Movement to a Successful Protest." In *Behavioralism in Political Science,* ed. Heinz Eulau. New York: Atherton Press, 1960.

——. "A Critique of the Ruling Elite Model." *American Political Science Review* 52 (1958).

——. "Further Reflections on the Elitist Theory of Democracy." *American Political Science Review* 59 (1966).

——. *A Preface to Democratic Theory.* Chicago: University of Chicago Press, 1956.

——. *Who Governs?* New Haven, CT: Yale University Press, 1961.

Dahl, Robert A., and Charles Lindblom. *Politics, Economics, and Welfare.* New York: Harper, 1953.

Davis, Lane. "The Cost of Realism: Contemporary Restatements of Democracy." *Western Political Quarterly* 18 (1964).

Easton, David. "The Current Meaning of 'Behavioralism.'" In *Contemporary Political Analysis*, ed. James C. Charlesworth. New York: Free Press, 1967.

——. "Harold Lasswell: Political Scientist for a Democratic Society." *Journal of Politics* 12 (1950).

——. "The New Revolution in Political Science." *American Political Science Review* 63 (1969).

——. "Political Science." In *International Encyclopedia of the Social Sciences* 12. New York: Macmillan, 1968.

——. *The Political System: An Inquiry into the State of Political Science*, 2nd ed. New York: Knopf, 1953.

Eulau, Heinz. *The Behavioral Persuasion in Politics.* New York: Random House, 1963.

——. "Political Behavior." In *International Encyclopedia of the Social Sciences* 12. New York: Macmillan, 1968.

Eulau, Heinz, ed. *Behavioralism in Political Science.* New York: Atherton Press, 1969.

Eulau, Heinz, and James G. March, ed. *Political Science.* Englewood Cliffs, NJ: Prentice-Hall, 1969.

Falco, Marie J. *Truth and Meaning in Political Science.* Columbus, OH: Merrill Publishing, 1973.

Fowler, Robert Booth. *Believing Skeptics: American Political Intellectuals, 1945–1964.* Westport, CT: Greenwood Press, 1978.

Friedrich, Carl J. "Political Science in the United States in Wartime." *American Political Science Review* 41 (1947).

"Grants for Research on American Government Processes: A New Program of the Committee on Political Behavior." *Items* 10 (1956).

Gross, Bertram M. *The Legislative Struggle: A Study in Social Combat.* New York: McGraw Hill, 1953.

——. "Review of *The Process of Government*." *American Political Science Review* 44 (1950).

Harris, J. P. "Relations of Political Science with Public Officials." *American Political Science Review* 35 (1941).

Harrison, Wilfrid. "Political Process." *Political Studies* 6 (1958).

Hill, David B., and Norman R. Luttbeg. *Trends in American Electoral Behavior.* Itasca, IL: Peacock, 1980.

Hunter, Floyd. *Community Power Structure: A Study of Decision Makers.* Chapel Hill: University of North Carolina Press, 1953.

"In Memoriam: V. O. Key, Jr." *American Political Science Review* 58 (1964).

Institute for Social Research. *A Quarter Century of Social Research.* Ann Arbor, MI: Institute for Social Research, 1971.

"Issue Voting Symposium." *American Political Science Review* 64 (1972).

Key, V. O., Jr. *The Administration of Federal Grants to States.* Chicago: University of Chicago Press, 1937.

———. *American State Politics: An Introduction.* New York: Knopf, 1956.

———. *Parties, Politics and Pressure Groups.* New York: Crowell, 1942, 1947, 1952, 1958, 1964.

———. *Public Opinion and American Democracy.* New York: Knopf, 1961.

———. *The Responsible Electorate: Rationality in Presidential Voting, 1936–1960.* With the assistance of Milton C. Cummings Jr. New York: Vintage Books, 1966.

———. "Secular Realignment and the Party System." *Journal of Politics* 21 (1959).

———. *Southern Politics.* New York: Vintage Books, 1949.

———. "The Techniques of Graft in the United States." Ph.D. diss., University of Chicago, 1934.

———. "A Theory of Critical Elections." *Journal of Politics* 17 (1955).

Key, V. O., Jr., and W. W. Crouch. *The Initiative and Referendum in California.* Berkeley: University of California Press, 1939.

Kirkpatrick, Evron M. "The Impact of the Behavioral Movement in Traditional Political Science." In *Essays in the Behavioral Study of Politics,* ed. Austin Ranney. Urbana: University of Illinois Press, 1962.

———. "Toward a More Responsible Two-Party System: Political Science, Policy Science, or Pseudo Science." *American Political Science Review* 65 (1971).

Kornhauser, William. *The Politics of Mass Society.* New York: Free Press, 1959.

LaPalombara, Joseph. "Decline of Ideology: A Dissent and An Interpretation." *American Political Science Review* 60 (1966).

Lazerfeld, Paul F., Bernard R. Berelson, and Hazel Goudet. *The People's Choice.* New York: Duell, Sloan and Pierce, 1944.

Leegge, David E. *The Development and Use of Sample Surveys.* Phase II Report for the National Science Board, Twelfth Board Report. 1979.

Lippmann, Walter. *Public Opinion.* New York: Free Press, 1965.

Lipset, Seymour Martin. *Politics and the Social Sciences.* London: Oxford University Press, 1969.

———. *Political Man.* New York: Anchor Books, 1963.

MacIver, R. M. *Social Causation.* Boston: Atheneum Press, 1942.

———. *The Web of Government.* New York: Macmillan, 1947.

McWilliams, Wilson Carey. "On Political Illegitimacy." *Public Policy* 19 (1971).

Miller, Eugene F. "David Easton's Political Theory." *Political Science Reviewer* 1 (1971).

Mills, C. Wright. *The Power Elite.* London: Oxford University Press, 1956.

Nie, Norman H., Sidney Verba, and John R. Petrocik. *The Changing American Voter.* Cambridge, MA: Harvard University Press, 1976.

Polsby, Nelson. *Community Power and Political Theory.* New Haven, CT: Yale University Press, 1963.

Ranney, Austin. "The Committee on Political Behavior, 1949–64, and the Committee on Government and Legal Processes, 1964–72." *Items* 28 (1974).

———. *The Doctrine of Responsible Party Government.* Urbana: University of Illinois Press, 1962.

Reid, Herbert. "Contemporary American Political Science and the Crisis of Industrial Society." *Midwest Journal of Political Science* 16 (1972).

"Research on State Politics: A New Program of Grants in Aid." *Items* 9 (1955).

Russett, Cynthia. *The Concept of Equilibrium in American Social Thought.* New Haven, CT: Yale University Press, 1966.

Ryan, Alan. *Philosophy of the Social Sciences.* New York: Pantheon, 1970.

Sayre, Wallace S., and Herbert Kaufman. *Governing New York City.* New York: Sage, 1960.

Schattschneider, E. E. *The Semi-Sovereign People.* New York: Holt, Rinehart and Winston, 1960.

Searing, Donald D. "Values in Empirical Research: A Behavioral Response." *Midwest Journal of Political Science* 14 (1970).

Somit, Albert, and Joseph Tanenhaus. *The Development of Political Science.* Boston: Allyn and Bacon, 1967.

Sorauf, Frank J. *Perspectives on Political Science.* Columbus, OH: Merrill Books, 1966.

Stokes, Donald E. "Interview with David B. Truman." *News for Teachers of Political Science* (1982).

Storing, Herbert, ed. *Essays on the Scientific Study of Politics.* Chicago. Chicago: University of Chicago Press, 1963.

Susser, Bernard. "The Behavioral Ideology: A Review and Retrospect." *Political Studies* 22 (1974).

Truman, David B. *Administrative Decentralization: A Study of the Chicago Field Office of the United States Department of Agriculture.* Chicago: University of Chicago Press, 1940.

———. "The American System in Crisis." *Political Science* Quarterly 74 (1959).

———. *The Congressional Party: A Case Study.* New York: Wiley, 1959.

———. "Disillusion and Regeneration: The Quest for a Discipline." *American Political Science Review* 59 (1965).

———. *The Governmental Process: Political Interests and Public Opinion,* 2nd ed. New York: Knopf, 1971.

———. "The Implications of Political Behavior Research." *Items* 5 (1951).

———. "The Impact on Political Science of the Revolution in the Behavioral Sciences." In *Behavioralism in Political Science,* ed. Heinz Eulau. New York: Atherton Press, 1967.

———. "The Politics of the New Collectivism." In *Trends in American Society,* ed. Clarence Morris. Philadelphia: University of Pennsylvania Press, 1962.

———. "Public Opinion Research as a Tool of Public Administration." *Public Administration Review* 3 (1945).

Turner, Julius. *Party and Constituency: Pressures on Congress.* Baltimore, MD: Johns Hopkins University Press, 1951.

———. "Responsible Parties: A Dissent from the Floor." *American Political Science Review* 45 (1951).

Van Dyke, Vernon. *Political Science: A Philosophical Analysis.* Stanford, CA: Stanford University Press, 1960.

Voegelin, Eric. *The New Science of Politics.* Chicago: University of Chicago Press, 1952.

Waldo, Dwight. *Political Science in the United States of America: A Trend Report.* Paris: UNESCO, 1956.

Waxman, Chaim I., ed. *The End of Ideology Debate.* New York: Simon and Schuster, 1967.

White, Leonard D. *The State of the Social Sciences.* Chicago: University of Chicago Press, 1956.

Whyte, William Foote. "Instruction and Research: A Challenge to Political Science." *American Political Science Review* 37 (1943).

Chapter 6: The Eclipse of Unity

Abbott, Philip. *Furious Fancies.* Westport, CT: Greenwood Press, 1980.

Bachrach, Peter, ed. *Political Elites in a Democracy.* New York: Atherton Press, 1971.

———. *The Theory of Democratic Elitism.* Boston: Little, Brown, 1967.

Bachrach, Peter, and Morton S. Baratz. *Power and Poverty: Theory and Practice.* New York: Oxford University Press, 1970.

Bell, Daniel. *The Coming of Post-Industrial Society.* New York: Basic Books, 1973.

Beardsley, Philip L. "Political Science: Case of the Missing Paradigm." *Political Theory* 2 (1974).

Berns, Walter. "The Behavioral Sciences and the Study of Political Things." *American Political Science Review* 55 (1961).

Best, Michael H., and William E. Connolly. *The Politicized Economy*, 2nd ed. Lexington, MA: Heath, 1982.

Boorstin, Daniel. *The Genius of American Politics.* Chicago: University of Chicago Press, 1953.

Burnham, Walter Dean. "American Voting Behavior and the 1964 Election." *Midwest Journal of Political Science* 12 (1968).

———. "The Changing Shape of the American Political Universe." *American Political Science Review* 59 (1965).

———. "The Constitution, Capitalism, and the Need for Rationalized Regulation." In *How Capitalistic Is the Constitution?*, ed. Robert A. Goldwin and William A. Schambra. Washington, DC: American Enterprise Institute, 1982.

———. *Critical Elections and the Mainsprings of American Politics.* New York: Norton, 1970.

———. "The Disappearance of the American Voter." In *Electoral Participation: A Comparative Analysis*, ed. Richard Rose. Beverly Hills: Sage, 1980.

———. "The 1980 Earthquake: Realignment, Reaction, or What?" In *The Hidden Election*, ed. Thomas Ferguson and Joel Rogers. New York: Pantheon Books, 1981.

————. "The Eclipse of the Democratic Party." *democracy* 2 (1982).

————. "The End of American Party Politics." *Transaction* 6 (1969).

————. "Party Systems and The Political Process." In *The American Party Systems*, ed. William Nisbet Chambers and Walter Dean Burnham. New York: Oxford University Press, 1973.

Caucus for a New Political Science. "Proposed Directions for the Caucus." Report of the Committee on Structure prepared for discussion at the American Political Science Association Meeting, San Francisco, CA, 1975.

Connolly, William E., ed. *The Bias of Pluralism*. New York: Atherton Press, 1969.

Crouch, Colin. "The State, Capital and Liberal Democracy." In *State and Economy in Contemporary Capitalism*, ed. Colin Crouch. New York: St. Martin's Press, 1979.

Crozier, Michel, et al. *The Crisis of Democracy*. New York: New York University Press, 1975.

Domhoff, G. William. *The Higher Circles*. New York: Random House, 1970.

Easton, David. "The New Revolution in Political Science." *American Political Science Review* 63 (1969).

Edelman, Murray. *The Symbolic Uses of Politics*. Urbana: University of Illinois Press, 1964.

Eulau, Heinz. "Communication to *PS*." *PS* 7 (1974).

————. "Communication to *PS*." *PS* 9 (1976).

Germino, Dante. *Beyond Ideology: Revival of Political Theory*. New York: Harper and Row, 1967.

Golembiewski, Robert T. "Group Basis of Politics: Notes on Analysis and Development." *American Political Science Review* 54 (1960).

Graham, George J., Jr., and George W. Carey, eds. *The Post-Behavioral Era: Perspectives on Political Science*. New York: David McKay, 1972.

Green, Mark. *Winning Back America*. New York: Bantam Books, 1982.

Green, Philip, and Sanford Levinson, eds. *Power and Community: Dissenting Essays in Political Science*. New York: Pantheon Books, 1970.

Greenberg, Edward S. *The American Political System*. 2nd ed. Cambridge, MA: Winthrop, 1980.

————. *Serving the Few: Corporate Capitalism and the Bias of Government Policy*. New York: Wiley, 1974.

————. *Understanding Modern Government: The Rise and Decline of the American Political Economy*. New York: Wiley, 1979.

Hale, Myron Q. "Cosmology of Arthur Bentley." *American Political Science Review* 54 (1960).

Huntington, Samuel P. *American Politics: The Promise of Disharmony*. Cambridge: Belknap Press of Harvard University Press, 1981.

————. "Paradigms of American Politics: Beyond the One, the Two, and the Many." *Political Science Quarterly* 89 (1974).

Irish, Marion. *Political Science: Advance of the Discipline*. Englewood Cliffs, NJ: Prentice Hall, 1967.

Kariel, Henry S. "Creating Political Reality." *American Political Science Review* 64 (1970).

——. *The Decline of American Pluralism.* Stanford, CA: Stanford University Press, 1961.

——. "Expanding the Political Present." *American Political Science Review* 63 (1969).

——. *In Search of Authority.* New York: Free Press, 1964.

——. "The Limits of Social Science: Henry Adams' Quest for Order." *American Political Science Review* 50 (1956).

——. "Political Science in the United States: Reflections on One of Its Trends." *Political Studies* 4 (1956).

——. *The Promise of Politics.* Englewood Cliffs, NJ: Prentice Hall, 1966.

——. *Saving Appearances.* Belmont, CA: Duxbury Press, 1972.

Landau, Martin. "The Myth of Hyperfactualization in Political Science." *Political Science Quarterly* 83 (1968).

——. *Political Theory and Political Science.* New York: Macmillan, 1972.

LaPalombara, Joseph. "Decline of Ideology: A Dissent and an Interpretation." *American Political Science Review* 60 (1966).

Lazarfeld, Paul, Lawrence Klein, and Ralph Tyler. *Behavioral Sciences: Problems and Perspectives.* Boulder: University of Colorado, Institute of Behavioral Sciences, 1964.

Leiserson, Avery. "Charles Merriam, Max Weber, and the Search for Synthesis in Political Science." *American Political Science Review* 69 (1975).

——. "Science and the Public Life." *Journal of Politics* 29 (1967).

Lipset, Seymour Martin. *Rebellion in the University.* Boston: Little, Brown, 1972.

Lipsky, Michael. *Protest in City Politics.* Chicago: Rand McNally, 1970.

Lowi, Theodore J. "American Business, Public Policy, Case Studies, and Political Theory." *World Politics* 16 (1964).

——. *At the Pleasure of the Mayor.* New York: Free Press, 1964.

——. "A Critical Election Misfires." *Nation* (1972).

——. "Decision Making vs. Policy Making: Toward an Antidote for Technocracy." *Public Administration Review* 30 (1970).

——. *The End of Liberalism: Ideology, Policy, and the Crisis of Public Authority.* New York: Norton, 1969.

——. "Four Systems of Policy, Politics and Choice." *Public Administration Review* 32 (1972).

——. "Party, Policy and Constitution in America." In *The American Party Systems,* ed. William Nisbet Chambers and Walter Dean Burnham. New York: Oxford University Press, 1967.

——. "The Politicization of Political Science." *American Politics Quarterly* 1 (1973).

——. *The Politics of Disorder.* New York: Norton, 1971.

Lowi, Theodore J., ed. *Legislative Politics.* Boston: Little, Brown, 1962.

Lowi, Theodore J., and Ben Ginsberg. *Poliscide.* New York: Macmillan, 1976.

Lowi, Theodore J., and Alan Stone. *Nationalizing Government: Public Policies in America.* Beverly Hills, CA: Sage, 1978.

McConnell, Grant. *The Decline of Agrarian Democracy.* New York: Atheneum, 1969.

——. *Private Power and American Democracy.* New York: Knopf, 1966.

McCoy, Charles, and John Playford, eds. *Apolitical Politics*. New York: Crowell, 1967.

Neustadt, Richard E. *Presidential Power*. New York: Wiley, 1960.

Nordlinger, Eric A. *On the Autonomy of the Democratic* State. Cambridge, MA: Harvard University Press, 1981.

Parenti, Michael. *Democracy for the Few*. 3rd ed. New York: St. Martin's Press, 1980.

——. *Power and the Powerless*. New York: St. Martin's Press, 1978.

——. "Repression in Academia: A Report from the Field." *Politics and Society* 4 (1971).

Paterson, Samuel. "Introduction to Avery Leiserson." *American Political Science Review* 69 (1975).

Petras, James. "Ideology in United States Political Scientists." *Science and Society* 29 (1965).

Piven, Frances Fox, and Richard Cloward. *Regulating the Poor*. New York: Random House, 1971.

"Political Change in America Symposium." *American Political Science Review* 66 (1974).

Pool, Ithiel de Sola. *Contemporary Political Science*. New York: McGraw Hill, 1967.

Pranger, Robert. *Action, Symbolism and Order*. Nashville, TN: Vanderbilt University Press, 1968.

——. *The Eclipse of Citizenship*. New York: Holt, Rinehart and Winston, 1968.

Ranney, Austin. "Toward a More Responsible Two-Party System: A Commentary." *American Political Science Review* 45 (1951).

Redford, Emmett S. "Reflections on a Discipline." *American Political Science Review* 55 (1961).

Ricci, David. *Community Power and Democratic Theory*. New York: Random House, 1971.

Rasmussen, Jorgen. "'Once You've Made a Revolution, the Same': Comparative Politics." In *The Post-Behavioral Era: Perspectives in Political Science*, ed. George J. Graham Jr. and George W. Carey. New York: David McKay, 1972.

Roettger, Walter B. "Strata and Stability: Reputation of American Political Scientists." *Political Science and Politics* 11 (1978).

Rogow, Arnold A. *Politics, Personality and Social Science in the Twentieth Century*. Chicago: University of Chicago Press, 1969.

——. "Whatever Happened to the Great Issues." *American Political Science Review* 51 (1957).

Runciman, W. G. *Social Science and Political Theory*. Cambridge, UK: Cambridge University Press, 1963.

Ryan, Alan. *Philosophy of the Social Sciences*. New York: Pantheon Books, 1970.

Schaar, John, and Sheldon Wolin. "*Essays on the Scientific Study of Politics*: A Critique." *American Political Science Review* 57 (1963).

Searing, Donald D. "Values in Empirical Research: A Behavioral Response." *Midwest Journal of Political Science* 14 (1970).

Spragens, Thomas A., Jr. *The Dilemma of Contemporary Political Theory: Toward a Post-Behavioral Theory of Politics*. New York: Duneller, 1973.

Storing, Herbert, ed. *Essays on the Scientific Study of Politics.* Chicago: University of Chicago Press, 1962.

Walker, Jack L. "A Critique of the Elitist Theory of Democracy." *American Political Science Review* 60 (1966).

Weinstein, Michael. "The Inclusive Polity: New Directions in Political Theory." *Polity* 5 (1973).

———. *Philosophy, Theory and Method in Contemporary Thought.* Glenview, IL: Scott-Foresman, 1971.

Wolfe, Alan. *America's Impasse: The Rise and Fall of the Politics of Growth.* Boston: South End Press, 1982.

———. *The Limits of Legitimacy: Political Contradictions of Contemporary Capitalism.* New York: Free Press, 1977.

———. "The Myth of the Free Scholar." *Center Magazine* 2 (1969).

———. "The Professional Mystique." In *An End to Political Science,* ed. Alan Wolfe and Marvin Surkin. New York: Basic Books, 1970.

———. "Sociology, Liberalism and the Radical Right." *New Left Review* 128 (1981).

———. "Unthinking about the Thinkable: Reflections on the Failure of the Caucus for a New Political Science." *Politics and Society* 1 (1971).

Wolfe, Alan, and Marvin Surkin. "Political Dimensions of American Political Science." *Acta Sociologica* 5 (1969).

Wolfe, Alan, and Marvin Surkin, eds. *An End to Political Science.* New York: Basic Books, 1970.

Wolin, Sheldon S. "Political Theory as a Vocation." *American Political Science Review* 63 (1969).

———. "Paradigms and Political Theories." In *Politics and Experience,* ed. Peter King. Cambridge, UK: Cambridge University Press, 1968.

Afterword

Almond, Gabriel A. *A Discipline Divided: Schools and Sects in Political Science.* Thousand Oaks, CA: Sage, 1989.

———. "Political Science: The History of the Discipline." In *A New Handbook of Political Science,* ed. Robert E. Goodin and Hans-Dieter Klingemann. Oxford, UK: Oxford University Press, 1998.

———. "Separate Tables: Schools and Sects in Political Science," *PS: Political Science and Politics* 21 (1988).

Bledstein, Burton J. Review of *Disenchanted Realists. Journal of American History* 72 (1986).

Burnham, Walter Dean. "Those High Nineteenth Century American Voting Turnouts: Fact or Fiction?" *Journal of Interdisciplinary History* 16 (1986).

Crick, Bernard. *The American Science of Politics.* Berkeley: University of California Press, 1959.

Dryzek, John S. Review of James Morone, *The Democratic Wish. American Political Science Review* 85 (1991).

Dryzek, John S., and Stephen T. Leonard. "History and Discipline in Political Science." *American Political Science Review* 82 (1988).

Eulau, Heinz. Editor's note. *Political Behavior* 7 (1985).

Farr, James. "The History of Political Science." *American Journal of Political Science* 32 (1988).

Farr, James, and Raymond Seidelman, ed. *Discipline and History: Political Science in the United States*. Ann Arbor: University of Michigan Press, 1993.

Farr, James, John Gunnell, Raymond Seidelman, John S. Dryzek, and Stephen T. Leonard. "Can the History of Political Science Be Neutral?" *American Political Science Review* 84 (1990).

Fine, Ben. *Theories of Social Capital: Researchers Behaving Badly*. New York: Pluto Press, 2010.

Freidel, Frank. *Francis Lieber: Nineteenth-Century Liberal*. Baton Rouge: Louisiana State University Press, 1947.

Greene, Donna. "Westchester Q and A: Ray Seidelman; How Nonvoters Affect Government." *New York Times*, January 7, 1996.

Gunnell, John G. "Handbooks and History: Is it Still the *American* Science of Politics?" *International Political Science Review* 23 (2002).

Haskell, Thomas L. *The Emergence of Professional Social Science: The American Social Science Association and the Nineteenth-Century Crisis of Authority*. Baltimore, MD: Johns Hopkins University Press, ([1977] 2000).

Helm, Charles J. Review of *Disenchanted Realists*. *Ethics* 98 (1988).

Holden, Matthew, Jr. "The Competence of Political Science: 'Progress in Political Research' Revisited." *American Political Science Review* 94 (2000).

Lowi, Theodore. *The End of Liberalism*. New York: Norton, 1969.

Lowi, Theodore J. "The State in Political Science: How We Become What We Study." *American Political Science Review* 86 (1992); reprinted in *Discipline and History*, ed. Farr and Seidelman.

Mansbridge, Jane J. *Beyond Adversary Democracy*. New York: Basic Books, 1980.

——. "Carole Pateman: Radical Liberal?" In *Illusion of Consent: Engaging with Carole Pateman*, ed. Daniel I. O'Neill, Mary Lyndon Shanley, and Iris Marion Young. University Park: Pennsylvania State University Press, 2008.

——. *Why We Lost the ERA*. Chicago: University of Chicago Press, 1986.

——. "Writing as a Democrat and a Feminist." In *Our Studies, Ourselves: Sociologists' Lives and Works*, ed. Barry Glassner and Rosanna Hertz. Oxford, UK: Oxford University Press, 2003.

Mansbridge, Jane J., ed. *Beyond Self-Interest*. Chicago: University of Chicago Press, 1990.

Miroff, Bruce. "A Science of Politics and a Science for Politics." Keynote address, New York State Political Science Association, Albany, New York, 2008.

New York Senate Bill S542A-2011 (April 11, 2012).

Putnam, Robert D. "Bowling Alone: America's Declining Social Capital." *Journal of Democracy* 6 (1995).

——. *Bowling Alone: The Collapse and Revival of American Community*. New York: Simon and Schuster, 2000.

———. "*E Pluribus Unum*: Diversity and Community in the Twenty-First Century." *Scandinavian Political Studies* 30 (2007).

———. *Making Democracy Work: Civic Traditions in Modern Italy.* With Robert Leonardi and Raffaella Y. Nanetti. Princeton, NJ: Princeton University Press, 1993.

———. "The Public Role of Political Science." *Perspectives on Politics* 1 (2003).

Putnam, Robert D., and David E. Campbell. *American Grace: How Religion Divides and Unites Us.* New York: Simon and Schuster, 2010.

Putnam, Robert D., and Lewis M. Feldstein. *Better Together: Restoring the American Community.* New York: Simon and Schuster, 2003.

Pye, Lucien W. "Political Science and the Crisis of Authoritarianism." *American Political Science Review* 84 (1990).

Ricci, David M. *The Tragedy of Political Science.* New Haven, CT: Yale University Press, 1984.

Seidelman, Raymond. *Disenchanted Realists: Political Science and the American Crisis, 1884–1984.* With the assistance of Edward J. Harpham. Albany. NY: SUNY Press, 1985.

———. "Political Scientists, Disenchanted Realists, and Disappearing Democrats." In *Discipline and History: Political Science in the United States*, ed. James Farr and Raymond Seidelman. Ann Arbor: University of Michigan Press, 1993.

———. Review of Clyde Barrow, *Universities and the Capitalist State. Journal of Politics* 53 (1991).

Somit, Albert. Review of *Disenchanted Realists. American Political Science Review* 81 (1987).

Somit, Albert, and Joseph Tanenhaus. *The Development of American Political Science: From Burgess to Behavioralism.* Boston: Allyn and Bacon, 1967.

Stanley, John. Review of *Disenchanted Realists. Contemporary Sociology* 15 (1986).

Whitfield, Stephen J. "Disciplinary Problems." *Reviews in American History* 14 (1986).

Index

Adams, Henry Carter, 23, 225
Adams, John, 4
Adcock, Robert, 245
Almond, Gabriel, 245, 246–47
American Economics Association, 26,
  252; and Wilson, 44
American Enterprise Institute, 197
American Historical Association, 118,
  252
American Political Science Association,
  44, 59, 61, 107, 152–53, 155, 158, 190,
  191, 196, 244, 249, 252
American Political Science Review, 187,
  196
American Science of Politics, 242
American Social Science Association,
  22, 251, 252–53
American Sociological Association,
  252
American Voter, 155, 166
Anti-federalists, 250
Aristotle, 86
Articles of Confederation, 6

Ball, Terence, 245
Barry. Brian, 221, 222
Beard, Charles: audience of, 64–65;
  and behavioralism, 94; biography
  of, 80–81; on civic education, 89–90;
  compared to Ward, 63–65; compared
  to Wilson, 64–65; on crisis of democracy, 81; on critical research, 89; on
  democracy and social science, 90–91;
  disenchantment with discipline,

91–92; *Economic Interpretation of
the Constitution,* 85–87; on expertise, 90; on the Founding, 81,
85–88; on groups, 86–89; *History
of the American People,* 80; later
thought, 92–97; on Madison, 88; on
"mindless empiricism," 84, 92; and
Merriam, 111–12, 115–16, 122–23; on
political science, 83–85, 92–95; on
professionalization, 81, 92–95; and
Progressivism, 15, 63–65; and return
to ethics, 92–95; and rejection of
New Deal, 95; science and politics,
82–84; and third tradition, 90–92,
96–98, 247. *See also* Progressive
political science
Behavioralism: definition of, 149–51;
  and Key, 155–56, 158–59; and
  Lasswell, 15–16, 102, 132; and
  Merriam, 15–16, 101, 107–09, 120;
  pre-World War II compared to post-
  World War II, 147–53; and reform
  political science, 145; as a science,
  148–50; and Truman, 155–56, 174–75,
  178–79,
Behavioral political science: audience
  of, 157, 183; and crisis of democracy,
  149, 183; failure of, 183; and philanthropy, 151; and professionalization,
  149, 151–53; and reform political
  science, 148; and third tradition,
  148–51; voting studies, 155. *See also*
  Key; Truman
Bellamy, Edward, 21